E AORDI XES

FO ERYDAY THINGS

EXTRAORDINARY
FIXES
FOR EVERYDAY THINGS

Reader's
Digest

Published by The Reader's Digest Association Limited
London • New York • Sydney • Montreal

About this book

Solving a knotty problem

We all love discovering clever, better ways of doing things. Such as a 'sneaky back way' to the local supermarket that detours traffic lights and jammed roads. Or the gadgets in DIY stores and the free catalogues that claim to solve problems we never knew we had. One of our contributors speaks proudly of the day he transformed a plastic milk container into a convenient, handled paint carrier that he could dip his brush into while standing on a ladder.

So you can imagine our collective delight when we heard about a truly superior way of tying shoelaces. There would be no more kneeling on the pavement to sort out errant laces. This technique, the inventor claimed, was easy to learn (because it's similar to the conventional knot you learned in primary school), never comes unbound and lets you quickly untie the laces in the usual way – by tugging on one of the ends. We won't go into detail on how the knot is tied, because you'll find that information, with illustrations, on page 131 of this book. But we all tried the technique then and there. It worked beautifully and we have been using it ever since. Our team are now the masters of shoelaces that were once uncontrollable and prone to coming undone at the worst possible times.

There's nothing more satisfying than finding a better, faster, easier way of doing something – even if it is just tying your shoelaces.

Going to unexpected experts

Perhaps we are slightly mad, but we consider that knowledge of a better way to tie shoelaces a great gift. Just a snippet of information, passed from one person to another – at no cost – and one more distraction has gone from our lives.

We hope you have a similar experience, several hundred times over, as you browse through and read *Extraordinary Fixes for Everyday Things*. To put this book together, our team of how-to writers tracked down some of the handiest people we could find in all walks of life. We spoke to builders, painters, mechanics, nurses, forest rangers, scoutmasters – all people whose expertise you would expect to find in a book like this. But we didn't leave it at that. We also grilled a fashion show manager, a lion tamer, a butler, a scientist who specialised in smells, Antarctic explorers, a rafting guide, a film-set builder and other intriguing people. Our quest was to provide a fresh approach to problems you confront every day, such as a chipped windscreen, water rings on a table top and a torrent of spam e-mails. And you'll find solutions to a few problems we hope you never encounter, such as what to do if you find yourself face to face with a great white shark.

Covering a wide range of problems

We've tried to make the scope of this book as extensive as everyday life itself. There are fast solutions to hundreds of problems related to your home. There are house cleaning and home-repair challenges that range from cleaning dirty carpets and scummy shower screens to fixing holes in walls, stopping leaking toilets and sorting out sticking doors and insect infestations. You'll also find solutions to problems related to organising and decorating your home and dealing with clutter and storage. There are solutions to how to deal with power failures, rebellious plumbing and other household emergencies. And the fixes extend to the exterior of the house and into the garden.

But the array of subjects covered here stretches far beyond your house and garden. You'll learn quick ways to handle unexpected food mishaps, such as burned roasts, over-salted or over-spiced stews and crumbling cakes. And you'll discover how to deal with problems with your clothes – such as popped buttons and stains – and appearance, such as impossibly frizzy hair. There are solutions to problems related to parties and weddings, such as handling difficult or unexpected guests and awkward social situations, such as who you should introduce to whom and how to offer condolences.

You'll find ways to tackle situations that occur every day such as what to do when you lose a wallet or when a credit card won't swipe, dealing politely with unwanted telesales calls, how to find a cheap flight and a number of ways out of hazardous situations on the road. There are even solutions to common health problems, including queasiness, rashes and a paper cut, as well as dangerous outdoor situations, such as getting caught in a rip tide or lost up a mountain.

The result of all this is, we believe, the largest and best collection of solutions to everyday problems ever put to paper. So gather up your gaffer tape, garden wire and bicarbonate of soda, start leafing through these pages and watch your daily hassles melt away. You can do it. It's as easy as tying your shoelaces!

The editors

Contents

PART SEVEN
Everyday life

PART EIGHT
Everyday health and hygiene

The extraordinary fixes philosophy

The joy of fixing things

Thomas the Tank Engine gets broken and his young owner is in tears. But it takes just a dab of glue and a little care and soon the engine is as good as new. The total cost of the repair: pennies. The hug you get in return: priceless. Or perhaps you have planned a special family Christmas for months. But on the day, everything conspires against you and you don't have enough time to cook the turkey. Don't despair – just boil the bird for an hour, roast it for another and you will have a wonderfully juicy dinner.

It feels good to fix things.

Despite the forces conspiring to create a disposable culture – ever busier schedules, ever available cheap consumer goods – the fix-it philosophy remains deeply embedded in the human psyche. Whether it's gluing a child's toy or rescuing a burned roast or mending a broken chair leg, it not only feels good to fix things, it is good – responsible, ethical and economical – to fix things.

Coping with the daily flood of problems

Fixing things was once part of everyday life. We had fewer possessions and part of being a good homeowner, parent or grandparent was the ability to run a household and keep it clean and working effectively. But times have changed. We're busier than ever, we have more possessions and the things we own are more complicated. As a result, problems bombard us daily in every aspect of our lives. Maybe it's the car (you've locked the keys inside), the house (the floor squeaks), your feet (they hurt or smell) or a party guest (she just won't leave). Having the know-how necessary to solve each and every dilemma is impossible. That's the nature of life.

And yet the problems keep coming. Many are trivial, many are humorous and some sap your spirit. When we set out to write this book, we sat in a room and brainstormed all the things that could go wrong in a typical day: around the house, in the garden, in the kitchen, with clothing and in social situations and on and on. At first, it was fun – and we had lots of fun dreaming up the silliest problems and situations. But as we got past 200 situations, then 300, then far beyond, the laughter stopped. Not just because of the large number, but also because so many of the problems on the list had actually *happened* to each of us. We may be an incredibly diverse bunch of people, but who among us hasn't had to deal with a popped button, hardened candle wax on the table, an unwanted visitor or a stuck window?

The search for fast and easy solutions

Extraordinary Fixes for Everyday Things was created to put you back in charge whenever you're faced with irritations like these – quickly. In the following pages, you will encounter an extraordinary assortment of remedies to hundreds of everyday problems that we are sure you have faced or are likely to face at some time in the future. Some of the solutions are absolutely ingenious. Some will strike you as basic common sense. (But when you're in trouble, common sense may be in short supply.) And all are tested and are proven to work.

THE MOTHER OF INVENTION

Every problem can be an opportunity to learn something new. And every so often problems inspire true innovation, not to mention fame and fortune. Here are a couple of small grievances that positive thinkers spun into gold.

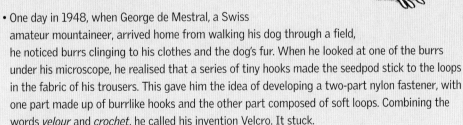

- One day in 1948, when George de Mestral, a Swiss amateur mountaineer, arrived home from walking his dog through a field, he noticed burrs clinging to his clothes and the dog's fur. When he looked at one of the burrs under his microscope, he realised that a series of tiny hooks made the seedpod stick to the loops in the fabric of his trousers. This gave him the idea of developing a two-part nylon fastener, with one part made up of burrlike hooks and the other part composed of soft loops. Combining the words *velour* and *crochet*, he called his invention Velcro. It stuck.

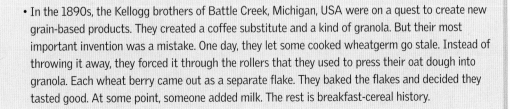

- In the 1890s, the Kellogg brothers of Battle Creek, Michigan, USA were on a quest to create new grain-based products. They created a coffee substitute and a kind of granola. But their most important invention was a mistake. One day, they let some cooked wheatgerm go stale. Instead of throwing it away, they forced it through the rollers that they used to press their oat dough into granola. Each wheat berry came out as a separate flake. They baked the flakes and decided they tasted good. At some point, someone added milk. The rest is breakfast-cereal history.

PROBLEM STOPPER

Know when to call a professional

Even the best fixers have their limitations. Call a professional:

• **When it will save you time and money.** Sometimes paying an expert works out more cost-effective than using your own free labour.

• **If you're too busy to do it right.** Temporary fixes tend to be more expensive in the long run than those done properly first time. Assess a situation and be honest with yourself about your time limits.

• **If you're just too busy.** Even if you have the skills to solve a problem, if you don't get around to it, your quick fix will be a continuing worry.

• **When it's just too big a job.** Know your limitations and you will stay safe and avoid expensive botched jobs.

• **When you've failed.** You can't fix everything. When you simply can't do it, call a specialist.

And what is just as important, all the solutions are fast and easy. Although we haven't taken a stopwatch to each task to determine how quickly it could be done.

We've also tried to make it as easy as possible to locate problems and their solutions. Our goal was to let you know a remedy for your problem within 60 seconds of picking up the book. A fast look at the table of contents should get you to within a few pages of your destination and a quick scanning of the headings should get you to the precise answer. Once there, each solution is succinct and clear. There are no long-winded discourses on tools, specialist techniques and materials.

Of course, you needn't wait for problems to occur to read further. We're sure you'll find this book great fun to browse through and read at your leisure. Not only will you learn all about fast, simple fixes, but you'll also be amused at our tales of astonishing mistakes, world-class fixes and secret tricks of the trade that some people with very interesting jobs have divulged.

Getting in the right mind-set

If you're not sure you're ready for this, you're in good company. Many people claim they are incapable of fixing things and are easily intimidated by tools, instructions or the risk of doing further damage. We understand. As we said before, the modern-day world is so complicated, so diverse that no one can possibly be master of every common skill.

But you don't need to be an expert. More important than expertise is attitude. To become truly efficient at fixing mechanical as well as health, kitchen, social and other problems, what you really need is the right mind-set. As you'll see, you almost never need expertise with a particular tool or in a special subject area to fix something. All you need is confidence and the willingness to give it a try.

We contacted some highly resourceful people to find out what it is they have in common. We didn't ask about specific skills; among the dozen or so questioned, one is a knot expert, another a salvager of architectural treasures, two more form an adventure photography team. Instead, we probed them for insight into their philosophy. As effective fixers, what makes them tick? We've distilled the results into a set of easily digestible principles. Read them, learn them and keep them to hand, as you would a kit of tools.

■ THE NINE RULES OF HIGHLY EFFECTIVE FIXERS

1 Be positive

You've probably heard the phrase countless times. *Stuff happens.* Minor frustrations are the norm, not the exception. Trying to pin blame on someone is usually a waste of time. Negativity clouds the mind. Avoiding the victim trap is an essential component of the fixer philosophy. If you drop and break a china cup, you can think 'unfair' or you can marvel at how long you and the cup defied gravity beforehand, given that it is a force powerful enough to move planets through the Solar System. Then you can focus on a solution.

You must get over the initial emotional response to a problem. Only then you will start to think of solutions. If you assume there is a way to deal with a problem, you'll probably find one. It's always likely to be a self-fulfilling prophecy.

2 Have a sense of humour

If looking on the bright side is an indispensable fix-it trait, sometimes it's also necessary to be silly, especially when things are so bad (a blocked toilet is flooding the hall, a downpour drenches your business suit before an important meeting) that the alternative is tears. If negativity clouds the mind, acute stress shackles bright ideas. Break the chains by being able to laugh.

3 Think fast, but take your time

It sounds like an impossible paradox. Such as 'What is the sound of one hand clapping?' But there is a key difference between thinking fast and acting fast without thinking. The latter is panic and has no place in the extraordinary fixes philosophy.

If your husband splashes chemicals in his eye while working in his workshop or the garden, he'll undoubtedly be very shocked – as will you. What should you do? Rush him to hospital? Yes, but thinking fast you can either put his head under a tap to get water into the eye or pour water onto it from a container to rinse the chemicals out. Get him to help by holding his eyelids open and rolling his eyeball. If his eyes are still hurting after you've rinsed them thoroughly, then drive slowly and carefully to accident and emergency to get them checked. A well thought-out fix will always be more effective than a botched attempt at a quick fix.

4 Be prepared

You might think being prepared means that you need the world's most complete set of tools: a different gadget for every loose nut, leaky pipe or damaged antique table. You don't, as you'll find out in the next section, 'The fixer's toolbox'. A garage-load of tools is expensive and can even be a burden. (Where is that three-tined, chrome-plated wotsit?) And not being able to put your hands on a tool can turn a five minute job into a two-month-and-five-minute job.

Along with the 'toolbox' section's specific list of versatile tools for a fixer's toolbox, here are some ideas on how to prepare yourself for the problems that punctuate our daily lives.

• **EXERCISE YOUR HANDS.** You may take them for granted, but your hands are your best tools, whether used alone or in conjunction with a screwdriver, scouring pad or garden rake. Practise fine motor skills with detailed work such as needlepoint or piano playing. Build strength by squeezing a tennis ball while watching television. Hone hand-eye coordination through artistic pursuits, such as sculpting, embroidery or calligraphy.

• **EXERCISE YOUR MIND.** Your mind is a computer database of past experience. Make a mental note every time a problem arises and you attempt a solution, whether or not it is successful. The database will build on itself, improving your effectiveness.

• **HAVE TOOLS AT THE READY.** You can get only so far using your hands and mind. Here is a good general tip for being prepared for most household fixes. As we suggest later, keep two bags of tools to hand – one filled with what you need for light repairs (claw hammer, small ruler, cordless screwdriver with two-way bit, pliers, screws, torch, pencil) and the other empty. When a special project arises, fill the empty one with just the tools that you need for the job so you won't be distracted by extra implements.

5 Think outside the box

Some fixes are straightforward. Others demand creativity. Perhaps you've made a small burn in the dining room carpet. The most straightforward approach would be to replace the carpet. But that's overkill, both time-consuming and expensive. You could, of course, patch it with a spare piece of carpet but that might not match. After a little creative thinking, taking a pair of sharp scissors and trimming off the charred tips of the carpet fibres is the best solution. If the burn wasn't very deep the problem will be fixed in minutes.

Here's another example: what do you do if the drawstring comes out of your pyjamas? Do you throw them away and buy another pair? Of course not. But you won't find a special pyjama-stringing tool at a hardware or fabric shop. Thinking creatively, you tie the end of the drawstring to a pencil and poke that through the waist of the trousers, bunching and smoothing the fabric until the tip pokes through the other hole. If you don't have a pencil or other tool to tie the string to, wet one end of the drawstring and place the string in the freezer. Once it has hardened, use the stiff end to work through the waistband. The extraordinary fixer knows that anything is a potential tool.

6 Know your enemy

Trying to tackle a problem that you don't fully understand can make matters worse. Perhaps you have seen a spate of mouse – or worse – rat droppings in the house. Your first response might be to set traps with poison everywhere that the rodents appear to be running. But if you're not careful about where you place the poison, it may be eaten by garden birds, by a neighbouring cat or your own beloved dog.

So study a problem. Analyse it. Break it down into its most elemental parts: rats, food source, access point between the two. Do your homework. (Contact a pest control firm for advice.) And then choose a solution. In this case, sealing up their entry point and placing a few traps may help to keep the invasion under control.

There simply isn't a ready-made solution for every one of life's little problems. But with a little creativity, anything, even frozen string, can become a tool.

7 Be flexible

A necessary ingredient for creativity is flexibility: the ability to adapt to new situations. Being flexible means keeping an open mind, whether that involves the tools you use or the results you seek. The key to flexibility when it comes to tools is to step back from the name of an object, which limits how it can be used. Take a tin that's usually used for baking bread, for example. If you view it as a deep-sided rectangular metal tray rather than merely as a tin for bread, a world of uses may open up.

8 Start simply

If the simplest solution doesn't work, move on to more involved ones. If your car doesn't start, you would first check the battery and maybe try jump-starting it. If that doesn't work, check the spark plugs. If it's not the spark-plugs, try the carburettor. There's no reason to expend time, effort and resources if the simplest possible solution solves the problem. Using a step-by-step approach – from simplest to most involved – gives you a problem-solving structure to follow.

9 Think it through

Cancer patients use guided imagery to overcome pain. World-class athletes depend on it for success. Author Dale Carnegie espoused it as a way to win friends and influence people. Also known as visualisation, guided imagery is the practice of mentally mapping out a sequence of desired results, such as a golfer visualising the perfect swing, the arc of the ball and where it will land on a fairway. Practising guided imagery can help the creative fixer to anticipate potential problems and achieve greater success.

Here's how visualisation might apply to a quick fix. Once you've settled on a solution but before you dive in and start gluing a chair back together, take a few minutes to walk through the sequence of events in your mind. See each step. Feel it. Try to experience it before you actually do it. Layer on details, such as the fit of the chair rungs and the dripping of the glue, to fill out the picture. Relax. Don't rush. Finally, linger on the most important image: the end result. Your goal is to start with success clearly imprinted in the mind.

The fixer's toolbox

Tools are the intermediaries between you and your environment. They allow you to turn a nut when your hands don't have the gripping power; to move a mountain of compost when you don't have the muscles or stamina to carry that much material all at once; and to cut materials that are too tough to break with your hands.

To carry out many of the fixes in this book, it is important that you have a good set of conventional tools, such as hammers, saws, screwdrivers and pliers. You'll find a description of these tools in the special feature starting on page 24. But in this section, we want to draw your attention to some often-overlooked tools and supplies that are versatile, inexpensive and durable time-savers. We questioned some of the handiest people we know about the unexpectedly useful tools and other supplies that a person should have on hand to handle the kinds of problems covered in this book. The results are given below. If you put these items on your shopping list and stock your home, car and workplace with them, 99 per cent of life's everyday fix-its will be within your grasp.

A first-rate fixer always has a good set of tools handy. But is there bicarbonate of soda and vinegar in your workshop?

■ SOME UNEXPECTEDLY USEFUL TOOLS AND SUPPLIES

✔ Gaffer tape

Gaffer tape is a fantastically useful item. It's strong, flexible and waterproof. You can cut it to any length your task calls for. And when its job is done, it is likely that the same piece will still be perfectly good. Just wrap it around the outside of the original roll and you can use it again. Gaffer tape comes in a variety of colours, the most common being silver.

On page 347 you can read about the photographer who improvised a dental cap for himself with gaffer tape when he broke a molar during an Antarctic expedition. This supertape seems to hold much of

Impromptu tools at your fingertips

Not every tool has to be bought off the rack at a DIY store. Scores of everyday objects around you will fill in nicely when 'official' tools are not available. Use a coin as a screwdriver for slotted screws.

• Use a belt buckle as a bottle opener.

• A credit card will scrape ice off your windscreen.

• Use a tie as a sling for an injured arm.

• A 2p piece makes a good measuring tool. Its diameter is 2.5cm. And a £5 note is 15cm long.

• Extend your arms out parallel to the ground at shoulder level. That distance, fingertip to fingertip, is equal to your height.

the rest of his life together, too. He uses it to keep little rubber caps from popping off his tripod, to protect wrists and ankles from mosquitoes, to fix a leaky canoe and restore a split paddle. He has even fixed a pair of trousers with a half dozen strips of red gaffer tape.

✔ Dental floss

Dental floss is super string. It's extremely strong and comes in a compact case. When you travel, you probably take some with your other toiletries, so all you need to do is remember that floss can do more than just clean teeth. Travellers swear by it for repairing torn bag straps and backpacks. (It helps if you've also packed a big sewing needle.) Dental floss is much stronger than thread and its slippery surface allows it to slide more easily through tough fabrics. You can also use it to tie a package closed or as a temporary washing line when you are travelling.

One of our contributors, doing charity work abroad, used floss to repair a broken necklace. She just threaded the loose beads onto a piece of floss and knotted the ends. The solution worked perfectly well until she could get the necklace home for a proper repair.

Dental floss has culinary uses, too. For instance, you can use it to slice a cake by holding the floss taut across the top of the cake, pushing down and then sliding it out the side. It can be used to slice cheese as well (unwaxed for soft cheese, waxed for hard).

✔ Sewing kit

Keep a compact sewing kit close to hand. Not only is it useful for stitching up split trousers in minutes, but the needles are also useful for extracting thorns, glass, splinters and other items from skin. (Remember to sterilise the needle with a match first.) At a minimum, include black and white thread in your kit; put in a few other colours for versatility. Stock the kit with three needles – small, medium and large (for tough fabrics).

✔ Multi-purpose tools

Going out and about with a case of tools is impractical. That's what makes the Swiss army knife, the Leatherman and other multitools so popular. These fold-up, many-tools-in-one devices are lightweight and compact. They come in a variety of models, so you can select the array of tools you'll be most likely to need.

For example, one model of Swiss army knife has two screwdrivers (flat head and Phillips), durable scissors, a bottle and can opener, a corkscrew, a nail file, a magnifying glass (to help you to read small print or start a fire with no matches) and two knife blades (one with a ruler on the blade). Other models have unexpected items such as tweezers, wire strippers and toothpicks. Some even have clocks, alarms and mini-torches.

Leatherman and its competitors are essentially a pair of pliers with a host of additional tools that swing out of the handles when needed. They tend to be more bulky than a Swiss army knife and can include heavier-duty tools, such as miniature wire cutters, files and saws. When you're contemplating your choice, here are a few things to think about besides the variety of models:

- Do the sharp tools lock in place, so they won't close on your hand while you're using them?
- Do several tools tend to swing out of the handle when you're trying to pull out only one of them?
- Does the frame come in a high-visibility colour? Multi-tools are easily lost when you're out and about, so choosing one in a bright colour is a good idea.

✔ Cable ties

Some people never go anywhere without cable ties. These strong nylon bands consist of a head (looking something like a belt buckle) and a slotted band. When you wrap the band around two or more objects, slip the tapered end through the locking head and tighten, the objects are bound fast.

Cable ties are great for holding car parts in place, bundling wires, binding newspapers, repairing fences, substituting for shoelaces, securing ponytails and more. You typically have to snip the tie to release the objects you've bound together, although some ties feature a release mechanism. Cable ties are sold in a variety of colours, range in length from 10cm to more than a metre and are available at DIY stores and a number of suppliers online.

✔ Galvanised wire

Galvanised wire (also known as baling wire) is a great way to fix one object to another. And unlike gaffer tape and cable ties (see above), galvanised wire can stand up to extreme heat, which means you can use it to secure a wobbly exhaust on your car or a loose carburettor on a lawnmower. This wire, which is 1.6mm thick, comes on a roll and can be purchased at hardware and DIY stores. It can be twisted and snipped with pliers. Among its myriad uses:

- When you've stripped the threads on a screw on an appliance, run some galvanised wire through the screw hole and twist it to hold things together until you can make a permanent fix.
- Galvanised wire can be used to mend fences in a variety of ways; for instance, you can use it to splice broken wires, fasten wire fencing to a post or reinforce a post that has cracked or broken.
- Use it to hang things up, such as pictures in your house, birdboxes, wind chimes or seasonal items stored in the garage.
- String some galvanised wire between two trees and throw a blanket over it to make a quick children's play tent.

✔ Staple gun

Which would you rather do: spend an hour tapping in tacks or nails with a hammer or accomplish the same task in a few minutes with a spring-loaded staple gun? Most people would opt for the latter. With the squeeze of a handle, a staple gun will fire a hefty two-pronged staple into wood and other hard but penetrable surfaces. Use it to put up holiday decorations in moments, to hold speaker wires in place, or to tack down plastic sheeting before a storm. Some people use their staple guns to create elegant window treatments, for draping and securing fabric and even for substantial jobs like re-upholstering furniture.

If you are likely to do a lot of stapling, consider a model that will allow you to adjust the firing strength of the gun or even consider an electric unit. If the stapling you're doing is meant to be temporary, wrap a strong rubber band around the staple gun so that it's right next to where the staple shoots out. This will act as a 'spacer', leaving the top of the staple protruding so it can be removed easily.

✔ Spray lubricant

Life is full of things that don't slide and glide as easily as they ought to – hinges, zips and pruning shears, just to name a few. For that reason alone, it's worth keeping cans of spray lubricant in your car, toolshed, office and kitchen cabinet. You can buy it just about anywhere, including supermarkets, hardware stores, discount stores, car parts suppliers and DIY stores. The most famous brand is WD-40, but other brands are available, too.

Aside from straightforward lubrication, there are scores of other inventive uses for spray lubricant, including these:

- Coat garden tools with it to prevent rust.
- For crayon marks on hard surfaces such as tiles, worktops, wood furniture and painted walls, just spray the lubricant on and wipe the marks away.
- Spray it on building ledges and eaves to repel pigeons and other birds from resting.

✔ Compressed air

For some cleaning tasks, you just need a blast of wind – and nothing more. Cleaning fluids will wreck some delicate items (such as dried flowers). And while you might think that just puffing up your cheeks and blowing onto an electronic game cartridge will do fine for dislodging dust, you are running a risk: your breath carries tiny water droplets, which can damage electronic parts. The solution is compressed air. Buy several cans at a computer store or photo shop or online and keep them in your toolbox, office, kitchen, near your TV, DVD and audio equipment and in the garage.

The following is just a sampling of other things you can clean with compressed air: cable ports on computers, cameras, CD and DVD players, computer screens, electric shavers, keyboards, power tools, sewing machines, slides and negatives, smoke alarms and typewriters. Cans of compressed air are also handy for cleaning in hard-to-reach places – the blades of a fan, for instance. Many brands of compressed air come with a little extender tube that can get the blast of air closer to hard-to-reach spots.

When you are using cans of compressed air, hold the can upright. Otherwise, you might get some of the propellant mixed in with the air, dampening something you didn't want to get wet. Also remember that the air is rushing out with considerable force and could damage delicate objects. You can reduce the force by moving the can farther away from the object being cleaned. And make sure your compressed air doesn't drive dust into the housing of the electronic equipment – perhaps, through the vents on the side of your computer monitor. For that kind of cleaning, a handheld vacuum cleaner is probably a better choice.

✔ Bicarbonate of soda

Sodium bicarbonate, also known as bicarbonate of soda, is the multi-purpose tool of the chemical world. You can use this non-toxic, mild alkali for scores of chores around the house, including cleaning, scouring, polishing and removing stains. But aside from cooking uses, bicarbonate of soda is probably most famous for deodorising refrigerators. Open a box and put it in the back of the fridge and it will absorb odours, keeping your milk from tasting like your leftover Chinese takeaway. Here's just a sampling of its other uses:

- Sprinkle some bicarbonate of soda on to a damp sponge and use it as a gentle scouring powder.
- Smother a grease fire on the hob with it.
- Brush your teeth with it.
- To remove a musty smell from carpet, sprinkle with bicarbonate of soda, let it sit for 3 or 4 hours and vacuum it up.
- Mix 2 tablespoons in a litre of warm water and use it to clean hard surfaces, such as tiles, worktops and stainless steel.

✔ White vinegar

White vinegar is another inexpensive and versatile household substance. Buy this mild acid at a supermarket or cash-and-carry store. Mix 50ml in a litre of water for cleaning hard surfaces, including windows. Vinegar kills germs and mould. It also removes stains, grease and wax build-up and does a superb job of breaking down mineral deposits on taps and showerheads.

Vinegar can even be used to remove soil from the hems of trousers. Use a cloth to dab the vinegar on until the mark is wet, let it dry and brush off the loosened soil.

More jobs for white vinegar:

- Use white vinegar as a hair rinse to neutralise the alkaline residue left by shampoos.
- If glasses come out of the dishwasher looking filmy, bathe each glass for a minute or two in vinegar, wipe with a sponge or dishcloth and rinse.
- To clean a coffeemaker, fill the tank with a half-and-half mixture of water and vinegar, put a new filter in the basket to catch loosened debris and turn the machine on. Let the coffeemaker run through its entire cycle, then run it through two more cycles with fresh water.

✔ Surgical spirit

Surgical spirit is a top-notch cleaner, stain remover and disinfectant. It's inexpensive and versatile. It also dries quickly, so it makes a great streak-free window cleaner and is good for removing dirt from electronic equipment that could be damaged by water, such as calculators, remote controls and keyboards.

- To make your own glass cleaner, mix 100ml surgical spirit, 2 squirts of washing-up liquid and 4 litres of warm water.
- To kill germs on children's toys and furniture, moisten a cleaning cloth with surgical spirit and wipe.
- To remove a lipstick stain from fabric, pre-treat it by blotting on surgical spirit. Then launder as usual.
- To remove an ink stain from fabric, pour some surgical spirit on a cleaning cloth and blot (don't rub) at the stain. Let the moistened stain sit for half an hour, then blot at the stain with a fresh cloth, adding more alcohol as needed. Keep moving to new sections of the cleaning cloth, drawing out more ink as you go. Rinse the stain with 50ml white vinegar mixed with a litre of water and rinse again with clean water.
- To remove a build-up of hairspray on a bathroom mirror, pour some surgical spirit on a cleaning cloth and wipe.

Be careful not to get surgical spirit confused with drinkable alcohol: surgical spirit is poisonous and is also highly flammable. Keep it well away from children.

Basic household tools

Ninety per cent of being a good fixer is being prepared for most common problems. So make sure that your toolbox is stocked with these essential tools:

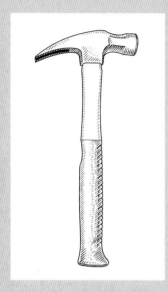

■ CLAW HAMMER

Every toolbox should have an average-weight (450g) claw hammer, with a two-pronged claw opposite the face, for driving and pulling nails and for light demolition work. Wood is the traditional handle material, but modern glass fibre and steel handles connect directly to the steel head. The handle should feel comfortable when you swing the hammer.

■ CORDLESS DRILL/DRIVER

For drilling and driving screws, a good cordless drill/driver is a must and given today's battery technology, a cordless drill can be used in place of a mains electric drill. For all-purpose use, choose a T-handled tool, which balances the battery weight better than one with a pistol grip. One with variable speeds allows you to use a low-rpm setting for driving screws and a higher one for drilling. Hammer action allows you to drill into masonry walls.

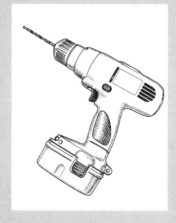

Buy a basic set of drill bits and a couple of driver bits. (For driver bit sizes, follow the advice about screwdriver sizes opposite.). If you own two batteries, you can always keep a charged one on hand when the other dies.

■ SPANNER

The most common and useful type of spanner, the crescent-pattern adjustable spanner, is great for turning square and hexagonal nuts and bolts. A thumbscrew opens and closes its parallel jaws, allowing for quick and easy adjusting. For maximum versatility, buy a medium-sized spanner.

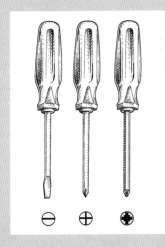

■ SCREWDRIVERS

Keep a collection of screwdrivers in your tool kit – at least three sizes of regular slotted screwdrivers (5, 6 and 8 millimetres) and two sizes of Phillips screwdrivers (No.1 and No.2). For cars and machinery, you will need at least two sizes of Phillips-head screwdrivers. Buy good-quality screwdrivers, which are still relatively inexpensive. Keep a cheap slotted screwdriver around for levering and gouging.

■ TAPE MEASURE

Tape measures feature spring-loaded, retractable steel tapes or 'blades'. They come in different blade widths and lengths. For around-the-house use, a 5 metre tape measure with a 19mm (¾in) blade is a good, compact choice.

■ PLIERS

Pliers are handheld levers (the joint being the fulcrum) that help you to get a grip on what you're doing. There are many types – some that lock, others which are adjustable – but for the basic toolbox, all you really need are medium-sized combination pliers and long-nose pliers.

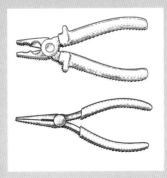

The former, made to fit the palm comfortably, are highly versatile. They have both flat and curved sets of teeth in their jaws, for gripping objects of different shapes and feature wire cutters near the pivot (and, sometimes on the outside). All 'electricians' pliers have insulated handles. Long-nose pliers, which also feature wire cutters, are useful for twisting and looping wire, fishing out dropped screws and delicate work, such as small-appliance repair.

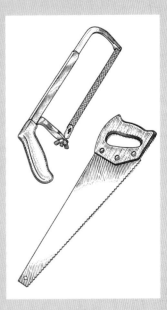

■ SAWS

Two saws that will cover most of your needs are a handsaw and a hacksaw. Tapering from heel (near the handle) to toe, handsaws, used for cutting across the grain of wood, vary in both length and the number of teeth per inch. The longer the saw, the fewer strokes needed to finish the job. The more teeth on the saw, the smoother the cut. A handsaw 500 to 550mm (20 to 22in) long with around ten hardened teeth per inch is a good choice.

continued overleaf

continued from page 25

Hacksaws are for cutting metal and plastic. They come with replaceable 300mm (12in) blades, which also vary in tooth count (18 to 32 teeth per inch). The thinner the metal, the more teeth the blade should have. Junior hacksaws with 150mm (6in) replaceable blades can be very useful for craft work and smaller jobs around the home.

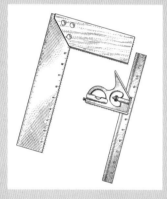

■ CARPENTER'S SQUARE

The simplest carpenter's square has a polished wooden stock and a steel blade and is mainly used to mark straight lines perpendicular to a board's edge. The combination square is a versatile variant with a base that features a level and allows you to mark both 90 and 45 degree angles. It usually has a tiny steel scriber.

■ FILLING KNIFE

Whether you're hiding nail holes with filler or scraping old paint from windowsills, a filling knife is a must for any toolbox. These come in various blade widths. A 50mm (2in) knife is not too wide for scraping paint, nor is it too narrow for spreading fillers.

■ LEVEL

A spirit level, which has a bubble of air inside a tube of liquid, can tell you if a surface is perfectly horizontal (level) or vertical (plumb). Levels come in different lengths. A 600mm (2ft) level is practical for household use.

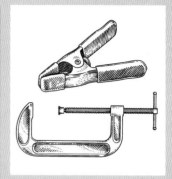

■ CLAMPS

Clamps are helpful for holding surfaces together while gluing or when you need a third hand for securing that piece of wood you're working on. They come in many styles and sizes. Common household clamps are G-clamps, which have an adjustable threaded jaw that closes on a fixed jaw and spring clamps, which can be opened and closed quickly by squeezing the handles.

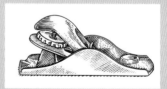

■ PLANE

Handheld planes, such as a block plane (shown above) or a bench plane, contain razor-sharp blades that lock in at adjustable angles. By pushing a plane evenly across wood, you can smooth and trim the surface or clean up the edges.

SAFETY GEAR

No matter how fast you can do a job, always wear safety gear appropriate to the job you are doing. Here are some tips on selecting what you need:

- **Safety goggles** Don't rely on ordinary eyeglasses to guard your eyes when particles may be flying. Wear special protective safety glasses with side shields (you can get them on prescription) or safety goggles that can be worn over your regular glasses.
- **Ear defenders** Wear ear protection when decibel levels start to rise. Ear defenders are easier to take off and put on than polymer foam earplugs and are harder to misplace. But both protect equally well.

- **Dust masks** For ordinary dust and paint fumes, you can use a simple disposable face mask. For more toxic dust, you need a respirator approved to British Standard EN 149: 2001 and marked with the level of protection it offers – FFP1 (fine non-toxic particles), FFP2 (fine toxic particles) and FFP3 (very fine toxic particles). Some respirators may be sold for specific uses (such as working with loft insulation) and some contain charcoal filters to remove chemical fumes.
- **Work gloves** Protect your hands from abrasive materials with sturdy cloth-and-leather work gloves. When dealing with toxic or irritating liquids wear heavy rubber or PVC gloves.

■ TRIMMING KNIFE

Even if you're just using it to slice up cardboard for recycling, a utility knife can be a handy tool to keep around. For safety's sake, choose a model with a retractable blade. Standard blades are double-ended (reversible) and spare blades can often be stored safely and conveniently in the knife's handle.

■ WOOD CHISEL

A chisel is a sharp, precisely bevelled tool used for deep-cutting or shaving wood. If you needed to mortise (or recess) a hinge in a door frame, you would use a chisel with a mallet. A 12mm (½in) chisel is a good general-purpose choice.

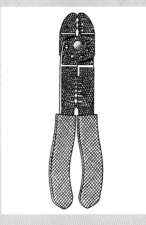

■ ELECTRICIAN'S CRIMPING TOOL

An electrician's multipurpose tool has many uses, including wire cutting, wire stripping and crimping wire to terminals. Small pliers on the nose also allow you to grip and twist wire.

PART ONE

Home care and repair

The key is stuck in the front door and a lightbulb has broken off in its socket. Or you've lost your Phillips screwdriver and found a white ring spoiling an antique table. The baby has been sick on the carpet and the dog has fleas. If any of this sounds familiar, read on and these dilemmas should be no more than a minor inconvenience.

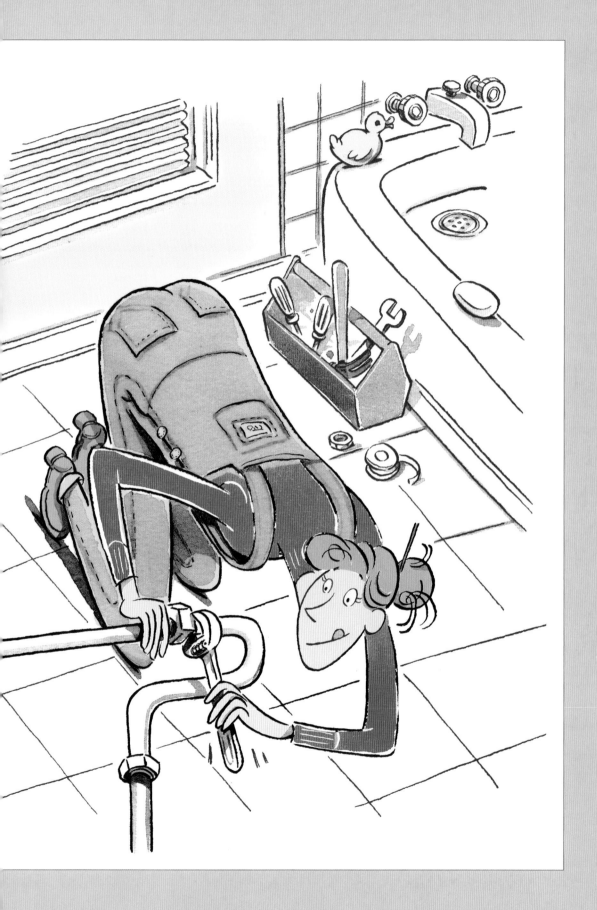

Cleaning the house

PROBLEM
STOPPER

**Keeping candles
from dripping**
Removing wax from a
candelabra is one thing,
but getting it off fine
furniture or tablecloths
can be a chore. You can
prevent the wax from
dripping in the first
place by putting the
candles in the freezer
for at least 24 hours
before lighting them.

■ HARD-TO-CLEAN ITEMS

My ceiling is too high to reach the cobwebs

TAPE A FEATHER DUSTER TO A POLE Using an extension ladder is not a
practical option here; you would never get around to it. The trick is
to attach a feather duster to the end of the kind of extension pole
that painters use to roll paint on to ceilings. Attach the duster using
gaffer tape (for a more permanent connection) or a couple of long
cable ties (if you don't want to commit the pole or the duster to
full-time cobweb duty). Then simply brush away the webs.

How do I clean my chandelier without making a mess?

USE AN UMBRELLA TO CATCH DRIPS You can quickly clean a crystal
chandelier without taking it apart by using an umbrella as you spray it
with an alcohol cleaning solution. Mix 2 teaspoons of surgical spirit
and 500ml of warm water in a spray bottle. Hang an opened umbrella
upside down, attaching the handle to the bottom of the chandelier.
Cover the bulbs and sockets with sandwich bags secured with twist
ties. As you spray the cleaner on, the umbrella will catch the dirty
drips. Because the umbrella is closer to the source, it catches a lot
more drips than newspapers or a dustsheet spread out on the floor.

My candelabra is covered with wax

PEEL AND THEN MELT THE REST WITH HOT WATER One popular trick for
removing wax from candlesticks is to put them in the freezer and
then peel off the hardened wax. But candelabras are often too big to
fit into a freezer. And if it contains several kinds of metals that freeze
at different rates, freezing could damage it. Instead, try the following
technique, which is faster and works like a charm: first, remove as
much of the wax as possible with your fingers. Then run hot water
over the candelabra in the kitchen sink. Hot water won't affect the
silver, but it will melt the wax off completely.

Candle wax has dripped onto the woodwork

USE ICE CUBES TO HARDEN IT To remove wax drippings, use the cold treatment. Carefully peel off the biggest chunks with your fingernails or a plastic kitchen scraper and chill the remaining wax with ice cubes in a plastic bag. Once chilled, the wax will be easier to break up and remove. Wipe off any remaining bits with a cloth moistened with paint thinner. Some people recommend warming candle wax to wipe it off, but try this only as a last resort, since the wax may melt and penetrate deeper into the pores of the wood.

Dusting my plants is tedious work

SHOWER THEM INSTEAD Don't dust indoor plants – just give them a shower. Place the dusty plants on the floor of the shower. Set the showerhead on a mist setting and gently spray the plants. If you're afraid of overwatering them, wrap each pot in a plastic bag, covering as much of the top of the soil as possible. Let the plants dry thoroughly before returning them to their normal locations.

WORLD-CLASS FIX

OLD-FASHIONED CLEANING METHODS

Before the days of powerful cleaning products, people had many ingenious ways of cleaning. At the Frontier Culture Museum at Staunton, in Virginia, USA, costumed staff members demonstrate some of those techniques. Here are just a few:

- To clean feather mattresses, they lay the mattresses on the grass on a rainy day. When the mattresses are soaked through, they are hauled to the barn to dry.

- They scrub wooden floors and tabletops with water and sand. After much elbow grease, they rinse the floors, let them dry, and sweep up the sand. In a way, it's like sanding off the top layer of wood.

- They 'sweeten', or remove mould or mildew, from wooden buckets by rubbing them with water and ashes, which are mildly abrasive and caustic. The insides of the buckets are then exposed to the sun's ultraviolet rays to sterilise them, destroying any bacteria growing inside.

- To wash woollen blankets, they plunge them in soapy, near-boiling water. Then they remove them and, without rinsing, hang them to dry. The hot water does not damage the preshrunk wool. And the old-fashioned lye-based soaps don't make suds and leave much of a residue. What little residue remains acts as a natural insect repellent.

- They scrub iron cooking pots with ashes and then season them with beef tallow.

My louvre doors are very hard to dust

USE A CLOTH-WRAPPED RULER Louvre doors can be dust magnets and a challenge to clean. Here's an easy way to clean them. Wrap a clean cotton cloth around a wooden ruler. Spray the cloth with the cleaner you use to dust. Then slowly run the flat end across each louvre to pull up the dust easily and completely.

Vacuuming my ceiling fan is a pain

USE AN OLD SOCK ON YOUR HAND TO CLEAN IT Ceiling fan blades are notorious for collecting mounds of dust. This remedy is faster and easier than trying to vacuum the blades. Place a sturdy stepladder under the fan. Pour a litre of water into a plastic bowl and add a squirt of washing-up liquid. Dip an old, clean sock in the solution and wring it out. Slip the sock over your hand, climb the ladder and run the sock-clad hand lightly over the fan's blades, making sure to clean both the top and bottom.

▥ WINDOWS

An old window sticker has left a mess

REMOVE LEFTOVER ADHESIVE WITH WD-40 You can spend hours trying to scrape sticker residue off windows. Even razor blades don't always remove all the sticky stuff. And as leftover adhesive collects dirt, you are soon looking at an ugly mark. Try this. Remove as much of the sticker as you can using your fingernail or a razor blade and then spray a little penetrating lubricant, such as WD-40, on to the adhesive that remains. Wipe with a paper towel or rag and the remaining bits will come off completely.

My windows always streak after washing

Washing windows is a tiresome chore, but it's even worse when your hard work leaves streaks on the windows. Here's how professionals avoid streaking when they wipe off their windows:

- Use a window-washing squeegee with a smooth, soft rubber edge. (Or use crumpled-up black-and-white newspaper.)
- Dry a 2.5cm strip at the top or side of each window and always start your squeegee there – starting on dry glass is one key to avoiding streaks.

- Don't wash windows in direct sunlight, because quickly dried glass is more susceptible to streaking. Evenings or cloudy days are the best times for washing windows.

My blinds are filthy

DUST OR WASH THE BLINDS Dust blinds regularly with a soft cloth, a duster with a handle and swivel head, or the dusting brush on your vacuum. (Be sure to dust both sides of the blinds.) If they're stained or spotted, it's time for a real cleaning. Though you can wash them in place (with a dustsheet over the floor and furniture), it's best to remove the blinds. Place one blind at a time across a table covered with a plastic sheet or shower curtain. Wash vinyl blinds using a sponge and a solution of 50ml white vinegar in a litre of warm water. Washing them in the bath is even easier. Run some warm water into the tub, add a squirt of washing-up liquid, and wipe each side with a large sponge. To rise, plunge them in clean water or hold them under the shower. Then wipe with a clean, soft cloth.

Many fabric blinds can also be washed, but take a very careful look at the care instructions before washing them. It's best not to leave them in the water for more than a minute or so.

My blinds are dust magnets

USE AN ANTISTATIC SPRAY To keep dust from piling up quickly, use an antistatic spray, on window blinds straight after you clean them.

There is mildew on my window frames

WASH WITH A BLEACH-DETERGENT SOLUTION Black or grey mildew spots on wooden frames can be cleaned away for good with a solution of 60ml of household bleach and 30ml of laundry detergent in a litre of water. Wearing rubber gloves to protect your hands, sponge the solution on the spots, let it sit for 10 minutes, and then rinse thoroughly with clean water.

My outside windowsills get dirty so quickly

APPLY A COAT OF FLOOR WAX Because exterior windows are exposed to the elements, they collect a lot of dirt. There is a very simple way to keep sills clean: just wipe on a coat of clear floor wax to protect them.

TRICKS OF THE TRADE

How to tell which side of the glass is streaky
When you clean windows, wipe the inside panes in a side-to-side direction and the outside in an up-and-down direction. If you do this, you can step back and easily see which side the streak is on, so you won't waste time recleaning the side that doesn't need it – and running the risk of introducing new streaks.

PROBLEM STOPPER

Keep venetian blinds clean
Keep grime from building up on metal venetian blinds by wiping a thin coat of clear car wax on to the blinds. The coating will keep dirt and dust from sticking, making it easier to clean with your duster or vacuum.

How to keep a mirror
free from lint
A lot of the materials
people use to clean
bathroom mirrors, such
as cloths and paper
towels, tend to leave lint
behind. Try using paper
coffee filters instead.
They make excellent
cleaners for glass
surfaces and mirrors
because they leave no
streaks or smudges.

■ BATHROOMS

My bathroom grouting is stained with mildew

SPRAY IT WITH VINEGAR Mildew on grouting is no match for the miracle household cleaning dynamo that is vinegar. Pour some white vinegar into a container, dip in an old toothbrush and scrub the mildew. Or pour the vinegar into a spray bottle, squirt it on to the mildew, and let it sit for 10 minutes. Rinse with water and scrub with the toothbrush if necessary.

SPRAY IT WITH A BLEACH SOLUTION Bleach is also effective in removing mildew from grouting. Fill a spray bottle with equal parts of household bleach and water. Spray the grouting, let it sit for a few minutes, and then wipe with a clean white cotton cloth. You can also use commercial-quality paste grout cleaners, but avoid pumice stones – using them takes far too much time and removes far too little mildew from the grout.

If you find it impossible to remove the stains in grouting, you may want to consider staining the seams with a darker colour. (See 'My grouting won't come clean', page 67.)

The mirror steams up when I have a shower

COAT THE MIRROR WITH GLYCERINE After a warm shower, you probably wipe off the bathroom mirror with a towel, but it just steams up again within seconds. Try this quick solution: when you clean the bathroom, wipe a little glycerine (available at chemists and some hardware stores) on to the bathroom mirror. Buff it lightly with a soft cloth. The thin coating of glycerine will prevent the glass from fogging and will last about a week. It will need doing more often if you have a lot of people taking showers.

My mirror is hazed with hairspray

WIPE IT OFF WITH ALCOHOL You probably have a fast, easy solution for a hair spray haze in your medicine cabinet. Surgical spirit will cut straight through the stubborn spray marks that are making a mess of your bathroom mirror. Pour a little surgical spirit on to a cleaning cloth or paper towel and give the mirror a rubdown.

My shower curtain is crawling with mildew

WASH IT OFF WITH A BLEACH SOLUTION Some shower curtains can be tricky to clean because they are big and cumbersome. Getting rid of mildew, especially during damp weather, can be especially challenging. Here is a solution that's quick, easy, and low-cost. Pour 4 litres of warm water and 100ml of household bleach into a plastic bucket. Wearing rubber gloves, soak a sponge in the solution, giving it a squeeze to avoid drips and then wipe. The mildew will vanish. Rinse using the showerhead.

I'm ready to throw away this filthy shower curtain liner

THROW IT IN THE WASHING MACHINE Don't throw away a polyester or nylon curtain liner just because it is covered in mildew and dirt. You can extend its life by cleaning it in your washing machine. Set the machine on the gentle cycle with warm water and 200ml of clothes detergent or 100ml of vinegar. If you have a tumble drier, spin it for 20 minutes on the lowest heat and it will come out clean and wrinkle-free. Or hang it on the line to dry in the breeze. Afterwards, rehang it immediately.

My glass shower doors are filmy

CLEAN THEM WITH VINEGAR, BICARBONATE OF SODA AND SALT Stubborn mineral build-up on glass shower doors or screens is no competition for a few common household ingredients – white vinegar, bicarbonate of soda and salt. Spray vinegar on to the door or screen and let it sit for a few minutes. Next, create a paste using equal amounts of bicarbonate of soda and salt. Use a damp sponge to rub the paste over the door, then rinse well.

My laundry basket smells unpleasant

PUT A FABRIC SOFTENER SHEET IN THE BASKET The solution is simple: place a sheet of fabric softener in the bottom of the laundry basket and change it every week. Or sprinkle some bicarbonate of soda in the bottom of the basket.

Bathroom mirror fogging up? A quick coating of glycerine will keep the steam off.

Here's an easy way to keep shower tiles free of mildew. Keep a spray bottle of household bleach mixed with water 1:4 parts bleach to water. Once a week, after your shower, spray the tiles with the bleach solution. Then rinse thoroughly. For just a few seconds' investment, you'll keep your tiles looking brand new. But be sure to keep the bleach solution out of the reach of children.

My brass fixtures look dull

POLISH THEM WITH BICARBONATE OF SODA AND LEMON JUICE Don't buy an expensive specialist brass cleaner. Save time and money by making a paste with equal amounts of bicarbonate of soda and lemon juice. Dip an old toothbrush in the mixture and lightly scrub the fixtures. Let the solution dry for a few minutes and then buff with a clean cloth. They will look brand new.

The nooks and crannies in my bathroom are hard to clean

USE AN OLD TOOTHBRUSH An old toothbrush is the perfect time-saving bathroom-cleaning tool. You can use it to clean the tracks of a shower's sliding glass doors. Simply spray bathroom cleaner on a paper towel and wrap the towel around the bristle end of the toothbrush. Then push the brush along the tracks to dislodge dirt. Or put the bristles to work on the grime that collects around the rim of a bathroom sink. Once the bristles have loosened the dirt, just mop it up with a damp sponge.

I hate the mineral deposits on my bathroom taps

USE AN OVERNIGHT VINEGAR WRAP No one likes crusty white deposits on a tap. Try this easy solution. Before you go to bed one night, take a bottle of white vinegar and three paper towels. Saturate the paper towels in the white vinegar and wrap them around the tap like a

THE BATHROOM OF THE FUTURE

In 1936, the architect and futurist Buckminster Fuller presented his prototype for 'the bathroom of the future'. Designed to be inexpensive, compact, efficient, and easy to clean, the Dymaxion Bathroom consisted of four pre-cast metal or plastic sections that bolted together into a single unit. Curved walls with smooth surfaces and large-radius corners eliminated germ-harbouring nooks and crannies and grime-collecting grout lines and made cleaning ultra quick and simple. The Fog Gun, a hyper-efficient hot-water vapour shower, used only a cup of water for each shower and cleaned without soap. The waterless Packaging Toilet shrink-wrapped human waste for composting. And downdraft vents swiftly drew steam away. The super efficient design even kept the mirror from steaming up and the sink from getting covered with splashes.

Sadly, the Dymaxion Bathroom was never produced commercially, although visitors can still see the prototype at the Henry Ford Museum in Dearborn, Michigan, USA.

cocoon. In the morning, remove the paper towels. Fill the basin with warm water, plus a squirt of washing-up liquid. Dip an old toothbrush in the solution and scrub the tap to remove the final bits of mineral deposit.

■ CLEANING THE KITCHEN

There's a burn mark on my laminate worktop

TRY BICARBONATE OF SODA ON LIGHT BURNS If the burn mark on the worktop is light brown, you may be able to remove it by covering it with a thick paste of bicarbonate soda and water. Let the mixture sit for 20 minutes, then scrub it off. If the burn has damaged the laminate, you may need to replace it completely.

My laminate worktop is scratched

HIDE THE SCRATCHES WITH CAR POLISH If the scratches aren't deep, you can hide them with a little car polish. Apply the product according to the directions. Buff with a soft cotton rag.

My expensive stone worktop has a stain

REMOVE WATER-BASED STAINS WITH HOT WATER Most stone stains come from liquids that seep into the stone's pores and then evaporate, leaving coloured solids. To remove the stain, you need to get the solids back into solution and extract them. To remove a water-based stain, such as fruit juice, pour hot (but not boiling) water on to the stain. Let the water stand for a few minutes and then soak up the excess. Lay a handful of paper towels on the stain, cover them with a piece of cling film and lay something heavy on top, like a pan of water. Let this stand overnight. In the morning, the paper towels should have drawn out the stain.

REMOVE OILY STAINS WITH ACETONE For oil-based stains, such as olive oil, follow the same procedure but instead of hot water, use (unheated) acetone. You can buy acetone at a hardware store or you can use most nail polish removers, which are acetone. The next morning, remove the towels and wash the spot with warm, soapy water. In either case, if the stain is still there, repeat the process.

The carpets near my kitchen are greasy

USE A SPECIAL GREASE-REMOVING COMPOUND The dingy film on the carpet near your kitchen is grease. When you cook, minute particles of airborne grease land on the kitchen floor, get picked up by your feet, and are transferred onto the carpet. Vacuuming doesn't help. Unless you remove the grease, it will sink deeper into the fibres, turning darker and darker as it collects more dirt.

You can buy dry carpet cleaners that are specifically designed to combat stubborn grease. They look a bit like moist bicarbonate of soda. They are available from specialist carpet cleaners and online.

1 Using water in a spray bottle, mist the high-traffic areas of the carpet where the grease has collected.
2 Sprinkle the product on to the dark spots and let it sit for half an hour to absorb the grease.
3 Vacuum up the powder.

My big family get-together was fun but we're left with a terrible mess

CLEAR UP THE WORST STRAIGHTAWAY Don't wear yourself out by trying to tackle the *entire* mess immediately. Spend just a few minutes dealing with the worst of the chaos and then do the detailed work in the morning. Assuming you have already put perishable foods away, here are the steps to follow:

1 Collect bottles, cups and glasses. Look out for spills and deal with them at once.
2 Empty half-filled glasses and cups into the kitchen sink. Throw away plastic and paper. Put the glasses on the worktop. Do the same with plates and utensils.
3 If you have one, fill the dishwasher with as many dishes as you can fit in and start it when it's fully loaded.
4 Gather up the rubbish in plastic bags, starting in the outer rooms and working your way toward the kitchen, so that you centralise the clutter there. Take rubbish out as soon as the bags are filled and tied, to prevent accidental leaks and any resultant odours.
5 In the morning, after a good night's sleep, finish up by dusting and vacuuming, again working your way toward the kitchen. Clean the kitchen last.

■ ACCIDENTS

Glass has shattered all over the floor

PUT THE PIECES IN A BOX, NOT A BAG Whether it was a wine glass, a lightbulb or a mirror that smashed to smithereens, here is how to quickly and safely handle shattered glass. More than anything, watch your step and warn other people away.

1 Wearing thick work gloves, pick up the large pieces first. Put them in a box or bucket, since a bag may tear and the shards inside can still stab you.
2 If the breakage was on a carpet, keep picking. Vacuum up only the smallest pieces.
3 If the spill was on a hard floor, such as wood or tiles, sweep up the fragments and then wipe the area with damp paper towels. Those near-invisible but still-dangerous slivers will stick to the moist paper. Throw away the towel after one or two swipes and use a fresh one, repeating until you have wiped the entire area.
4 When you've finished, seal the box, write 'Broken Glass' on the outside and put it out with your rubbish. Or find a nearby recycling bin and put it straight in there.

A rubbish bag has broken all over the carpet

PICK UP THE SOLIDS Get a new bag to put all the solid materials into. Don't be squeamish about the rubbish. You can wash your hands as soon as you've finished. Be careful to watch out for broken glass or sharp metal can lids.

BLOT UP THE LIQUID AND VACUUM Next, blot up any liquids with paper towels. Contain large spills by blotting from the outer edge to the centre. Take the vacuum cleaner and hoover up the small bits, such as crumbs and coffee grounds.

MIST AND BLOT REMAINING STAIN To prevent staining, lift the residue of any spilled liquid before it dries. The simplest stain-lifting technique is this: mist water on the stain with a spray bottle. Blot with a clean, dry paper towel. Repeat until the stain is gone. Dry by laying a thin stack of paper towels on the spot with a weight, such as a brick, on top. (Put the brick in a plastic bag or on top of a piece of foil.) Brush the carpet pile to restore a consistent texture.

As many carpets and rugs have padded underlays beneath them, don't soak the stains. Carpet underlays soaked with leftover cleaning solution can attract more dirt and lead to problems such as mildew and glue deterioration. Avoid rubbing the stain, which could push it deeper into the pile. Don't make a circular motion as it can destroy a the texture of a carpet.

I have spilled coffee on my sofa

USE A FIZZY DRINK TO GET IT OUT Quickly use a cloth or paper towel to blot up the liquid. Then pour a little soda water, or a fizzy lemonade drink such as Sprite, or 7 Up on to the stain and dab that up. The carbonation helps to bring the spilled coffee to the surface. Keep blotting the stain with an absorbent cloth to remove any liquid. Then rinse by dabbing it with fresh water.

I have dripped candle wax on the carpet

IRON IT OUT ONTO PAPER To get candle wax out of fabric or carpeting, you need to reheat the wax and soak it up with paper. First, pick out whatever wax you can with your fingers. Then place newspaper over the wax and apply a hot, dry iron to the newspaper. The wax will melt, and the paper will soak it up. If your carpet is a light colour, use white computer paper or a white paper towel instead to make sure that no ink transfers to the carpet.

▪ CLEANING UP AFTER CHILDREN

Unwanted felt-tip masterpiece on the wall? Get it off quickly with a paper towel – and perhaps a little surgical spirit.

My child has scribbled on the wall with a felt-tip marker

TRY INCREASINGLY STRONG MEASURES First try the simplest fix, which will be least harmful to the wall and then use tougher methods if that doesn't work:

- Wipe with dry paper towel. If the mark is still wet or the surface is smooth and non-porous, it may remove the mark.
- Then try moistening the towel with surgical spirit.
- As a last resort try paint remover. It is flammable, so be careful. It can also damage wall finishes, so test first in an inconspicuous area of the same surface.

A baby has vomited on the carpet

SPRAY WITH WATER AND BLOT Vomit is a protein-based stain, so avoid using warm and especially not hot water, which can lock the stain in the fibres of a carpet.

1 First remove any solids using paper towels.
2 Next, spray the area with cold water and blot. Repeat until the stain is gone.
3 If residue remains, soak the accident site in an enzymatic cleaner, the kind you can buy at pet shops to remove odours. Wash and rinse according to the product directions.

There is a piece of chewing gum on the carpet

FREEZE IT WITH ICE AND SCRAPE OFF Take some ice, put it in a plastic bag (to prevent leaking) and rub the ice on the gum until the gum freezes and hardens. Scrape away the hardened gum with a dull knife. If residue remains, remove it by blotting with a dry-cleaning solvent. Be sure to test the solvent first in an inconspicuous spot to make sure that it won't damage the carpet. This procedure will also work with upholstery.

CLEANING WITH PRODUCTS FROM THE KITCHEN

In your zeal to keep your bathroom clean, have you amassed a lot of specialised cleaning products? Do you have one product to clean the sink, another for the tiles and yet another to oust mildew from the shower curtain? You just don't need them. Keep a supply of bicarbonate of soda, white vinegar and surgical spirit on hand to conquer your dirty bathroom. Here are some tips:

- For sticky spots on bathroom worktops, dampen a cotton wool ball with surgical spirit and dab away the spots.

- To keep your toilet bowl clean, pour 50ml bicarbonate of soda into the water and let it bubble for a few minutes before scrubbing with a toilet brush and flushing.

- Other ways to clean a toilet: drop a denture-cleaning tablet (let it dissolve before flushing) or a can of cola (wait a few minutes before flushing).

- Mop a tiled bathroom floor using a mixture of 200ml white vinegar and 800ml warm water.

- To clean windows, mix equal amounts of distilled water and white vinegar in a plastic spray bottle. Spray the glass with the solution and follow by wiping with a clean cloth or paper towel.

My children have got crayon marks all over the kitchen table

USE TOOTHPASTE OR MAYONNAISE TO REMOVE THE MARKS These two common household items can help to remove crayon marks.

- For painted surfaces, put a dab of white, non-gel toothpaste on to an old toothbrush or dry rag and rub.
- For stained or untreated wood, rub real mayonnaise on to the marks with a rag, let it sit for a minute or two, and then wipe it off with a damp cloth.

▦ CLEANING UP AFTER PETS

My pet has made a mess on the carpet

USE AN ODOUR-CONTROLLING CLEANER Even the best-trained pets can have a mishap. Follow these steps to clean up the mess thoroughly:

1 Carefully remove the solid part of the mess using an inside-out plastic bag over your hand. Turn it right side out to fully enclose the contents.
2 Blot up any liquid content with paper towels.
3 Soak the accident site with an enzymatic odour-removing cleaner, available from pet shops.
4 Rinse the residue with plain water to avoid leaving any scent that might draw the pet back to use the same spot.

BE READY FOR THE NEXT TIME Put together a pet-accident kit: keep paper towels, plastic bags (for disposing of solids and paper towels), a sponge and an enzymatic cleaner in a labelled bag or box.

My pet has wet the rug

SOAK IT UP WITH PAPER TOWELS If the accident is fresh, soak up the liquid with a paper towel. Then lay a thick layer of paper towels on the spot. Cover the paper towels with newspaper. Stand on the padding for a couple of minutes. The pressure will help the paper to draw up the liquid. Do this again with fresh paper towels until no more comes through.

THEN USE AN ODOUR-REMOVING CLEANER Next, saturate the spot with an enzymatic odour-removing cleaner. This type of cleaner even works on old, dried-on urine stains. Rinse the area by spraying it with clean water and blotting up the water with paper towels. Avoid using fragrant cleaners, such as shampoos, soaps or vinegar to clean the rug. They may draw the pet to urinate on the same spot again.

I can smell pet urine, but I can't find it

USE A BLACK LIGHT TO FIND THE SPOT You don't always find a puddle when it's fresh. You may know nothing about it until you smell it and by then the puddle may be dry and invisible, particularly on a dark or patterned rug or carpet. To find the old stain, turn out all the lights in the room. Then use a black light to illuminate the old urine stains. A black light, sold in hardware stores, is an ultraviolet light that makes some compounds, such as those found in urine, glow in the dark. Outline the stains with chalk or string, so you can locate them when you turn the lights back on. Then clean as you would a fresh stain (see opposite).

My pet keeps urinating on the same spot

CLEAN WELL AND TRY RE-TRAINING Dogs and cats use urine as a territorial marker. In the house, it can ruin floors and carpets, and create foul and lingering odours. To stop them, you need to completely remove all traces of urine from the spot they've marked. After you've soaked up fresh urine using paper towels, take the paper towels to your pet's designated toilet area, such as a litter box or an area of the garden outside. Take your pet to the chosen spot and let it smell the urine there so that it makes the connection that the place is to be its toilet.

There's pet hair all over my furniture

VACUUM IT UP Pet hair can drive you mad. It turns up on sofa cushions and chairs, and then it ends up on your clothes. And it is the devil to remove. First, try the vacuum cleaner, but use a lint-brush attachment. These will help to dislodge even the short, wiry hairs that embed themselves in your upholstery.

WIPE IT OFF WITH A RUBBER GLOVE You can also wear a damp rubber glove and rub your hand across the cushions. This clumps together the hair for easy removal.

PROBLEM STOPPER

Keeping pet mess to a minimum

• To keep moisture and mud out of the house, carry a small towel on rainy or snowy walks for wiping the animal's paws.

• To catch food spills and speed up their disposal, cover the pet's eating area generously with newspaper. (But don't do this with a puppy you are paper training.)

• If a pet carries food away from its usual eating spot, keep moving it back until the animal gets the idea.

• If you bathe a dog in the bath, cover the floor with towels. Towel the dog as dry as you can – and don't open the bathroom door until it has shaken off all the water it can.

Tools and workshop

Stop wood splitting
To avoid splitting wood when you are driving in a nail, try blunting the point of the nail with a light hammer blow. Sharp nails spread the wood fibres apart as they are driven in; blunt nails crush the wood fibres. Another option is to try nailing into the lighter part of the wood, not the grain lines. The darker grain lines are harder and are more likely to start a split.

The best solution is to drill a pilot hole for the nail. To do this, select a drill bit that's slightly smaller in diameter than the nail. (An old trick is to clip the head off a panel pin, using the wire cutters on a pair of combination pliers and use it as a drill bit. Panel pins tend to become blunt rather quickly, so for large jobs use a drill bit.)

■ FASTENERS

I can't nail and hold boards together at the same time

USE SUPERGLUE TO HOLD THE PIECES An extra hand would be a great help when you are working alone in an awkward position – up a ladder or down on your hands and knees. But here's a fast, practical solution that some experts use: keep a tube of superglue, sold in DIY and hardware stores, handy in your pocket or tool belt. When you need to nail or screw two pieces of wood together and can't hold both pieces at the same time, dab a little of the superglue between them, hold them in place until the glue dries (a matter of seconds) and then drive your nail in. Make sure you use a fast-setting superglue, whose main ingredient is cyanoacrylate. This trick can also work for plastic, metal and other materials. It's the best solution – hands down.

Panel pins won't hold my mouldings in place

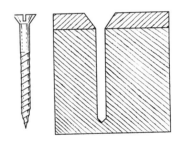

USE SCREWS If architraves and other mouldings won't stay in place and keep 'popping up', use small diameter countersunk screws to hold them in place instead of panel pins. Screws draw pieces together much better than nails. Drill a pilot hole for the screw through to the wood underneath and then a clearance hole and a countersink in the moulding. Fill over the screw head with filler.

I have dropped nails all over the floor

PICK THEM UP WITH A MAGNET This isn't a mess you can sweep under the carpet! If you have hundreds of panel pins, small nails or tacks scattered about the floor, it will take ages to pick them up one at a time. The quick solution is to go to the fridge for a magnet – the kind you use to put notes on the fridge door. If you drag a magnet across the spilled nails, you will be able to scoop up a dozen or more at once and be finished in no time. The bigger the magnet, the more effective it will be.

I keep dropping nails all over the garden

MAKE A HOLDER FROM A TENNIS BALL If you don't want to lug a heavy toolbox around to keep small fasteners in place, try this improvised container instead. Cut a slit in a tennis ball. Give it a squeeze and the slit will widen. Drop your screws or nails in and relax your squeeze to close it. Tuck the ball into your pocket and go outside to complete your project. Squeeze the ball again to open the slit and shake out nails and screws as you need them.

A slit tennis ball, if left empty, can serve another function. If you need to tap some delicate woodwork into place, slip the ball over the head of your hammer. It will give the hammer taps a gentler impact.

THE METRICATION MUDDLE

The United Kingdom has been messing about with metrication for more than 40 years. In 1965 the then Labour Government announced that the building industry would go metric 'within ten years' (in fact it went metric in 1970). In 1969 the Metrication Board was set up to oversee metrication, only for it to be abolished by the Conservative Government in 1980.

The way the system now operates is, frankly, a complete muddle. If you doubt this, stand in a timber yard for a few minutes and listen to what is being ordered – it will be a complete dog's breakfast of inches, feet, metres and millimetres. The problem is that with many things, the sizes or quantities haven't changed – only the units used to measure them.

So we have rolls of wallpaper measuring 10.05m by 0.52m (in fact 33ft by 21in), wood sized at 12mm, 19mm and 38mm (really ½in, ¾in and 1½in), plasterboard that comes in a thickness of 9.7mm (⅜in), plumbing pipe with circumferences of 15mm, 22mm and 28mm (the old ½in, ¾in and 1in sizes, but today the outside diameter is measured not the inside) – and the list goes on and on.

Continental Europe is, of course, completely metric (though they tend to use centimetres whereas we have gone for millimetres) as are China and Japan, while the United States seems to be making even slower progress than we are towards their declared aim of converting to the metric system. Australia is an interesting example of how a change in the system can be done effectively – they metricated completely between 1970 and 1981.

I keep whacking my fingers when I am hammering small nails

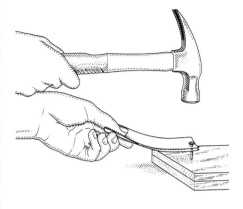

HOLD THE NAIL WITH A PIECE OF PAPER Gardeners get a green thumb; many carpenters get a red thumb – the swollen kind. To keep your fingertips out of harm's way when you are hammering a little nail or panel pin, stick the nail through one end of a folded sheet of stiff paper. (A panel pin is a thin nail with a small flat head, which can be punched below the wood surface.) Using the paper as a holder, drive in the nail. Before finally seating the nail, tear the paper away. The teeth of a comb, tweezers or long-nose pliers can also serve as nail holders.

I can't reach the place where I need to drive in a screw

MAGNETISE YOUR SCREWDRIVER The problem with driving a screw into tight spots is that you can't get a hand in there to steady the screw while you get started. You won't need to steady the screw if a magnetised screwdriver is holding it in place. You can quickly magnetise a screwdriver by dragging its blade over a magnet several times in one direction. Find a magnet on the fridge door.

A screwdriver that you have magnetised should hold its charge for about a week. To prevent the charge from draining out of it, keep it away from other metal objects. To demagnetise it, drag the blade over the magnet in the opposite direction. If you are often faced with this problem, consider buying a ready-magnetised screwdriver, which will keep its charge permanently.

TAPE THE SCREW TO THE SCREWDRIVER If the magnet trick isn't feasible, a little bit of adhesive tape will do the job instead. Tear off about 75mm of tape and push the screw through the centre of the sticky side of the tape. Insert the screwdriver in

TAPE

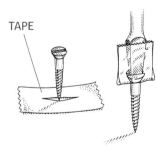

to the slot of the screw and then wrap the tape around the blade of the screwdriver.

USE BLU-TAK TO HOLD THE SCREW Yet another alternative is to dab some Blu-Tak on to the end of the screw and then insert the blade of the screwdriver into the slot.

I have damaged the slot in my screw

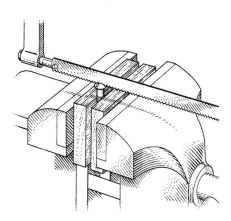

DEEPEN THE SLOT WITH A HACKSAW When you need to remove a screw and then drive it back in again, it's easy to chew up the screw's slot, especially if the blade of your screwdriver doesn't fit the slot. If you don't have a replacement screw available, a quick way to restore the old screw is to deepen the slot by running a hacksaw along it. With a cross-head screw, cut two slots at right angles. If you are repairing a screw when it is out of its hole, don't hold the screw in your fingers. Put it in a vice between two scraps of wood, so that you won't hurt yourself and can protect the screw threads.

▪ TOOL PROBLEMS

My spanner is too big for the nut

FILL THE GAP WITH A COIN Usually, bigger is better, but not when you need to remove a nut with an open-ended spanner that is a little too large for it. The solution is in your pocket or purse. Simply insert a

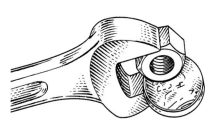

coin between the spanner and the nut. The coin will serve as a wedge, making it possible to turn the nut. You'll have to experiment to find out which coin best fills the gap. A washer will also work.

TRICKS OF THE TRADE

How to escape a scrape
When loosening a very tight nut or bolt, push the spanner handle with your open palm rather than grasping it with your hand. If the nut suddenly loosens or the tool slips off, you won't smash or scrape your knuckles.

I can't drill perfectly perpendicular holes

MAKE A SIMPLE DRILLING GUIDE For drilling straight down into a horizontal surface with a regular twist bit, make a drilling guide from two pieces of 19mm (¾in) plywood, 19mm thick and 50mm wide (¾in by 2in). Glue and nail the pieces together with panel pins to form a corner.

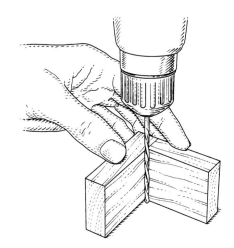

To use this guide, all you have to do is run your drill bit along the inside corner.

PUT A WASHER ON THE BIT SHANK When drilling a hole in a vertical surface, you can use the same guide block. But if you are using a wide spade bit, you will need a different approach. Slip a steel washer over the shank of the bit before you put the bit in the drill. If the washer slides forward or backward as you drill, you are tilting the

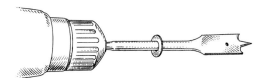

drill up or down. You will still have to use your eye to keep the drill straight from side to side.

I can't turn this nut with my spanner

EXTEND THE HANDLE WITH A PIPE What you need is a longer handle on your spanner to give you more leverage. Find a small piece of pipe, slide it over the handle of your spanner and use that to turn the stubborn nut or bolt.

I don't have a Pozidriv screwdriver

CUT A SLOT FOR A REGULAR SCREWDRIVER It's a frustrating case of incompatibility: you need to put in a Posidriv-head screw and all you have on hand is a conventional slotted screwdriver. As with the damaged screw head (page 47), a hacksaw provides a quick solution.

Use the hacksaw to extend one of the slots in the screw head so that it goes all the way across the screw's top. Then you can use a conventional screwdriver. You can use a Phillips screwdriver to loosen or tighten a Pozidriv screw – but not the other way round. It is better to have a socket screwdriver with a selection of bits.

My saw is all gummed up with resin

REMOVE IT WITH OVEN CLEANER When sawing soft, resinous wood like pine, you are bound to get a gummy buildup that will make your saw blade seem blunt. To remove the resin, spray the saw blade with oven cleaner, scrub with an old toothbrush and rinse with water. (Wear rubber gloves and safety goggles when you do this.)

■ ORGANISING YOUR TOOLS AND SUPPLIES

I can't keep my screws and nuts in order

USE OLD FILM CANISTERS You could buy one of those plastic cabinets for nuts and bolts, but sometimes it's good to have a smaller, more portable organiser. Old camera film canisters are an inexpensive, handy solution. They make great containers for small screws, nuts, tacks and drawing pins. And for those times when you are hanging on to a ladder or you don't want to put down a cordless drill or screwdriver, you can pop the top off a film canister with one hand. Label the canisters with masking tape and a marker. Or colour-code each canister with insulating tape, which comes in a rainbow of hues other than traditional black. But start saving the canisters now. With the ever-increasing popularity of digital cameras, film may soon be obsolete.

SURELY NOT

KNOW THE DRILL

It's a story that's repeated in do-it-yourself stores across the country. Every few months, a customer will come into the store to ask for a refund on a brand-new drill that does not work. The bit spins, he says, but nothing happens. No sawdust, no hole. Just smoke and the smell of burning wood. They're completely baffled – until the store explains that he has had the drill's switch set to reverse.

• To give your ladder skid-free traction on smooth surfaces, set the feet into an old pair of Wellington boots.

• To prevent a ladder from damaging wall-hung tiles, cover the top of the rails with old socks, gloves or mittens.

I keep losing the bits for my cordless drill

MAKE A MINI HOLDER FOR THE BITS One of the best tools to appear on DIY store shelves in recent decades is the cordless drill/driver. But it can be hard to keep track of small drill and screwdriver bits, especially when you find yourself in an awkward spot – working up a ladder for example – trying to alternate between two different bits. You can buy holders. But you can also make a bit holder yourself using recycled materials. Pull the rubber squeeze bulb off the dropper of an old medicine bottle. Tape the squeeze bulb, open side up, to the side of the cordless drill or tool belt or ladder – wherever it is handiest. Slip the bit in there when it's not in use. Make sure it fits snugly, so it won't fall out.

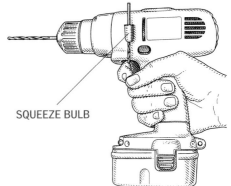

SQUEEZE BULB

STEP-BY-STEP LADDER SAFETY

If you are a homeowner, it is likely that at some point you will need to unfold a stepladder or lean an extension ladder against the house for a routine repair. Here is how to avoid becoming a ladder-injury statistic.

• Use a ladder of the correct length. Your extension ladder should extend at least 1m (3ft) over the roofline or similar working surface.

• Never stand on the three top rungs of a straight ladder. Never stand on the top step of a stepladder.

• Set straight ladders up at an angle of approximately 75 degrees (1 out, 4 up).

• Don't exceed a ladder's weight limit (user plus materials). This should be marked somewhere on the ladder. And never have more than one person on a ladder at a time.

• As metal conducts electricity, use a wooden or glass-fibre ladder when working near power lines or electrical equipment. Regardless of the material, never let your ladder touch a live wire.

• Position the ladder on firm, level ground. Use large flat boards to make adjustments for uneven or soft ground. Get a helper to hold the bottom to steady the ladder, if possible.

• Before mounting a ladder, make sure all the locks are properly engaged.

• Do not set up a ladder in front of a door that is not locked, blocked or guarded.

• When working on a ladder, keep your body centred between the rails. Do not lean to one side.

• Never leave a raised ladder unattended.

I can't keep track of my tools

GET ORGANISED WITH TOOL TRAYS Do you sometimes make half a dozen trips to the garage to find the right tool? Or, worse, can't find the right tool at all because your tools are scattered all over the house? Our favourite handyman has a solution. Get two heavy-duty plastic tool trays with side-by-side, lidless compartments and extra tool slots. Always return the trays to the workshop or garage when the job is finished.

USE ONE TRAY FOR LIGHT REPAIRS Keep one tray filled with what you need for light repairs. Here's what to keep in it:

- *450g claw hammer*
- *combination pliers*
- *adjustable spanner*
- *torch*
- *junior hacksaw*
- *tape measure*
- *trimming knife*
- *electrician's screwdriver*
- *cordless screwdriver with two-way bit*

USE THE OTHER TRAY FOR PROJECTS Keep the other tool tray empty. When a special project arises, fill it with the appropriate tools for that specific job. Be sure to unload the special-project tools when you have finished and you will always know where your tools are.

I need a funnel right now

MAKE ONE FROM A PLASTIC BOTTLE If you don't have a funnel when you need one, you can make one quickly from an old plastic soft drink bottle. Just use a sharp trimming knife to cut the bottle in half. Then use the spout end as a funnel.

Tools keep falling off my stepladder

USE LARGE RUBBER BANDS TO HOLD THE TOOLS
To save yourself numerous trips up and down a stepladder to retrieve tools that keep falling off the ladder, stretch two extra-large rubber bands around the top step or tool tray on the shelf. Slide your tools under the rubber bands and they'll still be there when you need them.

Spray can saver
To stop the nozzles on cans of spray paint from getting clogged with paint, when you have finished painting, turn the can upside down and spray onto a piece of scrap cardboard until only clear propellant comes out. That indicates that the nozzle is clear. Put the cap back on the can and put it away until you need it again. Be sure to store it where it will not freeze or be exposed to heat, as you would with other paints.

My extension lead is in a tangled mess

KEEP IT COILED IN A BUCKET The best solution when using power tools at a distance from a socket outlet is to have a proper extension lead, which you can wind back into its holder or onto its reel when you have finished using it. A home-made extension lead, fitted with a plug and trailing socket, is cheaper, but can get itself into an awful mess. Not only is the lead tangled, but every time you use it, you have to walk the lead out and re-coil the entire thing, even if you need to extend your reach by only a small amount. Here's a quick way to solve both problems:

1 Drill a hole large enough for the lead's plug to fit through near the bottom of a plastic 14 litre (3 gallon) bucket.
2 Feed the plug end of the lead through the hole from the inside of the bucket, leaving a short tail hanging out.
3 Coil the rest of the lead in the bucket.

When you need to use the lead, draw out as much as you need from the bucket.
When you have finished, simply coil it back again. As an added bonus, you can also use the bucket to carry tools to the site of a job.

■ SANDING PROBLEMS

My glasspaper is clogged with dust

SAND IT WITH ANOTHER PIECE OF GLASSPAPER It is frustrating – and wasteful – when the gritty surface of the glasspaper you are using quickly fills up with dust. But there is a fast and effective solution to this problem. Instead of discarding the clogged piece for a new one, lightly sand it with another piece of glasspaper. That will clear the dust and allow you to continue.

My house fills with dust when I'm sanding floors

TAPE OVER THE DOORS When you are doing a lot of sanding, especially sanding down wooden floors before applying a new surface finish, dust can get everywhere. In the room where you are using a floor sander, remove curtains, lampshades and pictures before you start and also remove any books from bookshelves (or cover them with a polythene dustsheet securely taped at the edges).

You will need to remove the door leading into the room so that you can reach the floor underneath it, so ask a helper to seal the doorway with a polythene sheet and strong adhesive tape from the other side once you are in the room with the sanding machines. This will ensure that dust does not spread into the rest of the house. Once in the room, open all the windows to allow the dust out. As sanding floors makes a lot of noise, warn your neighbours before you start work.

Sanding grooves on moulding takes too long

MAKE A MOULDED SANDING BLOCK If you would rather not be 'in the groove' any longer than necessary – especially if you have a lot to do – make a customised sanding block that exactly fits the pattern of the contoured wood moulding you are working with. Here's how:

1 Mix up some car body filler in a plastic bag.
2 Press the bag against the wood moulding before the filler hardens so that the mix conforms to the surface.

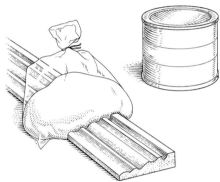

3 When the filler hardens, remove the plastic bag and shape the sides of the hard-filler block with a file or rasp for easy gripping.

Wrap a piece of glasspaper around the block and start sanding.

Furniture

**Polishing out
surface scratches**
If the scratch is in the
layer of finish – and
doesn't go into the wood
itself – simply buff with
a furniture wax polish.
That should remove the
scratch and restore the
lustre of the finish.

■ SCRATCHES AND DENTS

There is a dent in my sideboard

**USE STEAM TO SWELL THE
WOOD FIBRES** Small dents
can often be fixed with a bit
of steam. First make sure
that moisture can penetrate
the wood. Remove the
finish from the dented area
by sanding with fine-grade
sandpaper. Or just prick the
area several times with a
fine pin. Then cover the
dented surface with a pad
made by folding a wet
cloth, put a metal bottle top on the pad to spread the heat and press
the front tip of an iron on a high setting to the bottle top for a few
minutes. The resulting steam will make the wood fibres swell. Repeat
until the dent has disappeared. Sand the area and repaint or refinish.
Don't try this on veneers or near the joints of old furniture, because
the steam can damage natural glues.

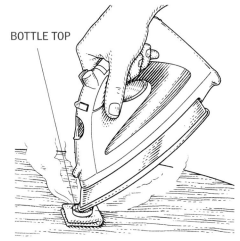

BOTTLE TOP

There is a scratch in my dining-room table

USE A NUT KERNEL OR SHOE POLISH For a scratch that goes deep
enough to expose the raw wood below the finish, here are some
ready remedies that you can find around the house:

- You can hide a small scratch on wood by rubbing it with
  a walnut, pecan or other oily nut. Olive or vegetable oil also
  works. Buff with a clean cloth.
- Use a cotton bud to apply a paste shoe polish that matches the
  colour of the wood.

USE A FURNITURE TOUCH-UP PEN OR CRAYON Furniture stores and DIY
stores sell touch-up pens and 'crayons' for scratches in wooden

The enemies of furniture

Many people wait until it's too late to face the forces bent on damaging the finish of their best furniture. Once a surface is scratched, stained or cracked, it may be expensive to fix – or it may not be possible to repair it at all. There are seven major enemies of wood finishes (not including young children). Know what they are and make sure you avoid them.

- **Liquids** One of the most common problems stems from sweaty glasses left on tabletops. Water and other liquids penetrate a finish film and damage the wood underneath, causing cloudy or chalky stains that are hard to remove. Use coasters and wipe up spills right away.

- **Heat** A hot cup of coffee placed on an antique finish can create a white ring, which resembles a watermark. Likewise, indirect heat can damage wood finishes. Use coasters for hot drinks. Keep furniture at least 60cm from radiators, open fires and other heat sources. Use caution when storing wooden furniture.

- **Dust** Silent and surprisingly destructive, dust can dull finishes by filling crevices and causing microscopic scratches. Dust at least every two weeks using a soft, lint-free cloth (an old T-shirt will work well), neither wet nor dry but lightly dampened. Every three months or so, use a spray-on furniture polish (but not if you previously waxed the furniture) or once a year or so, re-apply a paste wax.

- **Chemicals** Coasters can prevent water and heat marks, but be careful which kind of coaster you use. Some made of synthetic materials, such as artificial rubber, can soften and dull hard surface finishes. The same goes for plastic covers and pads. Avoid the use of such pads and coasters.

- **Acids** Body oils and perspiration contain lactic acid and salts that can break down wood finishes, leaving sticky, dirt-attracting areas. Plant and flower nectar can do the same thing. Place plants away from wooden furniture. Regular dusting and polishing will remove body oils. Periodically clean 'high-touch' areas, such as the arms of chairs, with a furniture cleaner, using a soft cloth or very fine (0000) steel wool.

- **Abrasions** Believe it or not, many furniture scratches and gouges may have nothing to do with children. Unlikely suspects, such as lamps, ceramics and other accessories with hard bottoms, are often the culprits. Place protective padding, such as stick-on felt sheets or pads sold in DIY stores and craft suppliers, on the bottoms of all such accessories.

- **Sunlight** We all know how dangerous the sun's ultraviolet rays can be to human skin. The same rays can wreak havoc on wood finishes, causing cracking and fading. The simple answer to preventing sun damage is not to place furniture in direct sunlight. But that's not always easy. You can use curtains and blinds, as well as UV-screening films, on windows to block out the sun. Planting shrubs in front of windows may help to block the sun. You can also move lamps and accessories around on wood furniture that is exposed to sunlight to avoid noticeable dark spots where the sun never gets a look in.

Rub away scratches on glass tops

You can rub away minor scratches in the glass top of a coffee or side table with a dab of white toothpaste. Use your fingertip to rub in the toothpaste in a circular motion. Let the area dry completely before buffing it clean with a lint-free cloth.

furniture. Match the wood as closely as possible, colour in the scratch and buff it with a cloth. You can also colour a scratch to match the wood using a cotton bud and a furniture stain, available at DIY stores and from specialist suppliers.

▥ STAINS

My antique sideboard has water rings

RUB THEM OFF WITH A MILD ABRASIVE Water rings only look permanent. Gentle scrubbing with a mild abrasive will usually remove the ring or white blemish caused by a damp coffee cup or glass on a wood surface. Here are three quick solutions:

- Rub metal polish into the area with very fine (0000) steel wool.
- Apply a dab of white toothpaste with a clean cloth.
- Mix cigarette ash with mayonnaise and rub the mixture in with a clean cloth.

Whichever method you use, rub gently in the direction of the grain and be patient – it takes slow-motion elbow grease to remove the stain without harming the piece's finish.

My wood furniture has a dark stain

BLEACH IT OUT WITH OXALIC ACID Dark stains on wood furniture are commonly caused by rust, alcohol, damp and ink. Sometimes, using the abrasive method described above for removing a water ring will work, but if the stain is too ingrained, you could try bleaching it with a special furniture bleach available from some DIY stores and specialist suppliers.

The wood bleacher is applied sparingly with a brush. Concentrate on badly affected areas. Allow to dry, check results and apply further coats if necessary. Rinse thoroughly with clean water two to three times and allow to dry completely before refinishing.

▥ BURNS

My table has a bad cigarette burn

SCRAPE AND FILL Will the burn leave a permanent scar? Not necessarily. Here's a nifty fix for burn marks in wood or veneer.

1 Start by removing the surface finish immediately around the burn with very fine sandpaper.

2 Using a small, sharp blade – a penknife blade for example, scrape away the charred wood, holding the blade at right angles to the surface and being careful not to gouge the wood.

3 If the surface damage is only superficial, you should be able to colour the wood with a stain, if the exposed wood is lighter than the rest of the table, or furniture bleach if it is darker.

4 Where the cigarette burn has gone deeper, buy some matching water-based wood filler to make the hole good. There are various different shades of wood filler to match different woods and you can mix two different colours together if you are between shades. Apply using a plastic scraper or filling knife. For best results leave enough filler to enable thorough sanding.

5 Allow the wood filler to dry thoroughly. Then sand back to the original surface level. Build up deeper holes in layers.

When you are happy with the colour of the finished wood filler (you can add a matching wood stain if necessary), apply a new finish over the repaired area, blending it in to the existing table finish.

I have a deep burn on my kitchen worktop

COVER IT WITH A TILE If a burn has eaten through the laminate, the easiest solution is to hide the burned spot with a glazed tile. Glue the tile over the damaged area and use it as a countertop trivet. Use a two-part epoxy adhesive to secure the tile.

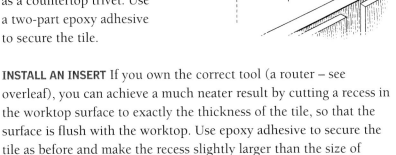

TILE

INSTALL AN INSERT If you own the correct tool (a router – see overleaf), you can achieve a much neater result by cutting a recess in the worktop surface to exactly the thickness of the tile, so that the surface is flush with the worktop. Use epoxy adhesive to secure the tile as before and make the recess slightly larger than the size of the tile so that there is adhesive surrounding it on all four sides.

**Fixing a burn in
leather upholstery**
You may be able to fix
small burn holes in
leather upholstery by
melting a little wax from
a crayon of the same
colour. Use a lighted
match or candle to
carefully melt and drip
the crayon wax into the
hole. Then use the back
of a spoon to smooth
the hot wax before
it dries.

A proper stainless-steel worktop hotplate can be installed in the same way, using a router to make a shallow recess (typically 3mm) in the worktop surface, cleaning up the corners with a sharp chisel, after using the hotplate itself to mark out the size of the recess. Holes need to be drilled in the bottom of the recess to take the securing bolts which pass through from underneath – you may have to remove a kitchen drawer in order to gain access.

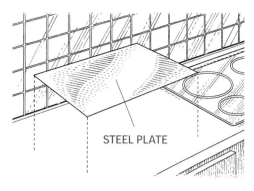

STEEL PLATE

■ VENEER AND INLAYS

The hardwood inlay on my table is loose

RESET IT WITH NEW The craft of adding plain or decorated hardwood strips to fine furniture is known as marquetry – and you can buy replacement stringing (narrow plain lines) and banding (wider decorative strips) by mail order from marquetry specialists.

1 Carefully pull up the old inlay and scrape out any old adhesive from the recess.
2 Cut the inlay to the correct size and shape, and use an offcut to spread contact adhesive carefully in the recess.
3 Spread more adhesive on the back of the banding.
4 When all the adhesive is touch dry, put the replacement inlay in place and use a wallpaper seam roller to press it down.

There's a blister in the veneer on my sideboard

Small blisters on most veneered furniture can be repaired with PVA woodworking adhesive and a few simple tools. Here's how:

1 Using the tip of a small, very sharp craft knife, cut a slit in the blister, following the wood grain.
2 Hold the slit open with the knife and use a fine-tip applicator bottle (available from specialist suppliers) to fill the blister with warm white vinegar. Let it sit for a few hours to dissolve the glue

around the blister. Let the area dry completely.

3 Now use a thin knife or the applicator (rinse the vinegar out and let the needle dry first) to insert a thin layer of adhesive across the surface of the wood beneath the veneer. Don't apply it to the veneer itself.

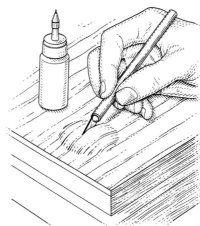

4 Lay greaseproof paper on the repair and slowly flatten the blister with a block of wood. Clamp it in place until the glue dries.

There's a blister on the veneer of my cabinet

IRON THE BLISTER If the veneer has bubbled up away from the edge, there may be a very quick solution. Iron it with a warm iron. Cut a slit as before and put a damp cloth on the surface to protect the veneer. The heat from the iron should re-activate the natural glue that was used on furniture until the early part of the last century. Weigh the area down with some heavy books after ironing it.

The veneer on my table has lifted

REGLUE THE LIFTED EDGE Veneer does sometimes peel, especially around the edges. The trick to repairing veneer is to remove the old glue and replace it with new glue.

1 If you can get under an edge, use an old knife to raise the loose veneer. But be careful. Wood veneer is thin and brittle. If you try to raise it too far, it may crack. If it's too rigid to lift, sprinkle a little warm water on it to make it more flexible. Lift it and gently scrape the underside with a craft knife or some other thin, sharp blade. Also scrape away glue from the base surface. Vacuum the dust and dried glue.

2 Once both surfaces are clean, use a small artist's paintbrush or the edge of the blade to cover as much of both surfaces as possible with woodworking adhesive. Press out as much of the excess glue as possible, wiping it away with a damp cloth.

3 Lay a piece of greaseproof paper on top of the veneer and weight it with a pile of books or another heavy, flat object.

4 When the adhesive has dried, remove the weight and paper and carefully scrape away any stuck paper with the blade.

I can't get the glue under the veneer

BLOW IT IN If you have trouble getting adhesive under old, brittle veneer, cut a length of plastic drinking straw and slightly flatten it. Then fold it in half and very slowly and patiently drip adhesive into one half. Slip the filled half under the veneer and gently blow in the adhesive.

▪ WEAR AND TEAR

My wooden drawer keeps sticking

LUBRICATE THE RUNNERS You probably need to lubricate the sliding parts. If the drawer is on wooden runners, a quick fix is to remove the drawer (and everything in it), turn it upside down and rub a white candle back and forth on the runners. Make sure there is no debris on the wooden tracks that hold the runners. If possible, rub wax on those as well. You could also use a dry spray lubricant, such as Dri-Lube, available at some DIY stores. Either one should solve the problem. If the drawer is on metal runners and uses some sort of ball bearing slide mechanism, a quick blast of WD-40 should get it sliding again.

My butcher's block has dried out

APPLY OIL Found in the best kitchens, a butcher's block is a hardworking, often unappreciated surface. Because it is used for cutting it is not finished with a surface varnish or finish. That means it tends to dry out and when wood dries, it cracks, splits and warps. Conditioning a butcher's block is easy. Most butcher's blocks are made of hardwood, which has tight grains and pores. First, clean the surface with a mild solution of water and a squirt of washing-up liquid and then blot it dry. Next, spread a liberal amount of butcher block oil (available by mail order from specialist suppliers) evenly over the wood's surface using paper towels or a clean white cloth. For best results, warm the oil for a few minutes beforehand by setting the container of oil in a bowl of hot tap water. Once you have spread the oil, let it stand on the surface overnight (or, if that's not possible, for at least 15 minutes). Wipe away the excess oil with a clean cloth.

TIPS FOR USING AND CARING FOR A BUTCHER'S BLOCK
- Wash well with a mild solution of washing-up liquid after every use, then rinse and wipe dry.
- After you have used the block for cutting meat or poultry, use a disinfectant cleaner or a mild (1:10) solution of bleach.
- Every so often, wipe freshly squeezed lemon juice onto the surface, leave for a few minutes then rinse off and dry.
- For a really fine surface, try applying beeswax (available in some DIY stores and by mail order from specialist suppliers). Apply with a clean cloth and buff off any excess.
- If your block is damaged (cuts, stains and scratches), use an orbital sander to clean up the surface before oiling and waxing.

My table's legs have come loose

WRAP THE SCREW WITH FABRIC Legs on tables or desks that screw directly into the wood on the underside of the table can be fixed by filling the hole with a thin piece of cloth so that the screw fits more snugly. First, unscrew the loose legs. Then cut a 25mm wide strip of old stockings or tights and drape it over the threaded end of the leg. Now screw the leg and its wrapping back into the table and trim away any cloth that shows. If it's still not snug, try the same process with a thicker piece of cloth, such as a strip from an old sheet.

My chair leg has broken near the top

GLUE IT BACK WITH A DOWEL If a turned chair leg has broken near the top, simply gluing the broken piece back into place will not work – the joint will soon break again. It needs the support of a central wooden dowel. Buy a length of hardwood timber dowelling at least half the size of the narrowest part of the leg and make sure that you have a drill bit of exactly the same size (12 to 14mm, say). The repair is done in five stages:

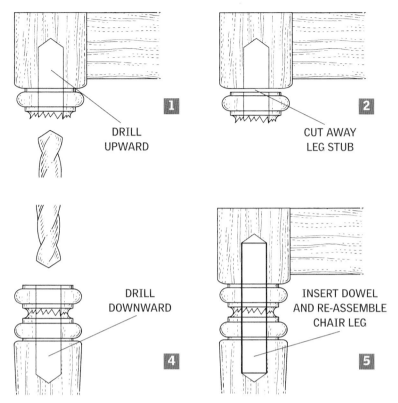

DRILL
UPWARD **1**

CUT AWAY
LEG STUB **2**

DRILL
DOWNWARD **4**

INSERT DOWEL
AND RE-ASSEMBLE
CHAIR LEG **5**

1 Keeping the drill bit square to the wood, drill upward through the broken stub of leg into the square top of the leg.

2 Use a very fine-toothed saw (such as a junior hacksaw) to cut through the leg stub, using one of the narrow diameters as your cutting line. This piece needs to be at least 25mm long.

3 Glue the cut-off stub back on to the remainder of the chair leg, using woodworking adhesive. Secure in place while the adhesive dries.

4 Drill down into the leg using the hole in the piece that you have just glued on as the drilling guide.

5 Cut a length of dowelling to just less than the depth of the two holes added together and re-assemble the leg to the chair with the dowel held in place with woodworking adhesive. Fix a clamp to hold it in place and wipe off excess adhesive with a damp cloth.

This method can also be used for repairing broken stair balusters; if the break is near the end and you can get the end out of its housing, you do not need to make a cut as you can glue the two pieces together and drill down for the dowel from the end.

A strand in my wicker chair has broken

REJOIN THE STRAND WITH TAPE For some reason a broken strand on a wicker chair can really draw the eye. A formerly pristine love seat is one step down the path toward dilapidation – at least in the eye of the beholder. But luckily the break is simple to disguise. Using your fingers, push the two sides of the broken strand back into place so that the ends meet. Then 'bandage' the two ends together by wrapping a thin layer of masking tape tightly around the break – two wraps will probably do it. Depending on how the wicker is woven, you may need to narrow the width of your masking tape by cutting it with scissors. Paint over the tape with the same colour as the original wicker. If the wicker has a natural finish, you may need to darken the tape or alter its hue with a brown or orange marker pen.

The rung on my chair is loose

REGLUE AND WEDGE THE JOINT
If a chair joint is shaky, you can often reinforce it quickly without having to undertake the tricky task of taking the chair to pieces. Pull the joint apart slightly and scrape off as much of the old glue as you can, using a trimming or craft knife. Then squirt white or PVA woodworking adhesive around the rung,  wiggling the pieces to work the adhesive into the joint. If the socket is enlarged, jam toothpicks (or wooden matchsticks) into the fresh adhesive around the edges. Trim the toothpicks and wipe off the excess glue with a damp cloth. After the adhesive dries, the rung will be secure and no one will ever notice the toothpick wedges.

My door hinge screws are loose

FILL THE SCREW HOLES WITH A DOWEL Loose hinge screws can be a common problem. Sometimes fitting larger or longer screws can be a good fix, but this is not always possible.

A neater solution is to remove the hinge, drill out the screw hole using a 6mm or 8mm dowelling drill bit and insert a fluted 6mm or 8mm dowel into the hole after coating it with woodworking adhesive. When the adhesive has dried, trim off any protruding dowel, drill a small pilot hole for the screw and re-fix the hinge.

Walls and ceilings

TRICKS OF THE TRADE

Fixing a small hole in the wall

To quickly fix a small hole in the wall when you don't have any wall filler, tear a few tissues or paper towels into tiny pieces. Put the pieces in a plastic container. Mix in just enough woodworking adhesive to make a thick paste the consistency of peanut butter. Stuff the paste into the hole and smooth it flush with the rest of the wall. The patch will dry within 2 hours. Disguise the patch with a little paint. Wallpaper adhesive can also be used with this technique, which is known as papier mâché.

▪ WALL PROBLEMS

There is a hole in my plasterboard wall

CREATE A CARDBOARD BACKING BEFORE FILLING Repairing large holes in plasterboard can be tricky, since there is usually no backing behind them. Ordinary wall filler just falls through the hole when you are trying to fill it in. Below is a technique that works well for holes up to about 50mm wide:

1 Cut a piece of firm cardboard slightly larger than the hole. Thread through a piece of strong string and knot it at the back. Put a little adhesive on the rim of the face of the cardboard. Push it through the hole and pull it towards you to form a tight backing that will support your patching material.

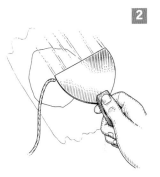

2 Apply fast-drying wall filler to the hole, filling it almost level with the wall surface. When the patch dries, cut the string flush against the wall. Score the surface of the patch. Apply more filler to make your patch level with the wall surface and smooth it. Then sand and paint.

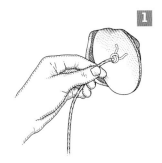

My plasterboard wall has hollows and bumps

Tiny bumps and hollows in plasterboard walls are usually caused by the nails that hold the plasterboard in place. Changes in moisture and temperature and movement of the building can all cause the nails to move, either creating a dimple (a small hollow) or perhaps pushing a disc of finishing plaster off the top of a bump. Both bumps and hollows are relatively simple to fix with only a few tools.

DRIVE IN A SCREW NEXT TO A DIMPLE If there is a dimple in the surface, drive a 32mm plasterboard screw through the same piece of plasterboard and into the same framing member (the wall stud or ceiling joist) a small distance away from the dimple. Sink the head of the screw slightly without breaking the paper on the surface of the plasterboard. The screw will keep the nail from moving again. Fill over both nail and screw heads; then paint.

PULL OUT A PROTRUDING NAIL If there is a bump, pull out the nail with a pair of pliers or drive it through the plasterboard with a nail punch. Drive in a new screw and fill in both holes as described above.

Cracks in my plaster keep coming back

COVER THEM WITH WALL REPAIR TAPE If you have an old house with plaster walls, it can be hard to get rid of stress cracks. Stress cracks occur when the house moves because of settling or seasonal swelling and shrinking. Even if you dig them out and apply so-called flexible fillers, the cracks will eventually reappear. The trick used by professional decorators is to use a thin self-adhesive wall repair tape, which is 50mm wide and very quick and easy to apply:

1 Make sure the wall around the crack is dry, clean and free from loose material.
2 Cut off enough tape to cover the length of the crack and press it down firmly into place making sure it is completely flat and crease free.

TYPES OF PLASTERBOARD

Plasterboard is essentially solid gypsum plaster sandwiched between two sheets of paper. The most common type of plasterboard used in houses has ivory-coloured paper on one side and grey coloured paper on the other. You fit it grey side out if you intend to plaster over it and ivory side out if you intend to paint or paper over it directly. But there are two other main types available.

- Foil-backed (duplex) plasterboard which provides moisture resistance and a small amount of additional insulation. It is notorious because it negates readings from pipe and cable detectors.
- Polystyrene-backed plasterboard (often called thermal board) provides considerable additional insulation and is good for insulating solid (non-cavity) walls.

---

3 Use a broad filling knife to apply fine wall filler (or finishing plaster) across the tape.

4 When the filler has dried, sand it smooth, taking care to 'feather' the edges to blend in to the surrounding wall and then redecorate (paint or wall covering).

The alternative way to repair a crack is to use the joint tape normally used for concealing joints when fixing plasterboard sheets for the first time. This is laid into a layer of jointing filler which has been pressed into the crack. A second layer of filler is then applied after the first one has dried.

I can't get wall fixings to hold in solid walls

CHANGE THE FIXING It's not uncommon that wall plugs put into solid masonry walls come loose or start turning with the screw. It happens either because the hole is too big or the wall material is too crumbly to hold the wall plug.

- If a wall plug turns in a solid brick wall, it is almost certainly because the hole is too big. There is a simple solution. Put in a larger wall plug; if this is too big for your screw, either use a bigger screw or fit a second, smaller wall plug inside the larger one (it might need to be hammered into place).
- If you are fixing into lightweight concrete blocks (usually grey in colour and used for the inner leaf of two-leaf cavity walls), there is a special wall plug you can use. This is a screw-in plastic plug with helical wings, which you first screw into a (large) hole that you drill in the lightweight block and then insert a woodscrew.
- In really crumbly walls (found in some 1930s houses), no kind of wall plug will stay in the hole. Instead, try drilling a large hole (25mm, for example) and mortaring a short length of 25mm dowel in place. Once the mortar has set, drill a pilot hole and you will then be able to screw directly into the dowel using a normal wood screw.

Gaps keep appearing around my doors and window frames

USE A FLEXIBLE BUILDING SEALANT Gaps between the brickwork and door and window frames are not only unsightly, but they can allow water in, leading to damp patches in internal walls and rotting of the timber frame itself. So fill them up as soon as they appear. Because the gaps arise from natural movement of the building materials (mainly shrinking of the wood), they should not be filled with a rigid filler as this will crack as the movement continues. Instead, use one of two types of flexible filler sold as building sealants.

Silicone sealant is similar to the sealant used around baths and along the back of worktops and is available in clear, white and brown to match the colour of your frame. It cannot be painted. Acrylic sealant also comes in different colours (typically white, dark brown and grey), but is easier to apply than silicone sealant and can be painted a different colour if required.

To apply a building sealant, you require a special applicator known as a 'caulking' gun.

1 Use an old paintbrush to remove dust and debris out of the gap and wipe the surface down with a damp cloth.
2 Use a trimming knife to cut off the tip of the cartridge at an angle: the closer to the end you cut, the thinner the bead of sealant that will come out.
3 Run the caulking gun down the gap, while squeezing the trigger firmly – try to fill the gap in one continuous movement.
4 If you want to over-paint acrylic sealant, leave it for a few days to allow it to form a hard skin first.

I just can't get my tile grouting clean

STAIN THE GROUT A DARK COLOUR Old white grout that has turned brown is nearly impossible to clean. Even bleach won't remove all the soaked-in dirt. And regrouting the joints is messy, labour-intensive work. The time-saving solution is to use a grout colorant, available in most DIY stores, which will give glazed kitchen or bathroom tiles a new look. As well as white, a range of colours is available. Here is how to apply it:

1 Make sure the tiles and grout lines are completely clean – if necessary, use a limescale remover – and dry.
2 Use the brush applicator provided to spread the grout colorant generously over the grout lines overlapping the tiles.
3 Leave for at least an hour (check instructions) and then use a clean sponge to wipe the colorant off the face of the glazed tiles.

▥ WALL ATTACHMENTS

I can't find a wall stud to screw into

USE A MAGNET ON A STRING Finding studs with an expensive store-bought gadget is a bit like using a divining rod to sniff out groundwater. It's hit or miss at best. For a better way that's also much cheaper, start with a small, strong magnet. (Suppository-shaped cow magnets, sold at specialist veterinary suppliers work exceptionally well.) Attach a couple of feet of string to one end using tape or glue. Dangle the magnet alongside the wall at about the height you want to drive in your screw. Slowly move your hand along the wall, raising it up and down if you

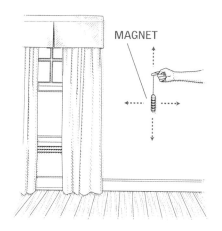

MAGNET

get no response. The magnet should be drawn to either a nail or a plasterboard screw in a stud. Mark the spot and use a level to draw a line straight up or down to the height you want. Then drive the screw home. This works well on walls covered with plasterboard but may be less successful on walls also covered with plaster.

(In case you are wondering, cow magnets are used for cows that are suspected of swallowing a nail or piece of wire. A vet will administer the magnet like a pill. Once it is in the stomach, the magnet stays there, attracting any pieces of stray metal to keep them from passing through the cow's entire digestive system.)

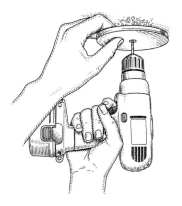

Plaster dust gets everywhere when I drill in the ceiling

USE A COFFEE JAR LID ON THE CEILING Drilling into the ceiling is tricky, because the dust can sprinkle into your face. To contain the dust, drill through the centre of a plastic coffee jar lid and leave the lid on the drill bit. Then, holding the lid steady with your free hand, drill the hole in the ceiling. The lid will catch any troublesome dust. Clear lids work better than solid-coloured ones because you are able to see the bit as you drill.

CATCH THE DUST IN A PAPER BAG Drilling into plaster or plasterboard can often leave an annoying sprinkling of white powder on the floor. Drilling can also chip the surface of the wall around the hole you are making. To avoid both problems, tape an open paper bag (or a coffee filter) under the location for the new hole, with the tape covering the spot that you intend to drill into. The tape will ensure that the drill bit doesn't chip away any more of the wall than you want it to and the bag will catch the plaster dust. When you have finished drilling, carefully peel off the tape and empty and re-use the dust catcher.

I can't hang pictures on my plaster walls

USE HARD-WALL PICTURE HOOKS Some masonry walls are so hard that when you try to hammer in a normal picture hook, it just bends. The answer is a special hard-wall picture hook, which is made from plastic and contains up to four tiny hardened steel pins.

You hold the body of the hanger against the wall and use a hammer to drive the pins through the body of the plastic into the wall surface. Most types can be used with hard walls covered with a thin coat of plaster, but none are suitable for heavy pictures. When you want to move a picture, it is not difficult to lever the hanger off the wall.

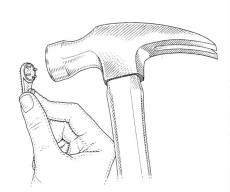

■ PAINTING PROBLEMS

I always spill paint when I stir it

MIX PAINT BY POURING IT BETWEEN CONTAINERS According to many decorators, paint tins were never meant to be stirred or dipped into with a paintbrush. Tins are only for transporting paint from the

**Clues that help you
to find wall studs**
In most homes the distance from the centre of one stud to the centre of the next is 400mm (16in) to match plasterboard sheet sizes, but sometimes it is another interval. In older buildings, spacing may be irregular.

• Look for plasterboard seams, especially when light hits at an angle.

• Look for a stud whose centre is 400mm from a major corner.

• Look for a stud next to a window or door edge.

• Look for nails in skirting boards that go into studs.

• Look for skirting board fixings (nails or screws) going into vertical studs.

A crude (but certain) way to find the location of a stud is to poke a bradawl blade through the plasterboard at intervals until you meet resistance. The problem is that you are left with lots of tiny holes to fill – unless whatever you are fixing will cover the holes up.

manufacturer to the shop and then to your home. To stir paint, they suggest a method that they call 'boxing'. Take two clean plastic containers that will each hold more than the amount of paint you will be mixing. Pour the paint into one of the containers, scraping as much of the thick stuff off the inside of the tin and into the container as possible.

Now pour the paint back and forth between the containers several times, as a method of stirring. If you will be using more than one tin of paint, box all your paint together to achieve a uniform colour. Even the colour of factory-mixed paint can differ between tins.

Whenever I paint or use filler, I end up with the stuff all over me

KEEP A BUCKET OF WATER NEARBY As well as getting it all over you, the paint and filler are probably also landing on other things that you don't want them on, such as floors and furniture. You can use a rag to clean up the paint and filler, but rags soon get coated themselves and can end up smearing everything.

If you are using water-soluble emulsion paint, a better approach is to have a rag in a bucket of water when you begin painting. Keep the bucket near you. When your fingertips get caked with filler or coated with paint, dip them in the bucket and wash them. If paint drips on the floor, grab the rag, wring it out and wipe up the paint before it has a chance to begin drying. With this method, the paint or filler dissolves in the water, giving you a fresh wipe for every spill.

When I touch up paint it always looks really obvious

DAB PAINT ON WITH AN ARTIST'S BRUSH It's aggravating when your attempts to touch up a wall to cover specks and grime ends up looking worse than before. The secret to an effective, invisible touch-up is in the touch. Say you have filled over a nail hole in plasterboard. Instead of brushing paint on to the white spot – a perfectly natural impulse when you have a brush in your hand – lightly dot the spot with the paint-dipped tip of the brush. It is very important to make dots, not create brush strokes. Use the smallest brush possible. An artist's brush is best. If the surrounding paint (and leftover paint) is no more than a year or two old, it should blend in perfectly.

When I am painting cupboard doors and shelves I get paint everywhere

REST THEM ON NAILS, TAPPED INTO THE TOP AND BOTTOM, WHILE THEY ARE DRYING You have removed a door or shelf from a cupbard to paint it. The problem is where to put the wet piece once you have applied the paint. Lay it across a portable workbench and you will spoil the paint surface. Lean it against the wall and you will leave a thin line of paint on the wall and floor. The safest way is to paint one side at a time, but if you are painting several coats, this could take forever. Try this clever trick to speed up the job. Tap a couple of panel pins – the size of the pin depends on the size and weight of the item you are painting – into the ends of each shelf or into the tops and bottoms of each cupboard door before you paint it. Drive them firmly into the wood, but not too firmly, since you will need to remove them later. Leave them sticking out 30-40mm. Paint the shelf or door. Lay a dustsheet or newspaper alongside a wall, stand the freshly painted shelf or door on one set of pins and then lean it

at an angle so that the top set of pins is against the wall, with only the pins touching. Once the paint has completely dried, carefully pull each pin out using a pair of pliers or pincers. If you use pincers (or the claw of a hammer), lay a cloth under the tool so that it doesn't damage the painted surface. Then quickly fill the tiny holes that are left and touch them up with paint.

▪ CLEANING UP PAINT

I can't get my paint rollers clean

It is essential to use good roller sleeves and to keep them clean. But too often, the paint soaks deep into the thick pile of the sleeves. Assuming you are using water-based paint, this is the best way to get a roller sleeve clean:

Better masking
When you are using masking tape to protect wood moulding during a painting project, firmly press down the edge of the masking tape with the edge of a flexible filling knife. This seal will prevent paint from seeping behind the tape.

Next time you paint
with oil-based paint –
even on a cloudy day
or indoors – first rub
waterproof sunscreen
into your exposed skin.
If you spill paint on
yourself, it will wipe
off, even after several
hours. Seth Smith, a
painter and decorator,
discovered this useful
side effect one sunny
summer day while
painting the outside of a
house. 'It was hot and I
had SPF 45 sunscreen
all over my hands and
arms. I was painting the
eaves and paint was
dripping down on me',
he recalls. 'I didn't clean
up for 4 hours, but the
paint still came off my
arms when I wiped
them with a clean rag'.

1 Scrape excess paint off the
   roller cover using the
   semicircular blade on
   a 6-in-1 painter's tool.
2 Fill a 15 litre (3 gallon)
   bucket with clean water and
   soak the roller cover
   overnight to loosen the
   remaining paint.
3 Using a paint roller spinner,
   spin the paint and water off
   the cover inside the empty
   bucket. The bucket should be
   tall enough to contain the
   spattering paint. Rinse with
   water and repeat.

You can buy 6-in-1 painter's tools and 15 litre (builder's) buckets
from most DIY stores. Paint roller spinners – known as paintbrush
or paint roller cleaners – are available online from specialist
suppliers. When you pull and push the handle of the device, the
roller sleeve (or brush) is spun round shaking off the water.

I hate cleaning paintbrushes after each use

WRAP THEM AND FREEZE THEM OVERNIGHT If you are in the middle of
long-term decorating, you don't want paintbrushes to dry out
overnight. The labour-intensive answer is to clean the brushes
thoroughly at the end of each day so that they don't turn cardboard-
stiff by the morning. But there is a much easier method: just wrap
the brushes in cling film and stick them in the freezer overnight. The
cold and the plastic will prevent the brush from drying out. They
may need to thaw a little when you retrieve them, but they will be
fresh and ready to use again in just a few minutes.

My leftover paint always goes bad

You have filled the hole your son made in a plasterboard wall while
playing Bob the Builder and it is now time to touch up the paint. But
the paint tins in the garage are all mixed up, they are rusty and the
paint in them has dried up. Here is an easy, effective way to store
leftover paint so that it will last up to three years:

USE THE RIGHT SIZE CONTAINER, SEALED TIGHTLY First and foremost, you need a container with a tight seal. Air dries paint out and leaves a thick, leathery skin on top. Some people wrongly think that all you have to do is remove that skin. But if you do that and you remove some of the ingredients that help the paint to dry properly and the next time you paint it will stay tacky for a week. The best way to keep air out is to use a container of the correct size for your paint. Some professional decorators suggest mason jars (used for bottling fruit and available in different sizes), but if you prefer to store the paint in the original tin (which in some cases is fine and more convenient), tap the lid on with a rubber mallet or by placing a block of wood on the lid and hitting it with a hammer. If you hammer the lid directly with something metal, you risk denting the lid and damaging the seal. If you keep the grooved rim of the tin paint-free, the lid will seal better. (Some DIY stores sell plastic rim covers that snap over rims to keep them clean when pouring paint.)

STORE PAINT UPSIDE DOWN Next, store the paint upside down. That way, the paint forms an airtight seal. Keep it in a relatively cool place. Put the tins on cardboard, in case they leak (although if you have sealed them tightly, they should not). Make sure the paint does not freeze or get too hot. Both extremes can ruin it.

NOTE KEY DATA ON THE CONTAINER Record as much information about the paint as possible on a strip of masking tape with a permanent felt marker. Include date of purchase (and/or when applied), brand of paint, type of finish, the manufacturer's colour code and which part of which room it was used for. Write this on the bottom of the container so that it is easy to read. If you put it on the side, it may get covered with dripping paint. (The bottom will be facing up if you store the paint upside down.)

It is a real hassle to dispose of old paint

CONTACT YOUR LOCAL COUNCIL Most local councils will have some kind of facility for disposing of partly-used tins of paint.

- Empty paint tins can usually be put in the normal household rubbish (leave the lid off) or recycled with scrap metal.
- With partly used emulsion paint, fill the tin with sand and leave it until it has solidified before putting it in the normal household rubbish.

When you prepare to paint a room, consider using a dustsheet made of canvas instead of plastic. Plastic is cheaper, but any paint drops that land on it stay wet for a while, increasing the chance that you will step on them and tread paint everywhere. Canvas dustsheets absorb paint spills, so the paint dries faster.

- Contact your local council to find out where in your area you can take partly used tins of other types of paint.
- If the paint is still usable, there are various community schemes that collect re-usable domestic paint for distribution to community and voluntary groups such as schools, churches and theatre groups.

Remember that you can minimise waste by calculating your quantities correctly in the first place. All paint tins should be labelled with the coverage rate.

Cleaning up paint takes such a long time

USE A PAPER PLATE AND MASKING TAPE You may consider yourself a Monet when it comes to selecting the right colour to paint a room, but you probably dread cleaning up because of all the spills and the time it takes to clean your brushes. Here are two tips that will help you to keep cleaning time to a minimum:

- Place a large paper plate under the opened paint tin to catch any over-the-side drips.
- Wrap masking tape around the brush handle, making sure that it covers 10 to 15mm of the bristles at the base of the brush. After you have called it a day, unwrap the tape and you will discover that the tape has prevented a lot of extra paint from soaking into the bristles. The cleaning up time will be greatly reduced.

Floors

▥ WOODEN FLOORS

My wooden floor is very scuffed

RUB WITH EXTRA-FINE STEEL WOOL A floor that's covered with scuff marks, shoe polish and paint splashes makes a room look weary. Get some extra-fine steel wool (grade 000) from a DIY store and rub the scuffs very lightly with it, taking care not to damage the floor's finish. You will be surprised at how quickly a gleaming, as-new floor is revealed.

Give wooden floors their good looks back with a quick rub with steel wool.

My wooden floor is scratched

STAIN AND VARNISH THE SCRATCHES The quickest way to fix small scratches in a wooden floor is to use furniture touch-up pens and crayons, available at DIY stores. Find a stain marker that matches the colour of your floor. (Stain from a tin will work as well.) After the stain dries, buff it with a cloth and use an artist's brush to cover the repair with polyurethane floor varnish, applying two or more layers to build the area up so it lies flush with the existing finish.

There is a dent in my wooden floor

STEAM THE DENT OUT Here's how to make a dent in the floor – or a piece of furniture – disappear like magic. The fix only works if the dented wood fibres have not been severed.

1 Remove any finish from the dented area. Sand off the top coat finish, such as polyurethane. Remove a wax finish by rubbing it with white spirit.
2 Fold a thin cotton cloth into a neat square that is larger than the dent. Soak the cloth in water and wring it out lightly.
3 Lay the cloth over the dent and place a steam iron, set on the hottest setting, on top of the cloth. The iron will heat the cloth, forcing steam into the dent and raising the grain of the wood.
4 When the wood has dried, sand it flush and reapply the finish, if necessary.

Many squeaky floors are caused by floorboards drying out – often as a result of central heating. This creates gaps between the boards and then you get the sound of wood rubbing on wood. You can often prevent squeaking by keeping your home's humidity levels more constant. Install a simple humidifier in areas with wooden floors and enjoy the sound of silence.

My floorboards are scratched and curling at the edges

IT'S TIME TO SAND THEM Old floorboards can be brought back to life by sanding them with an industrial floor sander. They are about the size of an upright vacuum cleaner and can be hired by the day. This will level the main body of the floor, but you will also need an edge sander – a large disc sander – to sand along the skirting boards.

Remove all the furniture and dustproof the room. Replace any damaged floorboards, fill gaps between floorboards (see page 78) and use a nail punch to drive home any protruding nails. Remove old floor polish using wire wool dipped in white spirit. This will avoids the continual sheet changing that will occur if you don't do it; nothing clogs a sanding sheet like old polish. Try to remove as much paint or varnish as you can from the floor, using paint stripper and a scraper. Remove all paint stripper with water or white spirit (depending on the type of stripper used) and allow the floorboards to dry thoroughly for a couple of days before starting sanding.

Using a floor sander is not difficult (you can ask to be shown how in the hire shop), but requires some care.

1 Fit a sanding sheet to the machine – for badly damaged floors, start with a coarse grade.
2 Sand diagonally across the floorboards in one direction and then in the other direction, changing sheets as necessary.
3 Vacuum the floor and switch to a medium grade sanding sheet, this time sanding up and down the floorboards until all the diagonal marks have gone.
4 Finish the main floor by sanding with a fine grade sanding sheet, again working up and down the boards.
5 Work around the edges with the end sander, again going through the grades of sheet from coarse to fine. Use a hand sanding block (or an electric 'delta' sander) in the corners.

Before you apply a new surface finish, sweep up all dust and debris from the floor and vacuum it thoroughly. If there is still some dust left, use a lint-free rag soaked in white spirit to remove it.

One of my floorboards is badly cracked

REPLACE IT WITH A NEW ONE When a floorboard is too badly damaged to be filled, you will need to replace it with a new one. It will probably be one that has already been taken up so removing the old board should not be too difficult. Lever it up from the damaged end and decide how much needs to be replaced – if you can't get the whole board up, saw through it next to a joist.

If the house is old, modern floorboards may be a different size. After cutting the replacement board to the correct length, you can use a bench plane to reduce it in width (to 2mm less than the size of the gap), but if it is the wrong thickness as well, you will have to do some clever fitting:

- For boards that are too thin, cut some supporting strips from thin timber moulding, stiff cardboard, hardboard or MDF to bring the level of the new floorboard up to the existing floor at every joist – but remember that cardboard will be compressed when weight is applied.
- For boards that are too thick, use a 25mm chisel to cut a groove in the board, using an offcut to check the new depth of the board once it is sitting over the joist.

To secure the new board at the end joist, nail a short batten to the side of the joist so that you can nail (or screw) the replacement board to that. Put nails (or screws) into all the other joists that are under the replacement board.

The satin varnish I used has turned out glossy

MIX THE VARNISH THOROUGHLY Even clear coatings, such as polyurethane varnish contain pigments. The less glossy finishes have more pigment, which is what gives it a satin finish. But the pigments are thick and may stick to the bottom of a tin of varnish like chocolate syrup in a glass of cold milk. For good chocolate milk, you need to stir the syrup. For a true satin finish, you must stir the pigment. But don't shake the varnish, because you will just get air bubbles that will ruin the surface of the floor or furniture. Instead, mix the varnish by 'boxing' it as you would with paint. (See 'I always spill paint when I stir it' on page 69.)

■ FLOOR SQUEAKS AND BOUNCE

My floorboards squeak

SPRINKLE TALCUM POWDER BETWEEN THE CRACKS Floorboards squeak for different reasons. Sometimes the floor isn't sufficiently well attached to the joists. At other times a cycle of swelling and shrinking causes the floorboards to rub together. If the squeak is caused by a surface gap between boards, try dry lubrication. Pinpoint the noisy boards and sprinkle talcum powder or graphite liberally into the crack. Lay an old towel over the powder and work it into the gaps with your foot. Wipe up the excess. If your floor has a wax finish, as opposed to a top coat finish such as polyurethane varnish, try pouring liquid floor wax, of the same kind that you would use to re-finish the surface, between the boards.

REPLACE NAILS WITH SCREWS As floorboards age, the nails holding them down to the joists can be become loose – especially with floorboards that have been lifted a couple of times. This causes the floorboards to squeak, rattle and roll. The answer is to pull the nails out with long-nosed pliers) and replace them with screws. If you are going to leave the screws visible in a bare floor, you may want to use brass screws – but it is generally better to use normal (zinc-plated) screws, driving them just below the floorboard surface and then filling the hole over the screw afterwards. Don't use too small a size of screw – something like 50mm No 10 screws should hold the board securely.

There are large gaps between my floorboards

FILL THEM UP Gaps between floorboards not only look unsightly if the floorboards are left bare, but the draughts coming up through gaps can discolour floor coverings (especially carpet) as they carry dirt and dust with them.

If the gaps are widespread and serious, the best answer is to re-lay the floor, taking up all the boards and putting them back down again closer together, but this is a huge job and most gaps can be filled either with a flexible filler or with thin strips of wood.

A flexible filler is applied either with an applicator gun or with a flat-bladed filling knife. Push the filler well down into the gaps between the floorboards and smooth it off. It is best to leave the filler slightly proud of the surface (it will shrink as it dries) and then sand it down lightly with an orbital sander or hand sanding block.

You can get suitable thicknesses of wood strip by going to the 'mouldings' section of a timber merchant or DIY store. Normally the mouldings will be hardwood (typically ramin) as softwood mouldings of this thickness would break. Each length of wood strip will have to be cut to size (use a tenon saw) and shaped to fit its gap. An orbital sander will help here – try to give the wood strip a slight taper, so that it wedges tightly into the gap. Then apply wood adhesive to both sides of the wood strip before hammering it into place with a rubber mallet, leaving it a couple of millimetres proud of the surface. When the adhesive has dried, use a bench plane to smooth down the strip.

▦ VINYL FLOORING

One of my vinyl floor tiles is damaged

USE A HEAT GUN TO REMOVE AND REPLACE IT The beauty of vinyl tiles is that they come in individual pieces. If one gets burned, stained or scratched, you can easily replace it. The problem lies in getting the underlying adhesive unstuck. And the quick solution is to carefully warm the tile with a heat gun, the kind used to strip paint. (If you don't have a heat gun, use a hair drier. Lift a corner with a filling knife. The tile should come right up. Soften the adhesive left on the floor with the heat gun and remove it with the filling knife. Apply new multipurpose floor tile adhesive to the floor, soften the replacement tile with the heat gun and insert it.

My sheet vinyl floor is damaged

PATCH THE DAMAGED AREA Here's a trick that makes repairing blemishes in sheet vinyl a breeze:

 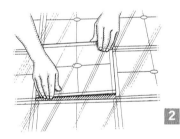

1 Lay some spare vinyl over the damaged part. Align the design on the replacement piece exactly with the design on the floor. Tape down the replacement vinyl piece to make sure that it does not move during cutting. Using a sharp trimming knife and a straight-edge, slice through both layers, cutting both the replacement piece and the piece to be replaced simultaneously. If possible, make the cut along a line in the design. Take your

Keep the spares
Whatever type of floor covering you have – vinyl tiles, sheet vinyl, wood strip, carpet or hard floor tiles – make sure that you store spare pieces carefully so that they are ready when you need to make replacements in the future.

How to work out how your floor is finished

If, like most people, you live in an older house, you may not know exactly how the wooden floors are finished. Here are some simple ways to work out the finish of the floor before tackling certain floor problems.

If you suspect your floors are coated with polyurethane, carefully scratch at the surface in a hidden corner of the floor. If you raise particles that look like flakes of hardened finish, it is probably polyurethane. If a yellowish goo comes up, it is probably wax. If it is wax, you should be able to feel the wood's grain when you rub the floor. And with a wax finish, you should be able to smudge it with your fingertip.

time. Now you will have an exact fit for the piece you want to remove. Remove the damaged piece and secure the replacement piece with double-sided adhesive tape (for stuck-down flooring, remove the old adhesive and apply new adhesive instead).

2 Insert the replacement piece and press it firmly in place. Cover the seams with a seam sealer, available at DIY and flooring stores. Make sure the sealer matches the finish of the floor.

There is an air bubble in my vinyl floor

SLIT IT AND SLIDE ADHESIVE UNDERNEATH It's hard to keep stuck-down sheet vinyl flooring free of air bubbles. They pop up and stand out as broad, flat, light-reflecting surfaces. For a quick fix, use a

trimming knife to make a slit along the length of the bubble in an inconspicuous place, such as a dark line in the floor's pattern. Use a filling knife to spread a thin layer of vinyl floor adhesive under the bubble on both sides of

the slit. Push up and down on the bubble to distribute the adhesive as widely as possible. Wipe up any excess adhesive and lay a piece of greaseproof paper over the area with a heavy object on the top to flatten it. Leave the weight in place overnight. In the morning the adhesive should be dry and the bubble will have flattened.

I have a damaged vinyl tile but no leftovers to match

REPLACE IT WITH A HIDDEN TILE You can usually find a vinyl tile that won't be missed under an appliance or permanent piece of furniture. Remove the tile by heating it with a hair drier to soften the adhesive. Prise it up carefully with a filling knife. (Pick up a replacement for the hidden tile at a DIY or tile store. It doesn't have to be a perfect match.) Remove the damaged tile the same way – by heating and prising – and discard it. Scrape away as much excess adhesive as possible, using the hair dryer to soften it. Apply new adhesive and install the replacement tile.

■ CERAMIC TILES

There's a chip in one of my ceramic tiles

TOUCH IT UP WITH PAINT Even in large ceramic tile floors, your eye will zoom in on the smallest chip or crack. The quick fix is to mask the defect with a touch of enamel paint so that your eye will overlook it. If the chip is deep, fill it before painting. Use a two-part epoxy adhesive. It is sold at hardware and DIY stores, mixes to a workable consistency, bonds tightly and holds paint.

I have a damaged ceramic floor tile but no leftovers to match

REPLACE IT WITH ONE FROM A HIDDEN AREA If you don't have any leftover tiles but need one to replace a conspicuous broken tile, look for a replacement under an appliance or permanent piece of furniture. Then put on your safety goggles and take these steps:

1 To remove your chosen tile, try to chip away the grout surrounding it by lightly tapping with a screwdriver or cold chisel and a hammer. You may have to sacrifice an adjacent tile to get access to the underside of the replacement.

2 Once you can get under the tile with a firm, flat blade, gently tap and prise, tap and prise, until the tile comes up.

3 Remove the broken tile or even pulverise it with a hammer. Go easy on this, too. Even though you don't need to preserve it, you may accidentally crack an adjacent tile. And particles of flying tile can scratch or dent wooden cupboards and plasterboard walls.

4 Remove as much as possible of the old adhesive bonding the tile to the floor, using a cold chisel.

5 Spread new adhesive in the area and lay the replacement tile on top. Once it is dry, regrout the surrounding joints.

6 To replace the tile (or tiles) you have removed from the hidden area, buy one of similar size and colour, using a shard of the broken tile as a guide. Out of sight like this, 'close enough' is fine. Install it in the same way as the method described above.

■ STAIRS

One of my stair balusters is broken

GLUE IT TOGETHER Balusters (the supporting posts for a stair rail) add character to a house and protect pets and children from falls. If a damaged baluster is not badly splintered, the best solution is to glue it back together. Put woodworking adhesive on both sides of the break and clamp the pieces together, using squares of cardboard under the clamp jaws to protect the wood. If the baluster is round or if you don't have clamps, use a tight spiral of

masking tape to secure the glued pieces. After the adhesive dries, repair holes with wood filler, sand and refinish.

My stair baluster is completely smashed

REPLACE THE BALUSTER To find an exact replacement for a damaged baluster, take the old one to an architectural salvage yard until you find a match. Or you may need to get a local wood turner to make a new baluster. Paint or finish a new baluster before you install it.

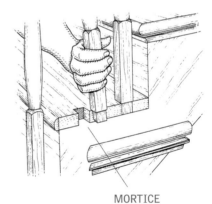

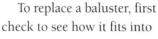
MORTICE

To replace a baluster, first check to see how it fits into the stair tread. If it goes into a slot (a mortice), here's how to proceed:

1 Carefully prise the trim off the end of the stair tread with an old chisel. Then lever out the bottom of the baluster.
2 Gently work the top of the baluster out of the handrail. If it is nailed, gently tap it out using a rubber mallet. Scrape out all the old adhesive at the top and bottom.
3 Test-fit the new baluster and cut it to fit as needed. Then put adhesive on both ends. Slip it in place and secure. Use panel pins and, to avoid splitting, drill pilot holes for the nails slightly smaller in diameter than the nails you are using.

If the broken baluster has a dowelled lower end, follow these steps:

1 Saw the old baluster in half to remove it. Give each half a sharp twist to break its glue seal. Clean out the old glue in the holes at both ends.
2 Cut the new baluster's upper end to fit into the handrail's hole with a 10mm space above.
3 Trim the dowel on the baluster's lower end to a 6mm stump. Test-fit the baluster by pushing it up into the handrail and letting it drop into the tread hole. You may need to trim the upper end more and bevel its edge.
4 Put adhesive on both ends and set the new baluster in place.

■ CARPET

There is a cigarette burn on my carpet

GIVE IT A TRIM WITH SCISSORS When you get a small burn on your carpet, give it a haircut. Get a pair of sharp scissors and remove the surface burns by snipping off the charred tips of the carpet fibres. If the carpet is plush, it helps to feather out the area by lightly tapering the nap in a circle a little wider than the damaged area. If the burn hasn't gone too deep, the charring will disappear.

My carpet has a ragged edge

SECURE IT WITH ADHESIVE Don't let the ragged edge run or your problem will be harder to fix. Try this solution. Trim the excess fibres and liberally smear a water-based latex adhesive that dries to a clear finish, along the bottom of the ragged edge, where the tufts are

SURELY **NOT**

WIRED FOR TROUBLE

Experienced carpet fitters see it time and time again – hi-fi enthusiasts who are so eager to run speaker wire throughout the house that they ruin a carpet. How? With drill in hand and daydreaming of their new stereos, they begin drilling holes up into floors for threading speaker wire from room to room. But they only remember the carpet that's on the floor when their drill bits grind to a halt in a tangle of carpet fibres.

Keep spare carpet in a convenient place
If you are installing wall-to-wall carpet in a room, always carpet the inside of the room's built-in cupboards, even if it seems unnecessary. The extra expense will be minimal. And if you ever need a carpet patch because of a stain, a burn or a tear, you can cut it out of the cupboard. Although it's easy enough to save a remnant for patches, remnants often go mouldy in the loft or are thrown out during spring cleaning. The cupboard carpet will always be there for you.

joined. When the adhesive dries it will be invisible and will lock in the fibres, preventing further fraying.

My loop rug has a tuft poking out

TRIM IT OFF Don't pull at the tuft. Loop rugs, such as Berbers, will run like nylon stockings and it will be impossible to make the rug look normal again. Take a pair of sharp scissors. Lie flat on the carpet and cut the tuft as close to the rug surface as you can. Do this the minute you notice a stray tuft. Otherwise, your vacuum cleaner's beater bar may catch it and cause it to run.

The seam in my carpet has torn open

SEW THE TEAR SHUT Most carpet tears occur along seams where two pieces of carpet were glued or sewn together. Pull the carpet edges together and hold them in place with nails driven about 150mm from the tear. Then use a curved upholstery needle and heavy fishing line to sew the pieces together. Make the stitch holes 15mm out from each edge and space them 10mm apart along the seam. For the least visibility, make the top of the stitch perpendicular to the tear and the underside diagonal. If you are rejoining a seam that was glued together, you will find that it is tough to work the needle through the old adhesive tape underneath. Use long-nosed pliers to help to push the needle. Secure the stitches with latex adhesive. When this has dried, cover the seam with a self-adhesive cloth tape.

There's a permanent stain in my carpet

PATCH THE DAMAGED AREA For permanent stains (and large burn marks) in a wall-to-wall carpet, the only solution is to cut out the damaged section and patch it. The procedure is basically the same as illustrated for vinyl flooring. (See 'My sheet vinyl floor is damaged', page 79.) Here's how to go about it:

1 Find a clean patch. If you have extra carpet, that's great. If not, take some from a cupboard or from under a large piece of permanent furniture.
2 Cut the patch slightly larger than the damaged piece you want to remove. (Cut just the carpet, not the carpet underlay.)
3 Place the patch over the stain or burn mark and use a trimming knife to cut though both pieces at once, ensuring a

perfect fit. To make sure the patch stays in place, put double-sided carpet tape on the underlay under the seams and then set in the patch. Don't use staples or tacks. They will pull down the underlay, making the patch obvious.

If the new patch doesn't match the original carpet in cleanliness and texture, consider making a double switch. Take a matching patch from an area, such as a hallway, where people are much less likely to notice a patch. Then replace the hole in the hallway with the clean patch. (Ask a carpet shop for a piece to patch a cupboard hole. It doesn't need to be an exact match, since no one will ever see it.)

Cutting carpet for a bathroom is very difficult

MAKE A TEMPLATE TO GUIDE YOU When cutting new carpet you need to get it right the first time. Cutting carpet for a bathroom is particularly tricky because of the curved shape of the toilet base and the odd shapes of bathroom cupboards. The secret is to make a paper template first.

Buy a large roll of lining paper from a DIY store. You'll also need scissors, a ruler, sticky tape and a pencil.

1 Start by placing a sheet of paper on the trickiest part of the floor. Trace and cut the paper to fit that area. Leave it there.
2 Go on to other sections of the bathroom floor until you have covered it all.
3 With all the paper sections in place on the floor, tape them together and check that the fit is perfect.
4 Remove the entire template and lay it over the carpet as a guide for cutting.

My floors are cold

USE BETTER UNDERLAY Ground floors in houses can often be cold as there is a cold, ventilated, space below the floorboards. Usually, the best answer is to upgrade the carpet underlay to one that has more effective heat retention.

If you are removing all the floorboards – either to replace or re-lay them or to carry out repairs to the joists – it is an ideal opportunity to insulate the floor before putting the floorboards back. You can use 100mm (or 150mm) blanket insulation sold in rolls for use in lofts. This is already the correct width to fit between the joists and can be supported by garden netting stapled to the joists.

Doors and windows

■ WINDOWS

I'm afraid that my windows aren't secure

LOCK THE SASHES WITH REMOVABLE NAILS It's very easy for burglars to open most latched windows. They smash a single pane, reach in, and open the latch. You can install key-operated locks, but it is expensive and time-consuming for a large number of windows.

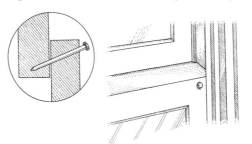

Here is a quick, low-cost solution for securing double-hung windows. Where the upper and lower window sashes overlap (when they are closed), drill a hole at an angle through the top of the lower window and extending about halfway into the bottom of the upper window. Drill the hole slightly larger than the nail that will be inserted into the drilled hole. (The nail should fit loosely so that it won't stick if the wood of the frame swells.) Now insert a nail so that the flat head is flush against the frame. Paint the head to match the colour of the frame. When you want to open the window, draw the nail out with a magnet.

My windowpane has broken

REPLACE THE PANE Most newer homes have double-glazed windows: contact the manufacturer or installer for a replacement pane. But many older houses still have windows with single-thickness panes that you can replace. Before you start, measure up the opening into which the window pane fits (scrape out old putty if necessary to make the measurement and take at least three measurements of width and height). Go to a glass merchant who will cut a new piece of glass to around 4mm less than your measurements (he will also advise you on the correct glass thickness for the size of the window). Buy putty and new glazing sprigs (the tiny nails that hold the window in place). Follow these steps to replace the broken pane.

1 Wearing thick work gloves and goggles, remove as much of the broken glass as possible.

2 Working on the outside of the window, use an old chisel or a glazier's hacking knife to dig out the old putty and glass fragments from the rebate. Use long-nose pliers to pull out the old glazing sprigs.

3 Knead some glazing putty as if it were dough to soften it. Then smooth a thin (3mm) layer on the inside edge of the groove. Insert the new pane and press it gently against the putty until the putty is squeezed flat all around.

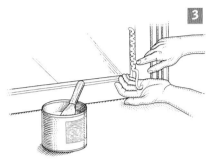

4 Insert new glazing sprigs in the frame to hold the pane in place. One or two sprigs a side will do with smaller panes; with a larger pane place the sprigs every 250mm.

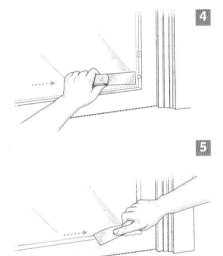

5 Roll more putty into a 'sausage' about 10mm in diameter and apply it to the front of the rebate over the edge of the glass. Use a clean putty knife to bevel and smooth the putty. Let the putty set for a week before painting it.

TRICKS OF THE TRADE

Replacing a pane in metal window frame
Replacing a window pane in a metal windowframe is very similar to the technique for a wooden window. The main difference is that the glass is held in place with clips rather than sprigs (save the old clips when you remove the broken pane) and that you use a different type of putty (glass merchants sell both types). You shouldn't need to paint the rebate unless it is rusty, in which case use a rust-killing primer.

My window is painted shut

WORK A SHARP KNIFE AROUND THE EDGES When you need ventilation in summer, a sloppily applied coat of paint on the windows will come back to haunt you. Find a sharp trimming knife and slide it along the crack between the window and frame, breaking the seal created by the paint. For stubborn cases, brush white spirit along the seal first; then work your knife along the crack.

Creaking casements
Hinged wooden
casement windows can
also sag because the
corner joints have
given way. They can
be strengthened (with
L-plates) in the same
way as sash windows
(right), but it is usually
better to remove them
from the frame first
(by undoing the hinge
screws), which allows
you to use a less
obtrusive method of
strengthening the corner
joint: drilling holes
and inserting adhesive-
coated wooden dowels.

My windowsills are rotting

USE A FLEXIBLE WOOD FILLER Common maladies in old houses with
wooden sills are when the grain splits, or entire sections of wood rot
and crumble. Instead of replacing the entire sill, try this simple fix:
use a high-performance wood filler which, although it sets rock
hard, is in fact flexible and will expand and contract with the
surrounding wood as the weather changes.

Start by cutting out all the rotten wood until you are back to solid
material. Apply Rot Wood Hardener to the whole repair area and
allow this to dry – the hardener strengthens and reinforces rotten
fibres to provide a solid base for the filler. Mix up the two-part filler
and apply it with a filling knife to the damaged area to the same
profile as the windowsill, leaving the filler slightly proud of the
surface. When the filler has set (it takes no more than 30 minutes),
use a chisel, plane or file to shape the filled area exactly, giving it a
final sand with fine abrasive paper.

For simple cracks, where the wood has not softened, you do not
need to use wood hardener: simply use the blade of your filling knife
to press filler down into the cracks before sanding and painting.

My window sash joints are sagging

STRAIGHTEN THE CORNER AND REINFORCE IT It is common for the
lower corners of a wooden sash window to absorb water and
eventually rot and sag. But you can prolong the life of your window
for years with this quick fix.

1 Thoroughly clean the area around the joint in the sagging
corner. (Work on the exterior side of the window.) Scrape with
a wire brush and rub with sandpaper to remove peeling paint
and rotted wood.

2 If you are working on an upper
sash, cut a batten about 25mm
longer than the distance from
the sill to the bottom of the
upper sash. Wedge the batten
under the corner of the sash
and tap the side of the batten
to gently raise the sagging
corner. (Protect the sill by
placing a thin piece of wood
under the batten.) If you are

working on the lower sash, raise the sash as far as it will go and use the same trick to straighten it. Fill cracks or gaps in the wood with exterior wood filler. Let it dry.

3 Attach a metal L-bracket to the exterior of the corner. (Use a galvanised bracket and screws so that it won't rust.) Do the other corner the same way, if necessary. Finish by re-painting.

My window sash cord has broken

REPLACE THE CORD Until the late 20th century, most double-hung windows relied on balance weights to raise and lower the sashes (that is, the frame and panes that form the movable part of a window). If you live in an older house, you know that the cords to these balance weights have a finite life span. When one breaks, the cord drops out of sight, and the window won't work properly. What's worse is that the window can slam shut, which often cracks the glass. When this happens, many homeowners get so frustrated that they install brand-new windows. You can save money – and save those solid old windows – with the following repair:

1 Remove the staff bead – the name for the narrow strip of moulding that holds the lower (inner) sash in place. It will probably be secured with panel pins: lever it off carefully with an old chisel, starting in the middle of the longer side pieces.

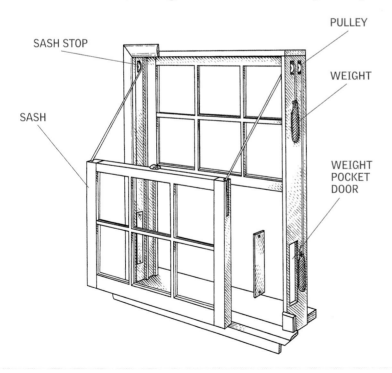

SASH STOP

PULLEY

WEIGHT

SASH

WEIGHT POCKET DOOR

2 Lean the bottom sash outwards as far as it will go, tie the end of a long length of string to the non broken cord and cut the cord off close to the window (if it's one of the upper sash cords that has broken, cut through both bottom sash cords). Carefully remove the bottom sash.

3 To remove the upper sash, first prise out the 'parting bead' (the thin strip of wood separating the two windows) by gripping it with a pair of pliers. Tie string to any unbroken sash cords as above and cut through them close to the window. Lower the upper sash gently into the room.

4 Buy enough spare sash cord to replace all cords (or you will have to go through this performance again when another one breaks which, you can be certain, won't be long): measure up from the window sill to the top of the window and then add two-thirds again for the length of each cord.

5 Use an old chisel (and, if necessary, a screwdriver) to open the pocket covers over the channels in which the sash weights run, reach into the pockets and pull the weights out. Cut the new sash cords to length.

6 Where there is a length of string over the pulley, tie one end of the new sash cord to the string and then use the old sash cord to pull the string and then the new sash cord into place – tie a pencil to the end of the cord to stop it falling through. If there is no string, tie a small weight (known in the trade as a 'mouse'), such as a screw, to the end of a piece of string and feed the mouse followed by the string over the pulley before drawing the new cord though as before.

7 Tie the weights to the ends of the new sash cords, using a double knot as before, place the weights back in their channels and put back the pocket covers (with screws if fitted).

8 Starting with the upper sash, use pincers to remove the nails holding the old cord in the groove in the top of the window, pull the weight right to the top of the channel and nail the other end of the cord to the side of the sash, with the sash resting on the window ledge (you may need a helper to do this). Repeat for the other side and put the sash back in place, checking that it operates smoothly.

9 Replace the parting beads, tapping them gently into place (don't use nails or adhesive) and attach new cords to the lower sash in the same way. Reposition the staff bead, but before finally hammering the nails home, check that the lower sash works properly.

10 Finish off by using quick-setting wood filler to make good any damage and touch up the paint and filler with an artist's brush.

My hinged window is draughty

FIT A SELF-ADHESIVE DRAUGHT EXCLUDER There are two main types of self-adhesive strip sold for draught-proofing hinged windows and both are simple to fix.

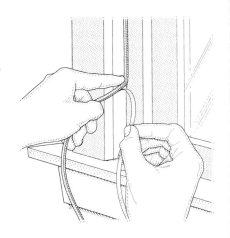

- PVC foam strip is the cheapest (but doesn't last long): choose a thickness to suit the size of gap you have. Foam strip is not very good at coping with uneven gaps and, unless vinyl-coated, gets dirty in use.
- Rubber strip is more durable and is better at coping with large and uneven gaps.

With both kinds of draught excluder, clean the frame first then simply peel off the backing paper and stick the excluder on to the window frame so that the window closes on it. Cut the strips to length with a trimming knife or kitchen scissors. Both types of excluder can also be used for hinged doors.

My sash windows rattle and let in draughts

FIT BRUSH-TYPE DRAUGHT EXCLUDERS Sash windows often rattle and one of the best ways to cure this is to fit brush type draught excluders, which will also keep out the wind. The excluders are rigid and are nailed in place to the frame surrounding the sash window so that the sash surface slides against the brush strip. Fixing nails are included with the strip.

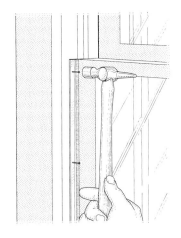

Although now usually superseded by nylon, hinged bronze strips were once very popular for draught proofing external doors and many houses still have them. Bronze weather stripping on a door can making an annoying scraping noise when the door brushes against it. An instant fix is to rub a white candle on the strip to silence it and keep it working smoothly. If you find any gaps between the strip and the door where air is sneaking into the house, use a screwdriver to prise the flap out to fill the gaps.

▥ DOORS

The screw hinges on my door are loose

PACK THE SCREW HOLES WITH TOOTHPICKS When door hinges come loose, the cause is usually screws that have torn through the wood that was holding them in place. You don't need to get new screws; you just need to repair the wood that holds them. First, determine which hinge is coming loose and on which side – the door or the door frame. Then follow these steps:

1 Open the door all the way and prop it into the correct position by tucking a book, folded towel, wooden wedge or some other object under its lower edge.
2 Using a screwdriver, remove the screws from the loose side of the malfunctioning hinge.
3 Take wooden toothpicks, dip them one at a time in woodworking adhesive, and insert them in the screw holes in the wood until you can pack no more in.
4 Using a trimming knife, cut the toothpicks flush with the wood. Let the adhesive dry.
5 Drive the screws back into their original holes, where they will now be held snugly in place.

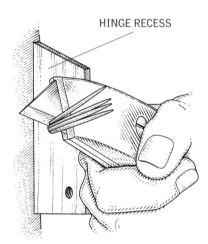

HINGE RECESS

PLUG THE SCREW HOLES WITH DOWELS An alternative to the toothpick method is to use a 6, 8 or 10mm drill to make a clean, round hole where each screw was before. Buy a wooden dowel (available in these sizes from DIY stores) of the same diameter as the drill bit. Slide the dowel into the hole to measure how deep it will go into the wood. Pull the dowel out and saw it off so that it will fit flush with the surface. Smear the dowel with woodworking adhesive and tap it into place. Repeat for each hole. Let the adhesive dry before you drive the screws back in again. You will need to drill a small pilot hole for the screws in the dowels to stop them from splitting.

My door rubs on the floor

USE ABRASIVE PAPER TO TRIM IT If a door sags slightly, it may just catch the high spots of a floor covering causing it to stick slightly every time you open it. The answer is simple: tuck a sheet of abrasive paper under the door, hold it with your foot and move the door back and forth over it until enough wood has been removed to create more of a gap between the door and the floor covering.

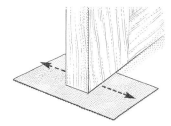

The doors in my house close on their own

CATCH

INSTALL A MAGNETIC CATCH Here's another way to solve the problem: Use a magnetic catch, the kind you find in kitchen cabinets, to hold the door open. Screw a magnetic cabinet-door catch to the floor on the spot where you want the door to stand open, and screw its striking plate to the back of the door. Make sure the catch is far enough out from the baseboard so that the doorknob won't hit the wall. If necessary, mount the catch on a small block of wood to raise it high enough to contact the bottom of the door.

I can't paint the bottom edge of the door

APPLY PAINT WITH A CARPET SCRAP When painting a door, you probably prefer to protect it from stray paint, but removing the door from its hinges is a lot of trouble just for the sake of painting the inaccessible bottom edge. This clever trick should work instead. Find a scrap of carpet that's several inches wide. Apply a generous amount of paint to the carpet. Then slide it under the door and rub it back and forth to coat the bottom edge.

Looking after locks
• Never oil a lock or latch. The oil will gum up the sensitive bits inside. Every few months, spray the keyholes with a cleaning lubricant, such as WD-40. Hold a cloth beneath the lock to catch the runoff. It will be black with grime. Keep spraying until the runoff is clear.

• If you need to paint a door, always remove the lock beforehand. Paint can ruin a lock.

• Be careful about installing draught proofing between the door and the frame. Locks and latches are meant to have some play to allow for expansion and contraction. Take away that play with draught proofing, and you may put pressure on the lock or latch, causing it to malfunction.

My wooden door is sticking in the frame

RUB THE DOOR EDGE WITH SOAP If damp weather has caused a wooden door to swell up and stick in its door frame, an instant solution is as close at hand as the bathroom basin. Take a bar of soap and rub it along the edge of your door to give it a thin coating. Now your lubricated door will slide into place with ease.

■ LOCKS AND LATCHES

My bedroom door latch won't hold

The cause is simple. The latch bolt on the door is not being caught by the striking plate on the door frame. But finding a solution requires a little detective work, because the latch bolt and striking plate can be out of alignment in several ways. Start by checking the striking plate for wear marks, and observe how the latch bolt hits the plate as the door closes. If you can't see how it hits, put a little lipstick on the end of the bolt and check the mark it leaves on the striking plate.

TAKE OUT THE STRIKING PLATE
If the bolt doesn't extend far enough to go into the plate – usually because the plate is recessed too much – you will need to put a thin piece of material, such as cardboard under the plate. To do this, take

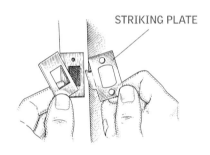

STRIKING PLATE

out the two screws holding the plate and use the plate as a template to cut a packing piece, complete with bolt and screw holes, from stiff cardboard. Put the packing piece under the plate and screw it back into place. You may need more than one thickness of cardboard.

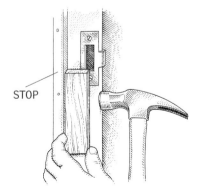

STOP

NUDGE THE DOOR FRAME STOP BACK
Sometimes the stop – the strip of wood against which the door closes on the frame – is too far forward, preventing the bolt from going into the striking plate. This can occur because the stop has swollen or shifted position with settling. You can usually use a block of wood with a hammer to

nudge the stop back slightly. If necessary, you may need to lever off the stop and re-nail it, or use a plane or chisel to trim it down.

ENLARGE THE STRIKING PLATE OPENING If the bolt and striking plate are only slightly out of alignment vertically, it is usually easiest to enlarge the opening in the plate a bit with a metal file. To do this, remove the two screws in the striking plate with a screwdriver. Then saw a slot in a heavy piece of scrap wood and push an edge of the striking plate into the slot to hold it steady while you file. After filing, screw the plate back onto the door frame.

MOVE THE STRIKING PLATE If the bolt and striking plate are more out of alignment vertically, you will have to reposition the striking plate up or down a bit to a position where it can do its job. (This is the last resort because it involves more work.) Remove the striking plate and use a chisel to extend the recess cut into the frame in which the plate sits and to enlarge the hole behind the plate that the latch bolt goes into. Then plug the old screw holes with toothpicks, matchsticks, or a dowel coated with woodworking adhesive. After the adhesive dries, drill new pilot holes for the screws and screw the striking plate into its new position. Fill the old recess area with wood filler.

RECESS

INSTALL A LARGER STRIKING PLATE If the old plate and frame are worn or damaged, buy a slightly larger striking plate from a DIY store and install it in place of the old one. It will look best if it completely covers the damaged area.

My rim lock has broken

JUST REPLACE THE CYLINDER Sometimes, a Yale-type rim lock can break – or you may want to replace it because it is worn or because you have lost the keys. You don't need to replace the whole lock: you can just fit a new cylinder.

The cylinder of a rim lock is the bit that you insert the key into. It is connected to the mechanism on the inside face of the door by a metal connecting bar – and it is this bar which can break. You can buy just the cylinder and bar along with a new matching mounting ring (which fits around the cylinder on the face of the door).

TRICKS OF THE TRADE

Keeping a door lock turning smoothly
Keep locks loosened up by lubricating them every six months. Simply rub the point of a B or HB graphite pencil along both sides of your key; then insert the key in the lock a few times. Or you can use a commercial lock spray or powdered graphite.

1 To fit the replacement cylinder, unscrew the main lock from the inside door surface. You will see the two screws holding the cylinder in place. Unscrew these and use the screws to fit the new cylinder in place.

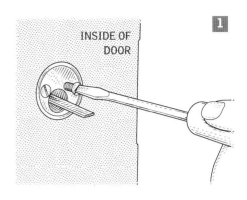

2 Insert the new cylinder into the hole and check that the connecting bar and screws are the right length so that it is correctly housed in the interior handle when the cylinder is in place.

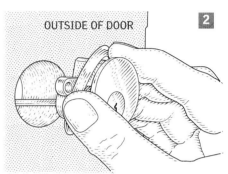

3 You may need to shorten the connecting bar (by cutting through it with a hacksaw) The bar is divided into breakable segments along its length.

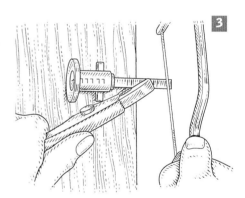

I have bent my door key

STRAIGHTEN IT IN A VICE A bent key is a weakened key. This means that at any time, it could snap off in the lock, creating an even bigger problem than you already have. So the best fix for this situation is a preventative one – get a new key. But if you simply have no alternative but to use the bent key, squash it flat in a vice. You may have one in your garage. If you don't, try flattening the key by placing it between two pieces of wood and hitting it with a hammer. If the key is not too badly damaged, it will still slide home into the keyhole and will allow you to open your door. But once you have managed to get into the house, get the back-up key and throw away the bent one. If you don't have a back-up, go straight to a shop that has a key-cutting service to have two copies made (one to use and one to keep in reserve).

My door lock is getting really hard to turn

CLEAN THE LOCK OR GET A NEW KEY If your lock is not operating properly, take the following simple steps to isolate – and fix – the problem. Operate the lock with the door open. If the lock is stiff, clean and lubricate the lock. Spray the keyhole with a cleaning lubricant, such as WD-40. The liquid that runs off will be black, so hold a cloth underneath to catch it. Otherwise, the run-off will stain your door. Spray until the run-off is clear.

If lubricating and cleaning the lock doesn't cure the stiffness, you may have a poorly cut key and need to have a new key made. If at all possible, find one of the original keys that came with the lock and try it in the lock. If it works, get it duplicated.

MOVE THE STRIKING PLATE If the lock functions properly when the door is open but is stiff when the door is closed, the problem is in the striking plate on the door frame. If you have to pull on the door to make the lock engage, move the plate toward you slightly. If you must push to engage the lock, move the plate in the other direction. Unscrew the plate, fill the holes with adhesive-coated wooden matchsticks, and drill new pilot holes for the screws in the right spots. You will need to slightly enlarge the recess in the door frame that the plate fits into as described on page 95.

I can't get the screws holding my door handle to stay put

CHANGE THE DOOR HANDLE OR THE DOOR LOCK When small door handles are fitted to large locks or latches (found in many older houses), the screws holding the door handle plate to the door simply don't have enough wood to hold them before the far end of the screw hits the embedded lock or latch. The solution is to fit a handle with a larger plate (so the screws are outside the area including the lock/latch body) or to fit a smaller latch/lock that will fit inside the area between the screws. The first option is generally easier; the second involves some carpentry and judicious hole filling.

My key is stuck in the door lock

GIVE IT A SHOT OF WD-40 This is usually a sign of an old lock, one whose pins are not aligning properly because the lubrication has dried out. Squirt some penetrating lubricant, such as WD-40, into the lock and then rotate and jiggle the key. Now try to remove the key. It should come out easily. If not, pinch the key so that your fingertips touch the lock and then work it out slowly. This pinching motion straightens the key and gives you leverage. Your next step should be to replace the lock's cylinder (see page 96).

I can't find the keyhole at night

MAKE IT GLOW IN THE DARK If you have trouble finding the door lock in the dark, dab a few drops of luminous paint around the keyhole for increased visibility. Luminous paint can be bought at DIY stores or from online suppliers.

My children keep forgetting their house keys

INSTALL A KEY SAFE Hiding a spare key outside for use by forgetful family members isn't a good idea. Soon everyone will know it's under the third stone from the doorstep in the front garden. Instead, install a key safe somewhere outside the house. Key safes are secure boxes for keys, with a combination lock on the front. Mount yours in a visible location to discourage tampering, and secure it to the wall of the house. Change the combination periodically if you give it to cleaners or workers outside the family. Key safes are available from locksmiths and online suppliers.

▪ GARAGE DOORS

My up-and-over garage door squeaks and groans

OIL THE MOVING PARTS With all those metal parts scraping together – no wonder. You won't eliminate all the noise of a moving garage door, but you can reduce the harshest sounds by lubricating the metal parts. First, use an aerosol form of 3-in-One lubricant (with added non-slip PTFE – also known as Teflon) to apply oil to rollers, tracks, hinges (if fitted) and springs. Keep the tracks clean and dry, so that the rollers won't drag. Don't use grease, and don't use WD-40, which will dry out more quickly than a regular lubricating oil. If the lubrication does not stop the problem, disconnect the door from the door opener (if it is automatic) and operate it by hand to see whether the noises are coming from the door or the moving parts inside the opener motor. Once you've pinpointed the source, lubricate as appropriate.

REMOVE ANY GREASE Never use grease on a garage door. Grease on the runners and rollers acts like a brake, especially in winter when cold temperatures harden grease into a sticky obstacle course. By making the door work harder to open and close, grease on the runners could be causing the noise. Use a spray-on degreaser, such as WD-40, to break down any old grease that you can see. Wipe away the residue with paper towels and then lubricate the parts with oil. Now open the door. And close it. Open it again. It should now run smoothly and quietly.

My automatic garage door won't close

CHECK THE PHOTO-ELECTRIC SENSORS Although the door slides down, before it can touch the ground, it heads back up again. It's not just a door with a bad attitude. On the contrary, this door means well. Something is triggering the door's safety feature, the one that keeps the door from closing on your car bonnet or an unsuspecting passenger. In the latest garage doors, this safety feature typically has an infrared beam source and a matching photoelectric sensor on either side of the garage door opening. They are located about 150mm or so above the ground. If the beam is obscured or is not properly lined up, it can malfunction. To fix the problem, try cleaning the beam lens, following the manufacturer's instructions. Make sure the indicator light (if it has one) signals that the feature is working and that the beam is aligned properly. Use a tape measure to check that the sensors are at the same height. Doors that don't move smoothly or are out-of-true could also be the cause. If so, try lubricating the door (see previous problem) or having it realigned.

PROBLEM STOPPER

Cut down the noise from a garage door
A cheap metal garage door is like a banjo. Thin and tinny, it amplifies all the noises its parts make. If your garage door makes too much noise, it may be time to get an upgrade. Buy a wooden or GRP (glass-reinforced plastic) door. While the working parts will still need to be lubricated to keep them moving smoothly and quietly, the layers of insulation will muffle any sounds the door makes.

Electrical problems

Replace flickering fluorescents

If you have a flickering fluorescent tube, replace it. Flickering tubes can burn out the fitting's ballast, which regulates the electric current travelling into the tube. If the ballast fails, you will have to pay for a more expensive repair.

■ LIGHTING

A bulb has broken off in its socket

REMOVE THE BULB BASE WITH PLIERS OR FRUIT Sweep up any glass on the floor. Turn off the electricity at the mains and remove the fuse for the lighting circuit you are working on (or switch off the relevant miniature circuit breaker) – switching the light off is not enough. For a ceiling or high wall socket, you'll need a step stool or step ladder. Wear protective goggles and gloves.

The best tool for removing the base of the bulb is a pair of long-nose pliers. Don't grab the remaining glass portion of the bulb with the pliers; it might break. Use the tip of the pliers to grab the edge of the bulb's metal base and turn it anticlockwise if it's a screw-in light bulb – or push and twist anticlockwise if it's a bayonet cap light bulb. If you don't have long-nose pliers, insert an orange, apple or potato into the broken base of the bulb and turn.

I can't unscrew my small halogen light bulbs

USE A BULB CHANGER The tiny flat-headed bulbs used in halogen lighting (both mains and low-voltage) can be difficult to unscrew. Little rubber suckers that you can use to grip the surface of the bulb may be provided, but otherwise you can buy a bulb-changer which uses the same principle. This tool, which comes in three different lengths up to a metre long, has a sucker on the end and, once applied to the bulb, can be used to twist or push and twist the bulb. A sliding switch on the handle then releases the bulb. Using a bulb changer will also extend the life of halogen bulbs as you can use it without grease from your fingers fingers getting on to the bulb. Halogen lamps get very hot and the heated grease causes the glass to deteriorate, significantly reducing the life of the bulb.

I can't unscrew my reflector bulbs

USE SOME STICKY TAPE ON THE BULB Large round reflector bulbs, found in many ceiling fittings, can be very difficult to get hold of when they need replacing. A suction bulb changer won't work (as the front of the bulb is curved), but you can use gaffer tape to make a makeshift handle to turn the bulb. Take a 150mm length of tape and fold the middle section over on itself, sticky side to sticky side, attaching the sticky ends to the surface of the bulb, going to the edges. Use the folded-over section as a handle to turn (or push and turn) the bulb; it should give enough grip to remove it.

My lightbulbs burn out too quickly

MAKE SURE THE BULBS REALLY ARE DYING TOO SOON Before you do anything, make sure the bulbs are, indeed, giving out prematurely. Check the package for the bulb's estimated life expectancy and then try to calculate how long yours are actually lasting. A bulb with a 1,000 hour life, for example, should burn for a little over four months (120 days) if it is used for an average of 8 hours a day.

KEEP THE BULB FROM OVERHEATING Check for heat, which will shorten the life span of a bulb. If it's a high-wattage bulb in a small shade, such as a tight glass globe, then the bulb might be overheating. If so, replace it with a lower wattage bulb. Bulbs in recessed fixtures surrounded by loft insulation can overheat as well. Go up into the loft and remove the insulation around the fixture. Unless the fixture is UL listed as safe for use with insulation, it shouldn't have any insulation around it.

WORLD-CLASS FIX

MIR HEROISM

Thanks to a quick-thinking fix by Commander Valeri Korzun, the crew of six on the Russian space station Mir escaped a fiery death in 1997.

Late one Sunday evening, Mir's master alarm sounded. Two-foot flames were shooting from one of the space station's oxygen-generating canisters. Sparks and molten metal were flying and smoke choked the central passageway. Wearing oxygen masks, crew members fought the fire, but the water-based fire extinguishers were useless against the burning lithium perchlorate. So the crew had to wait for the canister to burn itself out and hope that the flames would not burn through Mir's aluminum hull and cause the capsule to decompress 250 miles from Earth.

Thinking fast, Commander Korzun sprayed the wall with the fire extinguisher to keep it from melting. It took 14 minutes for the pressurised canister to burn out. When the smoke cleared, there was ash everywhere, but miraculously, the damage was minimal and no one had been hurt.

Inadequate venting, blocked hoses and vents, and a build-up of fluff are the main causes of fires in tumble driers.

When clothes take longer to dry or feel hotter at the end of the cycle the machine is in trouble. To avoid drier fires:

• Don't leave a drier, washing machine or dishwasher running at night or when you are out.

• Remove the lint from the trap after every load of clothes dried.

• Do not cover the vent or any other opening.

• Ensure the vent hose is free of kinks and is not crushed in any way.

• Use only the recommended vent hoses, and not improvised ones.

• Only vent the warm air to the outside of a building.

• Never put rags or materials into your tumble drier if they have been used to soak up flammable liquids such as petrol and alcohol.

KEEP THE BULB FROM SHAKING Check for vibration. Ceiling fixtures beneath springy floors can jiggle so much that a bulb's filament snaps prematurely. The same goes for lights on or near a wobbly ceiling fan or near a door that often slams shut. If you can't stop the vibration, use either a compact fluorescent bulb, which is not affected by vibration, or a shock-resistant 'rough service' incandescent bulb made especially for this purpose.

USE A LOW-ENERGY LIGHT BULB Low-energy bulbs (known as compact fluorescent lamps – CFLs) not only last eight to ten times as long as a normal light bulb, but cost only a fifth as much to run. With modern technology, low-energy bulbs now very much resemble the normal light bulbs they replace in both size and shape.

■ ANNOYANCES

My extractor fan rattles

CHECK THE OUTSIDE GRILLE Some extractor fans are naturally noisy, but a rattle is usually caused by the louvres on the exterior grill flapping in the wind. There are several ways to cope with this:

- Fit felt pads (such as those sold for use on furniture legs) to the back of each louvre.
- Replace the louvred grill with a fixed grille.
- Fit an extractor fan cowl over the grille.

My electricity circuit breakers keep tripping

CHECK OUT THE SYSTEM The wiring system in your home may have been designed for a time when people had far fewer electrical appliances and those they did have were used less frequently. It may be that it cannot cope with modern-day demands.

- A socket outlet circuit can only cope with 30A of current which is equivalent to just under 7kW – so if you have a washing machine, tumble drier, dishwasher and kettle (all with high-wattage water heaters) all running at the same time off the same circuit, it could well trip the circuit breaker. If this happens a lot, ask an electrician to install an extra circuit – either for the kitchen or for the laundry/utility room.
- Modern miniature circuit breakers (which have replaced fuses in most homes) are so sensitive that when a conventional

(tungsten) light bulb fails, the final surge of current in the bulb's dying moments can be enough to trip the circuit breaker. Replace tungsten light bulbs with compact fluorescents – see left.

- If your main circuit breaker (RCD – residual current device) trips a lot, it could indicate a fault. Have an electrician check out the circuit unless you can identify one particular appliance as the culprit that seems to trip the whole house more often than others.

My doorbell sounds muffled

VACUUM THE BELL'S INTERIOR You probably never think about your door bell or chime – much less consider cleaning it. But a blanket of dust can build up inside, giving it a fuzzy sound. So just remove the cover and vacuum inside with the brush attachment. Your chimes will return to their former clarity.

▪ LARGE APPLIANCES

My tumble drier is hot but the clothes don't dry

CHECK FOR A BLOCKED VENT If your tumble drier feels really hot, but your clothes seem to take forever to dry, the vent in the drier may have become blocked.

A blocked vent traps the excess hot air inside the drier's drum. But the low circulation of air keeps clothes from getting dry. This can be a serious problem – the extra heat can damage fabrics and can start a fire (see opposite) – but you can easily fix the problem yourself.

1 Start by checking the vent flap or hood on the outside of the house. Make sure that you feel a strong flow of air coming out when the drier is running. If not, try cleaning out the vent with a straightened wire clothes hanger.

2 If the vent flap is not the problem, check for a kink or sag in the hose and straighten it if necessary.

3 If a kinked or sagging hose is not the problem, disconnect the hose from the drier and with a torch look for blockages inside. To remove a blockage, shake it out or pull it out from the ends. If the hose is damaged, replace it.

My appliances wobble

ADJUST THE LEG HEIGHT There is an easy solution. The legs of most large appliances – fridges, as well as washing machines and driers – can be adjusted to level the unit. Some legs are threaded so that you can screw them in or out. You simply screw a leg in to lower a corner and screw it out to raise it. Put a spirit level on top of the fridge to work out which corner is low or high and adjust accordingly. If your refrigerator has rollers instead of screw-legs, use a screwdriver to turn the adjusting screw just above the roller. Bear these tips in mind when you are trying to level an appliance:

- If you have trouble screwing a leg in or out, tilt the appliance back slightly and prop it up with a block of wood.
- If the threads on a screw leg are locked tight, slide a wedge under the low corner. Use small squares of 3mm MDF (medium-density fibreboard) or plastic packer 'shims', available in various thicknesses.

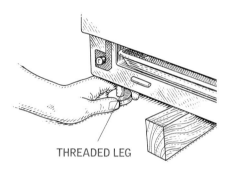

THREADED LEG

- If your fridge door doesn't close automatically from an open position, tilt the fridge backward ever so slightly. Fridges do need to be level to work properly, so some manufacturers make thin 'shims' (spacers) specifically to fit behind door hinges to deal with wonky doors.

My fridge rattles

CHECK IF IT'S OFF-BALANCE OR TOUCHING SOMETHING Make sure that the fridge is level (see above) and that it is not rubbing against anything, such as a cupboard or another kitchen appliance.

CLEAN THE COMPRESSOR COILS The problem could be a compressor that is overworked. Clean the dust from the compressor coils, which are usually located on the back of the fridge. You will have to roll the fridge out to access them. First, unplug or turn off the fridge, empty it and roll it out into the room. Then use a vacuum cleaner with a brush or crevice attachment to clean the coils thoroughly. Give the inside (and outside) a good clean before you put the food back.

Plumbing problems

▦ KITCHEN PLUMBING

There's a leak at the base of my kitchen tap

FIT A NEW SEALING WASHER(S) When tap washers need replacing, taps leak from the spout – but a leak from the base of a kitchen mixer tap, with water dribbling out where the movable spout meets the body of the tap, indicates a failed 'O'-ring washer. You may never have seen it, but there should be a tiny screw (a grub screw) on the tap which holds the swinging spout in place and once you have found this and unscrewed it (which will need a tiny screwdriver), you should be able to pull the spout out to reveal the sealing 'O' rings – there are usually two. (If there is no grub screw, line the tap spout up with the tap body and pull upwards sharply.) Take the whole thing – spout and 'O'-ring – to a plumbers' merchants to get a replacement of the correct size. Apply some petroleum jelly (Vaseline) when refitting the spout.

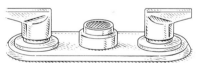

My hot water is too hot

CHECK YOUR IMMERSION HEATER If you heat your water with electricity with an immersion heater fitted in a hot-water cylinder, turn off the electrical supply to the immersion heater, remove the cover and check the setting on the thermostat inside. It should be no more than 60°C in a hard water area, 65-70°C elsewhere. If re-setting this doesn't cure the problem (or the thermostat is already correctly set), the thermostat has failed and should be replaced. Make a drawing or take a good photo of the wiring to the existing thermostat so that you can wire up the replacement (easily obtained from large DIY stores and plumbers' merchants) in the same way. You do not need to turn the water off.

CHECK YOUR HOT-WATER CYLINDER THERMOSTAT If hot water is provided by the central-heating boiler (via pipes taking boiler-heated water into and out of the hot-water cylinder), there should be a rectangular thermostat strapped to the side of the cylinder. Check that this is set to no more than 70°C – again, it may have failed and need to be replaced.

CHECK YOUR BOILER THERMOSTAT If there is no thermostat fitted to the hot-water cylinder, the hot water temperature will eventually reach the temperature of the water leaving the boiler. You can reduce this by turning down the boiler thermostat, but think about hiring a plumber to fit a hot-water cylinder thermostat (which may involve some pipe re-routing).

There's water coming from under my dishwasher

CHECK THE HOSES Water dribbling down the front of a washing machine indicates a failed door seal (which is not difficult to replace), but water appearing on the floor from under the machine will need a bit more investigation. The most likely cause is the failure of one of the washers at the ends of the supply hoses; the hoses themselves may have perished or split or the connection between the hose and the washing machine (or possibly hose and stoptap at the other end of the hose) may have come loose.

Before you start, unplug the washing machine (or isolate its electrical supply) and turn off the hot and cold stoptap that provide its water supply – these may be under the kitchen sink or next to (or behind) the machine. Normally, one has a red handle and the other a blue handle (note that dishwashers only have one supply hose connected to a valve with a blue handle).

Pull out the washing machine if necessary (lay hardboard sheets on top of vinyl floors to prevent the vinyl ripping) and examine the hoses carefully, which may mean disconnecting them at both ends.

Replacement washers (which fit inside the plastic 'nut' on each end of the hose) cost just a few pence, but if the hose is showing any signs of damage, it is worth replacing the hoses as well. You can buy extra-long hoses if it makes putting the machine back in place easier. You should not need to tighten the plastic nuts any more than finger tight to get a good seal, but if the hose can still be twisted once the nut is done up, use some waterpump pliers to give it a final tweak.

My enamel sink has a chip in it

FIX IT USING A REPAIR KIT Chips in enamel sinks, baths, appliances and basins don't have to be permanent. They are quick, easy and inexpensive to repair. There are several types of repair material available, from simple paints to tough epoxies. Two-part epoxies are best and are usually available in a variety of colours, so you should be able to find one that matches the damaged area.

1. Scrub the chipped area with soapy water. Then roughen it up slightly with a small piece of medium-grade glasspaper to remove rust or debris. Roughening also gives the damaged area some 'key' for the repair material to cling to.
2. Mix together equal parts of hardener and filler, following the manufacturer's instructions
3. Brush the epoxy onto the damaged area. Confine the repair to the damaged spot rather than trying to feather it out or blend the old with the new. If the chip is deep, don't try to fill it with one coat. Instead, wait 8 hours and then apply a second coat. Repeat the procedure if necessary.

You will need to wait 24 hours before getting the area wet and seven days before scrubbing it.

▪ TOILET TROUBLES

My toilet doesn't flush

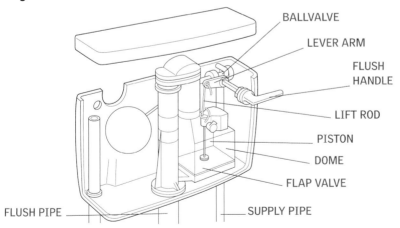

BALLVALVE
LEVER ARM
FLUSH HANDLE
LIFT ROD
PISTON
DOME
FLAP VALVE
FLUSH PIPE
SUPPLY PIPE

RECONNECT THE LINK GOING TO THE FLUSH VALVE If your toilet isn't flushing, it's probably a problem with the metal link that connects the handle to the flap valve at the bottom of the cistern. Lift the cover off

TRICKS OF THE TRADE

An impromptu toilet plunger
While staying in a log cabin in Canada, Jake Jacob found himself with a blocked toilet but no plunger.

His nifty solution was to cut an empty 1.5 litre plastic soft drink bottle in half. He then pushed a broom handle into the spout and secured it with gaffer tape. Then he used his makeshift plumber's helper in the same way as a plunger: He placed it in the toilet bowl, removed as much air from the bell end as possible and plunged it in and out to loosen the blockage. Jake's friends thought he was a hero.

**Testing for a
leaky toilet**

Here is a quick test to
confirm that you have
a leaky toilet:

1 Remove any colour-
producing in-tank bowl
cleaner so that you
start with clear water
in the toilet.

2 Colour the tank water
with enough food
colouring or powdered
drink mix to give it a
rich colour.

3 Wait half an hour.
If some of the colouring
has entered the toilet
bowl, your toilet is
definitely leaking.

the cistern and, inside, you will find a metal link that should be attached to the end of the flush lever and also to the top of the plastic lift-rod (to which is attached the piston plus the flap valve).

If the link has fallen off, re-fit it; if it is broken, replace it – you can make a temporary repair with a link fashioned from a length of metal coat hanger.

My toilet keeps running, even when I jiggle the handle

THE FLAP VALVE ISN'T WORKING PROPERLY If water continuously runs from the cistern into the toilet bowl, you have a failed flap valve (though with a modern WC cistern, it could be a failed float valve – see opposite). Normally the running will be obvious, but if you only suspect it, carry out the test described in the margin.

1 To replace the flap valve you must turn off the water supply to the cistern. If you are lucky, there will be an in-line isolating valve on the pipe leading to the cistern, which you can close with a screwdriver. If there is no isolating valve you will have to climb into the loft and turn off the red-handled gate valve at the bottom of the cold water cistern (see How do I turn off the water? opposite) – if you're not sure which one of two such valves to turn off, turn them both off.

2 Flush the cistern to empty it. If the flush won't work, bale or siphon the water out. Put towels on the floor and a container immediately under the cistern. Use a large spanner (water-pump pliers are a good choice) to undo the large nut that secures the plastic pipe leading from the cistern to the toilet bowl. Push this pipe to one side and now undo the larger nut that holds the flushing mechanism (the siphon) in place. Unhook the link connecting to the flushing lever and lift out the flushing mechanism.

3 You can now pull out the plastic innards. The flap valve is the piece of thin plastic, which covers the whole of the plastic plate at the bottom of the piston. Take the plate and the old flap valve with you to a DIY store or

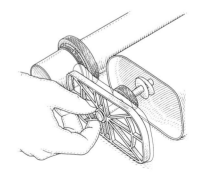

plumbers' merchants to get a replacement. If you cannot get an exact replacement, buy a larger flap valve and cut it just slightly larger than the shape of the plate with scissors – it should touch, but not drag on, the siphon's sides.

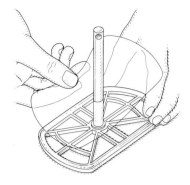

Reassemble everything, but before turning the water back on, fill the cistern from a watering can or bucket to test that the flap valve is working properly.

How do I turn off the water?

IT IS USEFUL TO KNOW HOW TO TURN OFF YOUR WATER SUPPLY In most homes, there are three places where you turn off the water supply:

- The main brass-handled stoptap (often under the kitchen sink), which turns off the kitchen cold tap and the supply to the main cold-water cistern in the loft.
- The cold tap supply (also supplying cold water to toilets), which is a red or orange handled valve on the lowest pipe leading out of the main cold-water cistern.
- The hot tap supply, which is on the cold pipe leading from the bottom of the cold-water cistern to the bottom of the hot water cylinder. This may be close to the cistern, but is usually found close to the hot-water cylinder.

There may be other stoptaps – those that turn off the supply to garden taps and electric showers, both of which are fed from the mains. And some taps (and toilet cisterns) may have in-line isolating valves on their supply pipes. When you have found all the water turn-off valves, label them so you know what they do.

How do I stop an overflow pipe running?

CHANGE THE FLOAT VALVE If the overflow pipe leading outside the house from your toilet is dribbling or running, it means that the float valve that controls the flow of water into the cistern is faulty. (some modern cisterns do not have outside overflow pipes – the

A better plunger
A plunger can become
a more effective tool
with the aid of a little
petroleum jelly. Just
smear some jelly
around the edge of
the suction cup. This
will create a better
seal between the
suction cup and the
drain. If the handle on
your plunger is loose
and pulls out of the
cup, use a hose clip to
secure the cup to
the handle.

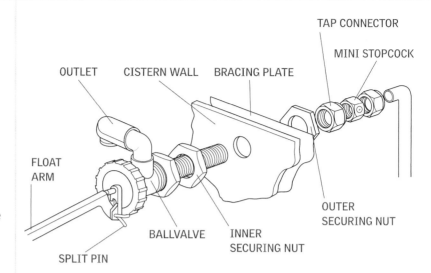

overflow runs directly into the toilet bowl, which could be a cause of
the toilet continuously running – see page 108)

Before buying a new float valve, check that the present one is
correctly adjusted: you can usually move the float up and down on its
arm so that the water level is around 25mm below the overflow pipe
when the valve shuts off the water. With an old valve, check that the
plastic ball is not punctured by corrosion so that water is getting in.

You can repair float valves, but they are inexpensive and you may
want to take the opportunity to fit a 'quiet' equilibrium-type float
valve instead of a noisy piston type. Make sure your new valve is the
correct pressure rating (high if fed from the mains, low if fed from a
cold-water cistern) and the correct type (bottom entry or side entry).

Replacement is straightforward: turn off the water supply,
unscrew the brass nut connecting the water supply pipe to the float
valve, undo the two plastic nuts holding the float valve in place and
pop in the new valve. There's a tiny fibre washer in the bit that goes
inside the brass nut – make sure that this is in place when
reassembling: if it looks worn, buy a replacement.

I can smell sewage when I flush the toilet

CHECK THE WATER LEVEL IN THE TOILET BOWL However clean your
toilet, it will reek if foul air is coming up from the drains. Escaping
gas could have several causes. Check the level of the water in the
bowl. If it is low, that may be allowing the air to escape. A pet may
be drinking from the bowl; keep the lid down to stop it. Evaporation
of water from a rarely used toilet (in an outhouse, for instance)
could be the problem. If so, flush it periodically to keep it full.

CLEAN THE RIM HOLES Bacteria can develop under the rim of the toilet bowl, giving off a foul smell every time you flush. This is more likely in hot, humid conditions. Kill bacteria with upward squirts from a toilet cleaner. With a modern toilet where the overflow discharges into the toilet bowl, pour several cups of bleach into the toilet tank's overflow tube (the one sticking up about half an inch above the water). This will flow through the rim holes and into the toilet bowl, killing bacteria hiding there. Flush the toilet to get rid of the bleach.

CHECK YOUR SOIL PIPE'S ROOF VENT Leaves or a bird's nest might be blocking the roof vent on your drainage system's main vent pipe, the soil stack, and this may block the path of escaping air. Other signs of a blocked vent are sluggish drains and basins, sink or baths that gurgle when you flush the toilet.

How do I stop my tap dripping?

REPLACE THE WASHER The majority of hot and cold taps in the UK still have flat circular washers that shut off the water when the tap is closed. In time, these become worn and needs to be replaced. Modern ceramic disc taps – which require only a quarter turn to open and close – cannot normally be repaired, unless you are able to buy a replacement cartridge.

To change washers on ordinary taps, turn off the water supply – if you are lucky – with an in-line valve on the supply pipes to the taps but if not, by turning off the orange or red-handled valves close to the cold-water cistern (for cold taps) or close to the hot-water cylinder (for hot taps): note that replacing the washer on the kitchen cold tap you need to turn off the water at the mains. Once the water has been turned off, open the tap you are working on to remove any water left in the supply pipe.

Arm yourself with a selection of spanners and screwdrivers. Take off the top of the tap (on most modern taps, the screw is hidden under the red or blue disc which can be levered out) and then undo the largest nut you can see (brace the tap body if necessary to prevent cracking a ceramic basin) which should allow you to remove the whole tap mechanism. The tap washer is on the far end of this and can usually be levered off, though it may be held in place by a small nut. Make sure that the replacement is the same size and clean any obvious grit out of the tap body before reassembly.

**Emergency
plumbing kit**
Keep a small box in a
place where you can
easily find it and keep it
stocked with the
following:
• Radiator key
• Tap washers
• Flap valve
• Fibre tap connector
  washers
• Tap 'O' rings
• Basin plug
• Chain for basin plug
• Vaseline
• Spare toilet cistern link
• Spare washing
  machine hose washers

■ ANNOYING PLUMBING

My pipes are banging

THERE IS A HAMMER IN YOUR PIPES Usually, the problem is something called water hammer, a pressure shock wave sent through a plumbing system by a sudden change in the flow of water when you shut it off. Apart from being annoying, water hammer can exert tremendous pressure that can damage pipes and valves, and weaken joints. Water hammer can often be cured simply by changing tap washers (see page 111) or by replacing the float-valves on toilet and cold-water cisterns with a modern equilibrium or diaphragm type rather than the old-fashioned piston type (see page 108). Sometimes, the solution is to close the main stoptap a turn or two.

If you have banging coming from central-heating pipes (or from the central-heating boiler, it is an indication that you might have corrosion in your central-heating system. In that case it is sensible to call in a plumber or central-heating contractor to check it out.

My radiators are cold at the top

LET THE AIR ESCAPE If radiators are hot in the middle and at the bottom, but cold at the top, it is a sign that air has got into the system. Before you do anything else, go into the loft and check that there is water in the small feed-and-expansion cistern next to the main cold-water cistern. It may be that the float valve has stuck shut (through under-use) and is left hanging high and dry over an empty cistern. Release (or replace) this first. When cold, the cistern should be only half full.

Removing air from radiators (with a half-full feed-and-expansion cistern) is easy: all you need is a cloth and a radiator key. The key is used to open the bleed valve at the top of the radiator (half a turn is normally all that is needed), with the rag held underneath to catch any drips. Leave the valve open until the hissing air turns to water and then close it. Do this with all the radiators in the house, starting with the highest one and finishing with the lowest – you may need to go round the system twice.

Note: if your radiators are cold at the bottom, it is a sign of corrosion in the system which is a far more serious problem.

Emergencies and home safety

▥ PLUMBING DISASTERS

My bath is overflowing

SOAK UP THE WATER WITH TOWELS Turn off the
running water and pull out the plug. Throw
old towels on any puddles. When they are
saturated, wring them out over the sink
or toilet and put them back down. With
big pools, contain the water by soaking it up
from the outside to the centre. Finish by mopping
and then air out the room. Take up loose floor covering to
avoid trapping moisture. Use a dehumidifier to dry the room faster.

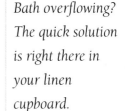

*Bath overflowing?
The quick solution
is right there in
your linen
cupboard.*

My toilet bowl is about to overflow

DON'T FLUSH! If a toilet looks like it will overflow after flushing, keep
calm. Most toilet bowls are designed to hold all the water in the tank
without overflowing. If you do flush again before the water level has
returned to its normal level, you may cause an overflow.

PLUNGE AWAY THE BLOCKAGE A blocked toilet can usually be quickly
cleared with a toilet plunger. Or you can improvise by wrapping a
plastic bag around a mop head and tying it on. If you have a set of
drain rods and a rubber plunger disc, fit this to one of the rods to
make a toilet plunger. Don't flush again until the water level is back
to normal. If the toilet remains blocked after vigorous plunging you
may need to call a plumber or drain clearing service. There may be a
foreign object lodged in the toilet trap. If you can see an object
blocking the drain, slip a plastic bag over your hand and pull it out.

I don't want my pipes to freeze when I'm away

SHUT DOWN THE SYSTEM OR KEEP THE HEATING TURNING OVER If you
are planning to leave the house unoccupied for any length of time

Flood control
Before you go on
holiday, consider turning
off the water supply
completely or partially
to prevent a flood while
you are away. Turning
off the water supply at
the mains stoptap will
minimise potential
damage. If this is not
practical, consider
isolating areas which
could be vulnerable to
leaks. On older style
washing machines and
dishwashers, ruptured
flexible hoses – which
carry the water to the
machine from the
pipework – were a
common cause of
household water
damage. Old hoses
which are weak and
fatigued can be a
potential source of
trouble, as they remain
under pressure even
when the appliance is
not in use. You can
usually isolate washing
machines and
dishwashers at the
appliance's stoptaps.

during the winter months, when freezing conditions are more likely, it may pay to drain down the system completely so that there is no stored water in the house and therefore no chance of it freezing and causing a leak. For shorter periods set the central heating on to low to keep the chill at bay.

My pipes have frozen

USE A MOIST RAG TO FIND THE BLOCKAGE You first need to locate the frozen spot in your plumbing, which is easy if the pipe has burst or is bulging. But if you are lucky, the frozen section of pipe will simply be plugging the water so that it can't run. To find the frozen plug, check the piping in the unheated areas of your house or exterior walls. On exposed pipes, you can pinpoint the frozen area by wiping the pipe with a moist rag. Frost will form as you hit the frozen spot.

THAW IT WITH A HAIR DRIER When you are thawing pipes, go slowly. Use a hair drier set on high to elevate the temperature. Never use propane torches – the heat they produce can turn water into steam, which could build up and burst the pipes. It can also melt the solder in the joints. Start thawing the ice in the frozen pipe from the side closest to a tap, so the melting ice will have somewhere to go. Work with the hair drier from the tap side back toward the frozen area. With the tap open, the water should start to run as the ice is thawed. Check for leaks along the section of frozen pipe, especially on the joints of compression fittings which may have been pushed apart.

There's sewage on the floor

DON'T TOUCH THE SEWAGE And don't make the situation worse by flushing the toilet or running water in the sink or bath. Use a neighbour's facilities if you can, until the blockage is fixed.

RODDING THE DRAINS A blocked drain outside may present itself as an unpleasant smell or an overflowing inspection chamber. If you are responsibile for the drains, it may be worth buying or hiring a set of drain rods before employing the services of drain specialists. Start by attaching a plunger disc fitting to the end of the first rod then screwing on two or three more rods. While you plunge the pipes keep turning the drain rods clockwise so that the fittings don't unscrew and get stuck in the pipe causing a greater problem. Wear heavy-duty rubber gloves for this work and clean your tools afterwards with a heavy-duty disinfectant-style cleaner.

KEEP A PLUMBING EMERGENCY KIT HANDY

You never know when you might encounter a plumbing problem, but it's worth investing a few pounds on some simple tools and equipment to keep in your tool kit just in case. There are a number of proprietary burst pipe repair kits available from plumbing merchants.

- **Buy a range of pipe repair kits** and store them in a brightly coloured box marked 'Plumbing' in an easily accessible place.
- **Special self-amalgamating tape** is available to cope with most burst pipes. It can even be placed straight over the leak while the pipe is under pressure. It helps to minimise the volume of leaked water, subsequently reducing damage. One roll of this tape in the tool box costs a fraction of a plumber's emergency call out fee.
- **For leaks other than pipes** a special putty is available which is useful where the other systems cannot be used, for example, on radiators.
- **It's also useful to keep a selection of tap washers** and washers for the ball valves that are found in toilets and cold-water storage cisterns. The spare parts that you keep in stock should match the taps and fittings that you have in the house.
- **A pair of adjustable spanners** is also useful to gain access to fittings.

▥ CHIMNEYS

Should I clean the chimney or hire a pro?

WHEN DECIDING, BE AWARE THAT IT IS A VERY MESSY JOB It is essential to have your chimney swept regularly. Keeping it clean will help to avoid chimney fires. Although you can hire or buy rods and chimney brushes and do the job yourself, you need to be aware of how much mess this job can create.

Cleaning up afterwards can be extremely laborious and the soot can also ruin conventional vacuum cleaners which may not have good enough filters to cope with the task.

CLEAN FABRIC AND METAL SURFACES Get rid of the lingering smoke smell by washing curtains and cleaning upholstery. Generally, cleaning upholstery is like cleaning carpets. You should never overwet the fabric and the cushion beneath it. Instead, apply a foam-type upholstery cleaner. Let it stand and then vacuum it off, following the label instructions. Before cleaning upholstery, always

PROBLEM STOPPER

What to do if you think there is a gas leak
- Open doors and windows.
- Check if the pilot light has gone out on your boiler. If any gas appliances have been left on, turn them off. If the pilot light is still on and your gas appliances are all off there may be a gas escape.
- Turn off the gas at the mains.
- Phone the National Gas Emergency Number immediately on 0800 111 999. (Do not call from a mobile phone.)
- Do not turn light switches on or off, use doorbells, mobile phones, or any other electrical switches.
- Do not smoke, light a match or use any other kind of naked flame.
If your mains tap is in an external meter cabinet, make sure you know where the key is.

HOME, SAFE HOME

The safety appliances and devices you install will help to protect your home, but you also need to prepare and plan for when things go wrong. Once these devices and plans are put in place, they need to be shown and explained to everyone in the house.

- **Smoke alarms** approved to BS5446 should be fitted to every storey in a house. A typical two-storey house could have one in the hall and one on the landing. Other alarms could be in bedrooms. Smoke alarms for existing homes can be battery operated, wired to the mains with a back-up battery or plugged into a ceiling light fitting. Some battery-powered alarms have indicators to show that the battery is still working; others give an audible warning when the battery is low. Plug-in alarms recharge when the light is switched on. Smoke alarms can be linked together so that when one is triggered they all go off. Clean with a vacuum cleaner nozzle, test the alarm and replace the batteries.

- **Carbon monoxide detectors** detect the lethal colourless and odourless gas. Have at least one on each floor, one close to the bedrooms and one near a boiler or heater. A carbon monoxide detector is only a warning device and should not be a substitute for regular servicing of heating appliances.

- **Passive infra-red lights** Automatic outdoor lights activated by PIR will welcome guests and deter burglars. They will light up dark areas which can reduce the likelihood of tripping. The sensor can be incorporated in the light or a separate unit operating a number of lights. Energy-saving versions are replacing the more expensive-to-run high-wattage halogen lamps.

- **Fire extinguishers and fire blankets** All-purpose fire extinguishers should be installed on escape routes and in areas where a fire is likely to start such as a kitchen. A fire blanket should be sited near to the cooker. A fire-prevention officer will be able to offer specific advice about the best type of equipment to purchase for your situation.

- **RCD protected circuits** 'Residual Current Devices' work by cutting the power supply to an appliance or circuit, fast enough to prevent an electric shock from being fatal. The latest wiring regulations require RCD protection on most new circuits in a house. Unless you have recently had your house re-wired to current standards there are probably areas which could be better protected. Get an electrical health check to eliminate unprotected circuits.

- **Planning escape routes** Ensure that the occupants of your house can escape safely from the house in case of a fire. This may mean investing in chain escape ladders which are stored upstairs and anchored to a wall. Make sure everyone in the house knows the escape drill and keep the routes clear of clutter, especially hallways and stairs.

- **Anti-scald measures** In some plumbing situations a shower or hot tap can become far too hot and can risk scalding the user. Thermostatic mixers and better water-heating systems can avoid this happening. Talk to your plumber about methods of ensuring that the water cannot scald, especially when used by very young or very old people.

- **A list of emergency numbers** Keep a list of up-to-date contact numbers that may be needed in an emergency. For example, energy and water supply companies, emergency gas leak reporting, your local council, the emergency services, environmental agencies 'floodline' (if appropriate) and your insurance company. Laminate this list and keep it close to a phone with a cord connection.

- **Whole-house surge protectors** These are available for electric, cable, and phone lines. Have them installed by an electrician.

check the label or tag for cleaning instructions. As smoke is drawn to cool surfaces, such as metal, wipe down exposed doorknobs, hinges, drawer handles and other metal surfaces with a domestic degreaser. This will also prevent the acidic soot from etching the metal.

My chimney is on fire

CALL FOR HELP AND EVACUATE If a build-up of combustible material in your chimney catches fire, you will probably see smoke and sparks shooting out of the chimney and you might hear a loud roaring sound. Chimney fires burn fast and furiously, melting flue liners, damaging chimneys and even igniting roof-covering materials. If your chimney is on fire, call the Fire Service and get everyone out of the house. Tell all the occupants to meet at the front gate, a safe distance from the house, so that all can be accounted for. The Fire Brigade recommend that you follow this procedure:

- Dial 999 and ask for the Fire Service. It will help if someone can wait outside to meet them.
- If you have a conventional open fire, extinguish the fire by gently splashing water onto the open fire.
- If you have a solid fuel appliance, close down the ventilation as much as possible.
- Move furniture and rugs away from the fireplace and remove any nearby ornaments.
- Place a sparkguard in front of the fire.
- Feel the chimney breast in other rooms for signs of heat.
- If a wall is becoming hot, move furniture away.
- Ensure that access to your attic or roof space is available for the Fire Service as they will want to thoroughly check this area for signs of possible fire spread.

AFTER A CHIMNEY FIRE After the fire is out, call a chimney sweep to come and inspect the chimney. And call your insurance company too. Most home insurance policies cover chimney fire damage. To reduce your chances of having a fire in your chimney:

- Get the chimney swept if you haven't used it for a while.
- Ensure a fireguard is in front of the fire at all times.
- Use sparkguards.
- Extinguish an open fire before going to bed or leaving the house.
- Never use petrol or paraffin to light your fire.

■ POWER CUTS

The power has gone out and I can't see

FIND A LIGHT SOURCE Find a torch. If you use a candle or gas light, take it with you as you move from room to room. Make sure a candle is well seated in a candlestick or other solid holder.

TURN OFF APPLIANCES Once you have an alternate light source, turn off all non-essential appliances – TVs, computers and stereos. Leave the central heating and fridge on. Keep the fridge and freezer closed.

DETERMINE THE EXTENT OF THE POWER CUT Look across the street and next door to see whether your neighbours' homes are also dark. If the power is only off in your house, call the power supply company.

USE OF YOUR CAR If you don't have a battery-operated radio, you can get the news on the extent and expected duration of a blackout from a car radio. You can also use your car to plug in a moble phone with a dead battery. Don't overdo using the car, especially if you are low on fuel. And don't run the car in a closed garage.

BE PREPARED FOR A POWER CUT

- Fill extra space in your freezer with plastic jugs of water (leaving enough room for the ice to expand). If the power goes out, this ice will extend the life of the food in the freezer. Put one or more jugs of ice in the fridge for the same effect.

- If you have an electrically operated garage door, check the instruction book and learn how to open it manually.

- Keep a cord-connected telephone in the house, even if you store it in a drawer or cupboard. Cord-less phones and answering-machine phones won't work when the power goes out. For your mobile phone, get a car charger that you plug into the car's cigarette lighter.

- During periods when there is an increased likelihood of a power cut, always try to keep your car's fuel tank as full as possible. When power goes out, service stations can't pump fuel.

- Consider getting a generator and having a supply of fuel for it on hand. But never operate one inside your house or in a basement. The fumes can be dangerous. Put it on a porch or in a carport.

- Keep a blackout kit handy. Make sure everyone knows where it is. Include:
  - a torch with extra batteries
  - a portable radio with extra batteries
  - drinking water (at least 4 litres)
  - a small supply of food that doesn't need preparation

Pests

■ FLYING INSECTS

I can't keep flying insects out of my house

CHANGE YOUR OUTDOOR LIGHTING Even if you keep doors and windows closed most of the time, moths, mosquitoes and gnats still get in and flit around the house, especially in summer. The cause may be your outdoor lighting. Porch and door lights that are on for hours at night attract lots of insects. When you open the door, they are drawn into the house.

Here are some ways to fix this problem:

- Turn on outdoor lights only when they are needed. Even better, install motion sensors, which turn lights on automatically when needed and switch them off after a few minutes – before the bugs have had a chance to congregate. Outdoor light fixtures with built-in motion sensors are available at DIY stores and electrical supply stores.
- Use yellow bulbs, which are not as appealing to insects as white bulbs.
- Consider modifying the outdoor lighting by the doors. Replace lights above doors with floodlights a few feet away, aiming them at the places you want to illuminate, such as stairs and paths. Another benefit of more strategic lighting is that there will be fewer spiders webs, since you will attract fewer insects.

Moths have munched my sweaters

FREEZE YOUR SWEATERS Clothes moths – or more precisely, the larvae of clothes moths – eat woollen sweaters. Usually we find this out when we pull a sweater out during the first cold blast of winter. Even if no moths are too be seen, how do we know the tiny larvae are gone? Here's a clever way to kill these unseen sweater-destroyers: freeze them. If it's below freezing outside, leave your sweaters on a porch or in an unheated garage. The cold will kill the larvae. Put the sweaters in plastic bags to keep them clean.

If it's not cold enough outdoors, put the sweaters in your freezer (or your refrigerator's freezer compartment if there is room). Leave them overnight and let them thaw out well before wearing. It's also a good idea to vacuum and wipe down wardrobes and drawers to make sure you reach the stragglers.

Clothes-moth caterpillars, which chew holes in clothes, hatch from eggs laid by clothes moths. Because the larvae are fragile, they don't usually survive in clothing that is worn regularly. Instead, they prefer stored clothes. Since they also seek out stains, such as perspiration, urine, fruit juice and other foods, make sure you wash or dry-clean all your clothes before you store them.

Fruit flies are driving me mad

MAKE A FUNNEL TRAP During warm months, these harmless but annoying creatures may enter your home as invisible eggs riding piggyback on fresh fruit. Before you know it, hordes of fruit flies are taking over the fruit bowl. You can solve the problem by putting the fruit you buy in the refrigerator and keeping a lid on kitchen rubbish. But if you don't like the idea of chilling fruits that ripen better at room temperature – bananas and peaches, for instance – create a fruit-fly trap. Put some banana peel or melon rind in the

WORLD-CLASS FIX

THE INVISIBLE ITCH

The problem may start like this: an office worker starts to itch. He swats at what he thinks are tiny bugs pricking his arms and neck with bites. Soon his workmates are itching and swatting, too. The office manager may call in a pest control company. But after monitoring for insects, the exterminators report that there are none.

The real culprit is static electricity. It frequently occurs in large offices where a lot of people are working on computers, which hold a tremendous static charge. The static electricity causes a prickling sensation. And the dry winter air that produces excess static electricity also causes itching. Experts suggest misting the air in the area with plain water to solve the problem. The water raises the humidity level and reduces the static charge. But take care not to spray water directly on computers and other sensitive electronic equipment.

bottom of a litre jar. Make a paper funnel (standard photocopier paper works fine). The small opening should be 10–12mm across, and the large opening should fit snugly into the top of the jar. Insert the small end of the cone in the jar and tape the wide opening to the jar's rim. Taking the bait, fruit flies will fly into the jar and lay their eggs, but they will have trouble finding their way back out again. Every couple of days, fill the jar with hot tap water and cap it to kill the larvae and flies. Discard them and start over with fresh bait and a new paper funnel.

USE FLYCATCHER RIBBONS Adhesive flycatcher ribbons – the kind you uncurl and hang from a hook – are also effective in capturing fruit flies. You can buy them or make your own with a length of sticky tape weighted at the bottom with a coin or a binder clip.

▦ ANTS

There are ants running all over my kitchen worktops

SEAL CRACKS AND ELIMINATE THEIR FOOD To get rid of ants, you need to follow these steps:

1 Wipe up any ants you see with soapy water. This erases the odour trails they leave for other ants to follow.
2 Look for their entry point – often a crack around a window or plumbing pipe – and close it off with a suitable sealant.
3 Eliminate all food sources, including crumbs, spilled sugar and fruit juice, pet food and rubbish. Sweep and vacuum often, especially around pet dishes and under children's places at the table. Set pet dishes in slightly larger pans of water with a drop or two of washing-up liquid, to create a moat. The detergent will break the surface tension so the ants can't float across.

Ants have made their nest in my houseplants

WRAP STICKY TAPE AROUND THE PLANTER Ants like dirt. And they love the honeydew that drips from aphid-infested plants. The instant solution is to wrap two-sided tape around the plant containers. The ants won't cross the sticky barrier.

THE ANT FARM – A BILLION SELLER

Some people are desperate to get rid of ants. But others are fans who are prepared to pay to keep them as pets! In 1956 the enterprising Milton Levine created the Ant Farm, a see-through ant habitat. Since then, his company, Uncle Milton Industries, has sold more than 20 million farms and shipped *1 billion* ants in the post.

The ants – known as red harvesters – are gathered in the deserts of the western United States. The only problem with mailing live ants is the weather. 'The big culprit is the outdoor mailbox', says a company spokesman. 'We won't ship them to places like Fargo, North Dakota, in the middle of winter, or you'd end up with antsicles.'

The ants come with simple instructions, including a useful tip for transferring them from vial to farm: put the ants in the fridge first for 15 minutes. The cold makes them groggy and less likely to escape.

Early on, Levine appeared on many radio and television talk shows. Once, according to the company spokesman, he literally got ants in his pants when – on national TV – the vial he was carrying in his pocket broke and dozens of red harvesters escaped. In the hot studio lights, the ants were anything but groggy. They scurried over his legs, biting furiously, while Levine tried to maintain his composure.

SET THE PLANTER IN WATER If the planter is small enough, you can place it in a tray or plate filled with water. This will create a barrier and discourage the ants from setting up home.

■ FLEAS

I think my house is infested with fleas

TRY THE WHITE SOCK TEST If you are not sure whether your home has fleas, stroll through the rooms that you are concerned about wearing a pair of white knee socks. If you have fleas, you will notice the creatures leaping onto the socks. Or create a trap by putting a lamp with a curved neck on the floor 15cm above a shallow dish of water containing a squirt of washing-up liquid. The fleas will jump for the light and drown in the water.

VACUUM THOROUGHLY To control fleas, you have got to attack them on all fronts, say the experts. The most likely reason for the infestation is that your pet has introduced them to your home. If so, treat the pet (see 'My dog is scratching, and I'm afraid he has fleas' below). And then treat your home, since the flea spends most of its life cycle off the host pet and in carpeting or upholstery in a pre-adult stage – egg, larva or pupa. For a couple of weeks, vacuum rugs and upholstery regularly, making sure to get under furniture and beneath chair and sofa cushions. Even if the vacuum cleaner bag is not full, remove it immediately, seal it in a plastic bag, and throw it away. It may seem wasteful, but you don't want to risk fleas hatching in your vacuum and spreading. Wash any rugs and loose covers that you can. Try to find easy-to-clean sleeping quarters for your pet – a washable bed on a tiled or vinyl floor – and clean the area frequently.

My dog is scratching, and I'm afraid he has fleas

USE A FLEA-KILLING SHAMPOO To make sure that it has fleas, roll your dog over and inspect its bare stomach. Or gently blow back the fur and look at the skin. If you spot fleas, you can wash your dog in a specialist flea shampoo, which will kill adult fleas and their eggs and is not as toxic as other chemical-based shampoos. (For a cat, ask your vet for a recommendation; some insecticidal products can be highly toxic to cats – and a bath is unlikely to go down well.)

CLEAN YOUR PET'S BED Wash your pet's bedding to kill flea eggs. Do it often, until all signs of fleas are gone. To make life easier, cover your pet's bedding with a blanket so you won't have to wash the cushion every time, only the blanket. Remove the blanket carefully, lifting it by all four corners so that the flea eggs won't roll off.

APPLY A FLEA REPELLENT For a quick and easy (though relatively expensive) long-term flea deterrent, try one of the topical liquids, such as Frontline, usually available only from vets. Typically, they work this way. You squeeze a prescribed amount of the oily liquid on the animal's back (the packs are sold according to the size and weight of the animal). This guards the entire animal against fleas for a month or more. Insect-growth regulators are another long-term solution. They don't kill adult fleas, but they prevent them from reproducing. And they do not harm the pet.

■ CREEPY BUGS

We have an invasion of silverfish

MAKE A TRAP WITH A JAR Silverfish are small, scaly looking insects that love warm, moist environments – cellars, kitchens and bathrooms. Trap them by wrapping the whole exterior of a small, clean glass jar with masking tape. Set it upright in an infested area, such as in a damp corner or around bathroom and kitchen plumbing. The silverfish can climb the taped sides, but once they fall into the jar, they are unable to climb the smooth glass surface inside. Either drown the silverfish in hot water or dispose of the captured insects outside. Reset the trap.

Eek! A spider

TRAP AND RELEASE IT If you want to get rid of a spider in your house, cover it quickly with a jar and then slide a stiff piece of paper under the jar to cover the opening. Pressing the paper firmly against the opening so the spider can't escape, carry the jar outside and let the spider go. Although their webs may seem to reflect on your housekeeping, spiders are mostly beneficial, because they trap other insects, including biting ones like mosquitoes. Many spiders do have venom glands, but they rarely bite humans. Poisonous spiders are rarely found in the UK and are usually escapees from specialist collections or the occasional refugee from abroad.

▪ MICE

I have mice in my home

SEAL ENTRY POINTS AND MAKE INVITING TRAPS Act the minute you see signs of a mice infestation. A female mouse gives birth to an average of six young – and can do it every three weeks. All those babies will be ready to mate in about two months. Under ideal conditions, a single female can produce 2,500 heirs in six months. At the first sign that you have mice in the house, follow these tips for eliminating them:

- Seal cracks and crevices, stuffing them firmly with steel wool, which the mice can't chew through. Fill gaps between the outside of the house and the inside.
- Set a series of traps around the perimeter of a room. Place the trap perpendicular to the wall, with the baited side facing and touching the wall. Mice travel along walls, whiskers touching the walls, for security. If you set enough traps in the right spots, say pest controllers, you shouldn't even have to bait them.

- Wear gloves when setting traps. Otherwise, mice may smell the human scent and steer clear. Rubber gloves work well.
- Bait with peanut butter. It's fragrant and hard to snatch without triggering the trap. Smear the peanut butter on the top and bottom of the bait pedal.
- Bait with a cotton wool ball. Cotton makes a great nest liner, so this will appeal to a mouse's nesting instincts. It is also useful for long-term traps – those you might set in the garage or basement to catch new intruders – because cotton doesn't get stale and moldy.

I'm not sure if I have mice

MAKE SOME TESTS If you suspect you have mice, test for their presence before you start spreading poison and setting traps. Mice are basically shy. They prefer places, such as cellars, where humans are rarely present. They are active at night and rarely travel into the centre of rooms, sticking to the walls instead. To test for them, sprinkle some unscented talcum powder on the floor next to the walls. Check the talcum powder in a day or two for footprints. Be sure to use unscented powder because any scent could put them off. And use only a sprinkling of powder because they might avoid

SURELY **NOT?**

A HAVEN FOR SNAKES

A US pest control company were once called by a woman in Pennsylvania because she had a snake in the house. When they arrived, they learned that she had allowed snakes to live in her basement, as they were a non-poisonous species that kept the rodent population in check. But during a party one Saturday night, a snake slithered across the living room floor, frightening the guests and the woman decided she had had enough. 'It was an old house with a stone foundation', recalled Dave Fisher, one of the pest controllers. 'There were snakes in the basement. Black rat snakes'.

The company's snake expert sealed himself under the house and spread wet sacks on the ground. As the moisture-seeking serpents crawled under the sacks, he grabbed them, put them in a sack, and handed them to Fisher. He did this for 2 hours at a time on and off for three weeks. By the end they had removed 33 snakes.

'The homeowner thought she had just one or two snakes living in the basement', says Fisher. 'She wasn't very comfortable with the idea of 33 snakes down there.'

Outwitting mice

Mice can quickly catch on to your attempts to trap them.

If you use snap traps, for instance, they will become wary when they see other mice caught in them. If an adult mouse skirts a trap because it knows there's danger there, its young will follow the example and grow up wary of snap traps. You could end up with a house full of mice that avoid your traps. A more thorough approach is to use a combination of snap traps and poison bait. You will need to get rid of 100 per cent of a population so that younger, more wary generations won't establish a foothold.

a heavy layer of it. Also be on the lookout for tiny black pellets, which also indicate the presence of mice.

I can't bear the sight of a dead mouse

PUT THE TRAP IN A PAPER BAG You are not alone. Lots of people are afraid of the sight of dead rodents. To avoid the aftermath of a mouse caught in a trap, set the snap trap in an open paper bag. Once the trap is sprung, throw the bag and its contents away.

My cat's caught a rat and I'm worried that there may be more

PREVENTION IS BETTER THAN CURE Rats need to be controlled as they can transmit disease to humans including the potentially fatal Weil's disease and salmonella. In a house, they may live under floorboards, in lofts, in wall cavities and in cellars. They can also survive in gardens, living in and beneath sheds and decks and by burrowing into compost heaps.

Good housekeeping is the best way to stop rat infestation. Keep your garden well maintained with overgrown areas trimmed back to restrict potential nesting sites. If you put out food to attract birds, hedgehogs or squirrels, you're also encouraging rats and mice. So don't put out more food than they are likely to eat. Make sure that household rubbish is disposed of securely and keep an eye on holes and cracks that may provide potential entry points.

If your cat catches a number of rats, you may have a problem. Contact your local authority's environmental health department who will send out a pest control officer to check the scene and put down traps or poison as necessary.

■ LARGER INTRUDERS

A bird is flapping around inside the house

CLOSE INSIDE DOORS AND OPEN WINDOWS A bird that mistakenly gets into a house through a window, door, or chimney usually panics and can't find its way out. To help a bird along, close all interior doors into the room so the bird won't be able to escape into another part of the house. Open the windows in the room and any curtains or blinds. Turn off the inside lights and, if it is dark out, turn on a light outside (your porch light or a security light, for instance). Your winged guest should be able to see an exit more easily.

Help! A bat has flown into my living room

CLOSE INSIDE DOORS AND OPEN WINDOWS
Occasionally, a lone bat will fly into your home through an open window or door. Don't panic: bats are typically not aggressive, although they can bite if handled. Caution: never handle a bat with bare hands. If the bat is active, do just as you would for a bird: Close all interior doors into the room, so the bat cannot escape into another part of the house. Open the windows, curtains and blinds. The bat should fly out.

CAPTURE IT IN A BOX If the bat has landed or is inactive, cover it with a shoe box or some other small box. Carefully slide a piece of cardboard (at least as large as the box opening) between the box and the surface the bat is on, nudging the bat into the box. Holding the cardboard firmly against the box, carry the bat outside and release it. Remember: wear sturdy gloves when dealing with a bat.

Five knots to solve knotty problems

There are many useful ways to knot a rope, but only the most dedicated sailors – and the occasional Boy Scout – know how to tie anything other than a basic square knot. Here are five supremely useful knots. Learn them, and you will be prepared any time you need to tie-down, haul, hoist or keep your shoelaces from coming untied.

■ PILE HITCH

Gives better grip on a thin rope

Thanks to great leaps in rope-making technology, today's ropes are thinner and stronger than ever. That's good in terms of price and reduced bulk but not so good when it comes to actually handling the rope. Tugging on rope can cut you, and there's not much surface area to keep your hands from slipping. This knot, the pilingspike hitch, is especially useful when you are tugging on rope when hauling or hoisting.

To tie this knot, you'll need some sort of 'spike', such as a screwdriver, a large nail or a dowel.

1 Bend the rope over an index finger. Grasp the two parts of the rope between your thumb and middle finger of the same hand, leaving some slack in the rope. Insert the spike, its tip pointing away from you, between the rope and your index finger, above the other fingers.

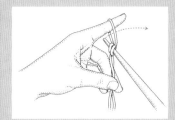

2 Rotate the tip of the spike away from you one-half turn and bring the spike tip up and through the loop that is around your index finger.

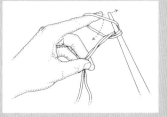

3 Push the spike up through the loop and take your index finger out to finish the knot.

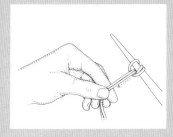

4 Pull on both ends of the rope to draw the knot tight. Now you can use the spike as a handle for pulling.

TIP If you're using slippery rope, make two turns of the spike before inserting the tip through the loop.

■ DOUBLE CONSTRICTOR

Binding knot for clamping things

Maybe a rubber hose has come loose in your car's engine or your washing machine. You need a way to secure it until you can buy a hose clamp. Here's an ingenious knot that can do the trick. It's called the double constrictor and it is a binding knot, used for clamping things. As well as clamping hoses, it will bind the ends of canvas sacks, keep ropes from unravelling, secure bundles of tubes or rods and splint a piece of cracked wood, such as a chair leg. But this knot is nearly impossible to untie. Don't use it unless you're prepared to cut the knot loose.

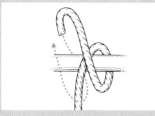

1 Lay the working end of your rope, pointing away from you, over the hose or other object to be constricted. Pass the working end around the hose and up, so that the rope crosses itself, forming an X on top of the hose.

2 Pass the rope around the hose again, forming a second X.

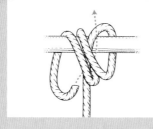

3 Pass the working end of the rope around the hose a third time, but this time bring it up on the outer side of the standing (or non-working) part of the rope. Bring the working end across the standing rope and thread it under the first two loops (between the loops and the hose). Pull the working end out between those loops and the third loop.

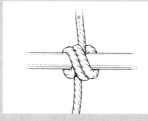

4 Pull hard on each rope end in opposite directions, drawing the knot tight.

■ BUNTLINE HITCH

Strong enough to tow a car

A strong rope will tow a car – but you need a strong knot to match. Compact, easy to tie, with a breaking strength of about 80 per cent of a rope's overall strength, the buntline hitch is one of the best when you need strength. Like all hitches, it is useful any time that you need to tie a rope end on to something else, like a climber's carabiner or the eye hook of a washing line pole. It's also good for tying down cargo.

1 Bring the working end of your rope toward you through the hitching ring. Cross the working end over the long end of the rope and then behind it.
  This will form a figure 8.

continued overleaf

continued from page 129

2 Pass the working end in front of the bottom part of the 8. This will divide the bottom part of the 8 into two sections, upper and lower. Then pass the working end behind the long part of the rope again and bring it out through the upper section of the 8's bottom part. Note that the working end comes out on top of itself.

3 Work all the slack out of the knot and push it down against its attachment point. Front and back views of the finished knot are shown here.

■ ALPINE BUTTERFLY KNOT

Versatile, stable and easy to tie

A hand winch, a block and tackle – anything with a hook on one end – can be hard to attach to a rope when you're hoisting something heavy.

The butterfly knot is the answer. While not as strong as the buntline hitch (60 per cent as opposed to 80 per cent of the rope's strength), the butterfly is more versatile, allowing you to create stable loops as small or big as you want anywhere in a length of rope, not just at the ends. It doesn't slip, is easy to tie and is handy when using extra-long rope. You can also use it for making handholds in a rope, so that several people can haul at once, and for clipping carabiners (sturdy clips used by climbers) to when climbing, hoisting gear or conducting a rescue operation.

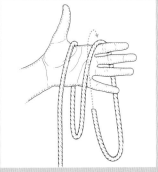

1 Make two loose turns around one hand. Start the turns on the palm side of the hand. Bring the end up to make a third turn, which should hang between the other two turns across the top of your hand.

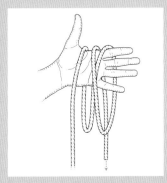

2 The three turns should now look like this.

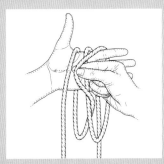

3 Pick up the turn farthest from your wrist. Pull it toward your wrist, over the other two turns.

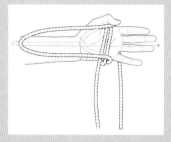

4 Pull the same turn back the way it came, but under the other two turns.

5 Draw up by pulling on all four parts that exit the knot. Pull on each, in turn, until the knot is firm.

■ SHOELACE SQUARE KNOT

A better way to keep shoes laced

The most common solution to loose laces – the double knot – is flawed. It often slips, especially with smooth-textured shoelaces. And it often jams, making it hard to untie. A better solution is a variation on the good old square knot that surgeons use for tying sutures. The next time you tie your shoes, try it.

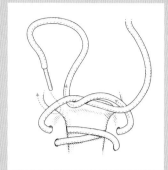

1 Begin as you always do, with an overhand knot. But before drawing it up, take one end around once more, forming a multiple overhand.

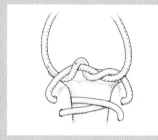

2 Now pull it tight. See how it stays put? The extra turn means more friction and more security.

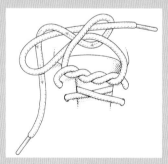

3 Now, as you always do, form a loop to make the first half of the bow. Again as usual, wrap the other end of the shoestring around the loop. However, instead of wrapping it around just once, wrap it around twice before pushing the string through the little hole to make the second half of the bow.

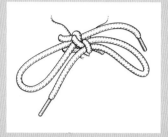

4 Pull it tight and the knot will stay put, will never jam and can be untied simply by pulling on either end. It's especially handy for runners, children – and anyone with a bad back.

PART TWO

Decorating and organising

Do you want to perk up a dreary living room? Or need some extra storage space to reduce clutter? Do you want to give a room more light? Are you fed up with people tracking mud into the house? Or want to give your house a new look in a hurry? Do you have a window blind that won't roll up? No problem – here are dozens of ingenious solutions for everyday problems all around the house.

Keeping up appearances

■ ROOM SPACE

I want to create a sense of space

USE LOTS OF SMALL MIRRORS You may know the time-honoured decorator's trick of using a huge mirror to make a room look larger. But large mirrors can be expensive. Small mirrors can create the same effect – or even a more interesting one – for pocket money. Buy several inexpensive small mirrors at car boot sales, junk shops or charity shops. Pick different shapes and sizes. If you like, spray-paint all the frames the same colour or use colours that will look good together. Decide which wall of your small room you want to mount the mirrors on and use masking tape to design a pattern for the mirrors on that wall. Mount the mirrors according to your design and then remove the masking tape.

An interesting collection of small mirrors is a quick way to open up a room.

How can I create an illusion of height?

DRAW THE EYE UPWARDS A combination of lighting, picture-placement and curtain-hanging strategies will create the illusion of height, making your room look more spacious than it is.

- Hang the pictures in your room 5 to 8cm higher than eye level to draw the eye upward.
- Use indirect lighting to illuminate the ceiling. (A light ceiling reflects light better.) Uplighters and lamps with heads that can be aimed upward will allow light to hit the ceiling and bounce off, bathing the rest of the room in soft light. This creates an illusion of height, making your room seem bigger.
- Raise the curtains. You can help to create the illusion of a higher ceiling in a small room by hanging the curtains higher. Instead of placing curtain rods at the level of the window frame, install them up against the ceiling (or at the moulding that edges the ceiling, if you have it). Then hang long curtains that reach the floor. This vertical treatment will add a sense

of height to the room. Drape the curtains to hide the wall above the window or add a stiffened fabric panel under the curtain to hide the wall.

My living room seems cramped

REDUCE CLUTTER AND USE LIGHT COLOURS You can make a small living room seem airier through a careful choice of furniture and accessories. Professional designers recommend these techniques:

- Choose just a few pieces of furniture – declutter.
- Choose light colours for the furniture and your walls and tone some of the furniture to the walls. Avoid busy prints.
- Choose low-slung, unobtrusive furniture and don't block windows or doors.
- Choose tables with glass or mirror tops.
- Choose sheer fabrics for window treatments and tablecloths.

This room feels like a corridor

USE STRIPES ACROSS THE SPACE If you have a long, narrow room, choose carpeting or rugs with stripes that run the width of the room rather than the length. This gives the illusion that the room is wider.

Dark wood panelling is making my living room seem dingy

PAINT IT WHITE OR OFF-WHITE Nothing opens up a room with dark wood panelling better than a couple of coats of satinwood white or off white paint. First, lightly sand the panelling to a smooth finish. Dab sealant on any knots in the wood and then apply a suitable paint. You may need two coats. You'll discover that the grooves between wood panels will provide a pleasing visual texture to the walls. If you have a brick fireplace, paint that too and the room will seem even cheerier and bigger. Add more colour with rugs, throws, decorative cushions, plants and vases of flowers.

A too-large sofa dominates the room

MAKE IT LESS CONSPICUOUS One way to solve the problem is to make the sofa stand out less. Place it against a wall – if possible against the

Using high ceilings to make up for limited floor space
Room is at a premium in the home of vet James Berry in Manchester. Luckily, his smallish loft apartment has 4 metre high ceilings. So instead of devoting a lot of his precious floor space to furniture, he tapped into his unused vertical space.

He painted his walls light beige to make the loft appear larger. His sleeping space is elevated, and he converted the cupboard under the stairs leading up to it into a mini-office with a desk, a computer and lots of shelves. He keeps his collection of CDs and books in tall, narrow bookcases. He also positioned his furniture to define separate kitchen, dining, and living areas. A tall cupboard against one wall holds his television and stereo. The cupboard is closed when not in use to give a clean, spacious look to his home.

Sometimes fixing a flaw in a room is not nearly as easy as drawing attention away from it. Jane Berry, a set and costume designer knows all about creating visual distractions and offers these tips.

If the structure of your room is irregular – say the room is oddly shaped or has sloping ceilings – use different shades of colour on the walls to attract attention to some areas while distracting from others. Similarly, if your room has something you don't want to be the centre of attention – an uninviting rough-textured wall, for instance – paint the wall on the opposite side of the room an interesting colour to draw eyes to it. Or cover ugly walls with fabric. Buy some inexpensive curtains and hang them on a problem wall to camouflage it. Or cover peeling plaster with a display of pictures, strategically placed.

wall with the main entry door for the room. If you do this, the sofa will not be the first thing that strikes you when you come in. Consider getting it a new slipcover that makes it less noticeable, preferably a light-toned solid colour that blends with the wall. Then keep other furnishings in the room to a minimum. In particular, avoid large upholstered chairs or recliners.

BUY A SMALLER SOFA In small rooms where you want to keep a cosy feeling but still have space to move around, you may want to consider using two comfortable upholstered chairs instead of a large sofa. Or consider a two-seater sofa, a love seat or a chaise longue as a quirky alternative.

Our expensive oriental rug looks overpowering in the living room

ADD MORE COLOUR You may have been proud – and a little nervous – when you spent a lot of money on a beautiful oriental rug for your living room. But you now realise that its bright colours and complex pattern totally dominate the room. Fight back with colour: add some multicoloured cushions and bright artwork to the room. Cover a chair in another vivid pattern. These strong new elements will force the rug to settle into the overall scheme of the room.

■ WARMTH AND COLOUR

I always have trouble choosing colours for my walls

PICK FROM YOUR FAVOURITE THINGS Look for inspiration in your favourite furniture, fabrics or china patterns. If your favourite living room furnishing is a chair upholstered in a multicoloured fabric that features sage green as a major part of the pattern, paint the walls to match this green. Use other colours in the upholstery fabric to help you to pick accessories for the room.

The colour I've chosen is much too dark

TEMPER DARK COLOURS WITH LIGHT COUNTERPOINTS Navy blue, bottle green and chocolate brown walls can make a dramatic statement in a room. But they need tempering with light-coloured, or even white, paintwork and upholstery fabrics, as well as window treatments. For example, a light-coloured painting or tapestry against a dark wall can create a beautiful focal point in a room. Make sure a room with dark walls also has plenty of light fixtures and lamps.

I want to reflect the changing seasons in my house

USE COLOUR ACCENT PIECES Without completely redecorating each season, a few well-placed cushions and throws can help to give a seasonal touch to your decor. In winter, place some red and green accents around. During spring and summer, use blues and yellows instead. When autumn rolls around, mix reds and yellows in with a little brown. When you find seasonal accents on sale, buy the ones you like. At the start of the appropriate season, place a few of these accents around the house. Out of season, store them on a shelf in the guest room or attic.

I want to give my house a new look in a hurry

CONCENTRATE ON THE WOODWORK If your walls are white, for example, paint the woodwork a contrasting colour, such as a grey-blue or misty green that picks up a colour in your curtains or upholstery. Or, if your walls are coloured, paint the woodwork white. The freshly painted woodwork will give the room renewed energy.

Redecorating is so expensive that I worry about making a mistake

BE CONSERVATIVE WITH LARGER ITEMS Interior designers suggest that you stick with neutral colours, patterns and styles for large, expensive items, such as sofas, dressers, carpeting or rugs, and specially made curtains. Express yourself with accessories, such as lamps, side tables and artwork. Smaller items are easy to move and the cost of your mistakes won't leave you with lasting regret.

I want to add sparkle to my rooms, but my budget is limited

TRY JUNK SHOPS AND CHARITY SHOPS You probably already know about the local charity shops, such as larger Oxfams and the Bethany shops in Scotland. You can often buy excellent secondhand goods at

PROBLEM STOPPER

How to make painting walls easier

• Wear clothes that you expect to get splashed with paint.

• Remove all doorknobs and other hardware and place each in a plastic bag with its screws.

• Cover or remove all furniture, rugs, and light fixtures. Cover the floor with dust sheets.

• Prepare a 'paint station' where you keep a paint tray, masking tape, brushes, rollers, sticks for stirring paint, can opener, cleaning rags, screwdriver, hammer, ladder and, if necessary, paint thinner or turpentine.

• Paint in this order: ceiling, walls, doors and woodwork.

• Don't rush. Give yourself plenty of time.

• When you've finished, keep a supply of paint for touch-ups in small plastic containers or glass jars with airtight lids. Label each with the colour and brand name of the paint.

A doctor who has braved 30 years of Scottish winters shares her top three tips for warming up a room:

1 Rearrange furniture away from cold windows and drafty areas. Move the main seating group close to a fireplace or woodstove.

2 Place a side table near your favourite easy chair and put a chess set or jigsaw on it, with the pieces arranged for action.

3 Give tabletops an inviting look by placing decorative runners across them and adding candles.

a fraction of the retail price at such places. For the best bargains, make sure you visit a secondhand shop in a more affluent area, where you're likely to find items donated by people who can afford to give away good-quality furnishings when they decorate. Find out the days when the shops tend to get new deliveries in and do your shopping then. That's when you are most likely to find treasures before anyone else sees them.

I don't know how to put together different types of wooden furniture

USE WOODS OF THE SAME HUE If you inherit furniture from relatives or buy bargain furniture at car-boot sales or junk shops, you may end up with pieces made from a variety of woods. Which ones will go together and which clash? The answer is simple: when decorating a room, stick with woods of the same hue to avoid a look of confusion. Don't mix a hard, dark wood such as cherry with a soft, light wood such as pine. But you can mix furniture made of cherry and maple quite effectively. And pine paired with walnut works well.

My bedroom needs a boost

USE A DECORATIVE FABRIC AS A WALLCOVERING Choose a fabric (it could be a bed sheet) with a pattern you like. Soak the sheet in full-strength liquid starch. The starch will act as a natural adhesive. Smooth the sheet over the wall behind the bed, starting at the ceiling line and working down. Use a squeegee to smooth out wrinkles. When you want to redecorate, you can easily pull down the sheet; the original wall finish will only need wiping down to be restored.

FIVE MINUTE DECORATING IDEAS USING A SHEET

A sheet is more than just a mattress covering. It can perk up a room for very little money, as in the following ideas:
- a tablecloth over a real or improvised dining room table
- a curtain, by threading a curtain rod through the broad hem across the top of a flat sheet and mounting it over a window, an open doorway, or an exposed cupboard on a tension rod
- a canopy to hang over a four-poster bed, with ribbons added to tie the ends to the four posts
- a cushion appliqué, by cutting out a pretty design from the sheet and stitching it onto a cushion
- seat cushion covers, by cutting decorative sheets to fit over padded seat cushions that have become faded or worn

■ ROOM LIGHTING

I can't get the lighting at the right level in the living room

INSTALL DIMMER SWITCHES You will have many more options for good lighting if you install dimmer switches on overhead lights and floor lamps. Dimmer switches allow you to control the intensity of light from each fixture. With a series of dimmer switches, you can regulate the light in each part of the room. (Dimmers come with instructions for installing them; it is not very different from installing an ordinary light switch.) To light a room properly, the first goal is to provide a uniform lighting that lets the eye scan from one end of the room to the other without interruption. Then you can concentrate on highlighting pieces of art or plant arrangements.

The lights in my living room seem to be getting dimmer

CLEAN YOUR LAMPSHADES Take a close look at your lampshades. Dust and household dirt can collect on them, cutting down on the lamp's illumination. You can remove the dust with a stiff paintbrush (keep it for lampshade cleaning duties only). Remove the lampshade from the lamp and go outside. Holding the lampshade steady in one hand, use the other hand to briskly brush the dust away. Start at the top and work down, slowly turning the shade as you go. Back inside, wipe off the lightbulb with a dry cloth before putting the shade back on the lamp.

No one ever uses the chair in the corner

ADD A NEARBY LAMP Maybe the problem isn't the chair, but the lack of light around it. A standard lamp can open up under-used corners of a room for reading, and adding a small table would give you a place to put a book or a cup of tea.

The chandelier looks lopsided

ADD WEIGHT TO ONE SIDE If a chandelier has arms that support several glass light globes, you may be able to rebalance the fixture yourself. Identify which light globe is higher than the others. Lift the globe off its holder. (You may have to remove the lightbulb first.)

Take some self-adhesive lead tape and wind it around the bottom of the holder to add a little weight. Make sure the tape is not on the lip that holds the globe so that it doesn't interfere with the way that the globe sits in the holder. Then put the globe back into place and check the balance of the chandelier. Add or remove tape as needed. You may have to put some lead tape in more than one holder to get the right balance.

■ ARTWORK AND FOUND ART

I don't have wall space for all the pictures I want to hang

ROTATE YOUR DISPLAY Install two or three long, narrow display shelves on a wall where you hang pictures. Arrange some of your favourites, putting several frames on each shelf and leaning them against the wall. After a few months, take these pictures down and put up some of the others. Store the pictures not on display in document boxes, where they will be protected from light and dust. You will catch your family's and friends' attention when you regularly change your gallery.

There is a lot of bare wall above my bedroom window

HANG A HAT If your bedroom has a low window or a high ceiling, you may wonder how to decorate the unexpected space above the window. An object such as a trimmed straw hat, a large, colourful plate or a fan will fill the space, hung on a hook centred directly over the top of the window.

A display shelf is the easy way to rotate your picture collection.

How should I light pictures on a wall?

BE WARY OF THE LIGHT FROM LAMPS If you want to bring out the best in your photos or mounted artwork, do not place them near a lamp with a shade. The shade tends to give the lightbulb a soft, yellow glow rather than the ample light you need to showcase your artwork. Instead use a white or clear glass lightbulb, which will attractively illuminate your prized piece of art. You can get small lights that attach to the top of the frame and shine on the artwork – but this can be distracting – or you can direct light at the piece from a track light.

I can't get my pictures to hang straight

TRY A LASER If you have trouble getting pictures lined up and level, consider getting a laser-powered level. This tool does the work of a spirit level and much more. It emits a level laser line in four directions, which makes hanging pictures (and installing bookshelves) easy. You can get simple ones for around £35.

I don't want to throw away this beautiful calendar

FRAME THE PICTURES Appoint yourself curator of your own art collection. Perhaps you have a calendar of paintings by Vermeer. Or you have brought back a calendar from China with exquisite silk-screen prints of birds, flowers and mountain scenes. Cut out or detach your favourite pictures from the calendar, place them in inexpensive frames and group them on a wall.

I need some new ideas for decorating

FEATURE NATURAL DECORATIONS Bring a little bit of the outdoors inside. There are lots of beautiful and entirely free items to be found in nature that will give your rooms a creative and distinctive look. Instead of hanging a landscape portrait behind your sofa, for instance, you could try placing an interesting branch or a piece of driftwood from your favourite beach. Arrange seashells as sculpture or pile pinecones in a basket or coloured pebbles in a fireplace.

Getting your house in order

■ ENTRANCE HALLS

My front hall is claustrophobic

HANG A MIRROR You may not be able to do anything to enlarge the space, but hanging a mirror in the hallway will make it seem bigger and brighter. A hall mirror is also great for last-minute checks on how you look before you head out the door.

I want my front hall to be welcoming

ADD LIGHT COLOURS AND FRESH FLOWERS For an inviting look in a hallway, choose light colours for paint and subtle patterns for wallpaper instead of dark colours or busy patterns. Install an attractive light fixture with a dimmer to control the light. Hang a small gallery of pictures or put a piece of treasured pottery on a table. And finally, nothing welcomes guests at the front entrance better than a vase of fresh flowers.

Vanquish the mess of muddy footware in your entrance hall with a cabinet.

On rainy days, muddy shoes pile up in the hall

BUY A CABINET FOR WET SHOES Look for a knee-high cabinet with a row of cubbyholes for shoes and boots. (Many home furnishings stores sell just such cabinets.) Each family member gets his or her own cubbyhole for wet shoes and boots, and the top of the cabinet makes a place to sit while taking them off.

People track a lot of mud into the house

USE MATS If you protect your doorways inside and out with large mats, you will cut down on all the things that shoes can track into a house. A rough waterproof mat outside allows family and guests to scrape their feet before coming in. Indoor mats long enough for several steps protect rugs and floors from wetness and debris.

I have new carpets and want my guests to remove their shoes at the front door

PROVIDE SLIPPERS A no-shoes-indoors rule is a good way to keep the house clean, but some visitors just aren't used to this custom. Adopt a Japanese practice and place 'guest slippers' in several sizes by the front door. This will give guests a hint of your wishes and make it easy for them to remove their shoes. Provide a chair or bench where guests can sit to take off and replace their shoes.

My front hall is always a mess

ASSIGN FAMILY BINS To straighten out your hall, assign everyone in the family his or her own in and out 'basket'. This could be a bin in a set of stacking bins, a drawer in a dresser or one shelf in a cupboard. People coming in can dump their school supplies, hats, briefcases and other such items in their own bins. And everyone can use the bins as a staging area for the next morning's departure. One specialist organiser calls this area the 'launching pad' for the house. Every few days, each person must be responsible for completely emptying his or her bin.

I am always losing my keys

DESIGNATE A BOWL OR BASKET It would be nice to think that everyone would carefully hang keys on a hook where they'd be easy to find when needed again. But the reality is that most people throw their keys on the first available table when they come in the door. Don't fight it: put a sturdy but attractive bowl or basket on the table by your front door and designate it for car keys, sunglasses, mobile phones and the other portable necessities of modern life.

■ LIVING ROOMS

Cushions won't stay on my wooden chairs

USE HIGH-FRICTION DRAWER LINER Cut a piece of high-friction drawer liner (designed to keep utensils or tools from sliding around) to fit

How to jazz up a room
Here are four easy ways to revive a faded room without opening a single can of paint:

• **Switch it around.** Rotate accessories from other rooms to create a new look. For example, move a vase of flowers from the bay window of your kitchen to the mantelpiece in the living room.

• **Rug trick.** Spice up a beige carpet with a bright-coloured rug centred on the living-room floor.

• **Focus on windows.** Maximise natural sunlight by opening blinds and shutters during the day. Accent window coverings with cheerful trimmings.

• **Personalise the decor.** Bring together items with common themes in one location in your family room. If you love golf, for example, dedicate an area of your room to a display of prized golf balls, tees and a framed photo of your favourite course.

the chair seat. Place it on the seat frame directly under the seat cushion. The liner, which comes in many colours, will grab the seat cushion and keep it in place.

My living room has turned into toy land

GET A TOY CHEST Buy a decorative toy chest with a lid in a colour that looks good with your living room furniture. Each day, allow your children to pick three or four toys or games to play with in the family room. Just before dinner, ring a bell to signal that it is time to pick up the toys and put them in the toy chest.

I need a way to showcase my fireplace

PAINT THE FIREPLACE WALL A DIFFERENT COLOUR When your guests walk into your living room, you want them to admire the splendid fireplace that should be the focus of the room. Paint the wall that includes the fireplace a different colour from that of the rest of the room. This will help to focus all eyes on the fireplace.

My fireplace is no longer safe to use

MAKE IT A DECORATIVE CENTREPIECE Even if the log-burning days of your fireplace are over, you can still use it as the focal point of your room. Buy a decorative fireplace screen and place candles in front of it. Or clean out the old burned logs and ashes, vacuum the area and place decorative candles of various sizes and colours on a low plant stand inside the fireplace.

■ WINDOWS

My window frames are not very attractive

HIDE IT WITH CURTAINS If you don't like the frames around your windows, the easy solution is to hang attractive curtains so that they cover the frames completely. Mount a curtain rod 5 to 8cm above the window opening and extend it at least 7cm to either side. On the other hand, if you have attractive window frames or woodwork, showcase these features by using blinds that fit only the interior of the window.

The pleats in my blinds are beginning to sag

USE THE BLINDS REGULARLY Over time, the pleats in fabric window coverings such as roman blinds tend to settle a bit, leaving billowy pleats at the bottom of the window and fresh-creased pleats at the top. The solution is to regularly open and close the blinds to help to keep all the pleats crisp and new looking.

I worry about washing sheer curtains

USE THE GENTLE CYCLE Most sheer curtains are made of synthetic fabrics that are machine washable in warm, not hot, water on the gentle cycle. Rinse with cold water and diluted fabric softener. Place the curtains in the drier with several hand towels and dry on the cool or permanent press setting for 2 or 3 minutes. Hang them back up so that they can shake out any further creases.

I'm always snagging sheer curtains when I hang them

COVER THE ROUGH EDGES To prevent snags, cover the end of the curtain rod with clear sticky tape or gaffer tape before pushing it through the pocket.

My curtain cords tangle easily

ADD A SMALL WEIGHT Keep cords straight by tying a small weight (such as a lead fishing weight) to each cord. Position the weight on the cord so that it hangs above the floor whether the curtains are fully opened or closed.

My curtains don't hang evenly

ADD WEIGHTS TO THE HEM Unruly curtains can be brought into line by adding weights to the bottom hem. You can buy weighted beads that can be threaded through the hem of sheer curtains to keep them from billowing in the breeze. To keep heavier curtains straight, sew small lead weights with two holes in them, like buttons, to the hem. The neatest way to do this is to sew the weights inside a tiny cushion of matching fabric to hide them and stop the metal from discolouring the curtain fabric. Many such weights now come already covered.

The easy way to keep curtain cords from tangling is to add a lead fishing weight.

I want an original look for some of the single windows in my house

USE NYLON CORD Hang 'found objects' in the window instead of a blind or curtains. Thread nearly invisible monofilament fishing line through beads, crystals, Christmas ornaments, children's toys or small pieces of driftwood and attach the lines at the top and bottom of the window frame with drawing pins. (You may want to hide the pins by touching them up with the same paint as is used on the windows.) Or use fishing line to tie together a latticework of beautiful dried branches from a small tree or shrub, with autumn berries or dried flowers attached.

■ FURNITURE

I want my wooden furniture to look new again

USE NEW KNOBS The easiest way to enliven chests, desks and dressers without the hassle or expense of re-painting or varnishing is to change the knobs or handles. A bright new set of knobs or replacing one style of pull with another can transform a piece of furniture.

My sofa feels much too soft

ADD A STIFF BOARD You can firm up a sagging sofa by placing a stiff insert of plywood covered with fabric under the cushions. Ask a timber merchant or DIY store to cut a piece of plywood of a size to fit under the seat cushions. Cover the plywood with a matching fabric if you're worried that the board might show.

My sofa is sagging

REATTACH THE SPRINGS A sagging couch may be easy to fix. First, turn it over. If the bottom is covered with plastic, fabric or gauze, peel back the covering to expose the springs. The springs are often attached to a bracket at either end with a simple hook and sometimes one or more springs can come unhooked if the sofa is subject to heavy use or someone sits down very suddenly and heavily. Simply reattaching the springs can be enough to fix the problem. But if the springs or pieces of the wooden frame are actually broken, that's a job for a professional repair person.

I have a living room cabinet with doors that won't open

RAISE THE CORNER Try lifting each corner of the cabinet 1.25cm and then testing the door. If a boost to one corner frees up the door, put a sliver of wood under that leg to push it up. Sometimes a cabinet warps slightly and a little lift is all it needs to regain its equilibrium.

My furniture doesn't match

USE ACCESSORIES TO CREATE CONTINUITY An eclectic look can be interesting and even very stylish. Instead of worrying about your furniture not matching, concentrate on using accessories to tie the room together. Choose cushions, planters, rugs and pictures that incorporate the same dominant colour. Coordinate fabrics for upholstery and curtains. The eye will be drawn to these elements and not to the mismatched furniture.

Where do you start when arranging living room furniture?

START WITH A CONVERSATION CIRCLE Designers say that the key to successfully arranging a living room is to first place the sofas and chairs in a rough circle suitable for encouraging conversation. None of these pieces should be more than 3 metres away from one another. After this arrangement is set, you can use other parts of the room for other purposes. You might want a listening area around the stereo system and you could also create a quiet space for reading.

SURELY **NOT**

I THINK I'LL JUST SIT RIGHT HERE

A tired visitor to a museum, in trying to take a load of his feet, suffered acute embarrassment when he sat in a chair in one of the exhibition halls and broke it into three pieces, sending him crashing to the floor. Unfortunately, the chair was part of the museum's collection. It was a 16th-century Ming dynasty piece from China, valued at around £230,000. The man apparently missed or ignored the 'Do Not Touch' sign posted beside the chair. Fortunately, the chair was insured and was fully restored.

PROBLEM STOPPER

Are your bookshelves taking a bow?
If your bookshelves are sagging under the weight of your books, try this trick.
To reinforce each shelf, screw a strip of wood along the front edge. Then, for additional support, screw an L- shaped bracket into the wall under the most heavily sagging section. In no time, your shelves should be shipshape.

How can I antique new brass hinges to use on an old cabinet?

AGE THE BRASS WITH SALT AND VINEGAR Use a small paintbrush to brush vinegar over the entire surface of the item. This oxidises the brass, which is actually what happens to the metal naturally over time. Painting on salty water will have the same effect, only it will take a bit more time and patience on your part.

BRASS CAN ALSO BE OXIDISED USING HEAT OR FLAME If you have ever heated up a needle to sterilise it, you will have noticed that the metal gets a rainbow effect that doesn't wash off. Brass will not develop rainbow colours, but the old and mellow look can be achieved by holding a flame close to the new brass. Caution: make sure the brass is not lacquered. The lacquer is flammable.

■ BEDROOMS

I am forever knocking things off my crowded bedside table

MOUNT A WALL LAMP To free up space on your bedside table, remove the lamp. Use a swing-arm floor lamp instead, or mount a swing-arm wall lamp above the headboard. Such fixtures allow you to adjust the lamp exactly the way you want it for reading. Install the lamp about 45 to 50cm from the top of the headboard for best results. If you don't have a headboard, position the lamp a metre or more above the mattress, so that it will be within easy reach but won't hit your head when you sit up in bed. With the lamp out of the way, you should have ample room on your night table for other bedtime essentials like your alarm clock, books and telephone.

My bedroom doubles as my home office

USE A DECORATIVE SCREEN You need to separate the two areas so that work worries don't keep you awake. Find a folding decorative screen to define the two spaces and block your view of your files while you are in bed. A screen, which you can find at DIY stores – and sometimes in junk shops, may not be cheap but it is infinitely flexible. Some screens have fabric panels that can be custom-made to match your curtains or bedspread.

I can't part with my souvenir T-shirts

MAKE A MEMORY QUILT For some people, a holiday or taking part in an athletics event is not complete without a souvenir T-shirt. But they can quickly fill up your dresser drawers. Still, how can you part with a T-shirt that proclaims that you survived a scary ride at an amusement park, visited a Hollywood movie set or ran a marathon? One solution is to save the memory and make rags out of the rest of the shirt. Cut out the logos from these cherished T-shirts and make them into squares. Then combine them to make a memory quilt that you can mount on the wall.

Small items in my drawers get jumbled

ADD DRAWER DIVIDERS If sports socks, casual socks and smart socks get all bundled together, you can solve the problem with a couple of drawer dividers. Buy them from specialised storage suppliers or make your own by cutting flat, narrow strips of wood so that the ends fit snugly at the front and back of the drawer.

To get rid of a drawerful of beloved T-shirts, cut out the logos and turn them into a quilt.

■ CHILDREN'S BEDROOMS

My children need more storage space

INSTALL SCHOOL LOCKERS The kind of lockers used in schools, gyms and sports centres provide excellent storage in children's rooms. You may be able to buy old lockers which can be painted in bright colours to match your child's room. Alternatively, they can be purchased new from specialist suppliers and you can put together the most useful combination for your needs.

My child throws everything on the floor

INSTALL A ROW OF HOOKS OR PEGS If you line a bedroom wall with a row of pegs or hooks, your child will have a place to hang up jackets and coats as well as small bags filled with such treasures as Lego, dolls and their clothes, and plastic models. Sacks often work better than a toy chest because they free up floor space and keep toys divided, so there is less chance of losing pieces.

I want to redecorate my child's room to celebrate a move from cot to bed

PICK TODDLER-FRIENDLY COLOURS AND TEXTURES Pick bold colours for walls and furniture; pastels can seem too tame to toddlers. Select objects in the room with tactile appeal, because young children love to touch different textures. Choose a faux fur bedspread or throw, for example, that your child can snuggle into. Or pick a rug with another kind of snuggly feel. Create an environment that will make your child feel secure and sheltered. Provide plenty of storage.

I don't want to be too strict, but my child's room looks like a rubbish tip

PUT UP A TENT Let your child exercise some creativity in his or her special personal space. If the room is large enough, put up a colourful small tent or build a little castle of cardboard and fabric in the room. Inside the tent or castle, your child can play with favourite toys, which will now be out of sight. The result will be a room that both you and your child will like and that will give the child some privacy.

■ BATHROOMS

I need to make my bathroom look bigger

USE A LIGHT COLOUR SCHEME As with any small room in your home, you can create the illusion of more space with a paler colour scheme. Use neutral or light colours for your walls, worktops and sink. Pick a clear or light-coloured shower curtain and accessorise with light-coloured towels to match.

The cabinets in the bathroom are a jumble of tubes and bottles

THROW OUT THE OLD AND ORGANISE THE REST Bathroom cabinets and shelves are one of the final frontiers of household organising. Attack each cabinet with a grocery bag in hand for disposing of unwanted items. Throw out anything that's more than two years old, that's past its expiry date, or that you don't think you'll use again. If there are items that don't belong in the bathroom, put them in the hall and put them in their proper places when you're finished with the bathroom cabinets. Organise the remaining things into groups of like items and cluster them together in zip-sealed bags, small boxes or plastic bins. If you use clear ones you'll be able to see what's there at a glance.

Bottles keep tumbling into the bath

PUT THEM IN A RACK There are only so many corners where you can store bubble bath, shower gels, shampoo and conditioner bottles around a bath before you start an avalanche. A simple solution is to move all the bottles to a waterproof rack that is mounted on the wall. These racks can be screwed to the wall or are available with suction pads so they can be easily removed and are available at bath and DIY stores.

My spouse and I fight over cabinet space

PUT SHELVES OVER THE TOILET If you don't have enough counter or cabinet space in your bathroom, consider a installing a cabinet above the toilet. You can buy units with several shelves, with and without doors, to store soaps and shampoos, extra toilet paper, tissue boxes and extra hand towels. Look in bathroom showrooms and DIY stores.

Cascading shampoo bottles? The simple solution is a wire or plastic rack.

I don't have enough towel rack space

USE A COAT RACK You may be able to maximise the space in a small bathroom by standing a coat rack in the corner. A coat rack is perfect for hanging towels and bathrobes. These items dry quickly without taking up much horizontal space.

Someone else is using my towel

COLOUR-CODE TOWELS Sharing a bathroom is difficult enough, but everybody in the family should at least have his or her own towel and facecloth. Try instituting a colour-coding system. Designate one colour for each person – say, blue for your spouse, red for you, green for your son and yellow for your daughter. Then make sure each person has at least two towels and facecloths, one to use now and one in the wash, in his or her colour. This system won't work if you want a coordinated look but is fun in an all-white scheme.

A bag for dirty clothes
Give an old sheet a new lease of life by converting it into a laundry bag. Hung from a hook on the back of the bathroom door, a laundry bag takes up less space than a laundry basket.

1 Use a double or king-size flat sheet.

2 Buy about 2m of sturdy nylon cord.

3 Make a 2.5cm hem in each short end of the sheet, keeping the ends open so that the cord can be threaded through. Then fold the sheet in half widthways and sew the two sides together.

4 Thread the cord through the hem. Tie the two ends of the cord together to form a drawstring.

5 Pull the cord to close the top and hang up your homemade laundry bag.

I have a burgeoning collection of hotel shampoos and conditioners

MAKE A GUEST BASKET There may be something in human nature that makes the complimentary shampoos, conditioners, hand lotions, shower caps and sewing kits provided in hotels completely irresistible. To make use of your collection, stock a small wicker basket with two hotel-size shampoos, two conditioners, two hand lotions and a shower cap. Put the basket in the guest bedroom whenever you have people to stay. The others can be kept to hand for short trips and weekend breaks. But don't collect any more until you have used up the ones you already have.

I need better light over the bathroom mirror

CHANGE THE LIGHTBULBS The harsh lightbulbs often used in bathrooms tend to throw shadows and make jobs such as applying make up and tweezing eyebrows, difficult. As the choices in lightbulb shapes and colours are almost limitless it's worth replacing exposed lightbulbs with incandescent globes that cast a softer light.

My bath towels never seem to dry completely

INSTALL A VENTILATING FAN You don't have to resign yourself to dank, damp towels. Instead, fold your towels just once and place them on towel racks. An immediate solution is to position a small oscillating fan on a bathroom shelf that is directed towards the towels and should help them to dry more quickly. When you have more time, consider installing an extractor fan in the bathroom.

■ LAUNDRY ROOM

I keep missing stains in my wash

INSTALL A BETTER LIGHT Maybe you don't see stains because it's too dark in your laundry room or near the washing machine. Try installing a wall-mounted spotlight by the washing machine. Look over each item of clothing under the bright light and you'll catch more stains for treatment before they go through the wash.

I have no place to hang wet clothes

BUY A RETRACTABLE WASHING LINE If your laundry area is too small for a drying rack, install a retractable washing line across a shower cubicle or in the hall. These devices can accommodate a lot of clothes – especially if you use hangers. Put a towel under the clothes to protect the floor if necessary. Or install an extra shower curtain rod above the middle of the bath which will give you a perfect place to hang and dry clothes.

I need somewhere to keep lost buttons

PUT UP A BULLETIN BOARD A laundry bulletin board goes a long way toward keeping the laundry organised. Tack up small, zip-sealed plastic bags to hold pins, threaded needles, spare buttons and other items for quick repairs. The bulletin board is also a good place to hang specific washing and drying instructions for favourite clothes that need special handling.

I struggle to lift large detergent boxes

USE A SHELF OVER THE MACHINE Buying laundry detergent in bulk saves money, but it can be too heavy to manage. To save heavy lifting, repackage the powder or liquid into smaller containers. An alternative, if you have room for a shelf above the washing machine, is to put liquid detergent into a large plastic container with a tap and dispense it as needed into a measuring cup.

TRICKS OF THE TRADE

To speed up bathroom cleaning Install a paper towel holder in the bathroom. When you need to clean the sink and the toilet lids, just reach for the spray cleaner and a paper towel. Then throw the used towel in the bin. Paper towels eliminate the need to keep a sponge under the bathroom sink, where its dampness can create mildew.

WORLD-CLASS FIX

LOW-GRAVITY LAUNDRY

Although there's never been a washing machine or tumble drier aboard a US space shuttle, astronauts have managed to change their underwear and even do laundry. John Grunsfeld, a veteran of four shuttle missions, recalls that he and his colleagues washed their dirty clothes by hand inside a plastic bag and then towel-dried them. With zero gravity, there was no need to use a washing line. Instead, the astronauts used 'towel grommets' – rubber discs, about 5cm in diameter, with an X cut into the centre – attached to the shuttle walls to hang their damp laundry. The astronauts would stuff a corner of a wet towel or T-shirt into the X and the item then floated in midair. 'The humidity is low on the shuttle', explained Grunsfeld, so the towels dried fast.

I need cupboards for laundry but don't want to spend too much money

USE OLD KITCHEN CABINETS If you have space for a laundry room, even if it is in a lobby or hallway, it's worth putting in some cupboards to hold the things you need. But you may not want to spend the money on new cabinets. At any given moment, somebody in your neighbourhood is probably installing a new kitchen. If you are lucky, you might see a set of discarded cabinets ready to be discarded that you can pick up at no cost. Secondhand furniture shops may also sometimes have kitchen or bathroom cabinets that are being sold off. Let them sit on the floor or put them up on the walls. Ask a carpenter to put them up if you are not very handy. Paint them to match the room.

I have nowhere to put my ironing board

BUY A WALL-MOUNTED IRONING BOARD You can install an ironing board on a door or on the wall of your laundry room or kitchen. These fold-down ironing boards are not only easier to set up than the freestanding models, but they are also sturdier. When you're not ironing, they simply disappear.

My children won't help with the laundry

USE PERSONAL BASKETS Designate and label a laundry basket for each family member. When you sort the clean laundry, put each person's clothing in his or her basket. Make each person responsible for folding his or her own items and returning them to the proper wardrobe, cupboard or dresser.

I spend forever folding laundry

MAKE FEWER FOLDS Reorganise your wardrobes, cupboards and drawers to accommodate clothes and linens with fewer folds. Fold a towel in half instead of thirds, for example. It may not sound like much, but an extra fold or two in each shirt, towel, sheet and pair of jeans adds up to many hours over hundreds of loads.

Coping with clutter

■ ORGANISING AND STORING

I want to store my magazines where I can find them

USE RACKS OR HOLDERS Space-saving magazine racks are available at DIY stores. You might attach a six-tiered magazine rack to the back of a door with wood screws, for example. Or keep magazines in upright magazine holders (available in office supply shops) on a bookshelf so they will be within easy reach but out of the way. After you have collected two year's worth of magazines in the holders, it's your signal to start discarding the older issues.

My house is inundated with catalogues

USE A LARGE FILE FOLDER Keeping catalogues 'just in case' can take up a lot of space and create clutter. Buy an accordion-style file folder to hold catalogues you are not ready to throw out. Give each catalogue a two-month life span. After that, throw them out. (You will undoubtedly get a replacement soon after.) You can also save space by jotting down the websites of each company and going online the next time you want to place an order.

The coffee table is littered with magazines

USE A BASKET OR BOX Keep the current issues of your favourite magazines within easy reach by placing them in deep wicker baskets or other decorative boxes. You could roll them up and place them in a bucket. Or designate a low shelf in the living room especially for magazines. Keep them organised in date order and you should easily be able to lay your hands on the issue you want.

Our CD collection needs storage space

USE SQUARE WICKER BASKETS You can organise your CD collection with wicker baskets. Pick square or rectangular baskets in colours and designs that match the living room or family room where you keep your collection. You could designate different colours for different types of music. Line up the CDs in the baskets so that you can read the titles. Baskets are often prettier and handier than specially designed CD holders and racks.

I can never find the CD I want

USE SIMPLE CATEGORIES You don't have to arrange all your CDs alphabetically by artist to keep track of them. An easier system is based on types of music – classical, big band, jazz and rock, for example. Designate separate sections – possibly colour-coded – in the CD holder for these categories. It will be easy to find what you want and even easier to put your CDs away later.

I need more storage space

USE CHESTS AND OLD SUITCASES All sorts of items can be adapted to act as storage systems. Ottomans and chests can act both as seating and as places to keep items out of sight including extra cushions, throws as well as CDs and DVDs. Or if you have some old-fashioned suitcases that you no longer use, these can make attractive feature storage in a hall, living room or bedroom. Pile two or three of a similar design on top of one another.

You'll be able to find your coat in seconds – if you keep only coats and jackets in the hall cupboard.

■ HALL CUPBOARDS

My hall cupboard is so packed that it is hard to find my coat

TRANSFER ITEMS TO OTHER STORAGE SPACE To reduce the clutter in a hall cupboard, don't use it for anything except coats, hats, gloves and scarves. Vacuum cleaners, kitchen supplies, spare lightbulbs and other kitchen or cleaning items should go somewhere else. Periodically check on old, unused or outgrown coats and donate them to a local charity. If the cupboard is still overcrowded, move out-of-season coats and boots to the attic or to a less heavily used wardrobe in another part of the house. This way, everyone in the family will be able to find what they need quickly and make swift exits for school and work. You will also have room for guests' coats.

I'm embarrassed to let guests open my hall cupboard

DECORATE THE INTERIOR 'Why not decorate your hall cupboard?' said one interior designer we consulted. The first step to an attractive entrance hall cupboard is to remove the extraneous junk. (See previous item.) But after that, why not decorate the inside with wallpaper, a coat of bright paint, an unusual light or an intriguing piece of artwork on the inside of the hall cupboard door?

I don't have a hall cupboard

BUY A COAT RACK Many flats and small homes don't have coat cupboards near the front door. Depending on your space, you should be able to improvise a satisfactory way to handle coats, gloves, scarves and hats. Buy a sturdy coat stand to keep by the front door, or install a row of hooks or pegs. A small table with a drawer or a compact chest of drawers can provide a place for gloves and similar items. Some entrance halls are big enough for an large wardrobe to hold coats. Include an umbrella stand for rainy days.

My children never hang up their coats

PUT HOOKS WITHIN REACH Your children may be staging a coat-hanging strike because they can't reach the hooks. On the inside of the hall cupboard or below your hallway row of pegs, install a second row of hooks at child height.

■ CLOTHES STORAGE

My wardrobe is overrun with shoes

Here are strategies for optimum shoe storage:

- Put the three or four pairs of shoes you wear the most at the front of the wardrobe.
- Store your shoes in clear plastic containers so you can quickly select the pair you want to wear. Or, if you prefer to keep the boxes that the shoes came in, carefully label each shoebox with details of the contents. Better still, take a Polaroid picture of the shoes and stick it on the front of the box, so you can easily identify what's in it without lifting the lid.

- Each time you buy a new pair of shoes, try to throw out or give away a pair of old or rarely used shoes.
- When shoes and boots are out of season, remove them from the wardrobe and store them in boxes under your bed or another clean, dry part of the house.

My wardrobe is bursting with clothes

MAKE UNDERBED STORAGE DRAWERS Try this simple way to store more clothes and shoes in your bedroom. Buy some inexpensive small casters at a hardware or DIY store. Screw them to the bottom of shallow wooden boxes or drawers from an old dresser. (Make sure the drawers, with casters attached, will fit under the bed.) They can easily be rolled out when you need an article of clothing. You may want to add covers to protect the clothes from dust.

I need even more clothes storage

USE BIG BASKETS Creative use of baskets can make up for a lack of wardrobe space. Large wicker baskets with flat lids that look like trunks can easily hold more folded sweaters or T-shirts than a drawer. And you can use these baskets as bedside tables or coffee tables.

I don't have much room to store out-of-season clothes

USE VACUUM-SEAL BAGS You can store rarely used clothes (such as evening gowns and dinner suits) in very little space if you use special vacuum-seal bags. Put the clothing in the special plastic bag and use a vacuum cleaner to suck all the air out before sealing the bag. The clothes compress and are totally safe from insects and dust. But they'll need a good pressing when you take them out.

I can't find my favourite sweater

REORGANISE YOUR WARDROBE Instead of grouping all your clothing by type (that is, sweaters, trousers and shirts together), group clothes by frequency of use. Put your most-used items on the most accessible shelves, which are those at waist height. Rarely worn clothes should go on top shelves.

Clothes you wear fairly frequently should be stacked on shelves below your waist. You will discover that this system can save you time in finding things.

■ KITCHEN STORECUPBOARDS

My storecupboard isn't big enough

ADD SHELVES TO THE DOOR If the walls and floor are jammed with cans and boxes, check to see whether the back of the cupboard door is being used effectively. Install narrow shelves or hanging racks on the door to hold frequently needed items such as spices, condiments and snacks. (Don't hang anything too heavy on the door, or the weight may cause it to drag on the floor.)

I'm wasting space under the stairs

USE THE BACK OF THE UNDERSTAIRS CUPBOARD Cupboards under the stairs often serve as convenient storecupboards. However, the space at the back, where the ceiling slopes down low, sometimes goes to waste. Here are ways to use that space:

- Store out-of-season items you don't need very often, such as barbeque equipment or Christmas lights, at the back.
- Buy boxes or bins on wheels, so that the items at the back can be rolled out.
- Install a second light at the back to make it easier to see what's lurking there. A battery-powered camping light will do.

I would like a wine cellar but don't have space

BE CREATIVE WITH DARK SPACES Unless you're a certified oenophile, you probably don't keep the quantity or quality of vintage wines to justify a full wine cellar. To store wines properly, you just need a dark, cool space. The ideal conditions are constant temperatures of between 12° to 17°C and between 60 and 80 per cent humidity. Wine should not be jostled, so keep it in a part of the house where the traffic is low. If you have room in a storecupboard, create a special space for wine. Or see if there is a cool space under the stairs that's not being used – you could make a pull-out panel. Since wine bottles should be stored on their side, look for adjustable racks that will fit on shelves or stand on the floor.

PROBLEM STOPPER

How to save plastic bags neatly for reuse
Whether you save them for recycling, as lunch bags or as pooper-scoopers, plastic bags quickly pile up. Here's a great solution from a professional organiser. Tape a medium-sized cardboard box closed and cover the top with attractive adhesive paper. Cut a hole 10cm in diameter in the top. You'll be able to stuff a huge quantity of plastic bags into this box, yet it's easy to reach in and grab a bag when it's needed.

Another way to make a holder is to sew a long cloth tube, elasticated at each end, that can be hung on a hook. Just stuff bags in at the top and pull them out the bottom.

PART THREE

Kitchen and cooking

The crucial ingredients just aren't there.
A Sunday roast has dived onto the floor. Unexpected guests
have shown up for dinner. Considering that the kitchen is the
logistical hub of most homes, it's no wonder that this room
can be at the heart of crises in the home. But don't phone for
a takeaway – we have a host of ingenious solutions that will
cure the most common culinary catastrophes.

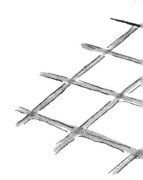

Food problems

■ SAUCES

My sauce is too thin

THICKEN IT WITH FLOUR The simplest and quickest way to thicken a too-thin sauce (or a stew) without altering its taste is to add some flour. Knead together equal quantities of soft butter and flour. About 50g each should be enough for most dishes. Now make marble-sized balls out of the paste and drop them into the simmering sauce one at a time. They'll dissolve instantly without lumps. Keep adding flour pellets until you get the consistency you want.

An alternative is to whisk a few tablespoons of fine grade flour into three times as much liquid (removed from the pan) and pour a small amount of the mixture into the sauce while it is on a low boil. Stir it in, turn the heat down, let it simmer for a few minutes, and then test the consistency. If it is still too thin, turn up the heat, pour in some more dissolved flour and repeat the routine.

REDUCE IT DOWN Often when a sauce is thin, it is because you have added too much water. If that is the case, thicken it up by reducing it down. Turn the heat up high and leave the lid off. Keep stirring, so that the sauce doesn't stick to the bottom. Let the excess water evaporate until the liquid level is where you want it. As only water has been lost, you will have a thicker sauce.

If you have a very watery stew that needs to be reduced, separate the liquid from the meat and vegetables. Either take the solids out with a slotted spoon or pour the whole dish into another pan through a colander. Reduce the liquid down to the consistency you want and then put the meat and vegetables back in. This will ensure that you don't overcook the meat and vegetables.

If your spaghetti sauce resembles red soup, the fast fix is to add tomato paste.

My spaghetti sauce is watery

ADD TOMATO PASTE If you want thick spaghetti sauce rather than a red soup, a simple solution is to stir in more tomato paste. But don't overdo it – add a tablespoon or less at a time until you get the thickness you want. If you don't have time to let the sauce simmer, add a teaspoon or so of sugar. The sugar will add a hint of caramelising flavour, making the sauce taste as if it has been cooking for longer. You can also add a pinch of bicarbonate of soda; it will neutralise the acid and bring out the tomato flavour. But if you do have time, let the additional tomato paste simmer in the sauce for a while, then taste to see whether it needs any last-minute seasoning.

ADD FLOUR Tomato paste has the advantage of being compatible with the taste of spaghetti sauce. But an alternative is to add flour, as you would to thicken a sauce or gravy. You shouldn't just dump the flour into the sauce. Either make flour-butter pellets, as described in the previous problem, or spoon 50ml of the sauce into a measuring cup, add a tablespoon of flour, blend well, then stir into the sauce.

My gravy is lumpy

STRAIN OUT THE LUMPS AND RE-THICKEN Gravy develops lumps because the thickening agent – flour or cornflour – has not been incorporated into the liquid. Once it clumps up, there is very little you can do to change its mind. You can't whisk away or press out or otherwise urge the lumps to dissolve. There is a simple solution to gravy lumps: get rid of them. All you need is a large colander with holes big enough for the liquid but not the lumps to seep through. Set it over a container, fill it half full of gravy, and gently press the liquid through with the underside of a ladle or large spoon. Throw away the lumpy material that's left behind. Repeat until you have strained all the gravy.

To get the thickness back (without lumps this time), put about as much flour as you think you have lost into a small bowl. Add enough water, wine or stock to dissolve the flour with whisking. Now slowly stir this mixture into the simmering, but not boiling, gravy. Add just a little at a time and let the gravy cool slightly each time before checking the thickness.

■ SOUPS AND STEWS

My soup has no taste

ADD A STOCK CUBE Surprisingly, the culprit often isn't inadequate seasoning or the wrong mix of ingredients. A soup usually tastes bland because the original broth or stock is weak. You can deal with

**How to ensure that
your vegetables are
perfectly cooked**
Give fresh vegetables
like green beans and
broccoli your full
attention and you
will never overcook
them again.

1 Before you do any-
thing else to prepare
a meal, drop your
chosen vegetables into
boiling water. Take them
out before they're done.
This is known as
blanching.

2 Plunge them straight
into a bowl of iced
water. (this stops them
from continuing to cook
while locking in the
colour and taste).

3 After the vegetables
have cooled down – a
minute or two – take
them out of the iced
water and drain them in
a colander over a bowl.
Forget about them while
you cook dinner.

4 When everything else
is finished, plunge the
vegetables into boiling
water again for less
than a minute. Drain,
season and serve.

that by whisking a beef, chicken or vegetable stock cube (or two, if it
is a big pan) in a little hot water to dissolve it and then stirring it
into the soup. Just like that, you will have boosted the taste without
changing the soup's volume or altering the ingredients. This flavour
booster works in a stew or sauce, too.

ADD MORE SPICES To bump up the taste a little more, there is no law
against adding more generous amounts of the spices than the recipe
called for. Recipes tend to be conservative about spices and what's
right for a cookbook aimed at a mass market may not be right for
your taste buds. Add and taste till you are satisfied.

ADD A LITTLE SALT 'Salty' doesn't equal 'tasty', but salt does bring out
the flavours that are locked into a sauce, stew or soup. So give the
pan a few shakes of salt, stir it in, let the liquid simmer a bit longer
and then taste again.

My soup is full of fat

USE AN ICE-COLD LADLE With almost any cooking
liquid – whether it is a soup, sauce or stew – fat
congeals at the top as it cools. Here is a shortcut
that the pros use to cool it:
fill a large metal ladle with
ice. Run the ice-filled ladle
bowl along the surface of the
liquid. Push the ladle down
far enough to submerge
most of the outside but
not so far that liquid
spills into the ice in the
ladle. Fat will stick to the
cold underside of the ladle.
Wipe it away with a paper
towel and keep skimming, adding more ice as needed to keep the
ladle really cold. You won't get every drop of fat out this way, but you
will definitely end up with a less greasy and fatty soup or sauce.

PUT IT IN THE FRIDGE If you have enough time, cool the dish in the
fridge for a few hours. Then simply skim the coagulated fat off the
top with a spoon. Sometimes fat forms so firmly that you can actually
lift it off.

■ OVERCOOKED FOOD

My vegetables have turned to mush

CONVERT THEM INTO A CREAMY SOUP Nobody likes mushy broccoli or asparagus or any other overboiled or oversteamed vegetable. But everyone likes cream of vegetable soup. The solution is to turn overcooked veggies into a creamy soup. And it is easy to do.

1 Drain the limp vegetables and throw them into a blender. Just a few pulses will yield a vegetable purée that nobody will ever suspect was once a soggy disappointment.
2 Bring a similar volume of chicken or vegetable stock to the boil in a pan on the stove; then turn the heat down.
3 Stir in the vegetable purée, add salt and any seasonings you want and let it simmer for 5 minutes. There is no need to add cream or milk. But if it is not smooth enough, run the whole thing through the blender again.

Serve the soup in a wide, flat soup bowl to further the illusion that you'd planned this treat from the beginning.

Help! I've burned the meat

The only problem with overcooked meat (once the burned parts are removed) is dryness. All you need to do is to make it moist again.

MAKE A CASSEROLE Here is a quick solution to meat that has been left on the grill or in the oven for too long:

1 Trim off the burned outer layer and discard it.
2 Cut the dry interior meat into thin slices.
3 Put the pieces in a casserole dish with some beef broth and some salsa if you like. This will add moisture.
4 Stir in some canned kidney or borlotti beans and, if you like, some canned or frozen sweetcorn and some chopped onion. Let it sit for a few minutes. Warm the mixture on the hob.
5 Grate a thick layer of Parmesan or Cheddar cheese on top. Put the whole thing, uncovered, into the oven for long enough to melt the cheese. Serve with warm tortillas or tortilla chips.

The real problem with overcooked meat is dryness, so the quick way to save your meal is to add moisture.

Take it easy with the salt

If you are worried about how much salt to use in a dish, it is better to err on the side of using too little. Salt is one seasoning that doesn't need to be cooked in; it can be added after the cooking is finished. Health concerns and changing tastes mean more people want less salt anyway, so let people decide how salty they want their food. Tell your guests that you haven't added much salt and that you won't be in the least insulted if they add more.

SHRED THE MEAT AND PUT IT IN GRAVY Here is another solution for burned meat. Trim off the charred outer layer and shred the dry interior meat with a fork or your fingers. (It should shred easily in the state it is in.) Stir the meat into 100-200ml of barbecue sauce, instant gravy or real gravy made by mixing flour with the roast's drippings. Then warm the dish on the stove for 5 minutes. Serve it with potatoes or a selection of root vegetables.

■ TOUGH MEAT

I'm afraid this roast will be really tough

BRAISE A LARGE TOUGH CUT If you have a large piece of meat that you know is tough, remember these three basics for tenderising it:

- Use liquid.
- Keep the heat extremely low.
- Cook it slowly.

Perhaps you have a 2kg chunk of chuck steak – tough stuff from one of the hardest-working parts of a cow, the shoulder. It will become even tougher if you roast it, so:

1 Rub the meat with flour, salt and pepper it and brown it briefly on all sides in hot oil in a flameproof casserole dish on the hob.
2 Turn off the heat and pour in a cup of seasoned broth, stock, tomato juice or wine along with some extra flavourings, such as chopped onion, crushed garlic cloves, thyme or a mixture of other herbs.
3 Cover the casserole dish, set the burner on a low simmer and let the meat cook for at least 3 hours. Turn the meat once or twice, but never allow the liquid to boil.

What you have done is braise the meat – that is, you have cooked it very slowly in liquid. The result will be a tender, moist delight (essentially a pot roast) that you would never have dreamed could result from the tough cut that you started with.

MARINATE IT AND MAKE A CASSEROLE You can also get tender results by cutting tough meat into large cubes and making a stew – the very essence of gentle, slow cooking in liquid. But there are still other options. For example, steep the tough chunk of chuck or rump in a marinade containing some kind of acid, such as wine or vinegar. Try 400ml water, 200ml dry red wine, some salt, a sliced onion and

1 or 2 teaspoons of a combination of the following: coriander, mustard, dill seed, allspice, bay leaves, cinnamon, ginger and cloves. Bring the mixture to a boil on the hob and then turn off the heat and let it stand. When it has cooled down, pour the marinade over the meat in a glass bowl, seal the top with aluminum foil, and put it in the fridge overnight or preferably for two days.

When you are ready to cook the meat, reserve the marinade. Brown the meat in hot oil on the hob. Then strain the marinade, pour the liquid over the meat, and let it cook for 2 hours in a 175°C / gas 4 oven. You will be amazed by the tenderness as well as the taste, which will be much like sauerbraten, a classic German dish that is marinated for up to three days before cooking.

I think this steak will be too chewy

POUND IT INTO A THIN MINUTE STEAK If you have sliced fresh meat that you fear may be too tough, your best – and fastest – bet is to pound it into submission. Pounding will break up the tough fibres and sinew. Lay the meat out flat on a wooden chopping board and pound it with a meat mallet or a rolling pin until it has been reduced to about half its previous thickness. Coat each slice generously with flour, cornmeal, or ground cornflakes (don't use beaten egg); then sear the meat for a minute or two on each side in hot oil over a burner turned to high. You will end up with meat so tender that you won't even need a knife.

■ TOO MUCH SALT

I've put too much salt in the soup

ADD MORE WATER It is possible that you haven't put in too much salt. A lot of water may have evaporated during cooking, leaving a salt-to-liquid ratio that is now too high. If that seems to be the case and the liquid volume has shrunk noticeably, simply put water back in. Add it a little at a time, taste-testing as you go.

ADD POTATOES If the problem really is too much salt rather than not enough water, add potatoes to the soup, along with a bit more water or broth. If you are lucky enough to have discovered the excess saltiness while the soup is still at an early stage of cooking, you can add the cut-up raw potatoes directly to the pot. But if the soup is already cooked (or very nearly so), you will need to turn it off and

TRICKS OF THE TRADE

Avoid contamination from meat
Bacteria from meat are easily transferred to other foods and merely cleaning kitchen surfaces and utensils with soap and water will not prevent contamination.

The solution is to mix ⅛ teaspoon of unscented bleach with 200ml cold water in a spray bottle and label it as a disinfecting solution. When you have finished preparing meat, clean all surfaces – cutting board, worktop, utensils, and such – with washing-up liquid and hot water.

Then spray them with the disinfecting solution and wipe with a paper towel.

cook the potatoes in a separate pan before adding them. If you don't have potatoes, add another form of starch, such as noodles, (cooked) rice or pasta, to absorb the excess salt.

ADD MORE OF ALL THE INGREDIENTS You can also increase the volume of the entire recipe, adding more of all the ingredients (except salt, of course) in their original proportions. Like the potatoes, the ingredients can be raw or cooked separately, depending on the stage at which you catch the problem.

I have put too much salt on the meat

ADD SOME SUGAR To rescue a cut of meat back from excessive salt, just sprinkle a pinch of sugar over it. It may seem a little strange to put sugar on meat, but the idea is to keep the amount small enough that you don't really taste it. At the same time, the sugar will subtly offset the excess salt.

These vegetables are much too salty

ADD SUGAR TO VEGGIES, TOO A touch of sugar is recommended to bring out the natural taste of vegetables, so adding a little bit to counteract saltiness is not such a radical idea. Or try a splash of vinegar or lemon juice. It probably won't neutralise the salt as completely as sugar will, but it will give a slight edge to the taste so that your taste buds won't focus on the salt.

■ HOT SPICY FOODS

This dish is much too spicy

INCREASE THE NON-SPICY INGREDIENTS The most common reason for an overly spicy dish is that you have added too much liquid hot sauce or hot chilli powder. The quickest fix is to add more of the non-spicy items. If it is a chilli dish, add more beans, beef broth or meat. For any sauce or other sauced dish that's too hot, increase the proportion of everything in the recipe except the hot spices.

SERVE WITH A STARCH For additional cooling down, serve your spicy dish over rice or with tortillas and soured cream. There is a reason such accompaniments are often on the same plate as spicy Indian, Chinese, Thai or Mexican dishes – they cool the heat.

PICK OUT THE HOT CHILLI PIECES Another reason for an overspiced dish is that you have put diced or sliced jalapeño, serrano or habañero chillies straight into the dish (for instance, Thai vegetables, or any other chilli-loaded recipe). Remove all the chilli pieces with a spoon or fork. Put the extracted chilli pieces in a small glass bowl and let people who adore fiery food serve themselves.

I've just bitten into a chilli

DON'T SWIG THE WATER Most people instinctively react to biting on a chilli by taking the worst possible course of action – flooding their mouths with water, beer or a soft drink. The sting in chillies comes from a chemical called capsaicin, which does not dissolve easily in water. Sloshing liquids in your mouth just spreads the pain.

If chillies ignite a fire in your mouth, flooding it will only make it worse. The fastest way to get relief is a little salt.

USE SALT, MILK OR BREAD INSTEAD In Mexico, where they *know* what hot chillies can do to unsuspecting mouths, three instant chilli-extinguishing remedies have proved themselves over the centuries:

- Salt is the quickest and most reliable pain reliever for anybody who is, as they say, *enchilado*.
- Milk, cream, yogurt or cheese will also help, thanks to proteins known as caseins in dairy products. Caseins disrupt the bond between the burning chemical capsaicin and your taste receptors, giving your tongue a break.
- A piece of white bread, a cracker or a tortilla popped into your mouth will help to absorb the pain-producing capsaicin.

■ MISSING INGREDIENTS

I need buttermilk for pancakes

ADD LEMON JUICE TO MILK Most homes don't have buttermilk to hand in the fridge any more. You can substitute sour milk for buttermilk. To make it, just add 1 tablespoon of lemon juice or white vinegar to 200ml of whole milk and let it stand for 15 minutes.

USE YOGHURT OR SOURED CREAM Depending on the recipe and your preference, you can also use an equal amount of plain yoghurt or use soured cream, thinned with milk to a pourable consistency, as a substitute for buttermilk.

Getting a sneak preview
Once you have baked a meat loaf or similar firm baked meat dish, there is nothing you can do to adjust the seasoning. Before you put the dish in the oven, steal a little piece and make a patty the size of a 10p. Cook it in a pan with a little oil.

Now taste it. If it is not flavoured the way you want it, adjust the seasoning. Re-test with another fried patty if you are still not sure. Then go ahead and bake, confident that there will be no surprises when it is done.

I've run out out of baking powder

MAKE YOUR OWN BAKING POWDER If you have cream of tartar and bicarbonate of soda, make your own baking powder by mixing ¼ teaspoon of bicarbonate of soda with ½ teaspoon of cream of tartar, which will yield the equivalent of 1 teaspoon of baking powder. Unlike commercial baking powder, your homemade baking powder will start using up its leavening power as soon as it mixes with liquid. So put any cake or other mixes in the oven at once.

USE BICARBONATE OF SODA AND AN ACIDIC LIQUID If you don't have cream of tartar, use bicarbonate of soda and an acidic liquid. Your choices are soured cream, buttermilk, yoghurt or a citrus juice, such as lime or lemon. Add the bicarbonate of soda to the dry ingredients, using about a quarter of the amount of the baking powder that the recipe called for. When it is time to blend in the liquid ingredients, add 120ml of your acidic liquid for every quarter teaspoon of bicarbonate of soda used.

I'm out of cinnamon, ginger or other spices

SUBSTITUTE ONE SPICE FOR ANOTHER If you don't have a spice that's called for in a recipe, substitute a similar one:

If you are out of...	try using...
Allspice	Equal amounts of cinnamon, cloves, and nutmeg
Caraway seeds	Aniseed
Basil	Oregano, marjoram, thyme, rosemary or savory
Cardamom	Ginger
Cayenne pepper	Ground chilli peppers
Chervil	Parsley or tarragon
Chilli powder	Cumin plus a dash of hot sauce
Cinnamon	¼ as much nutmeg or allspice
Cloves	Cinnamon, nutmeg, allspice, ginger or mace
Fennel seeds	Aniseed
Ginger	Mace, nutmeg, allspice, cloves, or cinnamon
Italian seasoning	Any mixture of oregano, thyme, basil, rosemary, savory, or marjoram, plus a little ground red pepper
Nutmeg	Allspice, mace, ginger, cloves or cinnamon
Poultry seasoning	Sage mixed with rosemary, thyme or marjoram
Rosemary	Savory, oregano, thyme, basil, rosemary or marjoram
Sage	Thyme
Tarragon	Chervil or fennel seed

The important thing to remember is that most sweet spices (cinnamon, nutmeg, allspice, cloves, ginger and mace) can be substituted for one another. And the same goes for herbs associated with Italian and other Mediterranean cooking (basil, oregano, thyme, rosemary and marjoram). When making spice swaps, start by using half the amount the recipe calls for and then add more (or another spice) until you are happy with the taste.

I don't have any barbecue sauce

MAKE YOUR OWN You probably have everything you need in your storecupboard. Start with a classic basic recipe:

> 300ml ketchup
> 200ml cider vinegar
> 70ml vegetable oil
> 70ml Worcestershire sauce
> 100g brown sugar
> 3 tablespoons prepared yellow mustard
> 3 cloves of garlic, minced
> Juice of 1 lemon
>
> Combine the ingredients in a stainless-steel, glass, enamel-coated or non-stick saucepan and heat slowly – for about 15 minutes – to blend flavours. Makes about 600ml.

To personalise the sauce, substitute tomato sauce or paste, honey, molasses, brown mustard or lime or orange juice for their obvious counterparts. Or add smoke flavouring, chilli powder, paprika, chopped and sautéed onion or celery, celery seed, cumin, French or western salad dressing or even ground coffee.

The recipe needs some white wine and I've run out

USE WHITE WINE VINEGAR Try this quick substitute: dilute white wine vinegar with water in a 50:50 ratio. Add a little sugar and use this concoction instead of the white wine called for. Nobody will be able to tell the difference.

USE DRY VERMOUTH Another solution is to keep a bottle of dry vermouth in the kitchen and substitute it whenever white wine is needed, using only half the amount called for. Add a little water or broth to make up for the smaller volume.

■ FLAVOUR FAILURES

My perfectly cooked meat has no taste

LIVEN UP THE SAUCE If your bland-tasting meat is in a stew or other liquid, there is a quick solution. Heighten the taste of the sauce or gravy and nobody will notice that the meat is bland. You can do this by adding a stock cube, more spices or salt, as described in 'My soup has no taste' on page 163.

MAKE A TASTY DRESSING TO ACCOMPANY IT What about meats that don't have a sauce that can be jazzed up? What if you have prepared a roast, steak or chop to lean and tender perfection, yet it is weak in the taste department?

If your problem is an underseasoned hamburger it can be jazzed up by a little ketchup or other sauce. But your perfectly cooked roast, steak or veal deserves better. Make it its own delicious little brush-on sauce that will garnish it subtly but with an unmistakable zing. Here are three quick, simple, sure-fire meat rescuers:

- Mix a salsa, as spicy as you wish, with an equal amount of apricot jam. Heat it in the microwave just long enough to marry the flavours (about a minute), and spread lightly on your slices of meat.
- Put together a sweet-and-sour sauce by blending apricot jam with apple cider vinegar to taste, again heating for just a minute in the microwave.
- Mix a bit of honey, horseradish, mustard and fresh chopped mint (or dried mint mixed with fresh parsley – or even mint jelly) to taste. This is sure to add taste to the blandest meat.

Any of these three taste enhancers can be helped along with a little lemon juice, vinegar, ground red pepper, curry powder or cumin. Add small amounts at a time and taste.

My potato salad is overloaded with mayonnaise

ADD BREAD CRUMBS Once you have stirred too much mayonnaise into a potato salad or coleslaw, you can't really take it out. But you *can* stir in a liberal amount of plain breadcrumbs as a quick fix. They will absorb the extra mayonnaise as they disappear into the dressing. Don't worry; your cold dish won't taste like breadcrumbs – and it won't taste like pure mayonnaise either.

■ NO TIME TO COOK

I don't have 4 hours to cook a turkey

BOIL THE TURKEY FIRST Assuming that you have a fresh turkey or one that you have defrosted, you can cut the cooking time in half – with the bonus of serving a bird that is tastier and juicier than usual – by boiling the bird before baking it. Here is how to proceed with a typical 5.5kg turkey:

1 Place the turkey in a large pan and add enough cold water to cover it. Add salt, pepper, cut-up onion and 2 tablespoons of combined parsley, thyme or other herbs.
2 Bring the pan to a boil on the hob and then lower the heat to a simmer (with tiny bubbles rising along the side of the pot). Simmer uncovered for an hour; then drain the turkey.
3 Prepare the turkey to roast as you normally would. Roast at 200°C / gas 5 and check to see whether it is done after an hour. (Pull a leg away from the body so that you are able to puncture the inner thigh near the hip joint. If there is no blood, the turkey is done.)

The result will be a succulent, moist turkey, in half the normal cooking time! Try it if you are tired of turkey with the consistency of polystyrene foam.

Believe it or not, you will get a better-tasting bird and it will cook faster if it gets a hot bath before roasting.

■ MARGINAL FOODS

My fruit is getting too ripe

TURN IT INTO A RAW PURÉE As long as the fruit isn't rotten or mouldy, cut away any parts that look bad, but don't throw it away because it is soft or mushy. Put the fruit in a blender, add sugar and turn it into a purée that you can blend into salad dressings, use instead of syrup on pancakes or pour over ice cream, pies and other desserts.

MAKE A COOKED PURÉE For flavour variation, cook down the fruit purée by simmering it in a pan for a few minutes and then letting it cool. You could add a little food colouring or some brightly coloured juice. Freeze whatever you can't use right away in sealable, portion-size plastic bags.

These salad greens are a little withered

SOAK THEM IN WARM WATER Slightly wilted lettuce, spinach and other leafy salad greens are still good; they've just lost water. They will perk up if left in a pan of warm water for an hour. Then drain them, splash them with cold water and let them drain again in a colander. When no more water drips out, shake them dry as best you can or use a salad spinner. Your greens will be resuscitated.

The cheese has gone mouldy

JUST CUT OFF THE MOULD The mouldy surface may look like a major problem, but it is usually not. Cut away the mouldy areas and enjoy the clean fresh cheese that's left.

Be careful not to reinfect the remaining cheese.

- Don't slice the cheese with the same knife or cheese slicer that you used to remove the mould. Wash the utensil first if you want to reuse it.
- Don't put the cheese back on the cutting board where the mouldy cheese was sitting. Wash the board first.
- Don't put the cheese back in the same packaging, which may harbour mould. Throw away the old wrapper and use a fresh piece of foil, waxed paper or cling film.

WORLD-CLASS FIX

You are alone in the kitchen

The late Julia Child, a noted US TV chef, took the snobbery out of French cuisine and made it fun and easy for amateur cooks across the globe. She also once imparted a wonderful all-purpose solution to many a kitchen woe.

Once, Child was demonstrating how to flip a potato pancake on her popular television show when she accidently spilled the contents of the pan on to the hob. As viewers watched in amazement, she promptly scooped up the spill and put it back in her pan and continued cooking, advising her audience, 'You can always pick it up if you are alone in the kitchen. Who's going to see it?'

The message was clear: what people don't know won't hurt them. As long as you are careful with hygiene, a so-called kitchen disaster is not a disaster at all.

Serving hitches

■ TOO MANY GUESTS

I have china for eight but ten to feed

MAKE THE MISMATCH LOOK PLANNED If the dinner is relaxed, it's unlikely that anyone will care or notice that two of the plates are from a different set. If the dinner is more formal, consider this quick solution: instead of using a full eight-piece formal china and two everyday settings, use five and five. Alternate the settings: formal, everyday, formal, everyday. The effect will be pleasing and look as if you planned it that way.

I've cooked for six but ten have turned up

MAKE EXTRA PASTA AND RELAX As soon as you know that there will be more people than you have cooked for, boil up some water for pasta. Once the pasta is cooked and drained, stir in a can of condensed mushroom soup (or something similar), add minced garlic, season liberally and add plenty of grated Parmesan or other grated cheese, the harder the better. Without delaying the meal much, you now have a delicious and filling dish that will guarantee that nobody will leave the table feeling the least bit hungry.

Pasta is not the only solution. If you have grilled six steaks, for example, what can you serve the extra four people? A simple and quick solution is put the entire meal on the table in serving dishes and encourage your guests to help themselves. Cut the steaks or other main meat dish into appetising slices or portions and arrange them on a serving platter. Display the vegetables in a casserole dish or vegetable bowl with a serving spoon. By some tacit rule of manners, people will help themselves to less meat than they would have eaten if served individually. And with the extra pasta and a generous basket of bread, what seemed to be insufficient should turn out to be a plentiful and enjoyable feast.

The second you find out there will be more mouths to feed than you expected, get some water on the stove and boil pasta.

■ A GUEST WITH SPECIAL REQUIREMENTS

What to do for an unexpected vegetarian

ASK YOUR GUEST WHAT HE OR SHE WANTS TO EAT Just as you are putting the final touches on your veal cutlets, you learn that the specially invited guest of honour follows a strictly meatless diet. What can you give the guest instead? Actually, there is only one person who can answer that question – your vegetarian guest. Ask the guest what you can prepare instead. It probably won't be the first time this has happened, so he or she may have an appropriate suggestion or two. Take your guest into the kitchen, apologise for not knowing, throw open your fridge and cupboards, and say, 'here is what I have. Let's see what we can do'. Your guest should eat happily and you will know that you did your utmost to cater to their needs.

Only one person can say what your vegetarian guest would prefer instead of the steak you have cooked. Feel free to ask.

■ LAST-MINUTE FOOD DIFFICULTIES

The butter's too hard to spread

MICROWAVE IT VERY BRIEFLY Your microwave oven will take care of that in 15 seconds – but no more than that. Put the cold butter on a dish and set the microwave onto the defrost setting. Remember that the inside of the bar will soften sooner than the outside, so be careful not to overdo it.

I squirt everybody when I squeeze a lemon

TWIST A FORK IN THE LEMON Squeezing a lemon into your drink or onto fish without embarrassing consequences is all a matter of control. To squeeze lemon juice into your glass or on food:

1 Take the lemon slice in one hand and your fork in the other.
2 Hold the lemon over your glass or food and stick the fork into the pulp. Then move the fork from side to side and twist it.
3 Remove the fork, pierce another spot and twist again.

Repeat this process until the lemon slice is used up. There will not be one unfortunate squirt.

■ WINE AND OTHER DRINKS

The punch is much too sweet

ADD LEMON JUICE OR DRY WINE Don't add water. By the time you dilute the punch enough to tone down the sugar, you will be stuck with a tepid, watery swill. Instead, add a tart juice – lemon or grapefruit – a little at a time until the punch's sugar ratio is just right. A dry wine will produce equally good results.

The same strategy works for cocktails that are too sweet. You can even use lemon juice or dry wine to reduce the sugary taste of puddings and pie fillings.

I don't have a corkscrew

DIG IT OUT WITH A SCREWDRIVER If you have a Swiss army knife, it is likely to have a corkscrew. If you don't, use a screwdriver tip to dig out the cork bit by bit. Once you have removed about half of it, you should be able to push the rest into the bottle and decant the wine – just as you would if the cork broke off during a normal opening process, as described below.

USE A LONG SCREW You will need some narrow pliers, a nail, a screwdriver and a long (5cm or more) wood screw. Place the tip of the nail against the centre of the cork and use the pliers to work it in about a centimetre to create a starter hole for your screw. You can also do this with a sharp skewer. Drive the screw into the hole, leaving enough protruding to grip with the pliers. Pull on the screw with the pliers, dragging the cork steadily straight out of the bottle. If the screw pulls free, make a new starter hole to the side of the old one and try again. Or, if the cork is far enough out, grab the sides of the cork with pliers and pull, twisting the cork slightly to loosen it.

The cork broke off in the bottle

TRY AGAIN WITH THE CORKSCREW First try to twist the corkscrew into the remaining half of the cork. It is a little tricky, because the now-jagged surface of the cork will be below the level of the bottle opening. But often you can penetrate the cork enough to pull it out.

PUSH THE CORK IN If you accidentally push the remaining cork into the bottle, don't worry. That was Plan B anyway. By pushing the

PROBLEM STOPPER

Always keep a corkscrew handy
To avoid not having a corkscrew when you need it, buy at least four wine openers. Keep one in the kitchen, one with your wine, one with the picnic gear and one somewhere for just such an emergency. You should never have to dig out a wine cork with a penknife again.

Add zest to a dull salad

Here is a simple but zingy salad dressing that will make taste buds snap to attention. It takes less than 5 minutes to make:

SUN-DRIED TOMATO BASIL VINAIGRETTE

1 tbsp sun-dried tomatoes (dry or oil-packed), chopped
1 tbsp fresh garlic, peeled
2 tbsp white wine vinegar (or white vinegar)
4 tbsp lemon juice, freshly squeezed
1 tbsp grated lemon peel
1 tbsp fresh basil, chopped
200ml extra virgin olive oil
¼ tsp salt
Black pepper, to taste

Blend the sun-dried tomatoes and garlic in a blender until smooth (about a minute). Add the remaining ingredients and blend until smooth (45 seconds to a minute). Cover and refrigerate until ready to use. Makes four servings.

remaining cork into the bottle, you have successfully opened the bottle and can pour the wine. Because bits of cork may be swimming around in the wine, pour the wine through a cone-shaped coffee filter into a decanter or a clean glass jug. If the floating cork makes it hard to pour the wine, use a kebab skewer or chopstick to hold it at the bottom of the bottle.

Dinner is ready and I've forgotten to chill the white wine

USE AN ICE BUCKET Don't put the wine in the freezer; wine bottles tend to get forgotten and end up freezing or exploding. Instead, fill a bucket half and half with ice and cold water and put the bottle in it up to its neck. You don't need a wine bucket. Any clean bucket that is almost as tall as the bottle will do. Some people believe that stirring salt into the ice and water helps the wine to chill faster. In about 10 minutes the ice-and-water treatment will chill the wine sufficiently. White wine should be just cold enough to taste light and fresh. Overchilling dulls the taste.

The red wine is too cold to serve

POUR IT INTO GLASSES Is it really too cold? Although most red wines are best served at or near room temperature, the tradition began centuries ago, when houses lacked central heating and the room temperature was considerably cooler than we are used to today. It is usually fine and sometimes preferable, to drink a red wine that is a little cool. If the bottle is really too cold (because it was stored in the fridge or left out in the car in winter), open it and pour the wine into wine glasses, just as you normally would. The liquid will warm to room temperature much faster once transferred from the thick bottle into thinner, airy glasses.

WARM THE GLASS WITH YOUR HANDS To warm wine even faster, use your secret temperature-control tools – your hands. Wrapping them around the bowl of a wine glass will warm the glass and get the wine to the temperature that's required surprisingly quickly. In fact, while wine glasses for white wine are made to be held by the stem (to keep the chill), the more bulbous wine glasses for red wine encourage the user to cradle them in the hand, which raises the temperature and releases the aroma, enhancing the taste. If you have guests, show them how they can warm the glass with their cupped hands.

I think the wine has gone off

DO A COMPARISON TEST Sometimes it is hard to tell whether a peculiar taste indicates that a wine has gone off or is just something you are not used to. If you have another bottle of the same wine, open it and compare. If the second bottle undeniably tastes better, the first bottle is not at its best.

GET ANOTHER OPINION If both bottles taste the same or you don't have a second bottle, get a second opinion. If you get a definite thumbs-up or thumbs-down from your co-drinker, consider the decision made. But if the other person is just as uncertain as you, err on the side of caution. Open something else and use the unproven bottle to cook with the next day.

■ DESSERT DISASTERS

My cake has dropped and my mousse is lumpy

MAKE AN ICE CREAM TOPPING Desserts, especially special ones, can go wrong just when you don't want them to. Cakes fall, bread puddings take on a strange consistency, mousses go lumpy and flans can become tough and chewy instead of light and fresh. These kinds of emergencies are the reason you should keep a good quality vanilla ice cream in the freezer. Take the ice cream out of the freezer and let it stand until it is soft. Then stir the ice cream with a spoon to help it to melt to the consistency of

SURELY NOT

CHAMPAGNE SURPRISE

A correspondent to wordbanquet.com tells of a family calamity of epic proportions. For a large Sunday luncheon, Mum had laid out a wonderful buffet for guests to enjoy. But before they could, Dad accidentally aimed the Champagne bottle at the fluorescent light above the table, launching a cork missile that sent a shower of broken glass on the food below.

The solution was a second-best meal of barbecued chops found in the freezer, followed by a dessert that had survived in the fridge. Of course, this will never happen to you, because you know to drape a towel over the cork, point the Champagne bottle at empty ceiling space, and hold the cork steady as you twist the bottle, not the cork.

Say goodbye to broken corks
There are two reasons why a cork may break when you use a corkscrew. One is that you did not twist it deep enough into the cork before you started to pull. So always twist the spiral part of the corkscrew in as deep as you can and remember that red wine bottles have longer corks than white ones.

   The other possibility is that the cork was either dried out or partially broken in the first place. If that's the case, there is a chance that the wine may have oxidised during storage, so sample it yourself before you serve to make sure it is drinkable.

a creamy sauce, but not a liquid. Add a little liqueur if you wish. Put individual servings of your failed dessert into bowls, chop the portions up (if you feel it will help) and then cover each serving with a generous serving of the ice cream sauce. You could top it with a cherry or another appropriate fresh fruit. Your guests may not be sure what they are eating, but they will know that it is cool, sweet and delicious.

My cake is just too rich and sweet

SERVE SMALL PORTIONS If you are worried that a chocolate cake or other sweet pudding or cake is simply too rich, serve half as much as you normally would. Announce to the table, 'This is extremely rich, so proceed with caution'. Then add that there is plenty more for those who want it. But stall a bit before obliging guests who ask for seconds. After 5 minutes or so, offer second helpings. Your guests may have realised how full they are and changed their minds.

   Smaller servings are also the best way to deal with too-rich main courses, such as quiches or casseroles. But you can correct rich sauces or cream soups by diluting them with vegetable or chicken soup stock. In these cases, the perceived richness is usually due to lots of butter, cream or cheese. The thin stock will tone down the richness without diluting the taste.

My pie is so runny that the slices are falling apart

MAKE A FAUX COBBLER There is a fast solution: spoon the entire pie into a bowl, break up the crust into medium-sized pieces and call it a cobbler – which is essentially what it has become. Put a large squirt of whipped cream on top and let the diners enjoy the taste, rather than dwelling on its former life as a pie.

Cleaning hassles

■ HARD-TO-CLEAN ITEMS

My coffee jug has an unattractive brown residue

USE ICE, SALT AND LEMON The glass jug that comes with a coffeemaker can quickly develop a brown, blotchy haze – especially when you leave it on for long periods of time. For the quickest cure, you will need some ice, salt and a lemon.

1 Fill the empty jug a quarter full of ice.
2 Cut the lemon into quarters and squeeze two of the quarters into the jug.
3 Add 2 tablespoons of salt. Swirl the mixture in the jug for 2 minutes and the inside surface will quickly come clean. Rinse under the tap.

The quickest cure for a brown, stained coffee jug is ice, salt and a lemon.

Tomato sauce has left orange stains on a plastic container

LET THE SUN BLEACH IT OFF Take the stained plastic container – the one that may have sat in the fridge for a week with a spaghetti sauce in it – out to the part of your patio or garden that gets the most sun. A balcony or even a sunny windowsill will do. Leave it there all day. When you retrieve it at sunset, the stain will be gone and your plastic container will look like new.

The only difficult thing about this method of cleaning plastic containers is believing that anything so easy really works. But the sun is a great bleacher of tomato-based stains, which are precisely the stains that often won't scrub off. Tomato-stained T-shirts and tablecloths will also come cleaner if you sun-dry them after washing.

USE A LITTLE BLEACH If you live somewhere where sun is at a premium, bleach is your best bet. Fill the container with water and a capful of household bleach and let it sit for at least an hour. With

Keeping tomato stains at bay

Avoid tomato stains in the future by spraying the plastic container with a spray cooking oil, before spooning in leftover spaghetti sauce or tomato soup. Or line the container bowl with plastic wrap (but never with aluminum foil, which the sauce will eat away). The surest stain-prevention strategy is to store tomato-based sauces in glass jars with tightly fitting lids.

most heavy-duty plastic containers, the stain should be gone when you rinse it.

A sun or bleach bath will also work for white plastic spatulas. But if the head is made of rubber, don't let the spatula sit out in intense heat for too long.

Burned-on food won't come off my pan

BOIL AND SOAK IT OFF The easy way to dislodge burned food from a pan is to fill it with water and a little washing-up liquid. Bring the water to a boil, turn off the heat, and let it sit for at least 15 minutes. The burned food should now be soft enough to scrape off with a plastic scraper. Then scrub the bottom of the pan clean.

If this treatment doesn't work the first time, try it again. Stubborn burned-on food may need three boilings. For extra power, stir 2 or 3 teaspoons of salt into the water. Or add a spoonful of vinegar.

I can't get the cheese off the grater

USE AN OLD TOOTHBRUSH This can be a bit of a challenge whether the problem is cheese or lemon zest, especially in a grater's smallest holes. There is no way to scrub them without shredding whatever you are scrubbing with. Instead, use an old hard-bristled toothbrush. Get it wet and brush away the stuck bits, inside and outside, top to bottom. Then wash the grater and rinse.

■ GREASE AND FOOD SPLATTERS

My kitchen walls are stained and greasy

WASH PAINTED WALLS WITH A BLEACH SOLUTION Most kitchen walls are painted. To clean them, add 100ml of household bleach to 4 litres of water and use it to wipe down the walls with a sponge.

If that doesn't work, use a specialist concentrated wall cleaner of the kind that mixes in water and includes a degreaser and disinfectant. Spray or wipe it over the entire wall surface, let it sit for about 10 minutes and wipe it off with a soft cloth.

WASH WALLPAPER WITH SOAPY WATER Wallpapered kitchen walls require a different strategy. First vacuum them, bottom to top, using the brush attachment. Then check to see whether your wallpaper is washable. Find a spot that nobody can see and use a sponge to wipe it gently with a mixture of water and washing-up liquid. If the wallpaper is not damaged, you can clean the entire wall with the soapy water. Rinse it off straightaway with a clean sponge and fresh water.

For wallpaper that can't be washed, hardware and DIY stores sell special cleaners that spread on like paste and then wipe off. Test it first in an out-of-the-way spot.

The inside of the microwave is dirty

STEAM OFF THE FOOD SPLASHES Water is all you need to get rid of dried-on food. And you don't need to scrub. Just put a glass of water in the microwave and heat it for about a minute, until the inside of the oven is steamy. Then let the glass of water sit for about 20 minutes with the door closed. The moisture condensing on the walls will soften the food residue. Finally, just wipe off the residue with a sponge or paper towel.

You have just spared yourself elbow grease – and saved money. Most microwave oven cleaners are nothing more than bags that release steam when they are heated. The glass of water will have accomplished the same thing without added chemicals, extra mess and unnecessary spending.

■ CHOPPING BOARDS

My chopping board is too dirty to use

SAND AND OIL A WOODEN BOARD If scrubbing with soap and water won't clean a wooden chopping board, sanding will. Use a very fine grade of glasspaper and press lightly. It won't take long to sand the entire surface. Finish with a coat of mineral oil or olive oil which will keep the wood from drying out and give the board a pleasing sheen and colour.

BLEACH A PLASTIC BOARD If you have a plastic chopping board, the best option is to spray on a 50-50 water-and-bleach solution (wear rubber gloves) and wipe it off with a paper towel. Bleach is not the best option for wooden chopping boards.

My wooden chopping board has deep cuts

SAND THEM DOWN If your chopping board is full of deep gashes and channels, it is time to sand it. But unlike sanding for surface cleaning, you need to start out with a coarse grade of glasspaper for this task.

The deeper the groove, the more roughness you need. Sand the whole surface evenly, not only the grooved areas. The trick is to use progressively smoother grades of glasspaper as the board starts smoothing out. (The higher the number, the smoother the glasspaper.) If you do this, you won't take off any more of the board surface than you have to.

When you have finished sanding, rub on a coat of mineral oil or olive oil to keep the wood from drying out.

■ KITCHEN ODOURS

My hands smell strongly of fish

RUB YOUR HANDS WITH LEMON Whether you have handled fish in the kitchen or while angling, this is an excellent way to get rid of a fishy odour: cut a lemon in half and squeeze each half over your hands. Rub your hands together and rinse.

WASH WITH SOAP AND SUGAR If you don't have a lemon handy, pour a teaspoon of liquid soap on to your palm. Add a tablespoon of sugar to the soap and rub the mixture thoroughly over your hands. Then rinse. The combination of soap and abrasion from the sugar will remove the odour.

The fishy smell lingering on your hands can be quickly killed by rubbing them on stainless steel.

RUB YOUR HANDS ON STAINLESS STEEL Some chefs swear by stainless steel as a way to remove fishy smells. Rub your hands against a stainless-steel sink or fixtures and then wash as usual.

The kitchen still smells of last night's dinner

BURN SOME TOAST There is nothing wrong with a kitchen smelling like food. But if a food odour becomes particularly unpleasant, a fast (if counter-intuitive) solution is to burn some toast to absorb the lingering odour. Just make sure the bread doesn't catch fire. Of course, you will now have a kitchen that smells like burned toast, but this odour at least won't linger for long.

SIMMER A LITTLE ORANGE PEEL For a food odour that appears to be fading, you can take less drastic action by creating a pleasant smell to overwhelm the unpleasant one. Simmer some orange peel and a pinch of cinnamon in a pan of water for a few minutes. Then turn off the flame and leave the open pan of warm, sweet-smelling water on the hob all day.

My kitchen is filled with smoke

GET THE AIR CIRCULATING If you want to eat in the kitchen and don't have time to wait – or if the smoke is working its way into the dining room where all your guests will soon assemble – you need to take action quickly.

Open all the kitchen doors and windows to get the air moving. Place a portable fan by a door or window that opens to the outdoors or that leads away from where the guests are or where you will be eating. Place the fan so that it will blow out through a door or window. The room should be clear in a few minutes – 10 minutes maximum if there really is a lot of smoke.

SET OUT A BOWL OF VINEGAR If you have time, there is a very easy way to rid a room of the odour of smoke. Set out a shallow bowl of vinegar, which will absorb the smell as the smoke dissipates.

■ FRIDGES

My fridge has smelt awful for several days

ABSORB ODOURS WITH BICARBONATE OF SODA, COFFEE OR CHARCOAL
The first course of action is obvious: quickly sniff out the source of the bad smell that's lurking in your fridge and get rid of it. To absorb lingering odours, bicarbonate of soda really works. You may already keep an open box in your fridge to prevent bad smells. But to get rid of a smell that's already there, pour a cup of fresh bicarbonate of soda on to a plate and leave it inside the fridge for a day. For stronger smells, fill a shallow bowl with dry unused coffee grounds and leave it in the fridge for several days. Freshly ground coffee beans work best. For sour smells, charcoal often works amazingly well. Just put several briquettes on a dish and leave them to soak up the odour for a few days.

Freshening up a fridge
For major fridge cleanings, follow the manufacturer's instructions. But to freshen up the overall smell, mix 50mg bicarbonate of soda with warm water and wipe the fridge's interior with a sponge. Be sure to get inside the flap or grooves on the gasket, the rubber seal that goes around the door to keep the unit airtight. Bacteria love to hide in there.

Rinse the surfaces with a clean water-soaked towel and then dry them off. Rinse the drawers and shelves in the sink or bath. Dry them before you put them back in.

STEAM WITH HOT LEMON WATER AND CLEAN If none of the above suggestions gets rid of the smell, you probably have a combination of food, mould, mildew and bacteria hiding in the fridge. Take out all the food and put it in a closed cooler with a bag of ice so you won't have to worry about it. Unplug the fridge. Squeeze a lemon into a cup of water, throw the peel in as well and heat the liquid on the stove. Pour the hot lemon water into a bowl, put the bowl in the fridge, close the door and wait a few minutes. This will start reducing the odour but, more importantly, it will also loosen any accumulations of food on the walls and shelves, making them easier to clean away. To give your fridge a quick cleaning, follow the instructions in the Problem Stopper box (left).

My freezer has iced up

HEAT IT UP WITH A HAIR DRIER If your freezer frosts up or accumulates ice, count your blessings. It must have lasted many years, since most new fridges are now frost-free. To melt the ice, unplug the unit. The ice or frost will melt eventually, but you don't want to keep the fridge turned off for that long. To help the defrosting process, get a hair drier and aim the hot air at the ice. Brush the resulting water into a bucket with a rag and soon the problem will melt away. Never stab at the ice with a knife. You could easily poke through a wall and burst a tube, letting coolant escape, a problem which is dangerous and expensive to repair.

■ ACCIDENTS

I have spilled oil all over the worktop

USE PAPER TOWELS, THEN SUGAR Quickly stop the flow with a dishcloth, paper towels or whatever is nearest at hand. Then get as much of the oil as you can up with paper towels or sponges. Sprinkle sugar over the remaining oil to absorb it, then wipe with paper towels. You still may have an oily film left, so spray a strong all-purpose degreasing cleaner on the surface and wipe it off.

A plastic bowl has melted onto the hob

PULL IT OFF WHILE IT IS WARM This sticky situation can happen with items such as plastic mixing bowls, plastic serving spoons and plastic chopping boards. As soon as you see it happening, turn off the burner and get as much of the melting plastic away from the heat source as you can by pulling from the end farthest from the hob. Heat won't conduct through the plastic, but you still should use a pot holder or oven mitt for safety's sake. If you are lucky, the melting end will still be hot enough to peel off the hob.

SCRAPE IT OFF SMOOTH SURFACES Once it cools, plastic sticks on hard. If you have an electric cooker with a ceramic hob, carefully scrape off the plastic with a single-edge razor. Scraping can also work on the smooth surface areas of any stove.

TORCH IT OFF ROUGH SURFACES If the plastic has stuck to an uneven surface, such as one of the burner grates on a gas hob or the pan underneath, remelting will get the plastic off more effectively than anything. But take great care when trying this solution and make sure there is someone else around. Remove the grate or pan and take it out to the driveway or patio. Then melt the plastic with a blowtorch – which is not as drastic as it sounds. You can buy small canisters of propane gas with screw-on attachments that will send out a modest jet of flame when you flick the little wheel like a cigarette lighter or use a small cook's blowtorch. Hold the grate or pan well away from your body with long-handled tongs. Or remove the grill rack from a barbecue and set it across two stools. Spread newspapers on the ground below so that you won't get melting plastic on the driveway or patio. Then carefully aim the blowtorch at the grill. As the plastic heats up, it will melt and fall to the newspapers below. When the plastic stops smoking, your problem should have melted away.

I have burned my finger while cooking

COAT IT WITH MUSTARD For quick first aid, some professional chefs cover the burned area of their fingers with mustard. Ordinary yellow English mustard will do. Don't stick your finger into the mustard jar. Just spoon some out, spread it on your finger and keep it there. You will feel a coolness and sufficient pain relief so that you can keep on cooking with one hand and most of the other one.

A BETTER TREATMENT If you have time, the proper first aid for a superficial burn on your finger is to soak it in cool water for several minutes and then treat it with aloe vera cream or an antibiotic ointment before covering the area with a dry gauze bandage.

TRICKS OF THE TRADE

Keep burned food off the floor of the oven When cooking a dish in the oven, line the rack below it with aluminum foil so that if anything spills during cooking, all you have to do is pull the foil out afterward. If you are baking something that is likely to bubble over – such as an apple pie – put an aluminum foil-lined pan underneath for double protection.

Kitchen clutter

■ TABLES AND WORKTOPS

My kitchen is littered with mail, newspapers and homework

GET A ROLL-AROUND FILE CABINET The kitchen is a great place for opening mail, reading newspapers and doing homework. The problem is the newspapers, magazines, letters, notebooks, books and other stuff that pile up on the table and worktops. These things need a place they can be stored in the kitchen but out of the way. If you have a reasonably-sized kitchen and a little spare space, an easy answer is a small portable filing cabinet on wheels, that can be found at any stationary shop. Put an in-tray on top for mail. Students get the filing drawer for homework materials. Simply roll the file cabinet under the worktop or the kitchen table or into an out-of-the way corner.

A filing cabinet with wheels is a fast fix for the collection of clutter on the kitchen table.

GET A POCKET OR A STAND FOR PERIODICALS The portable filing cabinet may come with a side pocket for newspapers or magazines. If it is not big enough, see if there is room in the kitchen for one of the wooden magazine racks that many people keep in their living rooms or downstairs toilets.

TRY MAKING A WORK SPACE As an alternative to the portable filing cabinet, consider a small permanent cabinet or a small two-shelf bookcase that you can position discreetly as a designated homework space. It may not be a typical kitchen design, but it will keep the rest of your kitchen clear for culinary pursuits.

■ FRIDGE CLUTTER

My fridge is full of leftovers

THROW OUT USELESS LEFTOVERS Accept a radical idea: it is sometimes okay to throw away food. The four squishy asparagus spears and the rubbery leftover hamburger patty wrapped in aluminum foil are no more 'wasted' in the bin than they are taking up space in the fridge. All vegetable waste can be put out onto a compost heap but meat leftovers cannot. But if you're strict, you can rid your fridge of many of its accumulated leftovers immediately.

MAKE A LEFTOVER SUPPER Plan on having leftovers for dinner. Take out and open every leftover you have saved – fridge and freezer. (The one exception is food you have frozen for a specific future use, such as spaghetti sauce.) If it looks or smells funny, if you can't tell what it is or if you doubt that anybody will eat it, throw it out. You may throw out a lot of old food and feel a bit guilty, but it is a one-time fix that's worth it.

Now, reheat (if appropriate) and serve for dinner all the leftovers that are left. You may end up with a dozen different small servings, a sort of mini buffet. Or you may need to cook more food to fill out the meal. Either way, nothing will be left over. It will either be eaten or thrown away and your fridge will be leftover free.

Sauces and dressings are taking over the fridge

TAKE CONTROL Sauces and dressings have a way of hiding when you need them and getting in the way when you don't. To take control, start by checking whether each condiment needs to be refrigerated in the first place. Ketchup is usually exempt from the 'refrigerate after opening' requirement. Check the expiry dates on all your sauces and dressings; then open them up and sniff for freshness. Throw out any that have expired or that have gone off.

KEEP EVERYDAY DRESSINGS HANDY Put the three or four items you use virtually every day – mayonnaise, mustard, ketchup or your favourite salad dressing – in a prominent, easily accessible part of your fridge, perhaps in a door shelf.

PUT THE OTHERS TOGETHER IN ONE AREA Keep the rest of the sauces and dressings together in their own home – in a contained space so that they can't scatter. Ideally, designate a fridge door shelf as a sauce and dressing zone. If space is tight, use a lidless plastic container to keep them together. You will always know exactly where your sauces and dressings are and access to them will be as easy as pulling out the plastic container.

Finding food fast in the kitchen

You will save yourself a lot of headaches looking for food if you follow a few simple principles, suggested by professional organisers:

• Turn cans so their labels face to the front, and line up boxes so you can see what's inside them.

• Stock cans, jars and bottles of the same item in rows on shelves, running from back to front. When you have just one left in the back, put that item on your shopping list.

• Group foods by meal type or ethnicity. Keep pasta and sauces together or group beans and pulses. Put all canned fruit in one area and dessert ingredients in another. You will not only know where everything is, but you will be able to quickly assemble the ingredients for a meal.

GIVE AWAY ONES YOU WILL NEVER USE AGAIN Get rid of 'single-use' sauces and dressings. Tartar sauce and mint jelly are not single-use items – you will want them for your next fish or lamb dinner. But the exotic banana chutney you bought for a special duck dish is probably unlikely to be used again. Give the unused portion and the recipe to a food-loving friend or neighbour.

■ FOOD AND SUPPLIES

I hate having to throw away food that's past its use by date

STORE FOOD SO YOU USE THE OLDEST FIRST If you frequently throw out packaged food because it has passed its use by date, use the LIFO (Last In, First Out) method of stocking. Put new purchases at the back of a shelf or the bottom of a stack so you will always use up the oldest (and easiest to find) food first.

My food cupboards are a jumble of bags and boxes

PUT LIKE ITEMS TOGETHER IN BASKETS To control the mess of boxes and bags in a cupboard, you need some flat-bottomed baskets or low-sided wooden boxes that are not quite as deep as your shelves and around 30cm wide. Kitchen shops can give you lots of attractive options, or you can simply cut down the sides of some cardboard boxes and use those. Line up the boxes on the shelves and assign a category of food to each. One box could hold sweet items – white sugar, brown sugar, syrup, vanilla, treacle, sugar cubes and so on. Another could be for baking-related items, such as flour, breadcrumbs and cornflour. Even breakfast cereals could have a box. However you organise your containers, future fumbling and searching should be limited to an area the size of your box or basket, which you can easily pull out and set on the table or worktop for hassle-free searching.

I can never find the can I'm looking for

INSTALL STEPPED MINISHELVES To control the chaos of cans in a food cupboard, try a staircase-style mini shelf unit. You can find these two or three-tiered shelves at kitchen shops or at Lakeland. Buy one about one can height short of touching the shelf above it and one can width less wide than the main shelf you will be setting it on. Fill the mini shelves with cans. Now you should be able to see the can you want, but you can also pull it out without toppling others.

Packets are falling from every shelf

PUT THEM IN TRANSPARENT CONTAINERS Use see-through, stackable plastic containers to hold loose packets of soup mix, hot chocolate drinks, tea and sauces. They'll be much easier to find than if they are tucked away in piles of plastic bags. Also re-package cereal, pasta, rice and beans – half-empty boxes and bags are space wasters and are almost impossible to keep tidy. Most dried foods can be emptied into large jars with tight-fitting tops or into airtight stackable plastic containers. Kitchen shops carry attractive sturdy glass or plastic containers or you can convert jars you already have. If you have space on a worktop or on top of wall cabinets, keep jars of dried foods outside the cupboard, where you won't forget where they are.

The same principle applies to dried dog and cat food. A large, rigid container on the floor, such as a big lidded bucket, will keep your pet's food easily accessible without incurring spills.

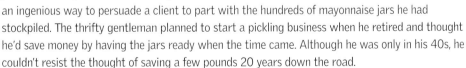

WORLD-CLASS **FIX**

THE COST OF KITCHEN CLUTTER

Today, there are people who actually get paid to suggest ways to de-clutter your home, including your kitchen. Identifying clutter sources is easy. Persuading their perpetrators to get rid of them is often harder. Christy Best, a professional organiser from Birmingham found an ingenious way to persuade a client to part with the hundreds of mayonnaise jars he had stockpiled. The thrifty gentleman planned to start a pickling business when he retired and thought he'd save money by having the jars ready when the time came. Although he was only in his 40s, he couldn't resist the thought of saving a few pounds 20 years down the road.

Best fought fire with fire. She calculated the total value of his mortgage plus household expenses. She divided that number by the square footage of his expensive home. The resulting figure explained to the jar hoarder how much it was costing him to store those containers. Surely there were better uses for such expensive space. Once he saw the figure, he got rid of the jars.

I don't have enough shelves for food

INSTALL WIRE SHELVES Use freestanding, plastic-coated wire units to create more horizontal space. These 'helper shelves' let you store twice as many cans, boxes or other items on a given shelf without perilously piling them on top of each other. They are widely available at home and kitchen stores and online at Lakeland.

I need more shelves for food

PUT SCREW-TOP JARS UNDER SHELVES If there is a lot of space wasted between shelves, try this trick from the workshop: attach jars with screw tops to the underside of the shelves. Using a small nail and a hammer, punch a hole into each metal jar lid. Then screw the lid to the shelf using 125mm wood screws. Install a lid about every 12.5cm. Then fill the jars with rice, dried beans and other ingredients and screw them into their lids.

I want a storecupboard but don't have space

CONVERT A SMALL CUPBOARD Even the smallest flat or cottage usually has a cupboard near the kitchen that can be treated as a storecupboard. The key is to adopt the same principles used in larger spaces. Organise the space by putting the most frequently used items in front. Group like items together. And use sliding shelves, lazy Susans and door-mounted racks or shelves to make the most of the space. Install a small light on the 'ceiling' of the cupboard to complete the pocket-sized storecupboard.

I have six half-empty boxes of snack bars

PUT THEM IN A BASKET Put an open-topped basket on a shelf and dump chocolate bars, cereal bars and similar items into it. It's up to you whether you make the basket easily accessible to your children (or yourself) or place it on a higher shelf out of reach of temptation.

I collect, but don't use exotic foods

MAKE SPECIAL MEALS TO USE THEM UP Instead of letting rarely used foods languish in your cupboards or throwing them away, use them as an excuse for creative cooking. Every month or so, explore your cupboards and pick out one or two things that you haven't used in ages. Now go through your cookbooks and create a meal plan that uses those ingredients. You will have more room in the cupboards and your family or guests will get a surprise meal

My spices are in permanent disarray

GET A SPICE RACK Store spices together in a way that you can see and choose what you are looking for without moving the rest. A spice rack is the best solution if your spices are in, or can be put in, bottles that fit the rack and if you have a convenient place to put the rack – a handy exposed wall or the inside of a cabinet door. But spice rack stuffed into a food cupboard with everything else will end up creating more disarray, not less.

GET A LAZY SUSAN If you have a potpourri of containers that don't always fit right in a spice rack, put them on a revolving lazy Susan. A lazy Susan can accommodate spice containers of any shape – tall skinny bottles, short fat ones, little bags, bigger bags and plastic containers as well as the classic little bottles. And as long as you keep it on a shelf at or near eye level, you can easily spot the spice you are looking for as you turn the tray.

I have more spices than will fit on a rack

FILE THEM IN A DRAWER If you are a true spice aficionado, do what many chefs do: buy a supply of sturdy medium-sized zip-sealing plastic bags. Except for the three or four spices you use most often, transfer each of your spices from its store container to its own plastic bag. Use masking tape and a permanent marker to label each spice bag. Date the bag as well, because spices do lose their potency and should be replaced after a year or even sooner. Give your spice bags their own drawer and simply line them up in alphabetical order. Provided you remember to put the spice bag back in its proper place, finding a spice is just a matter of opening the drawer and thumbing through the rows.

Utensil drawer
If your kitchen utensil
drawer is stuffed to the
brim, here is how to get
it organised. Start by
getting rid of anything
that's past its best such
as rusty or broken items.

Now select the
utensils you use most
and put them handle up
in a sturdy ceramic vase
or small stainless-steel
bucket heavy enough to
hold them without
tipping. Keep this
container on the
worktop near the cooker.

Put specialist
implements that you
may not use for months
at a time – turkey
basters, barbecue
equipment – in a
bottom drawer or a
storage area.

What does that leave
in the utensil drawer?
Just the things you
want easy access to, but
don't use every day –
garlic press, corkscrew,
rolling pin.

I'm always hunting for rubbish bags

KEEP THE BAGS IN THE BIN Bin bags often end up at the back of the cupboard under the sink where they may slip out of sight – particularly irritating on the day the dustmen come. To end this little annoyance, take some or all of the bags out of their cardboard box and off the roll and separate them from one another. Put the bags loose in the bottom of the bin. Every time you take out the rubbish, there will be a fresh bag lying there ready to be used.

■ POTS, PANS AND UTENSILS

My plastic food containers have got into a real mess

REPLACE THEM WITH NEW MATCHING CONTAINERS If your plastic food containers won't stack, don't have matching lids, take up too much space and fall out when you open the cabinet door, it's probably worth starting over again. If you have a typically random collection of plastic food containers – an assortment of yoghurt containers, margarine tubs and ice cream cartons, as well as better-quality items – get rid of them – ideally by recycling. Then go out and buy brand new matching plastic containers. Buy fewer than you think you need. Most importantly, get just one shape and style and just three sizes (large, medium and small). Now matching lids to containers will be easy and they will all stack or nest together.

To keep the lids and containers from drifting apart, keep your new storage container collection in its own drawer, plastic bin or box. And don't be tempted to augment your container supply. If now and then you need extra food storage, use the disposable food-storage containers sold at supermarkets.

The stuff in my floor cupboards is impossible to access

HANG UP YOUR MOST USED POTS AND PANS Here are some steps you can take to clean out the space. Start by putting your most-used pots and pans on racks. These are simple wooden or metal bars with hooks that attach to the kitchen ceiling or wall. The holes on most pot or pan handles will fit the hooks. Just like that, you will find that you have cleared out a fair amount of clutter from your cabinet and positioned your pots and pans for easy access.

GET MIXING BOWLS THAT NEST If you don't have a set of mixing bowls that nest, buy one and give away your old ones. Three or four bowls will now take up the same space as one old one. You can even keep them on the worktop or on an overhead shelf to free up more floor cabinet space.

GIVE AWAY OR EXILE NEVER- OR RARELY USED ITEMS What about bowls that don't nest? Pots and pans that don't hang? Or a paté pan and unused popcorn maker or juicer? If you won't ever use an item, give it away. If you use it less than once a month, store it in a distant cabinet or in a box in the garage. When you do need it, you can get it.

You will still have plenty of items to keep in the cabinets, such as jugs, casserole dishes and jelly moulds.

I find it hard to reach items at the back of my floor cabinets

PUT THE ITEMS ON SLIDING RACKS To make undercounter items readily accessible, place them on sliding racks that pull out like file cabinet drawers. You can find a rack that fits your cupboards at a kitchen or DIY store. All you need is a screwdriver to install it.

One glass is stuck inside another

USE HOT AND COLD WATER Don't use brute force to pull them apart. That could lead to broken glass and cut hands. Instead, take advantage of how materials expand or contract with temperature change. Put cold water in the top glass and wait a minute while the glass contracts. Then see if it lifts right out. If not, set the bottom glass down in an inch or two of warm water in the sink or a container. Then fill the top glass with cold water. That should help you to unstick them. A word of caution: if you use the hot-and-cold combination, never use water that's extremely cold or extremely hot as the glasses may crack.

PART FOUR

Outdoors

The world outside can seem fraught with peril: insects and other creatures lurking, unruly plant life, weather disasters. And that's just in your garden. Travel further afield and you can find that the problems are magnified. But don't worry – here are lots of creative solutions to solve any problems that you may face in the great outdoors.

Outdoor maintenance

■ OUTSIDE THE HOUSE

The porch light keeps going out

USE A LOW-ENERGY FLUORESCENT BULB Many outside light fittings use traditional incandescent light bulbs. When they blow out they are sometimes difficult to get at. Replace these conventional light bulbs with low-energy compact fluorescent lights.

They not only use four to five times less energy than the old bulbs, but will last longer, and greatly reduce the maintenance needed.

Energy-saving passive infra-red security lighting is also available, which will both deter thieves and cost less to run.

My awning has a tear

USE COLOURED GAFFER TAPE If you have an awning that pulls out to give shade to a patio, they can be susceptible to high winds and may sometimes rip. The trick with a tear in an awning or tarpaulin is to stop it from spreading any further. For a quick but very effective fix, lay equal-length strips of gaffer tape on both the top and underside of the tear. Strong and waterproof, gaffer tape will withstand the elements until you can properly patch the rip. For inexpensive tarpaulins, the gaffer tape patch should be sufficient. Car-parts suppliers and DIY stores sell gaffer tape in a variety of colours, so you should be able to find tape that is a reasonable match.

If you are always changing the porch light, a quick solution is a low-energy fluorescent bulb

I have a white powdery deposit on my wall

BRUSH IT OFF A white-coloured deposit known as efflorescence sometimes forms on brick or stone walls. It is caused by salt finding its way to the surface along with moisture as a damp wall dries out. If the wall has an underlying damp problem it must first be remedied; on a new wall the building process may have caused the materials used to become damp. To remove the efflorescence don't use water but instead use a dry stiff brush and repeat the process until the deposits stop forming.

My guttering and downpipes are blocked

WORK FROM THE BOTTOM UPWARD When water seeps from a joint on a section of downpipe this indicates a blockage in the pipe somewhere between the affected joint and the outlet. Try unblocking the pipe from ground level first. Cover the gully to keep debris out and push a length of stiff wire or a running garden hose up the pipe to shift the obstruction. Failing this unblock the pipe from the top using drain rods.

BLOW DEBRIS OUT WITH A LEAF BLOWER When rain runs off the roof and into the gutter – but it doesn't come out of the downpipe, some stray debris is probably blocking the pipe. Try blasting out the offending blockage. Stick the tube of a leaf blower into the bottom of the downpipe and give it a blast of air. The pressure should blow the blockage out of the top of the gutter, relieving you of the chore of climbing up to clean it out.

I want to stop my downpipe from getting blocked

DON'T LEAVE THE LEAVES If you live in a leafy area the fallen leaves can quickly fill a gutter in autumn and cause a blockage which can lead to trouble. Inspect gutters regularly and scoop out leaves and debris so that rainwater can run freely to the downpipes. You can make a scoop from an old plastic bottle. Stuff a rag into the top of the downpipe temporarily while you are scooping out the leaves so that you don't push debris into it and create a blockage. Finally, brush the inside of the gutter clean with a brush.

STOP BLOCKAGES BEFORE THEY START A wire mesh excluder fitted at the top of the downpipe will stop potential blockages such as leaves, moss and tennis balls from getting into the pipe in the first place. You can buy them at DIY stores and building suppliers.

I want to save rainwater

DIVERT THE FLOW If you are carrying out maintenance on your downpipes, consider fitting a diverter kit at the same time. Available from most DIY stores, a diverter will send rainwater along a smaller pipe to your water butt. When the butt is full the diverter returns water back to the downpipe to avoid the butt overflowing.

Preventing roof leaks
Once a year or so, inspect your roof for deterioration and missing pieces. Check for broken or slipped tiles or slates. Check the flashings around chimneys for deterioration. Check that ridge tiles are in place and that the mortar between them is in place. You don't have to climb up there to inspect it. A pair of binoculars is a great aid in getting a close-up view from the ground.

My gutters are always leaking

REPLACE LEAKING RUBBER GUTTERING SEALS Leaking guttering can be a major annoyance and can cause serious and potentially extremely expensive damage to the fabric of your house. On plastic guttering the source of the leak is often simply a perished rubber seal that is found on the unions between sections of gutter. On some makes of gutter you may be able to buy a replacement rubber seal, but on others you may have to buy the whole union as they are produced with the seals already bonded on.

How do I maintain old cast-iron guttering?

PAINT, CHECK AND SEAL JOINTS REGULARLY Many houses still have old cast-iron guttering and downpipes and many homeowners prefer the aesthetic appeal of the older material. But maintaining old cast-iron guttering can be far more of a headache than the plastic equivalent.

If you are a fan of your cast-iron guttering, the key points to bear in mind are these: keep out corrosion by regularly painting, checking and sealing joints with a proprietary roof and gutter sealant. If a section of cast-iron guttering or a downpipe becomes damaged you may be able to carry out a repair with self-adhesive flashing tape (see opposite) or a glass fibre repair kit. Otherwise you may need to make a trip to an architectural salvage company to find a suitable match. To preserve the metal on the inside of the gutter apply bituminous paint to keep rust away.

I want to paint my downpipe but not the wall behind it

SHIELD THE WALL Use a large piece of card to protect the wall when painting downpipes. This will ensure that you can paint right around the back of the downpipe without getting any paint on your brickwork or rendering.

I think I have damp on my wall – can I fix it without spending a fortune?

CHECK OUT THE DAMP-PROOF COURSE If you think you may have a rising damp problem on a wall in your house, search out the damp-proof course and make sure it isn't covered by a flowerbed, path or patio – before you call in the professionals. Also check that render has not been applied over the top of the course. Even piles of soil thrown against the base of a wall can bridge the damp course. Removing any material that is breaching the damp-proof course could solve your problem at little or no cost.

ROOFS

The lead flashing on my roof is loose

CLEAN OUT AND FILL Where the roof covering meets the wall there is an additional covering known as a flashing to seal the joint. Flashings that are fitted when a house is built are usually made of strips of lead which are then tucked into the mortar joints. If this kind of flashing becomes loose it is often due to the mortar cracking where the lead is tucked in.

To fix a loose flashing, rake out the loose mortar and push the edge of the flashing back into the gap between the courses of bricks. Wedge the flashing in place with blocks of wood and fill the gap with new mortar or a proprietary lead flashing mastic. When set, remove the blocks and fill the holes left with the same material.

USE FLASHING TAPE TO MAKE A REPAIR Leaking flashing can be repaired with self adhesive flashing tape. This tape comprises an aluminium foil backing joined to a bitumen adhesive compound to accommodate movement. It is supplied on a roll and comes in a variety of widths. Some brands come with a flashing primer which needs to be applied to the roof before the tape.

I need to replace a tile on my roof

KEEP SPARE TILES If you have an old roof with an unusual pattern of tile, search out some spares at an architectural salvage company. Or ask a neighbour with a similar roof covering if they can let you have a spare tile or two. It is always useful to store a handful of spare tiles or slates to match your roof covering. If one blows off during bad weather you will quickly be able to lay your hands on a replacement.

It is raining and my flat roof has sprung a leak

USE A SPECIAL RESIN COATING For a quick emergency fix, ask a roofing supplier for a resin-based fibre-reinforced coating: brand names for these products include Flag Roofix 20/10 and Rustoleum

How not to clean a deck

Don't use a pressure washer or a chlorine bleach solution to clean your deck. A pressure washer will erode the wood grain, making the boards rough. And chlorine bleach takes the colour out of the wood and weakens the fibres. It also corrodes the nails or screws.

Fillcoat. These are suitable for use on most types of roof including asphalt, roofing felt, metal, slate and tiles. You will need to clean the area thoroughly first to get rid of any dirt and debris, then apply the coating with a brush. The resin coating can even be applied to a wet surface – but it must be clean. Once the coating is in place it will be able to resist water straightaway.

There are blisters in the felt on my flat roof

PRICK THE BLISTER Use a trimming knife to make a cross-cut over the blister, taking care not to cut through the layer of felt below. Peel back the flaps and thoroughly dry the area underneath using a hot-air gun (you could also use a hair drier if you don't have a hot-air gun). Spread cold-applied felt adhesive to the exposed area and press the flaps back into place. When they have fully bonded, seal the cuts with heavy-duty bituminous mastic and replace the chippings.

My metal roof is covered in moss

TREAT IT WITH A FUNGICIDE If you live in a house with a flat roof that is covered in lead, zinc or copper you can prevent acid attack from moss or lichen by treating it regularly with a fungicide. You can patch any splits in the metal strip with self-adhesive flashing tape as described on page 201.

I need to be able to stand on my flat roof

STAND ON BOARDS Flat roofs are generally not designed for access. If you have to climb on one lay boards down to spread your weight. Don't walk on the unprotected roof – your weight will push the chippings through the felt-and take care not to drop heavy tools. If you stand a ladder on a flat roof, rest its feet on a board and secure the ladder so that the feet cannot slide outwards.

■ DECKS AND PATIOS

My decking needs cleaning

USE A SPECIALISED PRODUCT If your deck has become very dirty, use a product specifically designed for cleaning decks. After sweeping away as much debris as you can, brush the product into the wood, leave for about 20 minutes, then rinse off. Check that the cleaner you choose is suitable for your type of deck and wait at least two days before applying any protective coatings. For an eco-friendly and very cheap alternative, brush off debris and wash the deck down with a solution of warm water and soda crystals.

I need to age new paving stones so that they match the rest of the patio

KEEP THEM OUTSIDE If you install a path or patio made of bricks or paving stones, store some extras outside. When one becomes cracked or damaged you'll be able to replace it, as well as any others that may get damaged during the repair process. By keeping the replacements outdoors, they will weather at the same rate.

My patio has a sunken brick

PRISE THE BRICK OUT AND FILL UNDER IT It is easy to fix a sunken brick on a patio, but you must first remove it. Here's how:

1 Slide a thin chisel or a stiff filling knife into the crack between the sunken brick and a neighbouring one. Wiggle the tool back and forth to create a bigger gap. Repeat on all four sides.
2 When you have created a gap on all sides, use the tip or edge of the chisel or knife to prise the brick upward. You may need to prise it up from all four sides. Raise the brick far enough so that you can grab it with fingertips and pull it out.
3 Put sand into the hole from which the brick was removed. Tamp it down with a mallet or other heavy object. Keep adding sand and compacting it until the surface is level with the sand under the surrounding bricks.
4 Set the extracted brick back into the hole. Drive it into place by laying a short board over it and tapping it with a rubber mallet until it sits level with the surrounding bricks.

■ DRIVEWAYS

My concrete driveway is cracked

FILL IT WITH AN EPOXY COMPOUND If a concrete driveway or path is cracked, it is essential to attend to it as soon as you can, before water that has frozen inside the crack or the weight of a car passing over it has increased the damage. If you catch it early enough –

while the crack is half a centimetre wide or less – fixing it is very simple and takes just a few minutes.

Get a tube of concrete-patching compound at a DIY store. This is a special epoxy-type material that is slightly flexible so that it can expand and contract with the concrete. It comes in a tube that fits into a standard mastic gun.

First blow any dust and debris out of the crack or clean it out thoroughly with a wire brush. Be sure to wear goggles. Then, following the directions on the label, squeeze the material into the crack and smooth it with a filling knife until it sits level with the surrounding concrete. Allow the compound to dry before driving over the cracked area again.

My car has leaked oil on to the driveway

ABSORB IT WITH CAT LITTER You can buy absorbent products especially marketed for soaking up oil spills on your garage floor or driveway. But there's nothing that works better, is handier and is less expensive than cat litter. Just pour cheap, basic cat litter over the oil and let it soak up the liquid for one hour. Then sweep the litter into a dustpan and discard it.

▥ OUTDOOR FURNITURE

My metal garden furniture is rusted

POWER-BRUSH OFF THE RUST AND PAINT When the paint on mild steel or cast-iron furniture deteriorates corrosion will appear in the form of rust. If left, the rust will eat away at the metal as well as discolouring the surrounding paintwork.

Wearing safety goggles and a dust mask, remove the blistered paint and rust with a wire brush or sander. According to the scale of the job, there are various power sanders or wire brush attachments for power drills available to make this task less laborious. If the rust is widespread and the furniture is valuable, it may be worth considering a professional shot-blasting service to strip the furniture back to clean bare metal. (Normally, as the process creates a lot of mess, a contractor would take the item away to do this in a controlled environment.) Beware of sanding old lead paint which is poisonous. Once the furniture is free of rust and the finish is a bright bare metal, prime with a good-quality rust inhibiting metal primer and apply a suitable protective top coat. Rusty screws, nuts, bolts and washers can also be replaced with new ones – possibly ones which will not corrode in the future, such as stainless steel.

My plastic resin garden furniture has mildew

WASH IT WITH A BLEACH SOLUTION If you don't want to sit on your moulded plastic garden chair because it's already occupied by a lower life form (we're talking about mildew), there is a quick answer. Mix a solution of 1 part chlorine bleach to 4 parts water. Wearing rubber gloves, scrub the furniture with a sponge or brush dipped in the solution. Then rinse with a hose.

My aluminium patio furniture is tarnished

WASH WITH VINEGAR SOLUTION; THEN APPLY CAR WAX Polished aluminium will tarnish over time and corrosion will make it dull and pitted. To brighten aluminium furniture, wash it with a solution of 4 litres of water and 4 tablespoons of vinegar. If the surface is pitted, use a soapy steel wool pan cleaner to smooth it out. Rinse carefully to remove any traces of the steel wool, as rusting steel could discolour the furniture. Finally coat the aluminium with a thin layer of protective car wax.

My patio chair's webbing is unravelling

STOP THE FRAYING WITH A MATCH FLAME One little nick on the edge of a folding patio chair's plastic webbing and before you know it the fabric is fraying and unravelling, weakening the seat and turning it into a hazard for a potential sitter. But there is a simple solution: simply strike a match or turn on a lighter and run the flame quickly across the frayed edges. Apply just enough heat so that the material melts slightly and forms globs along the edge. Always do this outside and be very careful not to burn yourself with the flame or the hot edge of the material.

I want to keep wooden furniture looking good

CLEAN AND PROTECT IN AUTUMN Most wooden garden furniture will age and fade if it is not protected. Hardwood is the most durable, but treated softwoods such as pine are fine if they are properly maintained. To keep wooden furniture looking good, wash

Get a good handle on your tools
Sometimes the handle on a spade, garden fork, or other outdoor tool isn't up to the challenge of a heavy job and snaps.

To stop this hapening, condition the wooden handles on your tools with linseed oil once a year. Just soak a rag in the oil and rub it down the length of the handle. Dry handles become more likely to break; the moisture from the linseed oil helps to preserve their flexibility.

But to avoid having it slip out of your hands and cause an accident, wait until the oil is well absorbed into the handle before you use the tool.

Store your tools indoors or in a storage shed, too. Don't leave them exposed to the elements.

down the surfaces regularly with soap and water and treat with a wood stain or a coating such as linseed oil. The best time to do this is on a dry autumn day. Pay particular attention to horizontal surfaces that are exposed to more of the elements as well as areas that may collect water or are in contact with damp soil. If you want to keep the colour or finish of a table or bench it is worth protecting it with a sturdy tarpaulin.

■ BARBECUES

My barbecue is caked with dirt and grease

DON'T CLEAN THE INSIDE OF THE GRILL If it's been a hot summer and you've been making maximum use of your barbecue, it will probably be full of grease by the end of summer. But cleaning away a greasy, sooty build-up may be quicker and easier than you think. To start with, it's not necessary to scrub the interior of your grill, whether you have a charcoal grill or a gas grill. In fact, allowing residue from cooking smoke to accumulate inside the grill seasons it, imparting a better flavour to the food you cook. This is similar to seasoning a new cast-iron grill pan or wok with oil before you cook with it. You may even want to season a new grill before using it for the first time.

If you are bothered by flaky material falling off the inside of the grill, just remove it at the end of summer using a wet, soapy sponge, followed by a wipe with a wet, non-soapy sponge. That is all you need to do.

CLEAN THE GRATE WHILE IT'S HOT Although you will save time by not cleaning the inside of the grill, experts do advise that you regularly clean the grate that holds the food. Greasy clumps of burnt food that accumulate on this grate can give an unpleasant flavour to the next round of food you grill.

To clean the grate easily, first pre-heat the grill with the lid down for a few minutes until the grate is hot. Then scrub it with a long-handled brass-bristled brush. Be careful not to touch the hot grate with your hand.

Do this after you've finished cooking. If you clean the grate like this each time you use it, it should never get so messy that you need to remove it for a more heavy-duty cleaning.

Gardening problems

■ PLANNING AND TENDING

I need help in planning my garden

CHECK OUT NEIGHBOURS' GARDENS Gardening experts often say that planning a garden is just a matter of putting the right plant in the right place. But in practice, it can be hard to know what is the right plant for the right place. If you're new to gardening, where can you turn for help?

If you can, start with your neighbours. Walk around the neighbourhood and make a note of the gardens that catch your eye. Ask your neighbours what kinds of plants they enjoy and how much maintenance they require. Gardeners tend to love talking about their work. You will get ideas for plants you would like to have in your own garden, as well as tips on where to buy them and how to care for them. Neighbouring gardeners may even offer you plants or cuttings to get started with.

If you don't have helpful gardeners in your neighbourhood, attend local horticultural society meetings or visit a plant nursery or two. Some nurseries may offer gardening courses in spring and should be good sources of information about weather and soil conditions for gardening in your area.

If you are not sure what to do with your garden, an instant solution is to steal a good idea from someone else.

I would like to save money on seeds

COLLECT SEEDS FROM THE GARDEN Vegetable gardens are the gift that keeps on giving. If you collect the seeds properly, you won't have to buy new ones to start the new crop the following year. Keep these tips in mind:

- Find out whether your vegetables are hybrids. The packet they came in will have this information. If they are hybrids, don't bother keeping the seeds, because you will just get a wide variation in the quality of the vegetables next year.

Plan before you plant

Just sticking plants in randomly around the garden can lead to problems. When planning your garden, keep in mind the following questions:

• What kind of budget do you have? It will cost money to buy plants and to maintain them.

• How much time will you have to feed, water, weed and do the other chores a garden needs?

• What colours do you want in your garden? When during the year do you want them to peak?

• What kind of soil do you have? How well does it drain? How much wind, sunlight and shade do you get?

Once you have all this information, use graph paper to make a blueprint of your garden and where you would like the plants to go.

Old-fashioned varieties of vegetables are typically not hybrid, so seeds from plants grown from their seeds should be okay.

• Make sure you give the plant enough time to produce good seeds. Some vegetable plants, such as tomatoes and peppers, need to be ripe or slightly overripe. Before the seeds of beans and peas are mature they should be left in their pods to dry and sweetcorn should be left until the ears and kernels are dried on the cob. It is probably not worth trying to obtain seeds from carrots, beets, lettuce, cabbage, broccoli or radishes, as they don't produce seeds in the same year that they produce a crop.

• Take your seeds from fully ripe, good-quality large vegetables and spread them on paper towels in a warm, dry, shaded location for two to three weeks, until they are completely dry. Remove any bits of dried pulp or debris from the seeds – using your mouth to blow the material away sometimes does the trick. Then place the seeds in containers for storage.

• Store the seeds in a cool, dry place. They can keep for up to three years if they are stored well. A good spot for them is in a sealed jar or plastic container in a refrigerator.

• Take the seeds out of the refrigerator a week before you plan to use them and let them warm up to room temperature and adjust to the humidity. This is particularly important for beans and peas, which develop a hard coating during storage that can make sprouting difficult if they not been allowed to warm up before they are planted.

I want to start seeds indoors

USE PLASTIC FOOD CONTAINERS The simple solution is to start saving clear-topped containers from takeaway salads or delicatessens. These containers are perfect for starting seeds indoors, either at a window that gets a lot of natural indirect light or under an artificial plant light. Wash each container and fill the bottom with a lightly moistened seed compost. Place the seeds and close the lid, securing it with a rubber band. The clear lid allows light to pass through, holds moisture in and lets you keep track of your sprouting seeds. If the containers are next to a window, be sure to turn them regularly so that the seedlings don't tend to lean one way. Or place an aluminium foil reflector behind the containers to even out the light. Putting reflectors on three sides of – and under – the containers is a good idea if your window doesn't have sufficient light.

Herbs are hijacking my garden

PREVENT HERB ROOTS FROM SPREADING Whether the herbs are in the garden or on your plate, the same holds true: a few are nice, but you don't want them on everything. Gardeners soon discover that some herbs like to take over their surroundings.

Oregano, thyme and mints are particularly notorious for busting out all over and spreading by underground runners. To keep them in their place, cut the bottoms out of some large, wide-bottomed buckets. Sink the buckets 45cm into the ground and plant the herbs in them. The underground roots will be contained within the bucket deep underground and should not take over the rest of the garden.

I have a clump of perennials that's looking a bit past its best

DIVIDE PERENNIALS TO KEEP THEM HEALTHY Some perennials (plants that live over from one growing season to another) multiply by putting out adjacent roots and stems, so you can end up with a cluster of plants growing out from the centre, which may not be the effect that you are after. Moreover, the leaves and flowers at the centre of clumps of perennials may become sickly and weak looking, a signal that too many plants are competing for food and moisture.

The solution is to uproot the clustered perennials occasionally and divide them into pieces. The separate pieces, which will grow into replicas of the parent plant, can be planted elsewhere in the garden or you can pass them on to a friend or fellow gardener.

Here are some tips to keep in mind when dividing perennials:

- Divide plants when the flowers are dormant. For instance, if the perennial flowers in spring, divide it in late summer or in autumn. If it flowers in late summer, divide it in spring.

- Dig about 15cm around the plant with a spade or shovel. When the plant has been loosened, pull it out of the ground. Once it is out, experienced gardeners say, you can sometimes reach into the clump and pull the roots apart easily with your fingers. But if the clump is tightly bound, you will need to cut it in half or into several sections.

If you're not sure where one plant ends and another begins, put the cluster in a bucket of water and wash off as much soil as you can. This will help you to see where to divide the cluster.

I want to sow seeds in straight lines

USE A CORD AND STAKES To establish straight rows in a garden, tap in a small stake at each end of the row. Then stretch a cord between them. Carefully sow the seeds along the line made by the string. When you've finished planting the row, move the stakes into position to mark the next row.

■ NURTURING PLANTS

I keep feeding my vegetables, but they don't perk up

USE FERTILISER WITH CARE One mistake gardeners commonly make is to overfeed plants, which can damage their roots and lead to poor fruiting, poor flavour and excessive top growth. In fact, some horticulturists believe that many more problems can be attributed to overfeeding than to underfeeding.

Fertilisers, which provide nitrogen (N), phosphorus (P) and potassium (K), are a good way to give your plants the nutrients they need. (The three numbers prominently featured on fertiliser labels represent the percentages of these nutrients in this order.) You can test a sample of your soil using a kit from a garden centre (see box, right). If know nothing about its fertility, you can judge more accurately what type of fertiliser the soil needs.

Keep in mind that more fertiliser isn't better. In general, you should apply less than the bag suggests; certainly don't apply more than indicated. Most packages recommend using a strong dose so that you will need to purchase more product. Don't go above the recommendation on the package unless you know that your soil really needs the extra nutrients.

Most plants prefer a pH of 6.5 to 7 – the point where nutrients are most easily available. The soil type is determined by relative quantities of organic matter, rock and mineral particles. The pH of soil can be tested with a simple testing kit. The solution will turn yellow-orange for acid soil, green for neutral and dark green for alkaline. Ericaceous plants such as rhododendrons need acid soil, while others, such as lilacs grow better in an alkaline soil.

Another way of determining soil type is to pick up some damp soil and rub it between your fingers: clay soil is sticky and can be rolled into a ball; sandy soil feels gritty and loose; silty soil feels smooth and can be rolled but not balled; loamy soil is brown with lots of organic matter; chalky soil is light, does not hold water and is always alkaline; peaty soil is almost black, spongy and holds a lot of water.

My plants need an extra boost

ADD SOME BENEFICIAL FUNGI Whenever you plant seeds or seedlings or transplant a plant, consider adding some mycorrhizal fungi to the soil or sprinkling it on the roots of the plants before you plant them. These fungi are becoming a popular tool for gardeners. They form a beneficial relationship with the plant, improving its root system's ability to pull nutrients from the ground. This allows the plant to grow stronger and larger.

Brands of mycorrhizal fungi that you may find in nurseries or garden centres include Rootgrow.

I want compost – not a lifetime project

ENCIRCLE A COMPOST PILE WITH STRAW Some gardeners take their compost heaps very seriously. You can find entire books on the topic and you can spend a lot of time measuring ingredients and tending the heap. It is true that compost, which is a mixture of leaves and grass clippings, table scraps and other natural wastes, decomposes and enriches the existing soil with nutrients. But you don't have to lavish a lot of attention on your compost pile for it to be successful, say experienced gardeners.

Here is a simple way to generate compost if you have enough space in your garden. Buy a couple of bales of straw at a garden centre, and break them into chunks. Use these chunks to make a 1.2m circle. Fill it with leaves, grass clippings, table scraps, fruit and vegetable peelings and even weeds and old plants.

Avoid putting in meat, fat and bones or pet droppings, which can spread disease and attract pests. Sprinkle a little soil and some more straw on top. As your layers of compost grow taller, keep stacking

chunks of straw on the circle which should eventually start to look like a little igloo.

Let the mound decompose over several months and you will end up with superb compost to spread on the garden.

Composting takes forever

PUREE SCRAPS FOR FASTER DECOMPOSITION An easy way to speed up the composting process is to take the fruit and vegetable peelings, eggshells and other easily biodegradable scraps (no meat or dairy) that you have collected and put them in a blender along with a cup of water. Purée the scraps and pour the mixture on the compost pile. The mush will decompose quickly – usually in a few weeks. To minimise the mess, collect the scraps in a small plastic bag or a special bucket and purée them every few days.

■ URBAN GARDENING

My plot is too tiny for a proper garden

GROW PLANTS IN CONTAINERS Even if you have some outdoor space, you might not have enough for a fully planted garden. Growing plants in containers might be a solution. Just keep the following hints from gardening experts in mind:

- Use large enough containers to ensure that your plants will have plenty of room to grow. Ask a local nursery how much soil each plant will need. Although vegetables have been developed that don't require as much growing space, some still need a lot of soil. For example, you would need at least a 20 litre container for a single tomato plant.
- Use potting soil in your containers rather than soil from the ground. Potting soil is lighter, drains better and is sterilised to kill weed seeds and diseases that could damage your plants.
- Use a slow-release fertiliser in pellet form. As you need to water container plants frequently, an ordinary fertiliser would tend to wash right out of the soil. But in pellet form, a single application will release the plant food slowly and last for several months.
- Don't overwater your plants. Make sure that you thoroughly soak the entire container each time you water, but pour away any extra water that fills the saucer underneath the container.

Allowing a plant to sit in water encourages root rot. Since the signs of rot include wilting, many people think that the plant needs *more* water, which does even more damage. If you're not sure whether the wilting is from too much or too little water, gently pull the plant up out of the container. If the roots are brown and slimy, it's root rot. Water it less.

I'd love to garden, but I live in a flat

USE BASKETS AND PLASTIC POTS Even if you live in a high-rise building far above the nearest soil, let alone gardening space, you can still grow plants in containers and hanging baskets. For a successful high-rise garden keep these tips in mind:

- In tall buildings, balconies can get extremely hot and dry from sunlight reflected off the building, so you may need to water your plants every day. Since you'll probably be carrying water from your sink or bath tap, keep this chore in mind when you're planning how many plants to grow.
- Use plastic pots rather than clay pots. Plants in plastic dry out less quickly because the pots aren't porous like clay ones. Put 5cm of an organic mulch on top of the soil to reduce water evaporation.
- When you're planning for hanging baskets, consider how you are going to water them. Can you safely stand on a step stool and water with a watering can? Will you get tired of taking the basket down to water it frequently?

My house plants will die if I go away

ADD WATER-RELEASING GRANULES A fast, affordable and practical solution is to stock up on special granules that soak up and then gradually release water. Specific brands include SwellGel, which are sold by garden centres and garden products websites. When you add water to these polymer granules, they absorb many times their weight in water. By mixing them in with the soil in your containers and then watering, the granules soak up and then slowly release the water to keep your plants watered while you are away.

Be sure to follow directions on the label, because putting more granules in a container is not necessarily better. Since they expand when wet, if there are too many granules, they can swell up and damage your plant or push it out of the pot.

Patrol your garden daily

To minimise problems like insect infestations, diseases and wilting, spend 5 minutes every day walking around your plants and inspecting them. By giving plants a frequent once-over, you should catch problems early enough and you may be able to fix them quickly, as opposed to waiting until the damage is severe and requires a lot of work.

I am worried that the vegetables I grow may be contaminated

TEST THE SOIL AND CHANGE PLANTINGS ACCORDINGLY Researchers studying soil have found that people who grow vegetables in urban areas may be getting extra ingredients in their vegetables: traces of metals such as cadmium and lead.

Lead in particular is dangerous for unborn babies and children. It can cause developmental problems in the brain and nervous system, including mental impairment. Lead accumulates in soil in urban areas from chips of paint from older homes that were long ago painted with lead-based paint or from the exhaust of vehicles that burned leaded petrol decades ago.

Here is what gardening experts suggest you do if you are gardening in an older urban area that may have grown up close to polluting industries or if you live near a major road and are concerned that your soil may be contaminated. Take a soil sample and have it tested for lead. There are specialised companies that do this kind of testing. If you find that the soil has a high level of lead, you have these alternatives:

- Grow flowers instead of vegetables.
- Stick with 'fruiting' vegetables like tomatoes. They accumulate less lead. Steer clear of leafy vegetables, such as lettuce and spinach and root vegetables, such as carrots, potatoes and beetroot. They absorb more lead than other vegetables.
- Grow your vegetables in containers or raised beds. Fill the containers with potting soil. Fill the raised beds with new topsoil and compost that you have brought in from elsewhere. You should have the soil for your raised beds tested before you plant things in it to make sure that it is safe as well.

  If you use raised beds, first put down a plastic barrier between your old soil and the new soil and build the beds up to 30–45cm. That should give your vegetables enough new soil for growth and the plastic will keep the roots from tapping into the lead-tainted soil.

■ TOOLS AND TECHNIQUES

My gardening sessions leave me aching

PICK COMFORTABLE TOOLS AND WORK HABITS Thinking about your garden should give you a satisfied glow. But you find that it is giving you more of a dull ache in your back, you probably need to adjust the way the way that your garden is laid out, your gardening routines and the tools that you use.

- Make sure you're using tools that fit your body. (See 'Tool School' below.)
- Examine the repetitive movements you are doing that you may not have been aware of. Are you on your knees a lot? Are you constantly using your arms above your head? Are you continually bending and twisting? All of these sequences can cause or aggravate aches and pains. You may need to sit down on a bench rather than kneel, enlist some help in the garden or find new ways to do your gardening tasks that don't involve repetitive movements.
- Break up your tasks so that you're not repeating the same motion for hours at a time. If you must pull weeds, do so for only 15 or 20 minutes at a time, then rest or tackle another chore for a while.

The easy solution to gardening aches and pains is to change the way you work.

TOOL SCHOOL

No matter how pretty your garden looks, if it leaves you with aches and pains every time you have to work in it, your garden won't be a source of joy to you.

Here are some tips on how to keep gardening from taking a toll on your body:

- Before you buy a tool, be sure to practise the motions you will be doing with it in your garden. The tool should allow you to keep your body in a neutral position that doesn't require you to bend or twist uncomfortably. The handle should be the right length, the materials shouldn't be too heavy and the tool grip should be comfortable.

- Be aware of the kind of return policy that the garden centre or catalogue operates for tools before you buy them. You should be able to return a tool if it ends up not being comfortable for you.

- Look for ergonomic tools that are designed to be especially comfortable, particularly if you have arthritis or another painful condition. If you are using a tool that does not fit your hand or body comfortably, you are likely to have to use three times more energy for tasks than you normally would. This can cause extra pain and fatigue in your hands if they are already sore. These days, many garden centres and catalogues are stocking well-designed tools for people who have special physical needs. Be aware, though, that specially designed tools may feel a little strange at first and require a little time to get used to.

My fingers are sore from pinching out buds

USE GARDEN SHEARS INSTEAD By removing buds from plants such as chrysanthemums, you can make the plant flower later in the year. However, pinching off all the little buds can be a time-consuming chore. The advice from experienced nursery workers is to forget all that pinching and use a pair of garden shears or a stringed weed trimmer. They recommend that you cut the plant off about halfway up. This will also encourage the plant to become bushy and compact rather than tall and spindly.

■ SICK PLANTS AND PESTS

My vegetable plants keep getting diseases

CHANGE YOUR WATERING SYSTEM If your vegetable plot always seems to be full of weedy and diseased plants, the problem could be the way you water the plants.

First, refrain from watering at night, say experienced vegetable growers. When plants stay wet all night, they are more vulnerable to disease. Second, keep the spray from a garden hose off the leaves and other parts of the plants that sit above ground. These don't take up water; the roots underground do. Keeping water off the plants will help to cut down on diseases.

Vegetable plants also often get diseases because they touch the ground. If your plants are prone to disease, follow these guidelines:

- Mulch properly. Mulching is great for plants in general, since it holds moisture in the soil and organic mulches can supply some nutrients as they decompose. Mulch also keeps the plants, vines and vegetables from coming into direct contact with the soil. So make sure you have a 2.5 to 7.5cm layer of organic mulch, such as wood chips, shredded bark or grass clippings, in your vegetable garden beneath your plants.

- Get your plants up off the ground. If any crop can be trellised, staked or caged to force it to grow vertically, that's good, say experts. Tomatoes are grown this way, of course, but you can do the same with cucumbers and peas. You generally get less disease and better-quality vegetables. And picking them is easier, as they are higher off the ground.

My tomatoes have black bottoms

PLANT CRUSHED EGGSHELLS WITH TOMATO PLANTS Seasons that are very wet or very dry often spell trouble for tomato plants. The tomatoes may get a condition called blossom end rot. Particularly prone are container-grown tomatoes and those grown in grow bags.

Blossom end rot causes a very nasty blackening at the bottom of the tomato fruit that makes it unusable. The problem is caused by excessive water or hot, dry temperatures. Ideally, your plants will get a long soak each week or so, but nature – or your watering schedule with the garden hose – can sometimes provide them with too much or too little water.

A solution is to share your eggs with your plants. In February, start saving eggshells. Set them in a cool, dry place for 24 hours, so they can dry out and then crush them into a powder.

When tomato-planting season comes around, put the crushed shells from a dozen eggs into each hole before you put in a tomato plant. The plant will take in the calcium from the shells, which will greatly increase its ability to regulate its own reserves of moisture, experts say. No other type of calcium seems to work as well.

Further outbreaks are most easily prevented by making sure that the compost never dries out. Or give the plants a foliar feed with calcium nitrate. If you grow tomatoes in grow bags, place a 18cm deep and 18cm diameter ring full of compost over each of the three holes made in the grow bag and set your tomatoes out in these rings. This system will gives each plant extra compost and a larger root run which will be less susceptible to drying out.

My water garden has turned into a slime garden

ADD WATER-CLARIFYING PLANTS A pond in the garden can be a tranquil spot. But they do take some work if they are to stay fresh and clear. If the water in your garden pond or water garden has become green, murky and smelly and is encrusted with a film of algae, the solution is simple and involves adding two types of plants.

- First, make sure that two-thirds of the surface of your pond is covered with floating plant material such as water lilies, and perhaps, if your pond is deep or in shade, plants such as *Nuphar luteum* and *Nymphoides peltata*. The large leaves of these surface floaters create shade, which helps to thwart the growth of sun-loving algae.

PROBLEM STOPPER

Of hoses and roses
All sorts of problems with roses are caused by improper watering. Keep these tips in mind:

• Water roses before noon. If they sit in wet soil overnight, particularly if the soil is heavy in clay and doesn't drain well, roses will get root rot. If your roses develop this problem, you may detect a distinctive smell like rotten eggs. Furthermore, any water droplets that stay on the leaves during the bright afternoon sunlight will act like magnifying glasses, burning brown spots onto the foliage.

• When you prune roses, cut the stems at a 45 degree angle. If you cut them straight across, water droplets can sit on them and soak in, causing 'die back' or a brown colouration that spreads down the stem until it kills the plant.

- Second, add some oxygenating plants. Some of these seaweed-like plants are floaters and others need to be planted on the bottom, but they stay hard at work underwater keeping the water clear. In most ponds, you plant them in a pot and then sink the pot. Adding these plants, which are available at nurseries or garden centres, should help to clear the water in a few weeks.

Slugs and snails keep eating my flowers

SET UP A COPPER BARRIER Slugs and snails have a complete aversion to copper, say those who have successfully coped with the plant-eating molluscs. This gives you an opportunity to protect outdoor plants and decorate planters and raised beds at the same time. Go to a local garden centre or nursery and buy some self-adhesive copper tape. You can also order it online. Fasten a strip of copper around the planter midway between the top and bottom – or around the rim of the pot. It makes a good looking addition to the boxes and planters and posts a warning sign that says, 'No slugs served here'. You can also buy copper coated pot feet and specially designed slug rings that are placed in the ground around growing plants.

▥ TREES

I am afraid that strong winds will damage my trees

PRUNE WEAK BRANCHES
Big and strong as most trees are, they can take a beating when a powerful wind whips through their branches. Here's how to help yours to suffer fewer broken limbs the next time they tangle with the wind:

- A general rule of thumb is to avoid what experts call double leaders – two equal-sized branches that come out of the trunk at the same spot. This causes both of them to be weaker. Which one should you remove? Cut off the branch that's emerging from the tree at a narrower angle. Limbs that come out at a right angle are stronger than those at a narrower angle. The more limbs that grow out at right angles, the stronger your tree will be.
- Book a specialist tree surgeon to check out your trees and trim hard-to-reach, weak and dead branches so they won't break off and fall on your house, your car or your head.

A snapped branch has left a wound on my tree trunk

POSSIBLY TRIM IT, BUT OTHERWISE DO NOTHING For the most part, the tree will take care of itself. Trees naturally close off wounds to prevent rot and damage from spreading. Trying to help the process along might cause additional damage. For example, packing a cavity with insulation or painting a wound will only trap moisture and promote rot. What you can do to help your tree is to prune off any remaining portions of the branch in stages, as close to the branch collar as possible without cutting into the trunk. As a preventative measure, cut off any other dead limbs before they break off.

SURELY NOT

THE PLANT THAT ATE THE AMERICAN SOUTH

In 1876, Americans got their first look at an exotic Asian plant called kudzu at the Centennial Exposition in Philadelphia. Sixty years later, during the Great Depression, farmers and government conservation workers were paid to plant it liberally to reduce soil erosion. It also made good food for farm animals.

But the planting turned out to be a *really* bad idea. The lush, vine-like kudzu eventually engulfed about 7 million acres in the southeastern United States, where it still thrives. The plant can grow 18 metres every year and smother telephone poles, homes, old cars and fields in a dense green blanket.

**Killing weeds in
paving cracks**

You can use piping-hot
water to kill weeds
that sprout through
concrete joints without
endangering yourself
or the wildlife. Boil
water in a kettle, pour
it into the cracks and
watch the weeds wilt.
Be careful not to splash
the hot water on
yourself.

▪ LAWNS

Weeds are taking over my lawn

However consciencious you are about controlling weeds, the soil in your lawn is packed *full* of weed seeds that are lying there just waiting to pop up in a bare spot in your lawn. That's a little depressing to think about, but it's true. Three simple techniques – proper mowing, fertilising and watering – will dramatically cut down on weeds invading your lawn while minimising the need for chemical herbicides, say turf specialists. Here is how these three steps can keep weeds from taking over:

MOW HIGH AND OFTEN Most home owners typically mow their grass too short and wait too long between mowings. You should usually keep your grass between 5 and 7.5cm tall. Never mow off more than a third of the height of your grass at any one time, say experts. This may require measuring the grass with a ruler and checking the lawnmower's manual to learn how to set the blade to the right height.

By mowing the grass at the correct height, the leaves will form a dense canopy over your lawn. It will also help the grass to form more new leaf-bearing shoots. Both of these factors will help to crowd out the weeds.

FERTILISE YOUR LAWN REGULARLY Depending on where you live, you will need to fertilise at different intervals. In cooler climates, lawns need to be fertilised in May, early July, early September and again in late October.

Be sure to buy fertiliser that has package directions telling you what setting to use on the kind of fertiliser spreader that you have. The setting will determine how heavily your spreader will dispense the fertiliser.

Don't worry that you will be fertilising the weeds as well. They are so adept at utilising the existing nutrients in the soil that the extra fertiliser will make little difference to them.

WATER YOUR LAWN WHEN NEEDED Most of the grasses used in lawns require about 2cm of water each week during the growing season. Signs that a lawn is in need of water are that the grass turns bluish green rather than bright green or that your footprints remain in the grass after you walk across it.

The best time to water is early in the morning before the wind and sun cause water to evaporate. Avoid watering in the evening, since the leaves will stay wet overnight, raising the risk of disease and rot. The best way to water a large lawn is with a sprinkler but this may not be possible if you live in an area where hosepipe bans and droughts are common. But if you are able to use a sprinkler, use it efficiently. Use 'grey water' accumulated from baths and washing up and collected in a water butt. To find out how much water is coming out of your sprinkler and to ensure that it's hitting your lawn evenly, place a couple of large cans around 1.5 and 6 metres away from it. Check the depth of the water that the cans have accumulated after 30 minutes and multiply by 2 to estimate the hourly amount. Move the sprinkler accordingly to spread the water around.

If you find that water is puddling on the ground, turn off the sprinkler and let the water soak in fully before completing the watering in another two or three days.

There are lots of bare patches on my lawn

Bare patches on the lawn may occur for many reasons. Some are due to pests (see page 224) but most are not. Some of the most common reasons and their solutions are:

- Leakage of petrol from a lawnmower: check to make sure that the tank is not overfull before you mow.
- Uneven application of weed killer: if the damage is too great you may need to remove and re-seed the patches.
- Uneven application of fertiliser: this can be remedied by adding more to the bare patches.
- Poor preparation before seeding or turfing: buried debris or an uneven surface can be made worse if it is roughed up by a lawnmower. Always prepare carefully before sowing new seed.
- Waterlogging: check that the garden drainage is adequate. If it is not, water will pool after a wet spell and the grass may rot.
- Drought: water by artificial means if possible but remember that most grass will recover quickly after a wet spell.
- Overuse by children or pets: if the damage is severe you may need to reseed or returf; if not, installing a mesh in the areas where they play most may help to protect the lawn.
- Urine from female dogs: the chemical make-up of bitches' urine damages grass. If your female dog urinates on the lawn, douse the spot copiously with fresh water as soon as possible.

PROBLEM STOPPER

Scorched earth policy
A gardener who specialises in urban gardens tells a cautionary tale of a woman whom he met at a neighbourhood gardening function. He noticed that *everything* around her house was dying: shrubs, perennials, even trees.

The whole place looked as if it had weed killer on it, he recalls. The woman reported that she had indeed doused everything with herbicide in an effort to kill her weeds – mistakenly thinking that the chemicals somehow knew how to kill only the weeds, not the good plants.

Garden invaders

■ BIRD PESTS

Pigeons are nesting on my house

PUT UP A WIRE MESH BARRIER When pigeons and other birds build nests under your eaves, they often do their housekeeping on window ledges which can lead to a great deal of mess. To deter them from staying, change the ledge so that they won't have a level surface to land on. Take a length of stiff wire mesh – available both galvanised and coated in PVC from hardware shops, DIY stores and online – that is long enough to cover the ledge that the birds are roosting on. Use rustproof staples or nails to fasten one edge of the mesh to the wall a few inches above the ledge. Then pull the mesh taut across the corner and fasten the free edge of the mesh to the ledge. On each end, nail down a flap of mesh to cover up the hole so no little pests can get under the mesh. The invading birds will get fed up and find somewhere else to call home.

INSTALL A BIRD SPIKE Another way to stop pigeons from landing and roosting is to install specially designed bird spikes in places where they tend to settle including ledges, balconies and TV aerials. These can be purchased in a number of widths to suit even the narrowest ledge and quickly installed. The spikes are not intended to harm the birds in any way, merely to make the places that they are installed unappealing for them to land on.

Birds are eating my soft fruit

PUT UP A FRUIT CAGE Soft fruits like strawberries, raspberries, blackberries and red and blackcurrants are rewarding to grow in the garden. But their berries are extremely attractive to garden birds and sometimes squirrels which can decimate a carefully nurtured crop if it is not protected. To keep the birds away, it is worth building a fruit cage. You can buy these ready made with an aluminium frame covered with fine-gauge netting to keep the birds away. Or you could design your own, ensuring that the netting is attached securely enough all round so that no creatures can get through the gaps. Do remember to check the netting daily to ensure that no birds or animals are trapped.

■ INSECTS AND OTHER SMALL PESTS

Cutworms are slicing up my plants

SPRINKLE CORNFLOUR AROUND THE PLANTS Cutworms, which are actually moth larvae, live just below the surface of the soil and, true to their name, can tear right through your flowerbeds. They come in many colours and are from 2.5 to 5cm in length. One way to recognise them is to remember that 'C is for *cutworm*' – they usually curl up into a C shape when you touch them. You can quickly get rid of them with cornflour, say entomologists who specialise in non-toxic pest control. The cutworms like to eat the cornflour, but unfortunately for them they can't digest it, so they die. Sprinkle it on the ground around your plants and let them enjoy their last meal.

Snails are feasting on my veggies

ATTRACT THEM TO A SHADY RETREAT When snails proliferate in your garden, you can get rid of them in no time by putting a roof over their heads. Make a little table-like structure by nailing 2.5cm risers, such as short pieces of thick dowel rod, under the corners of a 30cm square of plywood or other board. Place this shelter wherever the snails are appearing and throw a few slices of raw turnip, carrot or potato under it as bait. Snails like to hide in dark, cool places during the day and they will gather together under the board after their night's activities. Each morning, collect up the snails from under the board and relocate them as you see fit.

Aphids are killing my garden

HOSE THEM OFF Research shows that simply blasting aphids with a hard stream of water from the garden hose is an easy way to kill most of the insects and chase away the rest. Cradle the plant with one hand and hit the aphids with a narrow stream of water. Most of the time you will get rid of them with the first session, but you may need to return the next day to get the stragglers. Though you may knock some petals from flowers with this approach, you're unlikely to damage the plant with a hard stream of water.

APPLY SOFT SOAP SPRAY Sold at garden centres, soft soap spray (also known as insecticidal soap), a combination of potassium salts or sodium combined with fatty acids, is also an effective tool against

aphids. When the soap lands on the aphid, the stuff washes away the protective coating on the aphid's body and causes damage to its cells, killing it. The spray will not harm birds, other animals or people. These soaps must be thoroughly applied by spraying them on to plants that you want to protect. Follow the label instructions carefully for proper use of the product; soap sprays can damage certain plants and should not be used in full sun or high temperatures.

ADD LADYBIRDS TO YOUR GARDEN Another way to annihilate aphids is to fight them with their worst enemy. Increase the population of ladybirds in your garden. These familiar red-and-black- spotted beetles rely on aphids as a primary food source. You can order ladybirds from a number of suppliers of organic pest control solutions. You can buy them as adults or larvae from Gardening Naturally (www.gardening-naturally.com) from around £14.95 for 25 adults. Scatter the ladybirds around your garden, making sure to follow directions from the company about what time of day to scatter them and how to make your garden attractive to them so they'll stay. You can also buy specially designed ladybird houses (or you could make your own from an piece of tree stump drilled with horizontal holes) which will attract both ladybirds and other beneficial insects such as lacewings. Note: you will also be encouraging native species of ladybird to fight back against foreign invaders.

Leatherjackets are gobbling up my lawn

KILL THEM WITH NEMATODES Leatherjackets are actually immature daddy longlegs. They live in the soil and eat grass roots, which can cause large patches of your grass to die. They are also are a food source that attracts animals that may be a pest in the garden such as pigeons and starlings. A simple, natural way to control leatherjackets is to attack them with nematodes. Nematodes are crudely built, microscopic worms that will attack and kill grubs underground. They are available from suppliers of organic pest control solutions such as Gardening Naturally (see above) and the Green Gardener (www.greengardener.co.uk) and you typically apply them to your lawn by attaching a container of them to a garden hose or by putting them in a watering can and sprinkling them on.

You should apply nematodes when grubs are closest to the surface, so the nematodes will work most effectively. The best time of year is usually early autumn, from September to October. Keep in mind that nematodes are fairly fragile, so follow the instructions for using them carefully. You should generally apply them in the evening, since they are killed by ultraviolet light. Then keep the soil well moistened so they will stay alive, but not so wet that they can't attack their prey.

There are hordes of ants marching everywhere in the garden

USE A BORAX AND HONEY MIXTURE If ants have invaded your garden, here's a low-toxic and effective way to eliminate them using a mixture of borax and honey. Ants, like people, adore sweet things, so the sweetness of the honey attracts them. They won't have to worry about cavities from the sugar, because the borax kills them.

Ants are nesting too close to the house

FLOOD THE NEST Encourage ant colonies to move away from your house without using poisons, which might harm your family or pets. Here are some measures you can take:

- Periodically flood the nest with the garden hose. For stubborn ants, pour boiling water on the nest.
- Put tomato or walnut leaves on the nest. These will repel ants.
- If the ants are climbing trees near the house, block their path by wrapping the tree trunks with double-sided sticky tape.

■ ANIMAL PESTS

The foxes are in my bins and messing up my garden again

SPRAY OR APPLY A DETERRENT PRODUCT If local foxes seem to enjoy strewing your rubbish bags down the street, chewing the fence or indulging in other antisocial antics in your garden at your expense, this may help. Spray the problem areas with a product called Scoot, a non-toxic formula that works by mimicking scent marking odours and leading foxes to vacate the area in the belief that another animal has taken over its territory. Scoot is totally safe for use in gardens, on plants and edible crops and is humane, biodegradable and very effective. Another possibility for gardens is Get Off My Garden, a citronella scented jelly granule product which can be used for defending soil areas such as flower beds or planters against fouling and digging. Another useful product is a spray called Wash and Get Off which both cleans up fox fouling and also removes the territorial scent, protecting the area from further attack. It is effective on hard surfaces such as patios and driveways so may be useful for preventing bin attacks.

The local cats are always leaving droppings all over the lawn

SCARE THEM OFF WITH CRYSTALS If you find muddy cat footprints all over your freshly washed car or little droppings left as 'presents' on your lawn, be careful in how you discourage the offenders. The last thing you want to do is to harm someone's beloved pet cat.

Try marking areas that you want to keep off limits to cats – around your driveway, for instance – with jelly-like crystals scattered around the cats' favourite fouling places.The crystals give off a strong odour which confuses the cats' sense of smell. Over a period of weeks it will discourage cats from using those areas again. The crystals are safe to use around lawns and flowerbeds and are also safe to use on concrete surfaces and paving.

I like moles but I don't want them to make mounds all over the lawn

APPLY A CASTOR-OIL PRODUCT With their velvet coats, pointed snouts and large, efficient claws, it's hard to hate a mole. But these underground pests can make a monumental mess of your garden with their tunnels and mounds. But here is a little secret: try using a non-toxic but unpleasant-tasting old-fashioned remedy – one that your mother or grandmother may have used on you – caster oil. Moles don't like castor oil any better than you do, say entomologists who specialise in pest management. So applying a product containing castor oil to your lawn will have the little tunnellers buying one-way tickets out of town.

One such product is called Biofume Mole Smoke. It contains a substance that when placed in an underground mole run and lit, emits a smoke containing castor oil which coats the walls of the run. Worms, the main food source for moles will avoid this oily substance and therefore the mole will soon leave as worms no longer enter their feeding tunnel. You need one 'smoke' to about three mole hills. Clear the mole hills and locate the runs. Seal all except the run where you want to introduce the smoke cannister. Light the fuse and place well into the run with the lighted end facing into the tunnel, seal to prevent the smoke escaping before it has coated the run with castor oil (contained within the mole smoke). This product is not toxic and will not kill moles, it will simply drive them away from the affected area. You may need to treat more runs if activity continues nearby.

Squirrels are trying to get into the loft

COVER HOLES WITH FINE CHICKEN WIRE Squirrels are wily and resourceful and may decide to use your loft as a cosy home in the winter months. If you want to deter them, cover any possible entrance holes with fine mesh chicken wire, securely fixed so that they can't gain access.

My traps aren't catching mice

BAIT TRAPS WITH PEANUT BUTTER If you are fed up with mice scurrying around your garden and invading your house, rethink how you bait your traps. Cheese is overrated as bait, as mice aren't instinctively attracted to it. Instead, bait your traps with a dab of peanut butter. And to make it *extra* appealing, put a shelled pecan or

DEALING WITH NEIGHBOURS' PETS

Pets are a common cause of friction between neighbours – whether it's a tomcat that sprays in your house or a dog that defecates on your lawn or driveway. Try this advice:

- **Assume goodwill at first** Calling the police or threatening to sue will usually make matters worse.
- **Talk to the neighbours** They may have no idea their pet is bothering you.
- **Say it nicely** Pick an opportune moment – a sunny afternoon when your neighbour is enjoying the garden, not a workday at 5.30pm when she is trying to get children and shopping into the house.
- **Look for allies** A dog-owning neighbour may write off one complaint as hypersensitivity, but if he hears the same complaint from two or three others, the message will be reinforced.
- **If you can't resolve the problem with your neighbours** Nuisance pets and pet owners can have legal action taken against them under anti-social behaviour and both noise and smell nuisance laws. This is usually the responsibility of your local authority's Environmental Health Department.
- **If you think a pet is being neglected or abused** Call the RSPCA who will go and talk to the owner in the first instance. They can take in animals that they believe are being ill-treated.

sunflower seed in front of the trap. A mouse will eat that as an appetiser and then attempt to snap up the peanut butter main course.

Deer are eating my plants

SPRINKLE THE PLANTS WITH HOT PEPPER If you live in a more rural area, hungry deer can be more of a problem for gardeners than urban dwellers could ever imagine. If deer have turned your garden into a salad bar, turn up the heat on them by giving your plants additional zest with powdered cayenne pepper. Sprinkle the cayenne on your plants and reapply after it rains. Eventually the deer will work out that the plants are hot – and will make someone else's garden their favourite mealtime destination. Buy cayenne in bulk to get it at a bargain price.

WRAP TREES WITH WIRE MESH If the deer are stripping the bark off the trees in your garden, wrap the tree trunks in stiff wire mesh. This wrapping of mesh will keep the deer from sinking their teeth into the bark. Local hardware stores, DIY stores, garden centres and nurseries will carry this material and it can also be purchased online.

Rabbits think my garden is a salad bar

PUT UP A CHICKEN-WIRE FENCE An easy-to-build fence will keep those bunnies from enjoying your vegetables before you do. Get a roll of 1 metre deep chicken wire and several metal stakes. Check for both at a local hardware store or DIY store. Pound the metal stakes into the ground, about a metre and a half apart, around the perimeter of your garden.

Unroll the chicken wire flat on the ground and, down one long edge, bend 15cm of the fencing out at a 90 degree angle. Stand the chicken wire up next to the stakes so that the bent portion is on the ground, facing outward. Attach the fencing to the bars using short twists of wire. When you have run the fencing around the enclosure and you are back at the starting point, attach the loose end of the fence to the post with a twist or two of wire. This will allow you to remove the fastening easily so that you can open and enter the enclosure when you want to work with the plants.

The fencing will keep the rabbits out and the portion at the bottom that sticks out along the ground will discourage them from digging under the fence.

You versus nature

■ HOT AND COLD WEATHER

I can't light my campfire and it's cold

CARRY A COTTON-WOOL BALL FIRE STARTER You light a match and set it into a little pile of pine needles, twigs and branches. The match goes out. You search for another, dreaming of a cosy fire. Unfortunately, you have no more matches. It's going to be a cold night. Here is the experts' ultimate hint for avoiding a situation like this.

Before you go out into the wilderness, take a cotton-wool ball and rub petroleum jelly all over it. Make sure you saturate the cotton. Do this to several cotton-wool balls, stick them in a film canister or a small sealed bag and put the container in your backpack or jacket pocket along with waterproof matches or a lighter.

The cotton wool is flammable and the petroleum jelly will keep the cotton-wool balls waterproof. When you need to light a fire, just assemble your pile of tinder and wood, tease some strands of fibre loose from a cotton-wool ball, insert the ball into the pile and touch your match or lighter to it. Even a spark or a quick flame will light the cotton, which will then burn for several minutes, greatly improving your chances of lighting your campfire.

Cotton-wool balls soaked in petroleum jelly are instant fire starters.

Everything's wet and I need tinder for a campfire

LOOK FOR AN EVERGREEN TREE You should find fire-starting salvation in a cone-bearing tree (a pine, for instance), say knowledgeable campers. The tree you select may be wet from rain or snow, but the base of the trunk is usually well protected from the elements. Two or three feet (60 to 90cm) up the trunk, you will find dead, dry twigs that will make great tinder for your campfire. The dead twigs snap off easily. If a twig bends without breaking, leave it alone. It is alive and won't burn well anyway.

Oddly enough, bundling up *too* warm for outdoor winter activities can leave you cold and shivering by the end of the day. A crucial aspect of staying warm is keeping your clothing dry. It doesn't matter whether the water in your clothes comes from rain or sweat; it will still make you cold. So when you're planning your outdoor activities during cold weather, plan on dressing a little on the cool side. You will warm up after a few minutes of activity and later in the day your clothes won't be so sweaty that they will sap your body heat. Dress in several layers so that you can easily shed the outer layers if you get too warm. Wear clothing made of thin synthetic material next to your skin – rather than cotton – so that it will wick sweat away from your body more easily.

I'm going to a sporting event, and it's bitterly cold

OPEN AN UMBRELLA Odd as it may seem, one of your best defences on a cold, windy day is a large golf umbrella, say a number of knowledgeable sporting enthusiasts. Open your umbrella, point it toward the wind and seat yourself close up inside the umbrella so that it protects you from the bluster. You will be surprised to discover how much warmer you feel in this makeshift shelter.

My car is stalling in the heat

STAY WITH YOUR CAR If you're motoring through a desert region (most likely abroad, rather than in the UK) and your car decides that it is not up to the challenge, feel free to be angry with the vehicle, but don't abandon it, recommend desert-survival experts. Pull off to the side of the road and stay near the car. Find some shade nearby – the car might even cast some shade for you. Don't go hiking for help. With any luck, another motorist will come along and help you out.

I am getting overcome by the heat

You were having such a good time out in the summer sunshine, soaking up the warmth and trying to store away some good memories to warm you through winter. But now you are *too* hot. That pleasant warmth suddenly feels more like a burning sensation. To avoid a medical emergency, advise hot weather survival experts, choose your next steps carefully, especially if you have been exerting yourself.

REST AND COOL OFF Common signs of *heat exhaustion* include a pale face, clammy skin and dizziness. These are all indications that you've pushed yourself too hard. You need to rest, cool off and get some water and salty snacks in you, say the experts.

HEAD FOR A HOSPITAL You may need to take more definite action if you are suffering from *heatstroke* – a medical emergency that requires prompt hospital treatment. Signs of heatstroke are skin that is red, hot and dry. You may also be confused and even appear to be hallucinating, so listen to your companions if they are concerned and take their advice.

■ DANGEROUS SITUATIONS

I am lost in the wild

Getting lost in the woods or when you are up a mountain can be very frightening indeed. Here is how to keep yourself alive until someone finds you or you find your way back:

DON'T PANIC Most people who die as a result of being stranded in the wilderness do so within 36 hours, but the average person can survive without eating for 40 days, say survival experts. If you keep your wits about you, you can last longer than you think. By panicking and running around frantically, you will burn up energy and get yourself sweaty, setting yourself up for potentially deadly hypothermia when the sun goes down.

KEEP WARM Staying warm and getting sleep so you can make rational decisions are crucial to wilderness survival. As your surroundings have changed, your habits may need to change, too. That could mean moving around at *night* to stay warm, preferably walking in a circle so that you won't injure yourself in the dark and sleeping during the *day* when the sun is out. Avoid lying down directly on the ground. The cold earth will draw the heat out of your body. Gather up a pile of leaves or whatever dry material is around and get into it. This will get you off the ground and trap your body heat.

DRINK WATER WHEN YOU FIND IT The water may have nasty microbes in it, but you can always visit the doctor when you get back to civilisation. If you don't stay hydrated, you might die, say survival experts. If you are in a forest or up a mountain, you can often find a creek flowing down between two large hills. Even a dry streambed typically has water in it if you are prepared to dig down a few feet. Or wipe your shirt on dewy grass and plants in the morning and wring it into your mouth.

The current is pulling me out to sea

THE PROBLEM IS A RIP CURRENT A rip current is a panic-inducing threat that can get you into real trouble at the beach. Many serious incidents involving swimmers being pulled out to sea are caused by rip currents.

Slow and steady will win the race, the old saying goes and it will also allow you to enjoy the great outdoors in a hot climate.

• Avoid going out in the heat of the day. Keep in mind that some asphalt roads in hot parts of the world can literally melt during hot periods and paved roads are tougher to walk on.

• Don't overestimate your heat-handling abilities. Many fatalities in the notorious Death Valley National Park in Nevada, USA, involve tourists from cooler climates who are simply unaware of the deadly effects of the heat.

It takes from five to twelve days to get acclimatised to temperatures over 30˚C. Stick to a '30-30' or a '40-20' rule: 30 to 40 minutes of activity, followed by 20 to 30 minutes of rest.

When waves travel from deep to shallow water, they break near the shore. When they break strongly in some places and weakly in others, rip currents – narrow, fast-moving strips of water moving seaward – can form. Rip currents (also called rip tides) often form in low spots or breaks in sandbars or near piers and other structures. The following are signs that there is a rip current: murky sandy coloured water, caused by sand stirred up off the seabed; foam on the water surface going out beyond the break; a rippled appearance, on a calm day, when the water around is generally flatter; waves breaking farther out on both sides of a rip on a day with heavier surf; a darker colour of sea, indicating deep water and debris (or people) floating out to sea

Most rip currents head straight back out to sea, perpendicular to the beach, but some go out diagonally. When people are caught in them, they often struggle in a futile attempt to swim directly toward the shore. But a strong rip current can make swimming seem like walking on a treadmill or up a down escalator, the experts say. Even strong swimmers may grow exhausted and panic.

SWIM PARALLEL TO THE SHORE If you are caught in a rip current, instead of struggling to swim against the current toward the shore, swim *parallel* to the shore, experts advise. Most rip currents are fairly narrow and you don't have to swim far to get out of their path. Once you're out of the current, *then* swim to shore.

REVERSE DIRECTION IF NECESSARY If you happen to be in a rip current that's headed diagonally away from shore, swimming parallel with the shore may put you into the swifter part of the current. If you feel as if you aren't getting out of the rip current quickly, turn around and swim parallel to the shore the *other* way.

I have cut myself badly and I'm miles from anywhere

CLOSE THE WOUND WITH GAFFER TAPE You've cut your knee badly and need stitches, but you're on a hike and are miles from a hospital. If you have the backpacker's staple, gaffer tape, in your pack, apply pressure to the wound to control the bleeding and then apply a strip of gaffer tape across it to hold the two sides of the gash together. This should allow you to walk to a place where you can get the medical help you need.

■ INSECT BITES

Ouch! I've just been stung

You are minding your own business when a bee or wasp gives you a painful sting. If you act quickly, you can minimise the pain and swelling. Here's what experts who have studied insect bites suggest:

PULL OUT THE STING Some insects, such as honeybees, will leave behind their stings when they sting. A widespread belief is that you should scrape away the sting with a credit card or knife edge to avoid squeezing more venom from the sting into your skin by pinching. But experts say most of the venom is injected within 20 seconds of the sting. You can easily take that long looking through your wallet or purse to find something to scrape with. Instead, pull the sting out of your skin and forget about scraping it.

TAKE AN ANTIHISTAMINE PILL Take an antihistamine, such as Piriton, after getting stung. This, too, will help to reduce swelling.

CARRY EPINEPHRINE IF YOU ARE ALLERGIC Remember that insect stings can trigger a life-threatening condition called anaphylactic shock in highly allergic people. This requires a more sophisticated level of treatment. If you know you have these reactions, consult with your doctor on how to treat insect stings. You may need to carry the drug epinephrine with you and, if you're stung, inject yourself with it before seeking emergency medical care.

The itch from a bee-sting is driving me mad

RUB IT WITH ICE The best way to minimise the itching of a sting is to rub ice on it, say medical specialists. Rub an ice cube or hold an ice pack on it for a few minutes and repeat as needed.

■ ANIMAL ATTACKS

A big, aggressive dog is growling at me

DON'T INTRUDE OR STARTLE IT Dogs are very territorial and may act aggressively to defend their turf. And dogs may attack if they're startled. So pay attention if you are walking or jogging and see a dog that hasn't noticed you; it may be startled when it sees you.

WATCH FOR PEAKED EARS AND BARE TEETH Dogs often exhibit warning signs that they are about to attack. They may hold their tails stiffly aloft, their ears may stick up, the hair on their backs may stand up and – not surprisingly – they may bare their teeth.

DON'T RUN OR SCREAM If you are confronted with a threatening dog, resist the impulse to scream or run. The dog's natural instinct is to chase and catch prey. And avoid making direct eye contact with the dog, because the animal will see it as a challenge. Instead, try to remain motionless until the dog has lost interest and leaves. Then slowly back away until it is out of sight.

Running or screaming is not the answer when faced with a threatening dog.

PUT SOMETHING IN THE WAY If a dog does attack, try to put something between it and you, such as a bag or package. If a dog bites you and holds on, avoid pulling away from it, because that can cause you further injury.

I've been bitten by a venomous snake

DRIVE TO A HOSPITAL OR CALL FOR HELP You are extremely unlikely to be bitten by a poisonous snake in the UK or Europe. But if you're travelling further afield it's not impossible that it might happen. Whatever you do, don't panic. People rarely die from snake bites within the first 24 hours, say snake experts. This gives you time to seek help calmly. The best first-aid tool for a snake bite is a set of car keys and a vehicle that's full of petrol, the snake researchers advise. Another good tool is a mobile phone. Call for help or drive to a hospital if you're not too far from civilisation.

DON'T CUT AND SUCK THE BITE OR USE A TOURNIQUET Forget about doing any DIY surgery on the bite. Many people are under the impression that cutting into a snakebite and sucking out the poison is a useful treatment. Unfortunately, say experts, cutting into the skin can damage blood vessels, nerves and other delicate tissue, particularly if the bite is on a hand or foot, which it often is. Besides, up to 30 per cent of bites from venomous snakes are 'dry' bites, which means they inject little or no venom. So people often inflict injuries on themselves trying to tend bites that weren't serious in the first place. Furthermore, if you have little cuts on your lips or gums and you *do* suck out venom, it could be absorbed through the open wounds just as if the snake had injected it.

If you are bitten on the arm or leg, don't tie a tourniquet around it. As soon as the tourniquet is removed, any venom and digested tissue that's built up in your limb will flood into the rest of your body, possibly causing serious damage.

I'm worried about a shark attack

FOLLOW COMMONSENSE RULES It's one of the most alarming images: the shark attack on a defenceless swimmer near a crowded beach but it's unbelievably unlikely to happen to you, especially in the UK. Although sharks attack several dozen people in the world each year in unprovoked incidents, the total per year since 2000 has been below 100, according to shark experts and naturalists. Over the past 100 years, the number of such attacks has been growing slowly but steadily, perhaps partly because the number of people who take holidays near the sea has risen, partly because there has been better reporting of incidents involving sharks and partly because of faster and more widespread media coverage of attacks. Given the number of people who take a dip each year, your odds of being one of those attacked is pretty slim. If you are holidaying abroad, follow these precautions, recommended by shark experts and you will improve your chances even further:

- Swim in groups. Sharks prefer solitary targets.
- Swim during the day. Sharks are most active during the night and twilight hours.
- Avoid swimming if you have an open wound or are menstruating.
- Don't wear jewellery that's shiny. The flickering light from jewellery looks like fish scales to a hungry shark.
- Steer clear of waters where people are fishing or feeding fish. If you see seabirds diving for food, shun those areas too.
- Be wary when you're between sandbars or places where the seabed drops away sharply.
- Don't get into the water if you know sharks are around.

TRICKS OF THE TRADE

Was there venom in that bite?
There is a simple way to tell whether the snake that has bitten you is cause for concern, according to snake experts.

- A venomous snake, such as a rattlesnake, copperhead, cotton-mouth or coral snake, will leave only one or two punctures in your skin.

- A non-venomous snake will leave multiple puncture wounds on your skin; 8 to 12 or more wouldn't be unusual. That's because venomous snakes use a fang or two to inject their venom, instead of their teeth. (Snakes do have teeth.) The non-venomous snakes bite you with their teeth.

PART FIVE

Clothing and appearance

If you've just lost a clasp from your earring, you'll find an easy fix in your child's school bag. Or need a brown rinse for your hair – and the chemist is closed? The answer is in the larder. Is a rough fingernail bothering you? Just pick up a pack of matches. Keeping yourself looking good can be hard work, but there are surprising and helpful solutions everywhere you turn.

Everyday clothing problems

CLOTHING MISHAPS

My button has popped off at the worst possible moment

WIRE IT BACK ON You're on your way to an important meeting and a button pops off. Find a thin piece of wire, even a plastic bag tie. (If you use the tie, strip off the paper or plastic covering, exposing the wire beneath it.) Thread whatever wire you use from the inside of the garment up through the hole where the original thread had been, through one hole in the button, down through another buttonhole and then through the second hole in the fabric. Twist the metal ends together until the button is secure. Bend the metal ends so that they will lie flat against the garment.

If you lose a button at a bad time, a wire twist tie can save the day in seconds.

My zip's pull has come off the track on one side

MAKE A CUT TO GET IT BACK ON TRACK If you are rushing to go out and you start to pull up your zip but discover that the glider is attached to only one side. Take a pair of sharp scissors and, at the bottom of the zip, cut between the last two zip teeth on the open side. Reinsert the glider here over the zip teeth. Zip up. Then, to keep the glider from coming off the track when you unzip, fasten a safety pin across the bottom of the zip on the inside above the cut.

I'm struggling to move my zip

LUBRICATE THE ZIP If your zip still has all its teeth, but it no longer moves easily up and down, lubrication is the answer. Rub the teeth on either side with a lead pencil, a dry bar of soap or a small ball of beeswax.

Either my trousers have shrunk or my waist has grown

PUT ELASTIC IN THE WAISTBAND If you put on a pair of trousers that you haven't worn since last season and they seem to have shrunk in storage, take a clever tip from maternity-wear designers. Buy a short length of elastic with buttonholes already in it from a fabric shop. Sew or pin one end of the elastic inside the waistband of your trousers. Use the button that is already on your trousers at the other end and in just a few minutes you've put slack in your slacks.

I'm always fighting static electricity

USE A FABRIC SOFTENER SHEET The easy solution is to keep a fabric softening drier sheet in your handbag or pocket. Rub the sheet lightly over your tights and on the underside of your skirt whenever you have a problem with static electricity. Residue from the sheet will prevent static build-up.

Here are two more ways to cope with the problem:

- Mist the underside of your skirt with hair spray, which will also prevent static electricity.
- Wet a paper towel or even your hand with water and lightly run it down the exterior of your tights and the interior of your skirt. This trick is used in the theatre by wardrobe supervisors, who often stand at the ready with a spray bottle of water to get the static out of costumes before performers go onstage.

My hem has become unstitched

STAPLE IT IN PLACE Both trousers and skirts are prone to having hems fall down, usually at the most awkward times. Unless the fabric is very delicate, a quick fix is to staple your hem into place. If you are careful, you can do this from the inside so that the staple will be barely noticeable. Staples only make tiny punctures in fabric and are easy to remove once you have access to a sewing kit.

My neckline keeps gaping open

KEEP IT IN PLACE WITH TOUPEE TAPE You're feeling great, except for a problem with the neckline on your dress or blouse. It keeps gaping open in a way the designer never intended. This is a problem that can be caused by wear and tear or improper fit. Double-sided toupee

Getting rid of pet hair quickly

If you're frustrated by dog or cat hair all over your clothing, lightly mist the hair-covered garment with water from a spray bottle. Then put the garment in the tumble drier with a damp towel, along with a fabric softener sheet. Tumble dry on a low setting for up to 15 minutes. The softener sheet will reduce the static electricity that helps the hair to stick to the clothing, while the tumbling and airflow pull the hair off the clothing and suck it out of the drier. (Be sure to clean the filter afterwards.)

tape will come to your rescue. Products such as Vapon Topstick will adhere to your skin and the garment at the same time and it won't hurt when you pull it off. The tape can be cut and shaped easily. Toupee tape is also great for stopping straps from falling off your shoulders. Look for it in beauty aid supply shops or online.

I forgot to pack a slip

SUBSTITUTE A T-SHIRT You're travelling and as you put on your favourite dress or skirt, you realise you need a slip and don't have one. A cheap T-shirt will come to the rescue. Snip the neck opening near the shoulder seam with scissors, a couple of centimetres on either side. Then pull the skirt up over your hips to your waist. If the first cut doesn't do it, snip a little more. If that still isn't enough, try sliding the T-shirt over your head rather than pulling it up to your hips. Once the T-shirt is on, cut off the arms at the seams, pull on your dress and noone should see what's underneath.

My clothes are crumpled and I don't have an iron handy

LET THE SHOWER STEAM THEM Hang your clothes in the bathroom, shut the door and run the shower on hot for five minutes. The steam from the shower will smooth out the wrinkles. You can even smooth out the clothes that you are wearing with this technique. And it's great for items that are difficult to iron.

For ultra efficiency, try spraying your outfit lightly with water and hanging it in the bathroom while you shower. Then shake the item and if you still have creases, press them out by laying the clothing on a flat surface and running your hand over it. With washable silks, spray the fabric, press it with your hand and leave it on a hanger for 15 minutes before wearing it.

PUT THEM IN A DRIER WITH A DAMP TOWEL If you have access to a drier, put a damp towel in with the outfit and turn it on to air dry. Your outfit should be wrinkle free in about 10 or 15 minutes.

My clothes smell musty and I have no time to wash them

SPRAY THEM WITH VODKA If your clothes are giving off a musty odour – or even a whiff of perspiration – and you don't have time to wash or dry-clean them, here's a trick that Russian theatre managers have used for centuries: put some neat vodka into a spray bottle and mist the garment. The vodka kills odour-causing bacteria (it's alcohol, after all) and because it is relatively odourless, you won't smell as if you've just came from a bar.

I have spilled greasy food on my shirt

ABSORB IT WITH TALCUM POWDER If you act quickly, you can rescue fabric from greasy stains (such as butter, peanut butter or greasy fast food). First, scrape away any food. Then sprinkle on a generous amount of talcum powder, enough to cover the spot completely and leave it for 5 minutes. The powder will soak up the oil. Flick off the powder and launder as usual. If the grease stain is older, follow the instruction in 'I have grease on my clothes' on page 249.

The seam in my trousers has split open

PIN OR STAPLE IT SHUT Your trousers have split and you're suddenly air-conditioned in a way you never intended. The classic solution is safety pins, if you have some at hand. Go somewhere private, remove the trousers and work on the interior of the garment. Gather a centimetre of material on each side of the seam and fasten the sides together with a small safety pin or two. Or staple the seam closed.

USE DOUBLE-SIDED TAPE A better remedy is double-sided tape, because it's less likely to show. Find a hardware or DIY store and buy the kind of tape used to hold carpeting in place. Find a private place where you can remove the garment and lay it out on a table or counter. Cut a strip of the double-sided tape just wide and long enough to fit invisibly between the two pieces of fabric that have separated and press it into place.

I have a run in my tights – and no nail varnish

USE SOAP TO FIX IT Yes, the traditional quick remedy for a run in your tights is a light coating of nail varnish. But if you don't have nail varnish, take a slightly wet bar of soap or even a small amount of liquid soap and gently rub it over the edge of the run. When the soap dries, it will harden and prevent further running.

PROBLEM STOPPER

Stop runs in your tights cold
You can reduce the likelihood that your tights will run with this cool tip: put your tights in a plastic bag and place them in the freezer. The temperature hardens the material, making it less likely to snag as you get dressed.

■ WEATHER-RELATED PROBLEMS

I forgot my umbrella and it's pouring

WEAR A PLASTIC BIN BAG Find the largest plastic bin bag you can find. Cut holes for your eyes, nose and mouth. Then slip the bag over your head. You may look like an alien, but your upper body will be well protected from the rain.

My coat is soaked from a downpour

DRY IT WITH A HAIR DRIER A rain shower has surprised you and there you are, dripping water in the foyer. Your sopping coat – not designed for a downpour – needs some special attention. You can't just stuff it in the wardrobe, where it will soak all the other coats. Hang it up on a good wooden hanger where there's plenty of air circulating to help to dry it out without it turning musty – the bathroom or laundry room will do. If you're in a hurry to go back out, hang the coat up and use a hair drier, moving it up and down the coat about 15cm from the fabric. Don't drape the coat on a radiator or near a heater: some fabrics are flammable and others may shrink. Hanging your coat near a cool fan is fine.

Hang your drenched coat on a wooden hanger and use a hair drier to get the moisture out of it in a hurry.

My shirt is dripping with sweat

USE A HAND DRIER A hot, humid day is taking its toll on you. You feel wilted and your shirt or blouse is showing signs of sweat. If you can't change your top, find a cloakroom with a blower-type hand drier and angle the spout so that the air can blow you and your shirt dry. Paper towels don't do the job quickly enough.

The snow's really deep and I don't have boots

WEAR PLASTIC BAGS INSIDE YOUR SHOES If you're going to be out in the cold for any length of time, keeping your feet dry is essential. Here's what to do: take off your shoes. If your socks are dry, slide your sock-covered feet into a pair of plastic bags (plastic grocery bags will do). If your socks are wet too, peel them off, dry your bare feet thoroughly, wrap them in rags and slip them into the bags. Then put your shoes back on. For extra weatherproofing, tape (with gaffer or packing tape) the tops of the plastic bags to the turnups of your trousers, the tops of your socks or your legs.

■ GARMENT WEAR AND TEAR

I have small pinholes in my garment

DAMPEN, RUB AND IRON THE HOLES You may have pin or staple holes in your clothing from tags from the shop or from pins that marked a hemline. In either event, they are probably not literally holes. More likely, the pin or staple has just pushed the weave apart. To close such holes, wet your fingertip and use your fingernail to gently move the weave closer together. Or dampen the fabric around the holes with a small wet paintbrush. Then ironing, using a pressing cloth, should close the weave.

Clothes hangers are puckering the shoulders of my dresses

STEAM OUT THE PUCKERS If you notice that hangers leave little pucker marks at the shoulders of garments that you take out of the wardrobe, the solution is to use a blast of steam from a steam iron to relax the puckered fibres. Or drape the garment over a towel rack in the bathroom when you shower.

I have snagged my sweater

PULL THE SNAG THROUGH TO THE INSIDE Your bracelet or watch catches a thread in your sweater and yanks it out into an ugly loop. Or you're playing with a cat and its claw snags. When knitted garments suffer this kind of damage, pull the loop to the inside of the sweater where it can't be seen. A needle and thread is all you need. Put the eye-end of a threaded needle through the fabric from the inside. Wrap the thread on the end of the needle around the snag and pull the needle and thread, and the attached snag to the inside of the garment. Don't cut the little loop – that will create a hole.

The cuffs of my sweater have stretched

DIP IN HOT WATER AND DRY WITH A HAIR DRIER If you are in the habit of pushing your sweater sleeves up your forearms and the cuffs have

PROBLEM STOPPER

Does pilling rub you up the wrong way? Pilling can be caused by items of clothing rubbing against each other in a washing machine or tumble drier or simply by friction caused when the garment is worn. To prevent pilling, wash your clothes inside out, so that the exterior surfaces never touch each other. This has the added benefit of limiting what is known as crocking – the dye from one fabric rubbing off on another. Denim, for instance, is usually dyed with indigo, which is very susceptible to crocking.

become stretched, and if the sweater is cotton or wool, a little hot water will do the trick. Dip the cuffs in the water and then dry them with a hair drier. But you might be out of luck, if the cuffs contain elastic, lycra or some other fibre that stretches. Once these materials lose their elasticity, they can't be fixed.

My sweaters are looking fuzzy

RUB LIGHTLY WITH FINE SANDPAPER Sweaters can look weary when little bits of material pill up on them. There is an easy fix for this. Before laundering, brush the fabric gently with a piece of extra-fine sandpaper. If you work gently, your sweater will look like new. Or try one of these higher-tech methods:

- Sweater Stone, a product sold at some sewing shops and available online has a pumice-like surface that removes fuzz.
- An electric fabric shaver, which costs around £10, will also keep your sweaters looking smart.

The buttons keep getting pulled off my sweater

ADD A SECOND BUTTON INSIDE When you are resewing the main button, sew a small clear button on the back of the fabric. Because it's clear and small, it won't be conspicuous when the garment is open. Line up the holes on both buttons and stitch right through from bottom to top and back again. The inside button will prevent the thread from pulling through the back of the fabric, a particular hazard in loosely woven or knitted cloth.

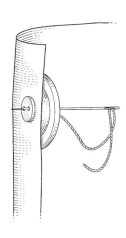

Everything I wear is missing a button

KEEP A BUTTON-FIXING KIT NEXT TO YOUR WASHING MACHINE Buttons work loose or come off completely quite regularly. When you are busy it is difficult to regularly check for and fix buttons that may be coming loose. Keep a miniature sewing kit right next to the washing machine. It should have three or four needles, each threaded in a different colour; scissors and a selection of buttons. When you pull a buttonless garment out of the machine, you can fix it on the spot. For buttons that pop off more than you think they should, stop the problem before it starts. Put a dab of clear nail polish on the centre of each button to seal the thread and prevent wear and tear on it.

I have a pull in my shirt

STROKE THE MATERIAL WITH YOUR FINGERNAIL A woven fabric such as linen, twill or denim may get a pull when a thread catches on something sharp, causing the threads to bunch up in an unsightly line. To fix the problem, stroke at the damaged material with your fingernail. This will pull the thread back into position.

The collar on my favourite blouse has frayed

BOND THE FIBRES WITH LIQUID SEALANT When everything on your garment looks fine except for the frayed edge of the collar, you can tuck the edge out of sight inside your collar, or you can just put clear tape over the frayed part. But a better solution is to use a liquid seam sealant that holds fibres together. These are available at sewing shops and online sewing websites with brand names such as Fray Stop and Liquid Stitch.

The crease in my trousers is gone

PRESS IN FUSIBLE THREAD If a trouser crease is not as sharp as it used to be, fusible thread can improve its appearance, especially in polyester and cotton trousers – but not silk or wool. You can buy fusible thread in fabric shops. Place a long length of the thread into the crease, on the inside of the fabric. Then press over the crease with an iron. The thread will melt onto the fabric, creating a permanent crease. Getting a straight crease can be tricky, so practise carefully on scrap material first.

The gathers on my little girl's dress have come undone

USE DENTAL FLOSS TO MAKE GATHERS If you don't know how to sew gathers neatly, dental floss is a real asset. Instead of using basting stitches, which are the longest stitches on a sewing machine, use a zigzag stitch over a length of dental floss along the fabric that you want to gather. Sew over the floss, but not through it, so that you can then pull on the floss to draw up the gathers until they look just right. Then sew across the top of the gathers to hold them in place and pull out the strip of dental floss.

When scissors can't fly
You know how modern
air travel is: tight
security and anything
that even resembles a
weapon is not allowed.
That can make it hard
for passengers who like
to keep busy with
sewing and needlework,
as scissors are not
allowed on today's
aircraft. But you can
solve the problem with
a disc-shaped metal
thread cutter, which is
safe and permitted on
planes. Made by a
company named Clover,
this thread cutter can
be worn as a pendant
or can be placed on top
of a spool of thread and
has grooves for cutting
yarn and thread. The
disc is available at many
sewing stores and
several websites.

■ SEWING GEAR

My sewing machine vibrates

PUT A RUBBER TREAD RUNNER UNDER IT When you are trying to put the finishing touches on a delicate sewing project, but your machine is vibrating all over the place, an easy solution is to buy a rubber tread runner, such as those used on outdoor steps, at a hardware store. Put the runner under the machine to absorb the vibration and help to hold the machine in place. Or buy cushioned, non-slip rubber shelf lining by the metre to use in the same way.

My sewing machine needs a good cleaning

USE A SQUEEZE BOTTLE TO BLOW AWAY LINT To clean out the little bits of fluff and lint that collect in tiny spaces in your sewing machine, an empty washing-up liquid squeeze bottle can come to the rescue. Clean the top and bottom thoroughly so that there is no detergent left and let both parts dry. Screw the top back on. Then simply squeeze the empty bottle so that it makes puffs of air. Aim it at the lint and the problem is solved. You can use this tool for cleaning computer keyboards, too.

My scissors don't cut well anymore

CUT THROUGH GLASSPAPER When scissors won't cut any more, use them to cut through a sheet of glasspaper several times. It will remove grime and sharpen the metal edges a little.

My hem is uneven and I don't have a skirt marker

USE A BATHROOM PLUNGER AS A GUIDE To adjust the hem of a skirt when the original hem isn't even, a humble bathroom plunger can help you. It has a handle and a firm base when you stand it up. Work out how high you want the hem to be from the floor and mark the distance on the handle of the plunger. Put on the skirt and have a friend use the plunger to mark the new hemline as you slowly turn.

Laundry problems

■ STAINS

My pen has stained my pocket

REMOVE THE STAIN WITH SURGICAL SPIRIT AND PAPER TOWELS
How many shirts have been ruined by a leaking pen. You can't
hear it and you can't smell it. But you can see the awful blue
or black ink stain at the base of a shirt pocket. Can you
rescue the shirt. If it's white cotton, the answer is yes, with
the help of surgical spirit. Put three paper towels, one on
top of the other and folded in half, on a flat surface, such
as a kitchen worktop. Put the shirt pocket over the paper
towels and pour surgical spirit onto the ink – just
enough to cover the area. The paper towels will absorb
the alcohol and draw the ink away from the fabric. Replace
the paper towels when they become saturated. Repeat the process
after about 2 minutes. The alcohol will loosen up the ink. Rinse by
pouring water onto the stained area, again changing the paper
towels. If there is still a slight ink stain, apply nail polish remover
(acetone) to a cloth and rub it on the stained shirt (always test a
patch first). Rinse with water; then pre-soak with a stain remover
such as Shout and let it soak for 15 to 20 minutes before laundering.

*If you act at once,
you can save an
ink-stained shirt.
You need surgical
spirit, but apply it
quickly for a
successful result.*

I have spilled coffee on my shirt

USE COLD WATER; THEN PRE-TREAT If you drink your coffee black, the
stain will be easier to remove than if you add milk, because the
protein in milk works against you. However you like your coffee, the
solution is the same. Hold the garment under a tap, stain side down
and run cold water through it for a couple of minutes. Next, rub
laundry detergent or a pre-wash product into the stain and let it
stand for 5 minutes. Then wash as usual.

My favourite garment has a mildew stain

REMOVE THE STAIN WITH BLEACH You threw a soaked sweatshirt into
the boot of your car and promptly forgot about it. When you finally
found it again, the sweatshirt had developed a mildew stain. If the

Removing a small bloodstain

If you get a small bloodstain on a favourite garment, if you treat it while it's still fresh, the stain will come straight out. What you need is an enzyme agent and your saliva is just that. Rub saliva into the bloodstain, rinse and watch the spot disappear. This is an old trick used by quilters, who frequently prick their fingers while stitching through several layers of fabric and batting.

shirt is white and all cotton and the stain is relatively new, you're in luck. Mix 2 tablespoons of chlorine bleach with 60ml water and pour it on the stain. Then launder. The bleach should kill the spores that caused the mildew. For coloured clothing and items made of synthetic fabrics, washing with an all-fabric bleach should do the trick. Remember, that the older a mildew stain is, the more difficult it will be to remove. In future, be sure to treat mildew stains as soon as possible.

The underarms of my blouse are stained

LAUNDER WITH BLEACH If your favourite clothes are being ruined by what appear to be sweat stains, which can show up as a yellow patch, you can tell whether it's actually caused by perspiration by feeling the fabric. Sweat may stain, but it will leave the cloth feeling normal. Stains from antiperspirant will feel either oily or stiff. For white cotton and linen, launder the garment with chlorine bleach, according to the package directions. Use oxygen (all-fabric) bleach on coloured and synthetic fabric. These methods should work whether the stain is caused by antiperspirant or sweat. Take a silk or wool garment to a dry cleaner and point out the stains with care.

My lipstick has left a mark

PRE-TREAT WITH LAUNDRY DETERGENT OR ACETONE Lipstick can easily stain clothing. Removing it is tricky because not all lipsticks are made of the same ingredients. First, try rubbing a lipstick stain with liquid detergent before laundering. If that doesn't work and the clothing is white, you can use acetone-based nail polish remover to remove the spot. Acetone can harm coloured clothing, so be careful. And even with white items, test it on an inconspicuous spot before you start to attack the lipstick stain.

I have grass stains on my trousers

PRE-TREAT AND WASH WITH AN ENZYME BOOSTER Grass stains can wreck a perfectly good pair of trousers in an instant. The sooner you treat such stains, the better. Rub liquid laundry detergent on the fabric; then rinse with hot water. If that doesn't remove the stain, rub more detergent onto the stain and wash the garment, adding a specially formulated Stain Devil or a stain removing product like Astonish, that will help to remove the protein in the stain.

Here are two other ways to remove a fresh grass stain:

- Mix 2 tablespoons of surgical spirit with 50ml water and spray it on the stain. Rub the area with an old toothbrush. Rinse the stain before the surgical spirit evaporates.
- Mix a few drops of household ammonia with a teaspoon of hydrogen peroxide. Rub it on the stain and then rinse with water as soon as the stain disappears.

Grass stains that are not fresh are tougher to remove, especially if you've washed the garment and then dried it at a high temperature.

A child has wiped his face on my clothes

CLEAN UP WITH BABY WIPES Tots tend to be exceptionally untidy eaters. Some of the resulting mess gets smeared from ear to ear and then on whatever piece of cloth is nearby. If that's the shirt or jacket you're wearing, there are a couple of solutions. First, get as much off your clothing as you can by blotting it with a paper towel. Then see whether the parents have any baby wipes; these are perfect for removing food smudges from clothing.

My favourite blouse has rust stains on it

TREAT THE STAIN WITH LEMON, SALT AND SUN If you have a persistent rust spot on a prized garment and it is washable, sprinkle salt on the stain; there is no need to wet it first. Then wet the area with lemon juice, either fresh or bottled. Lay the garment out in the sun, which helps to bleach the fabric, for a few hours. Then rinse to remove the lemon juice and salt. You may have to repeat the process a few times. On coloured fabrics, test the method in an inconspicuous place first. Take dry-clean-only garments to the dry cleaner.

I have grease on my clothes

ABSORB WITH POWDER AND DE-GREASE WITH DETERGENT Clothing, tablecloths, bedspreads and other fabric items face all sorts of greasy perils on a daily basis. Cooking oil from a frying pan, baby oil in the nursery and cosmetics in the bathroom can mean trouble. To remove such stains, follow these steps:

1 Blot up as much of the oil as you can with paper towels.
2 Cover the remaining spot with an absorbent powder, such as talcum powder, cornflour or bicarbonate of soda.

3 After about 30 minutes, brush the spot with a toothbrush or soft nailbrush. (Soft bristles won't damage or wear away the fabric.) Repeat until the powder has absorbed as much as it can.

4 Coat the spot with a clear de-greasing washing-up liquid. Brush it in with anoher toothbrush or rag. Let it stand for 2 minutes.

5 Soak the spot in hot tap water for 30 minutes to help to dissolve the grease.

The garment is now ready to be laundered in a hot water wash.

My shirt collar has a thick ring of dirt

PRE-TREAT IT WITH SHAMPOO The insides of shirt collars pick up oil and dirt from our skin, which leave a dirty ring on the cloth. Shampoo is the solution. Put a little bit of shampoo on the collar and gently rub it in with an old toothbrush. Then wash as usual.

Sticky pockets from gooey play dough? WD-40 will remove the stain in minutes.

My child left some Silly Putty in his pocket

SCRAPE IT OFF; THEN APPLY WD-40 You can work it like clay, you can bounce it like a ball . . . and you can seriously mess up fabric with this oozing plaything. Start by picking off as much of the substance as you can. Then scrape with a butter knife or some other dull, hard-edged object. Spray the stained area with WD-40, let it sit for 10 minutes and scrape again.

Spray the spot once more with WD-40, let it sit for another 10 minutes and blot the stain with a clean cloth. If a stain still remains, douse an unused area of your cloth in surgical spirit and blot the spot repeatedly. Then launder the clothing as usual.

I have water spots on my dress

DAMPEN THE AREA AND PRESS A little spill here, a little splash there and you can end up with watermarks on a garment. The first thing to be aware of is that the water didn't cause the mark. Rather, it's something in the fabric, such as dust, dirt, body oils or even fabric softener, that causes the stain. When water mixes with one of these substances, it creates a spot. The solution lies in more water:

1 Put an absorbent rag, such as an old gauze nappy or an artificial chamois, over the mark.

2 Spray this covering material with a fine mist of water from a spray bottle until the material is damp to the touch.

3 Press the covering material with an iron set at a temperature suitable for the fabric. The extra moisture will often disperse the ring, while the heat from the iron dries the sprayed water.

Alternative: Dampen a small artist's paintbrush, lightly brush over the water spot and use a pressing cloth to iron over the spot.

■ WASHING PROBLEMS

My white cotton top has come out of the wash with a pink blush

REMOVE IT WITH A BLEACH SOLUTION White or light clothing washed with darker colours can come out with an unwelcome new hue. But with a little patience you can sort it out. Soak white clothing overnight in a solution of 1 part household chlorine bleach to 10 parts water. Then rinse in cold water and wash as usual. Hang in the sun to dry (UVA rays will further lighten the fabric). If the dye isn't quite gone, repeat. The bleach and water solution also works on colours – say if a yellow top has turned a little pink. The dye in clothing is set chemically and professionally to stop it from running, so a diluted bleach solution can remove dye that has come from another item because it hasn't been set in the garment. But always do a patch test first to check the colourfastness of the original shade.

For delicate fabrics that can't be treated with chlorine bleach, use peroxide, which isn't as aggressive. To remove a colour stain, mix 50ml peroxide in 4 litres water. Soak for half an hour, rinse and wash as usual. Dry in the sun to help the peroxide to lighten the clothing.

I've accidentally spilled some bleach on my new navy skirt

RINSE WELL AND APPLY AMMONIA Bleach spilled on coloured clothes can ruin them. Laundry experts stress that time is of the essence. As soon as you see the problem, take these steps:

1 Rinse the garment with cold water. It takes a few minutes to flush bleach out of a fabric.
2 Put the garment on a counter with an old towel beneath it. Pour some ammonia, which deactivates bleach, over the area.
3 Wet a rag with more ammonia and rub from the outside toward the centre of the spill. This should take about 5 minutes.

Ironing needlework without flattening it
If you have cross-stitch or other embroidery on a tablecloth or clothing, directly ironing it normally against a hard surface like an ironing board will ruin the look of the stitches. Instead, lay a folded bath towel on the ironing board and gently iron the reverse side of the embroidery. This will provide enough pressure to get the ironing done without crushing the stitches.

The result may not be perfect; you may end up with a spot a little lighter than the rest of the garment.

Caution: Apply the ammonia in a well-ventilated area and only after the bleach has been thoroughly rinsed out of the fabric. The combination of bleach and ammonia can create a dangerous gas.

My white socks are dingy

BOIL THEM WITH LEMON White socks that have become a strange shade of grey or yellow, even though you've washed them with bleach, are one of the tougher laundry problems to solve. Your once washed socks may never be as bright as the day you bought them, but here's your best bet. Boil some water on the hob, drop in a slice of lemon and add the socks. Let them bubble away for 15 to 30 minutes.

I left my laundry in the washing machine for too long and it smells

RE-WASH WITH BICARBONATE OF SODA If you forgot to take out a load of laundry you may be greeted days later by an unpleasant smell. There's an easy solution: run the clothes through the wash cycle again with warm or hot water, depending on the fabrics in the load and 200ml bicarbonate of soda. Then put the laundry in the drier with fabric softener sheets. If a piece of clothing in the batch is something you need right away and it is dry, spray it with a fabric freshening product, such as Febreze which should neutralise the odour.

▪ IRONING PROBLEMS

I have lengthened my dress, but the crease of the old hem still shows

DAMPEN WITH VINEGAR SOLUTION AND IRON Even though you have carefully removed the stitches from a hem, lowered it and rehemmed it, the crease from the original hem still stands out like a beacon. Sponge the crease with equal parts of white vinegar and water, and then iron. Or sandwich the crease between two pieces of aluminium foil and press with a hot iron.

If there's a mark, as opposed to a crease, where the original hem was, use a spot remover to erase it. Or, if appropriate to the style of the garment, hide the mark by adding a decorative trim.

I have scorched my favourite dress with the iron

USE PEROXIDE ON THIN FABRIC With a flatter, thinner fabric, such as linen, cotton or wool, place the garment on a folded white towel. Then mix a 50-50 solution of hydrogen peroxide and water and pour it onto the mark. Leave the solution on for several minutes; then blot with a clean towel.

Here are two other ways to handle a burn mark:

- Make a paste with powdered dishwasher detergent and water and put it on the mark. Then lay the fabric in the sun to bleach.
- Use chlorine bleach for white cotton or linen fabrics and all-fabric bleach for synthetic fabrics. Leave either product on the scorch mark for 10 to 15 minutes. Then blot the area with water and launder.

Caution: Test any remedy on an inconspicuous area first. If you scorch a delicate fabric like silk, take the garment to the dry cleaners.

USE SANDPAPER ON THICK WOOL Sometimes you can smell the fabric overheating before you actually see the scorch mark. You end up with an ugly light-brown mark on your garment. What remedy you use depends on the fabric you're dealing with. On a solid-coloured thick, wool fabric (or heavy upholstery linen), you can use extra-fine grade glasspaper. Very lightly abrade the surface of the scorched fibres until you see undamaged fabric beneath the surface.

My iron has left lines on my clothing

PRESS THEM OUT If you've been heavy handed with the iron and one of your garments now has ridge lines and smashed-looking fibres or unwanted creases, you have four options, starting with the simplest:

- Place a pressing cloth over the area and see whether the heat of the iron will fix the problem. The pressing cloth can be a white tea towel, anything made of muslin or an old nappy.
- If that doesn't do the job, try steam. Don't put the iron right on the cloth, though. Hold the iron just above the fabric and let the steam spray. Then use your fingers or a brush to fluff the area.
- Still have a problem? Try misting the pressing cloth with water, then pressing.
- The last resort: Mist the press cloth with a half-and-half solution of water and white vinegar; then press without steam.

Scorched wool? Use some extra-fine grade sandpaper to remove the mark.

Appearance and accessories

■ HAIR PROBLEMS

Static electricity is making my hair stand on end

USE ANTISTATIC FABRIC SPRAY Static electricity will send your locks flying every which way, but never the way you want it to. To fix the problem, squirt some antistatic fabric spray on your comb and then run it through your hair. (It won't damage your hair.)

If you don't have antistatic fabric spray, dousing your comb with hair spray will also help. Misting your hair with water from a spray bottle is the last resort.

If you have hair-raising static, get it out in a jiffy with antistatic fabric spray.

My hair is so matted I can't comb it

LOOSEN IT WITH OLIVE OIL The solution is as close as your kitchen cupboards. Olive oil can help to loosen matted hair. First rub some oil into the matted area. Wait a few minutes and then slowly work out the matting with a large-tooth comb. After you've combed out the mats, shampoo your hair to remove the oil.

If you rub the oil into your entire scalp, it will act as a deep-cleansing conditioner. After rubbing in the oil, wrap your head in a towel for half an hour before washing your hair.

I'm frustrated with my frizzy hair

RUB IN SKIN LOTION Is your hair frizzy and uncontrollable and you don't have any hair-care products to hand? An easy remedy is to rub a generous amount of moisturiser onto your hands and work it into your skin. If you've used enough, you'll still have some residue left on your hands after a few minutes. Now rub your hands lightly over your hair. There should still be enough moisturiser left to smooth out the unwanted frizz.

My thick hair takes forever to dry

USE SUPER-ABSORBENT PAPER TOWELS People with thick hair face special challenges when it comes to drying hair quickly. A professional hair stylist says that super-absorbent paper towels are the answer. After drying your hair with a bath towel, scrunch sections of hair up in a paper towel, which can absorb more moisture than an ordinary towel. When the paper towel is saturated, throw it away and repeat with another. This technique should cut down the amount of time you need to use a blow drier.

My hair is really dry and dull

SPRAY IT WITH DILUTED CONDITIONER Some people have naturally dry hair. Others develop dry hair from exposure to heat and hair-styling chemicals. Dry hair owes its rough texture and dullness to raised cuticles on the hair shaft, which allow moisture to escape.

To treat dry hair, fill a spray bottle halfway with a hair conditioner and fill it the rest of the way with water. This makes a spray-on conditioner that you can leave in. If you have just washed your hair, spray the conditioner on your wet hair to help you to comb and condition it further. You can dampen dry hair a little with a spray bottle of water and then spray the conditioner on.

I have brown hair and I need an inexpensive colour treatment

MAKE A COFFEE RINSE Here is a low cost way to make brown or red hair richer and shinier. Brew some dark, rich coffee and let it cool. Mix 3 tablespoons of the coffee with a tablespoon of shampoo. Rub the shampoo into your hair and leave it in for 15 to 30 minutes. (Put on a shower cap if you want to walk around the house without making a mess.) Then rinse the mixture out of your hair and condition as usual.

Over-treatment has made my hair look like a bad wig

GIVE IT A BEER RINSE Even if you have loaded your hair with leave-in conditioner, anti-frizz products, hair-volume enhancers, mousse and hair spray, you can get it back to normal. Shampoo your hair and then pour a can of ale on to it. Leave the beer on for a few minutes and then rinse.

Food for your hair
If you have dyed, thick or dry hair, you can keep it healthy with a weekly deep conditioning. A professional hair stylist says you can use common ingredients from the supermarket: for example, mayonnaise or avocado well blended with a couple of teaspoons of olive oil. First shampoo your hair, towel it dry and comb either the mayonnaise or avocado oil mixture through your hair until it is saturated. Leave the treatment on your hair for 20 minutes or so before rinsing.

Mastering mascara
Some women pump the application wand up and down in the tube to get lots of mascara on the brush. But this technique allows air into the tube and makes it hard to get an even amount of mascara on the brush.

A better technique is to put the brush into the tube and twirl it. If there is already a clog in the tube, remove the wand and clean it thoroughly with soap and water. Add a few drops of spring water or distilled water to the tube. (Tap water isn't sterile.) Put the lid on tightly and shake the container. The water should dissolve any clumps.

■ FACE AND SKIN

My eyebrows are out of control

GROOM THEM WITH A TOOTHBRUSH If you are having a hair-raising experience with your eyebrows, get a new soft toothbrush, spray it lightly with hair spray and groom your unruly brows. (Keep it in a place where you won't mistake it for the one you use on your teeth.)

Rain has messed up my make-up

BLOT WITH TISSUE AND CLEAN UP WITH LOTION Getting caught in the rain can undo the make-up you so carefully applied in the morning, particularly mascara and blusher. To save face, first blot your face with tissues to absorb the moisture without removing or distorting your blusher and foundation. Then use hand lotion on a tissue to clean up smudges under the eyes. (Most mascara is not waterproof.) You can even use olive oil in an emergency, if you happen to be in a restaurant. Dab a napkin or tissue in the olive oil and then head for the cloakroom to remove the dark spots under your eyes.

I want to get rid of a spot

COVER IT WITH TOOTHPASTE Like many of life's little crises, spots turn up when they are least wanted. Ordinary white non-gel toothpaste has a drying agent that can help to heal a spot more quickly. Wipe enough toothpaste over the pimple to cover it and leave the toothpaste on overnight. The pimple won't disappear immediately, but the toothpaste should reduce the redness.

My skin is oily and I get spots

GIVE YOURSELF A HOMEMADE FACIAL Try a homemade facial mask to help with the problem. In a small bowl, mix one egg white and the juice of half a lemon. Apply the mixture to your face with clean fingers. As the egg white dries, it closes and tightens pores; the lemon juice helps to dry up oil on your skin. You can also make a facial mask by mixing bicarbonate of soda and warm water in a small bowl until you get a creamy consistency.

As the face mask dries, you will feel your skin tighten. Once the mask is completely dry, rinse it off with warm water. Then rinse your face again in cool water to help to close the pores. Apply moisturiser to rehydrate your face. Masks like this can be used once a week.

My lipstick doesn't go on neatly any more

PUT ON FOUNDATION FIRST As we get older, lipstick tends to 'feather' into the fine lines around the lips, giving the lips an uneven appearance. You can fix the problem by applying foundation to your lips as well as the rest of the face. Foundation will fill in the fine lines around the mouth, preventing the lipstick from spreading into them and also helps to keep the lipstick looking fresh longer. To further prevent the lipstick from feathering, you can create an added border with lip liner and then fill in with lipstick.

I had a late night and my eyes are puffy

PUT CUCUMBER SLICES OVER YOUR EYES If you have stayed up too late and maybe had a drink or two too many, the area around your eyes may have a puffed-up look by morning. You will have seen the solution in fashion pictures a hundred times: cucumber slices. Take a cucumber straight from the fridge. Cut two slices, about 6mm thick. Lie down and place the cucumber slices on your eyes for about 20 minutes. The cold cucumber, which is more than 90 per cent water, feels soothing. The moisture, plus the natural sodium in the vegetable and the cool temperature, will help to reduce the swelling under your eyes.

It's true! Cold cucumber slices really do help to reduce swelling on puffy eyes.

I have a snagged nail and no emery board

SUBSTITUTE A MATCHBOX If a ragged fingernail is catching on everything and you don't have an emery board, use a box or book of matches. Rub your nail against the little strip designed for striking matches. It's not as abrasive as an emery board, but it will help.

■ JEWELLERY PROBLEMS

The clasp on my earring has fallen off

SUBSTITUTE A BIT OF PENCIL ERASER If you lose the clasp that goes behind your earlobe on an earring for pierced ears, find a pencil with an eraser. With a sharp knife, a razor blade or a pair of scissors clip off a bit of the pencil's eraser, run the point of the earring shaft through the hole in your earlobe and press the bit of eraser onto the point to serve as an improvised clasp.

PROBLEM STOPPER

Keep jewellery from turning your skin green
Whenever you buy a new piece of costume jewellery, coat the inside – the part that will be in contact with your skin – with clear nail varnish. This will prevent the piece from tarnishing and leaving a green ring on your finger, wrist or neck.

My brass jewellery is turning green

MAKE A VINEGAR-BASED TARNISH REMOVER The condition may suggest that the plating beneath the surface may be damaged. But there is a way to take care of the green. Mix together a tablespoon of vinegar or lemon juice, a tablespoon of salt and a cup of hot water. Dip an old toothbrush or a nylon scrubbing pad into the solution and use it to wipe away the green. Dry completely with paper towels and a hair drier set on cool.

Ketchup can help, too. The acid in the tomatoes will eliminate the tarnish. Use a cotton swab or a toothpick to put it on the jewellery. Leave it on for 5 to 10 minutes and then clean the jewellery with a soft, damp cloth and dry it with a hair drier. Repeat if necessary.

My sterling silver jewellery is tarnished

SOAK IN A FABRIC SOFTENER SOLUTION There are three ways to deal with tarnish that has made sterling silver jewellery look dull, as long as the jewellery doesn't have stones set in it. The first is to soak the jewellery in a mixture of fabric softener, salt and water. Heat a litre of water, add 4 teaspoons of salt and stir to dissolve the salt. Then stir in enough fabric softener to make the mixture cloudy. Soak the pieces in the pan for an hour, remove, rinse under warm water and rub lightly with a clean, dry cloth. Repeat the process if you need a higher sheen.

RUB WITH A BICARBONATE OF SODA PASTE Put 2 tablespoons of bicarbonate of soda in a bowl and add enough lemon juice to make a paste. Brush it on the jewellery with a soft toothbrush. Let the solution dry a bit and then run it under water, using a clean toothbrush to remove the mixture. Dry thoroughly with a clean cloth.

USE ALUMINIUM FOIL AND BICARBONATE OF SODA Line a pan with aluminium foil (or use a disposable aluminium baking pan). Put the jewellery on to the aluminium. Dissolve a tablespoon or two of bicarbonate of soda in 500ml hot water and then pour the solution over the jewellery. You will see the foil getting darker and the jewellery getting lighter. Note: this method works so well that it will even remove tarnish from crevices in the jewellery. So if you prefer an antique look, use one of the first two methods. For silver jewellery with stones, use a paste silver polish and soft cloths; soaking stones can loosen or discolour them.

My gemstones have lost their sparkle

USE WINDOW CLEANER A little bit of an ordinary glass cleaner will get dull-looking gemstones to shine once more. Spray some commercial window cleaner on a clean, lint-free cloth, until it is barely damp. Then wipe it over the jewellery. This will also clean the metal around the stones.

■ EMERGENCIES WITH GLASSES

I have broken a stem on my glasses

FIX IT WITH GAFFER TAPE Make a temporary repair using that old favourite, gaffer tape. Using a toothpick or even a small, slender twig to serve as a splint, position it at the broken spot on the frame and wrap both together with tape. At a pinch, gaffer tape can also be used to secure the hinge.

I have lost the hinge screw on my glasses

FIX IT WITH FISHING LINE If a minuscule screw has fallen out of the hinge on your glasses and the stem is now separated from the frame, you'll find that a piece of nylon fishing line makes an excellent temporary repair. Move the loose stem to the open position, as if you were about to put the eyeglasses on, to get the proper alignment. Thread a piece of the nylon line through the screw hole. Then trim the excess line with scissors, leaving 1mm on each end. Heat the tip of a knife and touch it to each end of the line. The melting line will form just enough of a bead to prevent it from slipping through the holes. When it is time to make a permanent repair, snip an end off the line and slide it out.

The frames of my plastic sunglasses don't fit

USE HEAT TO RESHAPE THEM If they've been pulled around too much, plastic frames on sunglasses can get stretched into different shapes and may stop your glasses from fitting properly which can cause them to slip off. To get them back to the way you like them, immerse in hot water or heat them with a hair drier. The plastic should become far more flexible, allowing you to bend the frame back into shape.

How to keep from slipping in new shoes

A pair of slick-soled new shoes can have you sliding around like a slapstick comedian. To keep your dignity intact and prevent a fall, take a tip from professional models. Mix 4 or 5 teaspoons of sugar into a cup of cola soft drink and stir until the sugar dissolves. Then use a paintbrush or paper towel to smear the liquid on the soles of your new shoes. Let the mixture dry for several minutes and then put your shoes back on. The soles will now have enough tackiness to give you stable footing. Models use this technique when they strut the catwalk in fashion shows. It works well for plastic and leather soles.

■ SHOE PROBLEMS

My shoes are too tight

USE SURGICAL SPIRIT You need to stretch your shoes in the places where they are too tight. Put them on and apply surgical spirit with a rag or tissue to those snug areas. This will soften the leather and, with the aid of the heat of your feet, allow it to stretch to fit your foot better. The stretching will take a day. If they are too painful to wear all day, take them off and stuff them with socks or a pair of old tights to push them into shape. Some experts suggest that you dampen thick socks with surgical spirit and wear them in the shoes until the socks are dry.

My trainers smell

SPRINKLE THEM WITH BICARBONATE OF SODA Running and sweating will make your shoes stink. Bicarbonate of soda, famous for its odour-absorbing ability, is an easy antidote. Sprinkle some of the powder inside your shoes, leave it overnight and vacuum it out. For a longer-term solution, put your trainers in the wash and let them air-dry thoroughly afterwards.

A puddle has soaked my shoes

STUFF THEM WITH NEWSPAPER You have two problems when shoes get soaked. One is to get them dry and the other is to retain the original shape of the shoe. Crumpled newspaper can do both jobs better than paper towels because it holds its shape while absorbing water. Ball the newspaper up into tight wads and press them firmly into the shoe until it is well packed. Replace the newspaper stuffing every 20 minutes until the shoes are dry.

My shoes are caked with mud

LET THEM DRY BEFORE BRUSHING On leather shoes, wait until the mud has dried and then brush it away with a stiff brush. Rub a damp rag over the shoe to remove any remaining mud. Dry the shoes with a clean rag and then dab with a good wax shoe polish, which will penetrate the leather and protect the shoe from future stains.

I have white salt marks on my shoes

REMOVE WITH A VINEGAR SOLUTION A trudge home over a well-salted pavement on a winter day can leave your favourite shoes coated with stubborn salt stains. The quick solution is to mix 2 tablespoons of white vinegar with 100ml water and dab the mixture on the salt stain with a sponge or rag. The acidity in the vinegar will dissolve the salt. For suede shoes, first brush the stain with a suede brush and then apply a milder solution – 1 tablespoon of white vinegar in 100ml water. Machine wash canvas shoes.

The heel of my shoe has come loose

NAIL IT BACK ON FROM INSIDE If you're rushing out and the heel comes loose on one of your shoes – the only ones that go with the suit you're wearing – you need a quick fix. Find a short nail or thumbtack and a hammer, peel back the lining on the inside of the shoe and hammer the nail through the sole and into the heel. Shoe repairers will wince, but the heel will get you through the day.

I can't lace my frayed shoestring

DIP IT IN CLEAR NAIL VARNISH When the end of a shoestring is frayed, it's hard to thread the lace through the eyes of your shoe. The solution is to snip the frayed end off the lace. Then dip the tip in clear nail varnish to harden the material, wait for the varnish to dry and you'll be able to whip the lace through the holes in the shoe.

TRICKS OF THE TRADE

Is one foot larger than the other?
You could buy the size that fits the larger foot and pay extra for an insole to fill the space in the roomier shoe. Or, (if the difference is not too great) buy a pair of shoes to fit the smaller foot. Remove the lining and padding from the bottom of the shoe for the larger foot. There will be another layer of fabric underneath, which is perfectly comfortable. This method should work on virtually any kind of shoe.

PART SIX

Social life

A tipsy guest who's being offensive.
An acquaintance whose name you've forgotten.
Partygoers who don't know when to call it a night.
A sudden thunderstorm at an outdoor wedding.
The friends having a loud argument at your party.
In this part of the book, you'll find a safe passage
through all these potential social minefields.

Parties and weddings

A party planning countdown
Whether you are holding a party for 10 or 500, the best planning tool you can have is a timeline. This is simply a written checklist, broken down by day and hour, of what you need to do before the event. For example, you can use it to remind yourself when to have your cleaning finished, when to set up chairs and when to start cooking the different parts of the meal. This will keep you from forgetting anything important or starting a task prematurely.

■ PARTY PLANNING

I'm having a party at a smart venue and I'd like to save on the alcohol bill

SUPPLY YOUR OWN ALCOHOL Check with the venue if they are happy for you to do this. Buying the alcohol yourself will be cheaper than having the caterer or venue provide it. You will know your exact bill up front and how much your guests have drunk. (The caterer could exaggerate both of these and you would have no way of knowing.) And if you have any unopened bottles left, you can usually return them to the shop where you bought them. (Be sure that you are clear about the return policy before you buy anything.) When deciding how much alcohol to buy, consider the age of most of the guests (younger adults drink more), the time of day (people drink more at night) and how many guests drink in the first place.

An alternative: instead of buying your own, try to negotiate a flat fee for the alcohol from the caterer or venue.

I don't know how much food to get

FOLLOW THE CATERING RULES OF THUMB If you want to see party guests gathering their coats in unison, just run out of food or drinks and see how long the festivities continue. Fortunately, there are time-tested guidelines. Here are the basics:

- Overall amount of food: 700g a head for a meal; about 450g a head for a cocktail party
- Hors d'oeuvres: six pieces a head for a dinner party; 12 a head for a cocktail party (four to six pieces each per hour).
- Alcohol: two drinks a person each hour for the first two hours; half that amount later. A 75cl bottle of spirit (vodka, rum, whisky etc.) has about 30 25ml shots; a 75cl bottle of wine yields about five glasses
- Soft drinks: plan on three bottles of mixer for every bottle of spirit. Stock plenty of bottled water, as well as a good range of

soft drinks and juices for non-drinkers and to give drinkers of alcohol a break.

If you are serving an expensive, 'special treat' food item, such as caviar, plan on serving a lot of it, because that is probaly where your guests will go first. And remember, when planning the quantity of food, it is always safer to round up.

The weather forecast for my party is looking bad

HAVE A BACK-UP PLAN If you're planning an outdoor wedding or other major event, always take into account the possibility of rain. Talk to an equipment-rental or party-supply outlet about reserving a marquee that is large enough for your event. Keep an eye on the weather on the days leading up to the big day. If it looks like it will rain, go ahead and have the tent set up. Check whether you will be able to get your deposit back if you end up not using it.

If you are planning an event in a courtyard or other outdoor area at a large hotel, the establishment may provide you with an indoor room in case it rains. As these rooms are sometimes not very glamorous, watch the weather and have a plan in place to spruce up the room if you do need to move indoors.

Having a back-up plan in place can save a special occasion when Mother Nature wants to rain on your party.

 UNEXPECTED EVENTS

Fourteen people have turned up at a party for 12

KEEP SMILING AND IMPROVISE One of the most difficult situations you may face as a party host is accommodating guests who show up uninvited or come anyway after not responding to an RSVP. To reduce the risk of this happening, about a week before the party, call up any guests who haven't replied to your invitation to see whether they are planning to come. If surprise guests do show up, the polite thing to do is to overlook their impoliteness and make them feel welcome. If at all possible, rearrange the place settings to make room for the extra guests. If you are throwing a really big party, set up an extra table

Get a head start
Depending on how elaborate your party is, start planning early. Here is a sample timeline:

• Six to eight weeks before: plan the theme, activities and music; send invitations; hire entertainer and/or caterer.

• Two to three weeks before: order non-perishable supplies and decoration; hire helpers.

• One week before: call guests who have not RSVP'd; confirm the entertainer, caterer and helpers.

• Two to three days before: buy groceries; make any dishes that can be prepared and frozen; begin cleaning the house.

• The day before: thaw frozen foods; finish cleaning; decorate the space and set up table(s) and utensils.

• Party day: complete food preparation; do a final check of the space, bar and kitchen; give yourself plenty of time to get ready; take a deep breath and enjoy!

beforehand, just in case. And when you plan the menu and food amounts, assume that you will be feeding a few more people than are on your guest list. If you don't, you will just have to discreetly reduce everyone else's portions (before you serve them) in order to provide for the unexpected guests.

The food ran out before the party was over

GO TO THE SUPERMARKET DELI Experienced party planners keep extra hors d'oeuvres in the freezer for such moments. If that's not an option, get someone to nip out to the nearest supermarket. Most will have bags of prepared vegetables, special dips, cheeses and cold meats. Here is a quick-fix shopping list for a dozen hungry guests:

Amount	Item
500g	smoked salmon
500g	sliced cold meats
1kg	selection of good cheeses
1 jar	mustard
2 boxes	crackers
2 loaves	French bread or baguettes
1 jar	green olives
1 large bag	bite-size peeled carrots
2 small punnets	cherry tomatoes
1 large bunch	grapes
500g	dried apricots

I seem to be hosting a get-together I didn't know I was having

MAKE DO WITH WHAT YOU HAVE The phone rings and suddenly you find that eight people will be turning up in your living room in an hour. Don't panic. Here's a formula for throwing an instant party:

- Set the mood: light some candles and pick out a few background music CDs.
- Take an inventory of what's in the fridge and kitchen cupboards. Be creative. Check out a favourite cookbook. Don't be too ambitious. If you have potatoes and toppings (such as cheese, bacon, chives and soured cream), you have the makings of some party food that will appeal to most people.

- If you simply don't have any alcohol or enough food, you may have to make a quick run to the shops (see previous problem), but let your guests pitch in as well. Don't get stressed. Instead, turn the party into a participatory affair by asking your guests to bring their own choice of tipple or to pick up a specific item of food on the way to your house.

■ PROBLEM GUESTS

I need to get a shy person involved

MIX AND MATCH A shy, frowning, clearly uncomfortable guest is a danger to a relaxed, fun party and to your reputation as a host. If you see a guest sitting alone, corner someone who is a good talker or has something in common with the shy guest and introduce them to each other. Have a three-way conversation for a few minutes and then excuse yourself.

The trick to getting a shy person to talk is to avoid questions that can be answered with yes or no. Instead, try conversation starters that invite longer answers and follow-up questions: What travel have you done lately? What books are you reading – or what good films/theatre have you seen?

A big mouth is boring everyone else to tears

DEFLECT ATTENTION Although there are dozens of people mingling in your home, only one seems to be talking – standing in the middle of the room telling hearty jokes. Sometimes it's fine; a witty guest can keep the party rolling. But eventually the joking gets dull and you may want to shift the spotlight. What should you do?

Often the situation will resolve itself naturally. Guests will get up and move elsewhere and the dynamics will change. Or you can wait for a particular anecdote, then step in and say something like, 'Oh, that happened to Jenny, too. Jenny, tell us what happened.' But sometimes, as the host, it becomes *your* responsibility to absorb the loudmouth's good cheer. Tell the big talker that you need a little help with a task and ask him or her to assist you. By the time you return, other people will have had a chance to start up conversations.

As party host, it's up to you to get control of someone monopolising the room. A quick way is to ask for his or her assistance in another room.

A tipsy guest is making everyone else uncomfortable

CALL A TIME OUT Loud and out-of-control guests, especially those who are clearly drunk don't just spoil a good party; they can be a danger to themselves and to other people. If someone whom you have invited to your home is being loud and obnoxious, take him or her and say discreetly that while you are glad he or she is having such a good time, you would like him or her to tone it down so everyone else can continue to have a good time, too. If you don't know the person very well, get one of the guest's friends to try and calm him or her down. If the party is at a public venue, such as a hotel or pub, here are some other ways of reining in guests who have been seriously overindulging:

More light and less music quickly signal to your guests that it's time to head for the door.

- Ask the bartender to stop serving them drinks.
- Ask the venue manager to intervene.
- If the guest is really making trouble, call security.

Caution: Do all you can to keep a guest from driving under the influence of alcohol. Offer to call a cab for anyone who isn't sober enough to drive. If you know the person well enough, offer to let him or her sleep it off overnight on your couch or in the spare bedroom. Or discreetly slip out and give the person a lift home.

Two friends are arguing loudly at my party

INTERVENE WITHOUT TAKING SIDES Here's a technique that will help you to defuse the situation. Walk up to the two arguing people and say, 'Is this a matter that you two can resolve? If not, I'm afraid I'll have to ask you to leave.' This simple expression of question and consequence usually quashes the argument. It makes both people accountable for their actions, regardless of who is in the right. And you, the host, are not forced to take sides.

My guests don't know when to call it a night

LIGHTS ON, MUSIC OFF The party is rolling along nicely: the guests are having a good time, the music is playing and no one wants the evening to end. No one except you, that is. When it's one o'clock in the morning and you just want the last remaining guests to leave so you can go to sleep, take your cue from the entertainment industry. Half an hour before you know you want people to leave, start telling them that the evening will soon be coming to a close.

Start putting away drinks and food, turn on a few lights and turn down the music. In half an hour's time, thank any stragglers for coming and help them to the door. Be polite, but firm.

I'm at a party with someone I hate

KEEP CIRCULATING Maybe it's a colleague who's after your job. Or a neighbour who keeps looking at your spouse the wrong way. Whatever the case, you find yourself face-to-face in a social setting with someone you really dislike. The key is to keep your animosity from ruining the party. At your first encounter, greet the person as cordially as possible and move on. Parties are all about mingling and circulating, so there's no reason to linger with someone you dislike, much less air your grievances. If the party is a sit-down dinner and you know beforehand that this person is on the guest list, inform your hosts of the situation so that they can keep you well apart.

Keeping everyone happy with the music

USE A LITTLE CREATIVE DECEPTION It's inevitable that at wedding receptions or other parties with several generations of guests, young people will want the music turned up *and* older people want it turned down. If you can't reach a happy medium, try an event planner's ploy: simply tell your noise-sensitive guests that you have noted their wishes and had the music turned down, but don't actually do it. This is a psychological trick that usually makes the listener think the music is indeed quieter.

▥ WEDDINGS

I'm afraid that my wedding day will turn into chaos

APPOINT SOMEONE TO OVERSEE THINGS FOR YOU Having 'too many cooks in the kitchen' all issuing orders on your wedding day can lead to confusion and chaos. Choose a 'wedding marshal' – one person who will be in charge on the day. Pick as your overseer a responsible friend or family member who will be at the wedding but who doesn't have a specific duty or isn't already deeply involved in the day. Don't choose a bridesmaid, best man or the mother of the bride, as they already have enough to do. Give your coordinator a to-do list and specific instructions on how things should be done. They can make sure the flowers are in their proper places, the chairs are set up in the right places and that all the caterers and other helpers are where they need to be. Make sure to work with your wedding marshal well ahead of the event, rather than just handing him or her a list on the morning of the wedding.

I'm afraid that I won't be prepared for any wedding day emergencies

PUT TOGETHER A WEDDING DAY TOOLBOX A well-organised bride, mother of the bride or other person in charge of a wedding will keep a wedding day 'emergency kit' ready to handle little last-minute incidents that can arise.

The kit should include scissors, needle, thread and safety pins to repair accidental rips and tears in the wedding gown or bridesmaids' dresses. Put in a little can of hair spray and a travel hair drier, for hair emergencies and a painkiller, such as paracetemol to treat headaches and some plasters for the occasional cut or scrape.

Another good tool in the kit is a small bottle of laundry detergent. One wedding planner used it to fix a panic-stricken bride's train after it was dropped on to a dirty pavement before the wedding. A little detergent and water dabbed onto the spots sorted out the problem.

I'm not sure how to thank our best man and bridesmaids

JEWELLERY IS ALWAYS APPRECIATED It's appropriate to give your wedding attendants a token of your appreciation and esteem. If it is within your budget, one gift your attendants will really appreciate is assistance with all or part of their wedding day clothing or accommodation costs.

Less expensive alternatives include cufflinks or a good leather wallet for the best man and ushers and jewellery for the bridesmaids that can be worn on the day of the ceremony. Gift certificates for spa treatments are also a popular choice for bridesmaids.

Manners and social obligations

■ AWKWARD SITUATIONS

Someone has a trolley full of shopping in the express queue

TALK TO THE MANAGER The shopper who abuses the express till queues poses the kind of problem that really makes people cross in our pressurised times. Some of these shoppers, with their bulging trolleys, are just being rude. But others may be making an innocent mistake. It is not up to you to confront them or ask them to go to another queue. It is the shop's responsibility to enforce their six (or eight) items or less rule. If you notice that this problem happens a lot, ask the manager if he or she can do anything to keep express queues moving quickly. And be sure to check your own trolley or basket before you start glaring at others. If you find yourself with an item or two over the limit, that's probably all right. But if you realise you are way over the limit, graciously find another till queue.

If the express till queue is regularly misused, it may be worth speaking to the manager to make sure they are aware of the problem.

I've forgotten someone's name

ACKNOWLEDGE IT WITH A SMILE Don't be mortified when you forget the name of an acquaintance or colleague. These things happen to everyone. Just say, 'Oops, I've forgotten your name' and lightheartedly promise to remember it next time. When the person reminds you of his or her name, repeat it aloud as a way of helping you to remember it better.

I've called someone completely the wrong name

SAY YOU'RE SORRY AND LET IT GO What may be worse than not remembering someone's name is calling the person by the wrong

Keeping guests out of the kitchen

When your kitchen is a mess of pots and pans, hot hob and oven, and dirty dishes, it's not a place where you want guests to congregate. But asking them to stay out can be awkward. Keep them in the right part of the house by planning ahead. Don't put anything in the kitchen – no food or drinks.. By keeping such items out of the kitchen, guests will be more likely to stay in other areas of the house. If possible, shut the door to the kitchen. People are reluctant to go through closed doors in other people's homes.

name. For instance, if you are speaking to a friend's new husband and you call him by the old husband's name. Or you refer to your new boss by a sacked boss's name. Try to acknowledge your mistake with a little humour. Perhaps say, 'Oh, I really know you're Mike and not Tom.' Apologise for your slip-up and let it drop.

If your mistake has obviously insulted a person of authority, such as your boss, who wasn't impressed with how you recovered from the error, you might want to send a quick note later, again apologising for the lapse.

I have really put my foot in my mouth

DON'T DENY, JUST APOLOGISE PROFUSELY Perhaps you wrote a nasty e-mail message about someone and accidentally sent it to them. Or mocked an acquaintance whom, you discovered too late, was standing nearby. As the floor isn't going to open up and swallow you whole, much as you wish it would, you have to deal with the situation you have created. You must offer an apology and it must be a good one. Don't say, 'I didn't really mean it.' You probably did mean it and denying it will just compound the error. In other words, don't apologise for what you think, feel or said about the person. Instead, apologise for the effects of what you said. Try saying something like: 'I cannot apologise enough for making those careless comments about you. It was heartless, it was stupid and you don't deserve whatever embarrassment or irritation I have caused you'. Apologise profusely and sincerely and then be done with it. Don't stretch out the explanation or keep bringing up how sorry you are later.

I have bumped into a friend who didn't invite me to his wedding

FORGIVE AND FORGET Your circle of university friends swore that you would be friends forever. So your feelings were hurt when, five years after graduation, one of the guys invited everyone except you to his wedding. You have just bumped into him at a reunion and you feel awkward. In this case, take the moral high ground and don't mention the wedding. Perhaps you lived far away from the ceremony and your friend didn't want you to feel obliged to make a lengthy journey. Or perhaps the other friends had stayed in closer touch with the groom than you had. Whatever the reason, don't make a big deal of it. When you see your friend, simply congratulate him on his marriage and wish him and his wife the best.

A stranger has asked me a personal question

REPLY POLITELY BUT KEEP IT SHORT Perhaps you are pregnant. Or your child has a birthmark or disability. Or one of your children is adopted. You would think these matters would be your business alone, but unfortunately there are a lot of nosy people out there. Although such questions are undeniably rude, bluntly telling the questioner to mind his or her own business is not the way to deflect the questioner. People don't mean to be rude. Give him or her the benefit of the doubt. Have a few polite responses ready, but don't offer too much information. Say something like, 'Yes, I'm expecting' or 'Yes, she's adopted.' Continue with, 'I'm in a hurry' and don't get involved in any further discussion.

My friend has bad breath

OFFER A MINT How do you tell a friend that he or she has bad breath? An easy, roundabout way is to pop a mint or into your own mouth and then offer one to your friend. If you do this, you won't be saying anything outright and if he or she accepts your offer, everyone wins. If not? Well, it depends on how strong your friendship is. You either risk offending your friend with the truth or ignore the problem and excuse yourself to get a breath of fresh air.

WHAT IS THE POINT OF ETIQUETTE?

Etiquette isn't just for stuffy Victorian tea drinkers or members of the aristocracy. It is a series of codes that is intended to help make your life better, no matter what job you do or your station in life. Here are some insights into how good manners benefit everyone from people with experience in the etiquette business:

- 'People say to me that etiquette is pretentious. It's not. Etiquette is about kindness, courtesy and respect.'

- 'Etiquette is just a set of rules that evolve as our culture evolves. We have travel etiquette, death etiquette, phone etiquette and Internet etiquette. There are rules for everything.'

- 'Etiquette helps smooth the way through different situations. It's about being considerate and respectful and honest and kind. It's based on consideration and respect – being able to empathise with how other people might want to be treated. A lot of it is common sense and a lot of it depends on the situation.'

If you have flatmates or close neighbours, it's likely that one of them will do something at some point that you'll find irritating. Advance planning can prevent many problems and the next-best solution is to deal with the problem immediately. Here are some pointers:

Set ground rules up front with flatmates. Decide how often boyfriends or girlfriends can stay. Decide when and how loudly everyone can play music or watch TV. Decide how bills and chores will be divided. All are common problem issues.

If your neighbours do things that intrude on your peace and enjoyment of your home, meet with them as soon as you can to come up with a solution. You will save yourself a lot of pent-up anxiety and hard feelings.

■ PHONE ETIQUETTE

My telephone call has been cut off

CALLER REDIALS A disconnected phone call is a minor inconvenience, but the solution can be a major hassle. Who should redial and resume the conversation? If both people redial, both get busy signals. If *neither* redials, thinking the other person will do it, both people waste time staring at the phone. In general, the person who instigated the call in the first place should do the redialing. But if you know that the disconnection was at your end – maybe you pressed the 'disconnect' button on the phone – *you* should call back.

I'm in public and my mobile is ringing

BE DISCREET AND DON'T DISTURB OTHERS Improper mobile phone usage is a major and mounting source of irritation these days. The general rule is to avoid making or receiving mobile phone calls if you are going to intrude on people around you. That includes settings such as restaurants, cinemas, libraries, public transport and places where you should be interacting with others (on a date or at a meeting, for instance). You should not disturb strangers with your conversation (especially if it involves intimate details) and don't make friends and acquaintances feel second best when you take a call during your time with them.

If you know that you're going to be receiving an important call during a meeting or get-together, tell your companions ahead of time that you will be called away at some point. Set your mobile phone to vibrate instead of ring and head to a secluded area when you get the call. If the call could be an emergency issue – say from your child's babysitter – you will be forgiven for going ahead and taking it where it would normally be impolite. Just be as discreet as possible.

■ SOCIAL COMMUNICATIONS

I'm never quite sure when a thank you note is required

WHEN IN DOUBT, WRITE Thank you notes are on the endangered-habits list. Etiquette experts plead for you to do your part to bring them back from extinction. Write a thank you note within a day or two of receiving a gift. (After a wedding, you have six weeks to send your thank you notes, but sooner is always better.) Sit down with your children and see to it that they write thank you notes for their gifts they receive, as well. This is a habit that is best started when they're young. Steer clear of pre-printed cards which say something along the lines of 'Thank you for the _____.' Cards like this don't really convey much appreciation.

Gifts aren't the only reason to send notes. After you have dinner in someone's home, it is proper to thank your host in a call the next day, followed by a quick thank you note. And *always* send thank you notes to potential employers after an interview, thanking them for their time and interest. This habit is fading away nowadays and a note will make you stand out from other candidates. If the employer is likely to be making the decision very soon, an e-mailed thank you is appropriate.

I would like to offer my condolences to someone quickly

IT'S OK TO E-MAIL If someone you know suffers a tragedy or loss, you are expected to express your sympathy. Ideally, you should offer your condolences in person. If that's not possible, a written note should be your next choice. However, if you want to offer comfort immediately, e-mail is a good way to send the bereaved person a quick message. E-mails are preferable to phone calls, which might come at an inconvenient time and can't be dealt with later. Just be sure to follow up the e-mail with a visit or handwritten note later. E-mail should *complement* these methods, not replace them.

I need a card for someone who's terminally ill

TRY WRITING YOUR OWN You want to offer sympathy and support to a friend who's in a struggle that he or she is not likely to win. But what kind of card is the right one? Obviously, don't choose 'Get Well Soon', a message that fails to acknowledge the seriousness of your friend's problem and conveys a wish that probably won't come true. Choose a card with a message such as 'My thoughts and prayers are with you'. But only send a card with a specifically religious theme if you know that the recipient shares those beliefs. Probably the best option is simply to pick a pretty card that's blank on the inside, so that you can express your own thoughts and best wishes.

I keep forgetting birthdays

KEEP TRACK MANUALLY OR DIGITALLY It's not that easy to remember everybody's birthdays and other special occasions. The basic strategy for keeping on top of such things is to compile a list of every date you need to remember, buy a calendar and jot each one down. You will of course have to remember to check the calendar. Or better still, have the calendar programme in your computer, mobile phone or Blackberry do the remembering and reminding for you.

What if you still keep finding yourself empty-handed on gift-giving occasions? Avoid the situation by stocking up on cards and gifts in advance. Go to a card shop and buy several cards that are appropriate for the occasions you observe, plus some tasteful-but-generic blank ones that will do for just about any occasion. Keep a laundry basket or cardboard box full of small gifts and wrapping paper. Pick up a selection of attractive gifts at sale prices after Christmas. You should find plenty of useful gifts that you can put away safely whenever you suddenly remember that you need to celebrate someone's birthday.

My Christmas cards often go astray

DO AN E-MAIL ADDRESS CHECK We live in a fast-moving society, so keeping track of friends and acquaintances can be tricky. When it is time to send out Christmas cards, it's important to have everybody's contact information updated. To make sure your address book is accurate, send an e-mail to all your friends and family in October, asking them to e-mail you back with their updated contact information. (Give them yours as well.) When December comes, you will have everyone's addresses handy and won't have to scramble to get the address at the last minute.

▪ DATING

My date is very boring and I want to get out of here

DON'T RUN AWAY Even if you are not having a good time, think twice before abruptly rushing away from a date who is not to your liking. First of all, it's rude. But there's another good reason to try to leave on a good note: you never know who you might meet through this person. Your date may be no fun, but that doesn't mean his or her brothers or friends are. Stay on good terms with the person and you might be able to meet other people, one of whom might turn out to be a better match for you. This is particularly important for singles who have trouble meeting eligible dating candidates.

At the end of the date, just say, 'It was nice meeting you', and leave it at that. If you feel like calling later, you will have set the stage for it. But if you don't call later, you didn't promise that you would.

Even if your date is not what you'd hoped for, leave on good terms. You never know who you might meet through this person.

I'm dating a high-powered woman and don't know how to behave with her

KEEP CHIVALRY ALIVE Treat her as you would any other woman. Chivalry may be dying, but it is still a great asset on a date, even if she earns lots of money. Open the door for her. Let her go first through a door. Pull out her chair at the dinner table. And send flowers if you really like her – check with the florist which flowers are currently elegant and fashionable but don't send ones with a specific romantic connotation unless you want to give that message.

I have a first date – but not much money

KEEP IT SIMPLE AND ACTIVE If you've finally had the nerve to ask someone on a date, but money is tight and even if you had more cash, you are not sure what sort of activities she would enjoy. What should you do? First, don't get concerned about making a first date a lavish event. Your only two goals are to discover whether you are really attracted to the other person and whether you enjoy being with this person. So don't get tense and nervous, wondering whether you've finally found 'the one.'

Instead of spending £100 on dinner and a film, keep the first date simple, aimed at simply having a good time. Choose a Saturday afternoon. In summer, go for a bike ride or a walk through a park. In winter, go ice-skating and get some hot chocolate. If all goes well, the date can extend into the evening and if not, you can say you have plans with friends later. If you both decide to continue the date, stick with the simple, low-key theme. Have a bite at a café, for example, and save the expensive dinner for the second date.

■ GIFT GIVING

I've been invited to a dinner, but I don't know what to take

WINE OR CHOCOLATES ARE ALWAYS WELCOME When your hosts have been kind enough to invite you to their home, it's polite to return the kindness by bringing a small gift. A few rules apply. Unless you have the host's blessing in advance, never arrive bearing a dish of food, such as a casserole, that needs to be eaten immediately. It might clash with the rest of the dinner. Nor should you bring a gift that requires attention, such as fresh flowers that need to be cut and put in water. Your host already has enough to do. Bring a small potted plant, a bottle of wine, a box of chocolates or some other small token of your appreciation. Don't expect to get a taste of the wine, though; the host isn't obliged to open it and serve it with dinner.

I'm not attending the wedding; should I send a gift?

YES, YOU SHOULD If you were sent a wedding invitation, but it is too far away to attend or you have another commitment, you should still send a gift. A wedding present isn't intended as repayment for taking part in the wedding ceremony and reception. It is a way of expressing your good wishes for the couple and responding to the regard they showed you by asking you to share in their big day. What you send depends on how well you know the bride and/or groom. If the bride is a close relative, you will obviously want to give a meaningful present. If the wedding is that of a distant acquaintance, something more modest is fine. Have a look at their wedding list. It is likely that they have put together a list with a wide range of prices and you'll be able to find something suitable.

Should I give a gift every time a friend marries?

DO SEND ANOTHER GIFT You gave a friend a fondue set in 1980, a VCR in 1987 and microwaveable serving dishes in 1995. Now it's the new millennium and your friend is getting married again. And yes, you do need to send another wedding gift. You always need to give *something*, but what, exactly, depends on the situation. If you only gave your friend an expensive wedding present two years ago, it's appropriate to give more of a token gift this time around. If your friend's last wedding was 15 years ago and the spouse has since died and your friend is finally remarrying, a more substantial gift to mark the event would be appropriate.

I didn't receive a gift from someone who came to my wedding

IT'S APPROPRIATE TO CALL AND FIND OUT IF IT HAS GOT LOST If you're not sure why your aunt didn't send you a gift even though you are close to her, it is worth calling her to ask if she intended to get you a gift. Although this may seem like the *opposite* of good manners, etiquette experts explain that while it may seem as if you're pressuring her for a late gift or trying to make her feel guilty, what you are really doing is trying to find out whether her gift was lost in the post or the order was misplaced by the shop. If that is what happened, it would be inconsiderate to allow your friend or relative to spend money on a gift that you didn't receive. Discovering that the gift was actually lost may also prevent any future strain or awkwardness in your relationship.

▪ FOOD ETIQUETTE

Yuck! Someone's bitten into their food and put it back into the dip

ALERT THE HOST Taking a bite out of food and then putting it into a dip again is both inconsiderate and unhygienic. It also puts you, as the observer, in an awkward spot. It wouldn't be polite to confront the offender, but then it also wouldn't be right to say nothing and allow others to sink their food into a now questionable dip. The solution is to discreetly tell the host or someone on the serving staff, 'You may want to replace that dip'. Don't go into detail, just say it's tainted and leave it at that.

I've just spilled my drink on a dining companion

ASSIST, BUT DON'T TOUCH, YOUR VICTIM Although your first instinct may be to grab a napkin and help to dab away the drink you have just knocked over onto a dining companion, restrain yourself. No matter how helpful you intend to be, touching the person you've spilled drink on intrudes into his or her personal space and might make him or her feel even more uncomfortable. Discreetly gather napkins, sparkling mineral water or any other items that might be useful in cleaning up. Offer to pay the cleaning bill for the stained garment. But it's best to keep your hands to yourself.

■ BUSINESS INTERACTIONS

Is it appropriate to hand out some business cards at a friend's party?

IF YOU DO, DO IT SPARINGLY AND CAREFULLY Business cards are a great way to share information about yourself, leave behind a little reminder of your presence and encourage new business. But networking without careful thought at a social engagement can potentially leave the wrong impression and devalue the card. Make sure that when you give someone your card, there is a certain amount of importance attached to it. Not only should you be sparing with your cards, but you should also make sure that you hand them out at the right moment and to the right person – someone with

EATING STYLES: WHEN IN ROME...

European and American styles of eating are differentiated by how the knife and fork are held during a meal. In the American style, a person cuts food by holding the knife in the right hand while holding the fork, tines down, in the left hand. Once the person has cut a piece, the knife is placed on the plate (blade facing toward the eater) and the fork, with tines up, is switched to the right hand to convey the food to the mouth. In the somewhat more efficient Continental style, there's no switching of the fork. Food is taken to the mouth with the fork held tines down in the left hand, while the knife remains in the right. Both styles are acceptable, but what is never acceptable is to cut up more than one piece of food at a time and then shovel the cut pieces into your mouth with the fork.

whom you will actually be able to do business or who works in a business that is related to yours. The best way to handle a situation like this is to ask someone for his or her card first – if it is appropriate and you have been discussing your line of work – then ask if you may then return the favour by giving him or her your card.

I would like to know how to introduce people properly

THINK RANK, NOT AGE OR GENDER Whether you're at a business or a social function, there is one basic rule you need to follow when introducing two people to each other. Don't worry about their gender or their age. Instead, always introduce the person of lesser authority to the person of greater authority. So you should not say, 'Joe Bloggs, this is Ambassador Horace Massingham-Smythe', but rather, 'Ambassador Horace Massingham-Smythe, may I present Mr Bloggs'. If everyone is of the same rank, you may want to introduce the younger person to the older one.

There is a question on my voice mail that I don't have an answer for yet

CALL BACK WITH A PROGRESS REPORT If someone at work calls (or e-mails) you with a business-related question that you know will take a while to answer, you may be tempted not to respond until you know the answer. This is not a good idea. Instead, reply immediately with a progress report and say that you will come back with the requested information as soon as possible. If you think that you can definitely stick to it, give the person a specific date by which you will have delivered the answer to the question.

The finer points of elbows
This may come as a surprise, but propping your elbows on the dinner table isn't a complete faux pas. As long as there is no food on the table, it's completely appropriate to rest your elbows on the table before and after the meal and between courses. But keep a check on your posture and don't sprawl your upper body across the table.

PART SEVEN

Everyday life

Cars came first but the dented bumper was not far behind. When e-mail was invented, spam followed soon after. When mobile phones became ubiquitous, so did problems with poor reception. Every innovation of modern life, it seems, creates a new universe of potential mishaps. But for work, play, commuting, computers, travel, shopping, children and more, we've got plenty of useful answers.

Modern living

Copy your wallet
Losing your driving licence is one thing; losing your entire wallet or handbag is an entirely different matter. Few things in life can make you feel more helpless. That's why it's a good idea to photocopy every important document that you keep in your wallet or handbag, from credit cards to gym memberships. If you do this, you'll know exactly what you've lost and whom you have to call to report it.

■ LOST, MISPLACED AND STOLEN ITEMS

I've left something in a taxi

NOTIFY THE TAXI COMPANY AND HOPE FOR THE BEST As soon as you become aware of a loss, contact the cab company, if possible and see if the cab driver has handed in your lost item. If you lose something in a London black cab, they will automatically hand it in to the police who then forward it to the London Lost Property Office (Tel: 0845 330 9882) which will search for your item for 21 days after the reported date of loss. You will have to give proof of identity to get your items back from them. To improve the odds of recovering your item or avoiding a loss in the first place:

- Whenever you get into a cab, note the taxi number. This will make it a lot easier for the taxi company to at least identify the cab you travelled in.
- If you have already got out of the cab, try to get the licence plate number, for the same reason.
- Put your name, address and phone number on particularly important items, such as briefcases, laptop computers and address books.
- Whenever you exit a cab, take note of everything that you were carrying with you, especially your wallet and mobile phone, two items that can easily slip out of your pockets.

I have lost a contact lens on holiday

GET YOUR PRESCRIPTION SENT THROUGH The advent of disposable soft contact lenses and online vendors has made losing contacts much less of a problem than it once was. (When was the last time you saw someone on all fours looking for a tiny piece of clear plastic?) But if you are travelling and run out of disposable lenses or lose one of your special hard lenses, it could really spoil your holiday. The most obvious solution is to travel with an ample supply of disposables or an emergency spare set of rigid lenses. But if you didn't think ahead and find yourself without lenses, here's what to do. Contact an optometrist, optician or ophthalmologist where you are staying and make sure that office accepts prescriptions by fax or email. If it does, call your dispensing optician and get a copy of the prescription faxed through. If this isn't possible, you will need to be examined for a new prescription.

I can't find my driving licence

REPORT IT TO THE POLICE AND THEN THE DVLA If you have lost your licence, first make a lost property report at a local police station. Although you probably won't get your licence back, at least you will have started a paper trail to show that you are trying to get a new one. Try to ensure that they give you a reference number – this will be useful if you are stopped before you have managed to replace the licence. Then get in touch with the The Driver and Vehicle Licensing Agency (DVLA) (Tel: 0870 240 0009 or go online at www.dvla.gov.uk). You may be able to get a new licence over the phone if you have a licence with a photocard, but if you have one of the old-style paper licences you will need to apply in person at a Post Office or fill in the form D1 'Application for a driving licence' and post it to them along with any documentation they require. If you do find your licence again after requesting or receiving a new one, you'll need to write to the DVLA enclosing your old licence and explaining what happened.

My bag has been snatched!

CANCEL YOUR CREDIT AND DEBIT CARDS
If your handbag is stolen, it has probably gone for good. The police do not recommend that you or a good Samaritan chase after the thief. What you should do is phone and cancel your credit and debit cards immediately. If you don't have the card numbers handy, call home and ask someone there to find some old credit-card receipts. Tell your credit-card company where and when your bag was stolen. If you report the loss before the thief uses the card, you won't be liable for any unauthorised charges. If the thief does run up charges before you call in, your liability is limited to £50. Follow up the initial call with a letter to the credit-card company listing the account number, the time and place of the theft and the date you reported the loss. And remember to keep checking your statements carefully, as you'll need to report each unauthorised charge to your credit-card company in writing. Finally, be sure to report it to the

Don't run after the person who grabbed your bag – phone the police and your credit-card companies instead.

police. Not only might it help in apprehending your bag snatcher, but it will also come in handy if the credit card company questions your reported loss.

I can't find my wallet

GET OTHER PEOPLE TO JOIN THE SEARCH Stop looking by yourself. You will just keep looking in the same places over and over again. Bring a fresh set of eyes into the equation. For instance, if you've lost your wallet around the house, enlist your neighbours' children to look around your house and car. The person who finds the wallet gets a £10 prize. It would be money well spent.

■ TAXES

I'm missing some of my tax paperwork

CHECK LAST YEAR'S RETURN Not everyone in the UK needs to file a tax return. But if you're one of them, you've left it rather late and you discover to your horror that you're missing some paperwork with information you need, here's what you can do:

- Find last year's tax return. Most people's tax returns do not deviate much from year to year, so last year's return should be a good indicator of the documentation you're missing this year.
- If you're looking for deductions, get out old bank statements and credit-card bills. If you can't find all of them, call your bank and credit-card companies and get them to send you a copy of your yearly transactions. Most charge a nominal fee.
- If you need verification of mileage, ask your mechanic, who will have jotted down the mileage when the car was serviced. This will help you to estimate the miles you can deduct.

I'll never make the tax deadline

FILE ONLINE (OR HAVE A GOOD EXCUSE) Since 2008, if you want to file a paper tax return, you must send it to your tax office by 31 October following the end of the tax year. If it arrives later than 1 November, you are automatically fined £100. But switch to online filing and you get an extra three months until 31 January. You'll need to register which involves waiting for security details to arrive by post – allow seven working days. The HM Revenue & Customs (HMRC) software is free and covers the most commonly used sections of the return. If your tax affairs are unusual, you might need to buy commercial software; the HMRC website (www.hmrc.gov.uk/sa/file-online.htm) has a list. The final deadline is 31 January. If you miss it there is a £100 automatic fine with a further £100 if you still have not filed six months later. In extreme cases, HMRC can fine you up to £60 for each day you delay. 31 January is also the deadline for paying any tax due and you'll incur penalties and interest on tax that is paid late.

You can apply for the £100 late-filing fines to be reduced to an amount equal to any tax you owe if it is less. This means that, even if your return will be late, paying the tax on time can reduce or eliminate the late-filing penalties. HMRC may also waive the £100 penalty if you have a reasonable excuse for filing late. Reasonable excuses might include for example: an unforeseen postal strike; records lost through fire, flood or theft and you could not get replacements in time; you had a serious illness or your spouse, civil partner, unmarried partner or a close relative died immediately before the deadline. Excuses that HMRC will not accept include pressure of work and difficulties getting the information you need.

■ MONEY AND BUYING

I always spend too much money at the supermarket

STICK TO YOUR LIST There are so many temptations in supermarkets these days. Here are a few ways to keep costs down while shopping:

- Don't go shopping on an empty stomach.
- Shop with a list and stick to it.
- Don't dawdle. The faster you shop, the less you'll spend.
- If possible, don't take children with you. But if you have to take them, give them a task, such as picking items like breakfast cereal, pasta and bread, so that they are not pulling out every confectionery item on the shelves.
- Buy staple foods, such as rice, pasta and flour, in bulk. Buying in bulk is cheaper, and you might be able to go without shopping for a few days and save more money.
- Use coupons. Make use of the coupon circulars that sometimes come through the door or that are handed out when you

accrue enough points. Trade coupons that you don't want with those you do with a friend who may have some you do want.

- Keep an eye out to see if there is a pattern to the way that your supermarket offers one-day, unadvertised specials. If there seems to be a particular day when the specials are on, make sure you check in on that day or ask sales staff what is the best day to get discounts.

My credit card won't swipe

TRY WRAPPING IT IN PLASTIC You're in a rush at a cashpoint and it tells you that your card 'cannot be processed. Please try again'. Or your debit card won't register in the supermarket's card terminal. It may be that the magnetic strip on the back of the card is scratched, preventing the machine from reading it properly. Try taking a thin piece of plastic – a grocery bag is perfect – and wrap it very tightly around the card. When you swipe it again with the plastic in place, it should work. The extra layer of plastic will fool the machine into thinking that there are no scratches on the strip.

Card won't swipe? Wrapping plastic around it will quickly solve the problem.

I'm in the market for a mortgage

GET AN 'AGREEMENT IN PRINCIPLE' AND SHOP AROUND Buying a house may be exhilarating, but it's stressful, too. And no part of the process is as stressful as securing a mortgage especially while lenders are reining in offers because of the 'credit crunch'. To avoid disappointment, ask for a mortgage agreement in principle before you find your dream home. You fill in a form similar to a full mortgage application, giving information about your income, job status, and so on. The lender assesses your credit worthiness and, if you pass, issues a certificate showing how much you can borrow. The certificate is usually valid for three months. It is not a guarantee that you'll get a mortgage; that depends on the information you gave being verified as correct and the lender accepting the property you choose. But the certificate does prove to sellers that you are serious and will give you the edge over buyers who have not sorted out their finances. Here are a few guidelines to securing a good mortgage deal:

- Shop around. A broker can help but some lenders only offer their mortgages direct, so check out the market yourself using a web comparison site, such as www.fsa-gov.uk/tables.
- Make sure you have a deposit – in 2008 – at least 15 per cent was required. First-time buyers with household income below £60,000, buying a newly built home, may qualify for a five-year, interest-free loan to cover the deposit under the government's HomeBuy Direct scheme – see www.communities.gov.uk for details.
- Don't just compare interest rates, look at the mortgage fees too. Check whether any are refundable should your mortgage not be approved or if you choose to pull out.

It's time to pay the restaurant bill, and I've forgotten my wallet

LEAVE YOUR WATCH WHILE YOU FETCH YOUR WALLET Don't panic. Offer to leave behind something of value while you dash home for your wallet works in most cases. Explain your situation to the manager and offer to hand over your watch, mobile phone or briefcase. Another solution is to call home to try and get a credit-card number.

I'm getting too much unsolicited mail

TAKE YOUR NAME OFF THE MAILING LISTS If you are inundated with junk mail, what can you do to stop the flow? With mail from companies, cut it down by going to the Mailing Preference Service (MPS) a free service funded by the direct mail industry. It enables UK consumers to have their names and home addresses removed from or added to lists used by the industry. The MPS holds a list of names and addresses of people who wish to limit the amount of direct mail they receive. Contact them by phone on 0845 703 4599, in writing at Mailing Preference Service (MPS), DMA House, 70 Margaret Street, London, W1W 8SS or online at www.mpsonline.org.uk to register your name on their preference list.

Being registered with the MPS can remove your name from up to 95 per cent of direct mail lists. It will not stop mail sent from overseas, un-addressed mailings or mail addressed to The Occupier. You can expect to continue to receive mailings from companies with whom you have done business in the past. You may also receive mailings from small, local companies. If you want to stop these as well, you will have to notify these companies directly. It will take up

Argue like an umpire
When you get into
discussions that lead
to arguments, you know
you are always right.
The problem is in
persuading others of
your point of view. The
challenge is even more
pronounced for sports
referees, officials
and umpires.

Next time you are in
a conversational mess,
think like an umpire. He
will usually try to explain
how he saw a situation
and say something like,
'If it happened the way
you saw it, then I'm
wrong. But that's not
how I saw it'.

In other words, a
little give-and-take can
go a long way in getting
your point across. Ask
questions and force
your opponent to sup-
port his theories. One
question that always
works is, 'Did you see
the whole incident or
do you *think* you saw
the whole incident?'

to four months for the MPS service to fully come into effect although
you should notice a reduction of the mail during this period.

■ PUBLIC PROBLEMS

I always forget my lines when I speak in public

USE AN OUTLINE AND THEN AD-LIB You're not alone. If you keep
forgetting your lines when speaking in public, experienced speakers
advise that you throw away the script. It's hard to remember the
words if you're trying to follow a script that is too detailed. Speaking
without a script is the best way to ensure a smooth presentation,
because it gives you more flexibility. Jot down the main points you
want to make so that you'll have an outline to remind you. Put them
in the sequence in which you want to bring them up.

I said something very stupid in a meeting

MAKE A JOKE, IF YOU CAN; OTHERWISE, APOLOGISE No matter who's at
the meeting, once you've said something stupid or inappropriate,
you may become the focus of attention. What should you do? The
sharp-witted among us may be able to diffuse the situation with a
joke. It's not a bad idea, but only if you've come up with something
truly funny that won't offend anyone and make matters worse. For
the rest of us, the best way out is to apologise gracefully. Say
something along the lines of, 'I am very sorry. I really did not mean
for that to come out the way it sounded. 'What I meant to say is …'
Most people will let you off the hook at that point.

If you don't feel that what you did deserves a *mea culpa*, you
may be able to pin the blame on the business-world mainstay:
brainstorming: 'I was just thinking out loud – brainstorming!' As
any mid-level manager will tell you, there are no stupid ideas
during a brainstorming session.

I'm in a karaoke bar and I know I'll have to sing

PRACTICE AND RELAX Public speaking is not the only thing everybody
is afraid of; singing in public is far more terrifying. Here are some
tips to help to make a karaoke experience less nerve-racking:

- Pick songs that you like and that are easy for you to sing.
- Practise at home. Sing along with the original recording to
  make sure you can hit all the notes. Watch yourself in a mirror

to make sure that you don't make too many silly faces. Record yourself if possible.

- Even though you will have the karaoke screen to prompt you, you'll feel more confident if you know the words by heart.
- Before going 'onstage', take a drink of water to lubricate your throat and vocal cords.
- You will have a microphone, so you don't have to shout. And don't forget to breathe.
- Remember, this isn't the Royal Albert Hall. Relax, smile (if it's a happy song) and have a good time. If you're having fun, so will your audience.

I feel guilty about ignoring beggars

GIVE A GIFT OF FOOD, NOT CASH You're actually doing the right thing, according to social workers and you shouldn't feel guilty. Unfortunately, many beggars have substance abuse problems or are mentally ill. While giving them money may stop them from hassling you, the donation is likely to feed self-destructive behaviour and end up in the coffers of a pub or a drug dealer. Here's how to make a more positive contribution. The next time you are in a fast-food restaurant, buy a few gift vouchers. Hand one of them over the next time you are approached by a beggar – or take them in and buy them a burger. It may not be what they really want but you will know that you've been able to provide a meal. Another way to help is to make a donation to a local homeless shelter.

A salesperson is being very rude to me

COMPLAIN TO THE MANAGER – AFTERWARDS All you want to do is to buy a pair of jeans, a few apples or perhaps a new TV. Dealing with an obnoxious salesperson is not on your agenda at all. What should you do? Complaining to the manager may not get you very far, because unless managers actually witness gross misconduct, they often feel compelled to side with their employees. The best time to complain to the manager is later, after you either make or don't make your purchase, not in the heat of battle. Here are some other strategies for dealing with a rude salesperson:

- Turn around and walk away, especially if you're in a shop where the sales staff work on commission.

Practising may not get you to the Royal Albert Hall, but it makes singing karaoke a lot less stressful.

- Kill the salesperson with kindness. You won't win in a battle of who-can-be-the-rudest, so be extra nice – it's hard to maintain rudeness when the other person doesn't respond in kind.
- Keep calmly repeating your questions. This may make the salesperson angry and might attract the attention of a manager.

■ SPILLS

My overloaded plastic bag has ripped

IMPROVISE A CARRIER Oranges rolling one way across a supermarket car park and canned tomatoes rolling in the other direction are the last thing you need in the middle of a busy day, but if you're wearing an anorak style jacket with a zip, you can improvise a solution. First, put down your other grocery bags and gather the contents of the split bag. Take off your jacket and spread it out on the ground. Place as many loose grocery items as possible inside the jacket, zip it up and tie the arms of the jacket together to form a loop, folding the bottom of the jacket through the loop so your items won't spill out. Hoist the loop of your impromptu carrier over your shoulder and tuck any remaining loose items in the good bags.

I have spilled a box of beads

WRAP TAPE AROUND YOUR HAND A bevy of beads scattered all over the kitchen floor is a handicrafter's nightmare. But there is an easy answer in the utility drawer – a roll of masking or sticky tape. Hold one of your hands out flat, fingers pressed together. Wrap the tape, sticky side out, around your hand until the palm and fingers are covered. Then lightly press your taped-up hand against the beads, lifting up to 20 at a time. Brush them off the tape into a container and then go after more escapees until the job is done.

■ LOCK OUTS

I have locked my keys in the car

HAVE YOUR NUMBERS ON HAND If you're locked out of the car, your best option is to contact one of the motoring organisations (if you are a member), a locksmith, or a local garage. The following free telephone numbers will connect you to a local contractor: Scoot 0800 192192; Talking Pages 0800 600900. The police may help you if there is a child or distressed animal locked in the car, or you are caught in a dangerous or isolated spot late at night or are a disabled driver. Even if this is the case, the police may still need to break in to gain access to the car.

If the above options are not open to you and you don't belong to a motoring organisation, you may either have to break a side window to gain access, or call a locksmith. But, if a window is open just a crack and you have manual locks with a 'mushroom' shaped button, and a wire coat hanger, the following might work. Straighten out the hanger and bend the end into a U-shape. The idea is to get the U around the base of the door lock. Once you manage to get it round the base, slowly pull the hanger up in the hope of catching it on the wider part at the top. Once you are able to do that, slowly pull it up again and the lock should pop up, opening the door.

If the car has power locks, it may be easier to use the hanger to press the button on the side opposite the slightly open window if you can find a rod or hanger long enough. Keep pushing the hanger down until you find the button and you may be able to push it open.

I'm locked out of the house

YOU MAY HAVE TO BREAK IN If you're locked out of the house and no one else has a key, you are faced with two choices: Call an emergency locksmith (expect to pay £65 to £100) or break a window. While breaking a window is not something we're exactly recommending, there is a right way to do it. Pick a window close to the ground and make sure you can fit through it before you start breaking in. Next, find a heavy rock or brick that you can fit into your hand. Hold it against the window using a piece of cloth (a shirt or jacket will do) to cover your hand and then, very carefully, start tapping the rock or brick against the window, close to the lock. Tap until the glass shatters, then use the jacket to clear away any hanging glass near the lock. Put your arm though the hole and open the lock.

Now you will need to get your window fixed, so you will need to read 'My windowpane has broken', on page 86.

■ LEGAL PROBLEMS

I've been arrested

SAY NOTHING WITHOUT A LAWYER Here are some things to do – and not do – should you find yourself in the backseat of a police car.

- Keep your mouth shut. Be co-operative and do what the police ask, but do not answer any questions or offer any information except to give your name and address. You must, however, provide a sample for a breath test if asked to do so.
- Ask to see a lawyer. If you cannot afford one, a solicitor will be provided. Do not answer any questions until you have seen a lawyer in private.
- Make sure you understand why you have been arrested. The police cannot usually detain you without charge for more than 24 hours (36 hours for serious offences). Make sure that the correct time of arrest is logged on your record.
- Ask for someone to be notified of your arrest (you do not have the right to make a phone call yourself).
- Don't sign anything unless advised to do so by your lawyer. Sometimes police officers will ask you to give a statement and sign it. Don't do it.

My bank and credit-card statements contain items that I don't recognise

ACT QUICKLY AND CONTACT YOUR BANK AT ONCE You may be a victim of identity fraud. Here's what to do:

- Check all your other card, bank and building society accounts for unusual transactions. If someone is using your accounts fraudulently, the bank will take action
- Make sure your passport, driving licence and other important documents are all safe and secure. If anything is missing, contact the issuing agency at once
- If there is any possibility that your mail is being stolen or redirected without your knowledge, contact Royal Mail, especially if you have recently moved house, or live somewhere where other people can access your post
- Obtain a copy of your credit report and check that there are no entries from organisations that you do not recognise. If there are, contact the organisation straight away. If you are a victim of fraud, the credit reference agency will advise you what to do. (Credit reference agencies include Call Credit: www.callcredit.plc.uk; Equifax: www.equifax.co.uk; Experian: www.experian.co.uk)
- If you suspect that someone is using your name or address to apply for credit, contact CIFAS, the UK's Fraud Prevention

Service (www.cifas.org.uk; tel 0870 010 2091). You can apply for Protective Registration, to set up a password to use for any future credit applications in your name

- Keep a record of everything you do, including organisations you have contacted, dates and the name of anyone you speak to. Keep copies of all correspondence and send all letters by recorded or special delivery.

■ PASTIMES

I'm just not getting any better at golf

LOWER YOUR EXPECTATIONS AND PRACTISE PUTTING The object of the game is to keep hitting a little ball until it falls into a hole 400 metres away. Some days, that can seem more like punishment than fun. If you have just taken up the game and find that you are struggling to improve your golf, here are some secrets from the pros:

- Do not play with any expectations of how you will perform. Banish thoughts like, 'I'm going to break 80' from your head.
- Don't spend a lot of money on clubs. There are millions of pounds of golf equipment sitting unused in garages all over the world. Try car boot sales, check out eBay or ask around at your local club to see if anyone is upgrading their clubs and find yourself a set of good clubs cheaply. (Use inexpensive balls, as well.)
- Try playing late in the day, when the 'serious' golfers have finished and are off the course.
- If you have whacked the ball ten times on to one hole without finishing, don't waste any more time. Pick up the ball and move on to the next hole.
- If you have just two shots to try to get out of a sand trap and you are still stuck, throw the ball out.
- If you must practise, practise on the putting green, not the driving range. Good putting is the best way to cut the most off your score.
- Walk the course; don't use a buggy. Not only is this good for your heart, it's also good for your game, as it gives you more time between shots.

Banishing impossible dreams and practising your putting are the fast ways to improve your game.

Making use of time spent waiting in line

When you're stuck in a long line, relax and use the time productively, says storyteller Dennis Goza. He carries flash cards that he has made to help himto learn Chinese characters with him. 'I practise "writing" the characters by tracing them in the air with my finger – which helps to ensure that other people don't crowd me too much', he says.

I'm going to a racecourse for the first time and don't know how to place a bet

LEARN THE TERMINOLOGY Here are a few basic terms that will help you to decide what kind of bet you want to place and where to do it.

- A stake is the amount of money that you are willing to gamble.
- The odds, or price express the perceived probability of that horse winning the race.
- Winnings or returns are calculated according to your horse's odds. Prices can be odds against, even money or odds on. With an odds against bet, if your stake is £1, a winning bet at 2/1 will return £2 plus the original stake, giving £3. With an even bet, if your stake is £1 you will get £1 plus your stake, making a total of £2. An odds on bet is less lucrative: a successful £1 bet at 1/2, will return 50p plus your stake, making a total of £1.50.
- Sometimes instead of odds being expressed as a fraction, they may be referred to as simply 'long' or 'short'. Long odds such as 50/1 indicate that a horse is very unlikely to win, while short odds such as 2/1 show that a there's a good chance of a win.

WHEN BETTING, YOU HAVE THREE OPTIONS It's up to you to decide which horse you bet on – you can study the previous 'form' of the horse and/or jockey or you can make a decision based on the look of the horse on that day. You can then place your bet on the Tote, with a course bookmaker or at the racecourse betting shop.

BETTING ON THE TOTE If you are betting for the first time, the Tote is probably your best option. You can place bets in a number of ways based on your horse winning or being placed. The money is pooled and then distributed at the end of the race on a pro-rata basis depending on the amount of money put in by each individual. Tax is deducted from the total before the money is distributed.

USING A BOOKMAKER With a bookmaker you can only bet to win. Remember to shop around to get the best odds, always give the name of the horse, keep your card as a receipt and don't throw away a bet until the 'weighed in' signal is given.

THE RACECOURSE BETTING SHOP At a racecourse betting shop you can make a variety of bets at much smaller stakes. You fill in a slip and hand it over with your stake. You are then given a receipt, which you return to the counter for payment if your bet is successful.

Electronic life

■ TELEPHONE HASSLES

Finding numbers in directories takes too long

GET FREE DIRECTORY ENQUIRIES FROM YOUR LANDLINE It can be time consuming finding the number you want from a phone directory, if you have one to hand in the first place. It can also be pretty expensive dialling directory enquiries to find the number you want. It is possible to find your number for free using one of the free directory enquiry services from your landline: The Number on 0800 118 3733 and Free Directory Enquiries 0800 100 100. Both are able to offer numbers without charge in return for playing you an advert each time you call.

I keep getting an engaged tone

LET YOUR PHONE TELL YOU WHEN THE LINE IS FREE It can be pretty frustrating and time consuming if you keep dialling a number and it is constantly engaged. But with most phone companies you can get your phone to let you know when the line becomes free by using a ringback service. With British Telecom (BT), for example, if the number you dial is engaged you press 5 on your phone and hang up. Once the line becomes free, within 45 minutes your phone will ring and if you pick it up the number you want should be ringing. BT charge 30p for the service – there is no charge if the line doesn't become free within 45 mins. Check with your phone provider if they offer ringback and how much it costs.

Recorded phone menus drive me crazy

BYPASS THEM WITH A FEW KEYSTROKES It can be frustrating when companies use automated menus if all you want to do is talk to a person. But you don't need to spend ages listening to recorded messages and choosing menu options – you can bypass them simply by pressing 0, * , or # repeatedly. You can also often get through to a person simply by doing nothing. Once you speak to a person ask for a direct number that you can call them on next time.

I can't get good mobile phone reception inside this building

GO TO A WINDOW You can improve the reception of any indoor antenna – mobile phone, TV or radio – by moving it close to a window. Broadcast signals penetrate buildings most readily through glass. So that is the best place to position the antenna for your FM radio tuner or the aerial for your TV and it is the best place to stand when talking on your mobile phone.

If your mobile phone is breaking up, simply moving near a window can quickly restore the signal.

Cold callers keep wasting my time

FOLLOW YOUR OWN SCRIPT If you feel rude hanging up on cold callers, it doesn't mean that you have to listen to them. Follow this script and you should be off the phone in 20 seconds:

1 Cut the person short as soon as you realise it is a sales pitch.
2 Say that you have a strict policy of not doing business with strangers over the phone; if they wish, they may send literature.
3 Ask to have your name removed from their calling list and say that you forbid them to rent it to other companies.
4 Confirm that they heard what you said; then politely thank them and hang up.

Remember: You have no obligation to listen to cold callers. They are intruding on your time and a pleasant rebuff is fair and appropriate. Never say yes to a phone offer unless it is a company you know and have complete faith in. Scams are everywhere.

I need to curtail long phone calls

'THE DOORBELL'S RINGING. I HAVE TO GO' Forget cold callers – just try cutting off a long-winded relative. You don't want to be rude, but sometimes you just have more important things to do. Try these strategies for ending a call without hurting anyone's feelings:

- Open the front door and ring the doorbell, thereby alerting your chatty caller that a guest has just arrived.
- Say the battery is dying on your cordless phone.
- If things get really desperate, disconnect in the middle of your own sentence. The person on the other end of the line will assume there was a problem with the phone. Leave the phone off the hook for a while in case your talkative relative calls back.

■ INTERNET PROBLEMS

Searching on the Internet is frustrating

LET GOOGLE, MSN OR YAHOO HELP With today's powerful search engines, finding what you're looking for on the Internet has never been easier, which is why it is so maddening when you can't find something. Keep in mind, though, that even Google, the Web's king of search, is only looking at about 10 per cent of all the Web pages out there. So if you're searching for something really esoteric, you will find these tips that apply to most search engines handy:

- If you're looking for information about Manchester United football club and you simply type *Manchester United* in the search box, you'll not only get Web pages containing references to the team, but also pages that refer to Manchester itself and eventually, to sites containing just the word *united*. But put *Manchester United* in quotes – '*Manchester United*' – and only sites that refer to the entire phrase will pop up.
- Suppose you want to know all about Washington State, but nothing about Washington, D.C. If you simply type in *Washington*, you will get sites about each place. To weed out sites about the US capital, insert a minus sign before D.C.: *Washington –D.C.* (don't forget the space before the minus sign).
- Most search engines ignore words such as *the* and *and*. If those words are important to your search, put a plus sign in front of them. So if you're searching for the musical *The King and I*, type in: +*The King* +*and* +*I* (or put the whole phrase in quotes).
- If you don't know how to spell something, don't worry: type it in and if it is close enough to a word in the dictionary, most search engines will ask you if that is what you actually meant.

I'm overwhelmed with junk e-mails

FILTER OUT, OPT OUT, FIGHT BACK 'Junk', 'spam', 'trash', 'bulk', whatever you call it, there it is, taking up space in your e-mail account. Here are some ideas for stemming the flow:

- Use your e-mail's filter programs. Set them on High to weed out anything that looks like junk. In the beginning, you will have to check the trash folder regularly to make sure that important stuff isn't getting blocked as well, but after a while, you should only need to check occasionally.

TRICKS OF THE TRADE

Getting specialised information
To find really specific stuff, use a specialised directory. These directories will find sites on the Internet for almost any subject or interest. They will collect pages that the major directories might miss. Start by searching a directory that lists such directories, such as the Open Directory Project (www.dmoz.org), a comprehensive human-reviewed web directory.

- Use different e-mail accounts for different purposes. Have a business e-mail, a home e-mail and an e-mail solely for commercial uses.
- Opt out. When you are buying products online, many vendors will ask if you want to receive e-mailed updates or other announcements. The answer should always be no.
- Go to the website of the Direct Marketing Association at www.dmachoice.org/EMPS/ and sign up to its e-mail preference service to get your e-mail address purged from commercial lists. This won't eliminate all the junk, but it will help.
- Don't reply to spam. This confirms your e-mail address as real and will result in more spam.
- Don't post your e-mail address online or at least do it rarely. This is where e-mails are harvested.
- In the worst-case scenario, you may have to get rid of your old e-mail address and set up a new one. Then follow the rules above to ensure you minimise spam.

Pop-up advertisements are driving me crazy

TRY SPYWARE OR A POP-UP BLOCKER Nothing can slow your Internet experience down more than pop-up ads. To stem the tide, try downloading some free programs to rid your computer of 'trackers,' little bugs that electronically attach themselves to your computer, allowing pop-ups to come flying in. The best way to do this is to go to a site that lets you download software free, such as download.com or cnet.com, type *spyware* in the search box and then pick a program that is compatible with your computer and operating system, which will be Windows in most cases.

Another way to try to rid yourself of pop-ups is to download a pop-up blocker. The Google and Yahoo search engines both offer this feature free and both seem to work well. Go to their websites, type in *toolbar* and then follow the simple directions for download. You can also search for 'pop-up blocker' on a free-software site to obtain a program that stops pop-ups.

I am afraid to give out personal information online

READ THE SMALL PRINT FIRST Many unsuspecting consumers get their identification and credit card numbers stolen through a variety of nasty tricks. Here are some ways to protect yourself online:

- Do not disclose your information without understanding how it will be used. In other words, read the small print. Most reputable websites will not give away your information, but some will. Avoid those that do not have a privacy notice or do not guarantee confidentiality in their privacy notice.
- Never use your main e-mail address when you order anything online. E-mail addresses are available free from dozens of online vendors and your own Internet service provider may offer you extra ones. If you set up a few e-mail addresses for making purchases and rotate your use of them, online thieves will have a harder time keeping track of you.

My Internet service keeps freezing up

CLEAR THE CACHE When your browser won't load, it is most often the fault of the Internet provider. First, make sure all your cables and connections are still plugged in. If that doesn't help, call your provider's helpline number to verify whether it is the provider's problem and, if it is, how long it will take to fix.

If your provider says all is running smoothly at its end, take a harder look at your own computer. More likely than not, the problem has to do with your cache. This is where your browser keeps the Internet pages you have recently visited so that you can get back to those pages quickly. A problem with one of those pages can wreak havoc with your entire cache and keep you from accessing the Internet. The solution is to clear the cache. Here's how to do it for some common browsers:

SURELY NOT

A BIG SERVING OF SPAM

In the autumn of 2001, a supplier for a major computer maker sent an e-mail to about 2,900 customers who had ordered a software upgrade. Unfortunately, the sender entered the e-mail addresses in the 'To' field, where all of them would be visible to each recipient. An unscrupulous spammer could have easily harvested those names and then filled the customers' In boxes with junk e-mail. One analyst likened the blunder to giving away a customer database. That is a painful reminder of how important it is to BCC all the recipients of a mass e-mail.

The surest way to avoid being 'phished' (see next page) is to give your personal identification only to sites that you have gone to on your own, not sites that you reached by clicking on an unsolicited e-mail.

- For Windows Internet Explorer: quit all other programs. Open your browser and assuming it is not working, hit the Stop button. Then go to the Tools menu and choose Internet Options. Click on the General tab and you will see something called Temporary Internet files. Click the Delete Files button, then hit OK. You should now be able to get online.
- For Explorer on a Macintosh: quit all other programs and hit the Stop button on your browser. Then choose Preferences from either the Edit menu (OS 9) or the Explorer menu (OS'X). Click on Advanced under Web Browser and then, under the header labelled Cache, click Empty Now. You should be able to get online.
- For Netscape on either type of computer: hit the Preferences button, then the Advanced button and then click on the little arrow. Look for Cache and click on that. Then hit Clear Cache and try to get online.

I have sent an embarrassing e-mail to the wrong person

RECALL IT, IF YOU CAN Beware the Reply All button. It makes it so easy to send things out to the wrong people. We've all heard stories of unfortunate people who sent out embarrassing e-mails, only to end up sacked, divorced or worse. So what if that happens to you?

If you're lucky enough to be on a closed (controlled access) e-mail system at a company or an institution – specifically, one that uses Microsoft Outlook for its mail server – it is possible to actually recall an e-mail message, as long as it hasn't been opened. To do that, follow these instructions. But remember that this probably won't work from your home computer.

1 Select View and then select Folder List.
2 Click Sent Items.
3 Open the message you want to recall.
4 On the Actions menu, click Recall This Message.
5 To actually recall the message, click Delete Unread Copies of This Message.
6 Click OK. Outlook will attempt to recall the message.

If your embarrassing e-mail wasn't sent from such a system, your options are limited. One idea is to call the recipients and ask them to delete the e-mail before they open it. Not very likely? Well, here's another, more devious suggestion. Send another e-mail to everybody who got the problem message. In the subject header, type something like VIRUS ALERT!!! In the body of the e-mail, tell them that you think your system has been infected by a virus and that they should immediately delete any e-mails received from you recently. Cross your fingers and stay away from the Reply All button in the future.

■ COMPUTER PROBLEMS

My computer keeps crashing

THINK SOFTWARE RATHER THAN HARDWARE Life without Google or Yahoo or MSN? No thanks. When your computer keeps crashing, try some of these fixes before you take it to a £50-an-hour computer repair shop:

- Make sure there are no disks in either the floppy or CD drive. Sometimes a disk will interfere with the computer's operation.
- Turn everything off when you shut down the computer. This means printers, outside drives, monitors, everything. If you leave some components on, 'bad' information can pass back and forth, corrupting the whole system. So shut everything down, unplug everything and then start over again.
- More often than not, the problem will be software-related. If one program in particular seems to be the culprit, try erasing it from the computer and reinstalling it using the CD that you bought originally.
- Finally, give the computer a good thump. But not too hard. Many computers, especially those in an office environment, will collect dust inside the unit. So turn it on its side, to dislodge any dust and then give it a good whack or two. Any dust that is interfering with the connections will clear out.

My mouse is misbehaving

CLEAN THE BALL AND ROLLERS Few things are more annoying than an out-of-control cursor caused by a dirty mouse. Fortunately, there's an easy cure. If you're using a mouse with a ball underneath, clean it out. Disconnect the mouse, turn it over and, using both thumbs, twist the ring that holds the ball in place anti-clockwise. When you get the ball out, use a cloth moistened only with water to wipe the

ball clean. Then blow into the hole to get rid of any dust lying around. Inside, you will see three rollers. Use a fingernail or a pair of tweezers to scrape away any grime built up on the rollers. Once the ball is dry, pop it back in and then twist the cover back on.

If you are using a cloth mouse pad, throw it away and replace it with an easy-to-clean plastic or vinyl one. A cloth pad collects dirt, which will get back into your mouse.

If your mouse is of the optical variety and it is suffering from the same problems, check your desk surface. If it is glass or a solid material, the mouse might be having a hard time 'reading' the surface. Try putting it on a patterned surface or even on a piece of paper.

Some of the keys on my keyboard are sticking

SHAKE AND BLAST If your computer keyboard gets a fair amount of use, some keys will probably start sticking eventually. Built-up dirt is usually the culprit. The most rudimentary way to clean a keyboard is to disconnect it, turn it upside down and give it a good shake over a waste bin. You can also use a can of compressed air, sold at computer or camera stores, to blast debris out from under the keys.

If shaking and air-blasting don't work, go to an electronics or office-supply store and buy some contact cleaner, a chemical solution that won't interfere with electrical connections. Spray the solution on the stuck keys, let them dry and see what happens.

If all else fails, unplug the keyboard and pry off the stuck key with a flat-head screwdriver. Clean off the key with some compressed air or even a hair drier. Use contact cleaner to get rid of heavier dirt.

Caution: Don't take off the space bar, as it is nearly impossible to snap back on correctly.

To save a flooded keyboard, unplug it immediately and take it to the sink.

Help! I've spilled a drink on my keyboard

DISCONNECT IT IMMEDIATELY They do make waterproof keyboards. But, chances are, yours is not one of them, so you're going to have to act quickly if you do spill something on it. The first thing to do – right away – is either unplug the keyboard or turn the whole computer off. Do this within seconds of spilling the drink to limit the chances of permanently damaging the computer. Liquid in the keyboard can act as a conductor and cause a short circuit.

Once you've shut down the computer, take the unplugged keyboard over to the sink. If you spilled only a little water on it, turn it upside down and let it drain and dry out. If you have spilled a lot of water or – worse – juice, sweet milky coffee or a soft drink, you'll need to clean out the keyboard. Pour distilled water, which contains no minerals or other impurities that might conduct electricity when you plug the keyboard back in, over the spill. Use just enough water to do the job; don't splash the whole keyboard. Turn the keyboard upside down and let it drain. Once it is completely dry, plug it back in. If the spill didn't do any damage, it should start up again. If it did, then you may need to get it repaired or consider a replacement. Laptop keyboards, which are more complex and fragile will probably need professional help whatever you do.

■ ELECTRONIC GEAR

A tape is stuck in my video recorder

REMOVE THE VCR TOP AND LIFT OUT THE TAPE One minute you're watching home movies, the next minute the tape is jammed. But all is not lost. Do not try to force it out. Instead, unplug the VCR and unscrew the top. You'll find the screws either on the top or the sides of the VCR. Once you get the top off, you'll see the tangled tape. Untangle it manually and lift the cassette out of the VCR.

If the tape is not too badly mangled, you can thread it back into the cassette. However, if it is creased, ripped or otherwise damaged, you'll need to go to an audio/video supplies vendor (or to the Internet) and buy a splicer and splicing tape – you can buy a kit with tape and splicer for around £10. The splicer will expertly cut out the part of the tape that is damaged. Use the splicing tape to tape the two pieces back together. The better of these splicing machines do this job in one fell swoop. Don't worry. Even a few inches of tape will contain just a second or so of lost memories.

My CD or DVD won't play

CHECK THE DISC FIRST Digital technology is wonderful, except when it doesn't work. There are no gears to check or tape to untangle, so figuring out why something's not working is just about impossible. However, there are ways to get things moving again. Before throwing away your faulty CD or DVD player, try the following:

TRICKS OF THE TRADE

Keep your favourite CD from skipping
If a CD is skipping, try cleaning it with car wax. Apply the wax to a 100 per cent cotton cloth and wipe it on the disc. Let the wax dry completely and then buff it with a clean cotton cloth, wiping in a straight line from the centre circle to the outside edge. (Don't use a circular motion.)

• Make sure the disc itself is not the problem. A dirty disc is likely to cause problems. Check the back of the disc for dirt. Place it upside down and wipe it with a damp cloth. Wipe it from the centre outward, as this is how the information is stored. Clean it and try it in the machine.

• If a disc still doesn't play after cleaning, check for scratches. Most are superficial and are easily removed – with toothpaste! Use ordinary white toothpaste, not the gel kind. Apply to a clean soft cloth and wipe from the centre outwards. Then rinse the disc under water. You can also try a window cleaner with alcohol if the scratch is a little deeper.

• If the above methods don't yield a disc that works, your problem may be with the player and specifically, its counter-weight, which centres the CD/DVD in the machine. Unplug the player and turn it over a few times. This may be enough to rebalance the counterweight.

• If all else fails, it may be time to start taking things apart. Dust may have settled inside the machine. A CD that sounds as if there is static on it or a DVD that breaks up on the screen is a telltale sign of dust in the player. Unplug the machine and unscrew the top. Using a straw – or even better, a can of compressed air – blow on the inside of the player to rid it of dust. It's pretty delicate in there, so try not to touch anything or use any foreign objects.

I can't get the CD or DVD out

JEMMY OUT THE TRAY If your machine won't release a disc, you will have to do it manually. Find a paper clip and turn it into a hook, place it over or under the tray and pull the tray out just a little. From there, you should be able to pull the tray out with your fingers to release your disc from captivity.

Family life

■ INTERACTIONS BETWEEN CHILDREN

My children are fighting over toys

GUIDE THEM TO A NEGOTIATED SOLUTION Few things are as exasperating as listening to children fighting over a toy or anything else. While your first inclination may be to banish the toy from existence, there's a better way to restore peace. Take advantage of the situation to teach your children how to negotiate. The goal is to get them to share the toy or whatever it is they are fighting over. Direct them toward a compromise, but let them work it out themselves. Suggest possible solutions, such as that Max gets the toy for the morning and Jack gets it for the afternoon. Teach them that every either/or situation can be turned into a 'Why not both?' agreement. And make sure they understand that sharing the toy does not mean losing it for good.

A fight over a toy provides a chance to give your children an instant lesson in the art of negotiation.

My children argue all the time

CALL A TIME OUT WHEN NEEDED Just because siblings are related doesn't mean that they are necessarily compatible. Fighting and arguing are a normal part of growing up with brothers and sisters. Here are a few ways to keeping the bickering under control:

- Establish clear and firm limits on unacceptable behaviour – no hitting, screaming or throwing things – and enforce them.
- Provide a distraction. Put on some music and tell the children that it's time to dance. Or invite a friend over for each of the squabbling siblings.
- Try not to get overly involved in the cause of the disagreement. Encourage the children to work it out themselves.
- If the arguing gets out of hand, call a cooling off period for each child in separate places.
- Use positive reinforcement. Praise your children when they are getting along.

Memory calendar
They may be toddlers now, but in the blink of an eye they will be leaving home for a job or to study and you will want to remember every moment of your children's youth. Photographs will do the trick, if you can bring yourself to edit the mountain of snapshots you have accumulated.

Another way to permanently preserve achievements and events in their lives is to place a display calendar in each child's bedroom. At bedtime each night, make an entry for that day on the calendar – jot down an amusing thing the child said or a significant thing he or she did. In time, you will have an interesting, accurate memory tool that you and your children will enjoy reading in the future.

My child shies away from group activities

GET THE CHILD INVOLVED INDIRECTLY Not all children adapt readily to group settings. If your child or a child you're responsible for (such as a visiting playmate), refuses to participate in group games, one approach is to get the child involved without actually playing the game. If it's a sports game, for example, ask the child to help to keep score, be the referee or help to decide disputes. This will give the child a stake in the outcome and may encourage him or her to give the game a try next time.

My child is being bullied

ENLIST A FRIEND'S SUPPORT Research shows that one of the best ways to deal with a bully is to have a friend around. The friend does not necessarily have to be big or trained in martial arts. Just having someone who is there often helps. Get your child to stick with a friend on the school bus, in the playground or wherever the bullying is occurring. When that's not possible, your child should be equipped with appropriate responses to disarm the bully. Here are several steps your child can take:

- Ignore the bully and walk away.
- In an assertive but not aggressive way, tell the bully to stop.
- Report the bullying to an adult.

Make it clear to your child that he or she could make matters worse by falling apart, crying, making a snide remark or letting the bully know that he or she is scared or upset. Make sure your child doesn't blame him or herself for the bullying; the problem is with the bully, not with your child.

■ BEHAVIOUR PROBLEMS

My child won't eat

MAKE FOOD FUN The threat is probably as old as civilisation itself: 'You're not leaving the table until you clean your plate.' Thankfully, there are better ways to get fussy children to eat their food. Here are some of them:

- Involve your children in menu planning and food preparation.
- Offer your children foods cut into interesting shapes or that are otherwise visually appealing.

- Every once in a while, switch meals around: pancakes for dinner, a hamburger for breakfast. When meals are surprising and fun, children may eat more.
- Negotiate. There will be no seconds of a favourite food – say, spaghetti – until your child has tried some of the vegetables.
- Encourage your child to at least to try a new or rejected food, but don't insist that they finish something they don't like. Give them a small portion to start with. Watching you eat and enjoy a rejected food might get them interested in it.
- Take a relaxed approach and don't turn the dining table into a battleground. As long as your children are healthy, fluctuations in food intake are not a cause for alarm. Offer a variety of nutritious options and let your children develop their own tastes and preferences.

I want my children to pick up after themselves

MAKE IT A REQUIRED CHORE Children are very good at making a mess, but less good at cleaning it up. Here are a few pointers:

- Every child's routine should include a regular household chore suited to his or her age and abilities. Make it clear to your children that putting away their toys, for example, is a requirement, not an option.
- Praise your children when they do well; remind and cajole them when they don't.
- If your children still resist picking up after themselves, a good old threat now and then won't do permanent damage. Tell them that if they don't clean up right now, you're going to take three items lying around the floor to a charity shop. (Be prepared to follow through with your threat.)
- If you have two or more children, make a contest out of cleaning up. Whoever does it best or the fastest wins a prize.

Getting my child to sleep is a challenge

STICK TO A BEDTIME ROUTINE Going to sleep can sometimes be the most trying part of a child's day – for you, the parent. Here are some ways to help to speed the process along:

- Establish a bedtime routine – with set times for bath, brushing teeth, slipping on pajamas, reading a story and lights out – and stick to it. Give your children a little notice so that they can finish what they're doing before starting to get ready for bed.

- This tactic works particularly well for babies, but is good for toddlers, too: strap the child in the car, put on some calming classical music and take a slow drive around the neighbourhood. The movement of the car, the darkness and the soothing music will probably put the child to sleep.
- If children are really hyperactive, it is next to impossible to get them to lie still. Turn this negative into a positive by playing a quick game of tag in the house. After 10 or 20 minutes, everybody should be exhausted from running around.
- Children can be creative when it comes to avoiding bed. Don't cave in. It is fine to insist that they stay in bed and go to sleep.

Shopping with my children is an ordeal

KEEP THEM OCCUPIED AND INVOLVED Small children and shopping are often an unhappy combination. But there are ways to make the experience less exasperating for you.

- Try to avoid going shopping with your children when they are tired, hungry or not feeling well.
- Keep the children occupied and distracted. Bring along toys and books and make sure to interact with them.
- It can be frustrating for a child to watch you pick item after item from your list and have all his or her requests turned down. Instead of saying no each time your child asks for something, say instead, 'Let's add it to the list'. When you've finished shopping, read back the items on your child's list and let him or her pick one or two of those items.

My children keep whining

THREE STRIKES AND IT'S TIME-OUT You've probably heard the old adage: 'Your child knows your magic number.' Your children ask for something – sweets at a supermarket checkout, for instance, or an extra 30 minutes of TV – and you say no. Then they will keep asking, over and over, until they hit the magic number of noes, when you either give in or lose your temper. The old adage has even been backed up by research. Here is a simple solution (also backed up by research): the next time your children ask for something, such as sweets and your answer is no, say no. If they whine or keep asking for the sweets, wait 5 seconds and then give a warning, such as, 'if you ask me again, you'll have to go to your room' (or whatever punishment is appropriate). The third time, follow through. Stick to this simple routine and the magic number should become 1.

My child has had a bad day

LISTEN AND EMPATHISE When children come home from school or the playground complaining about having had a bad day, because they got into a fight, for example, or lost a favourite toy, parents have a tendency to both downplay the incident and problem-solve. These responses can seem insensitive to children and may even keep them from confiding in you in the future. It is likely that what they really need is empathy. A good way to demonstrate empathy is through a technique called reflective listening, in which you gently repeat what your child is telling you. This makes your child feel that you are really listening and sharing his or her emotional experience.

Fear of the dark keeps my child awake

TURN ON A NIGHT-LIGHT AND COMFORT YOUR CHILD What child isn't afraid of the dark at some point? Night-lights or desk lamps help some of the time, but not always, especially not if your child is having vivid nightmares. Often after bad dreams, your child will want to sleep in your bed. For the child's benefit and yours, don't allow it. Walk your child back to his or her room and sit for a little while, if that helps, rubbing your child's back or singing a song. Create a calming ritual. But do not linger too long. You want your child to overcome his or her fears independently.

■ OTHER CHILDHOOD PROBLEMS

My child has lost his favourite toy

IT'S NOT LOST – IT'S GONE ON AN ADVENTURE Losing a favourite stuffed animal or other special toy can be very upsetting for a child. To help them to come to terms with it, try the 'Toy Story' strategy: tell your child that the toy has gone off on an exciting adventure. You could even take it to the next level by sending letters or e-mails from the toy to your child. When the toy eventually turns up, arrange for your child to be the one to find it.

TRICKS OF THE TRADE

Getting children to study
Simply forcing children to do homework doesn't always get better results. Here are some suggestions:
• Establish a clear, consistent after-school schedule, with time for relaxation, activities and study. Homework doesn't have to be done straight after school, but it shouldn't be left to the end of the day either, when everyone is tired.
• Provide the right environment. Some children can work happily at the kitchen table; others need quiet.
• Try to be on hand when children are doing homework. Sit with younger ones and study with them. Make it fun. If memorisation is required, try singing the material.
• Don't interfere too much in your children's homework. Guide your children to the answer; don't give it to them.

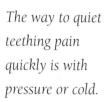

My baby is teething and is suffering

APPLY PRESSURE OR COLD There are many ways to help to soothe teething pain, but the most effective methods involve pressure or cold. With a clean finger, gently massage your baby's gums. Or give the baby something cold to chew on – a wet facecloth chilled in the fridge or even a frozen bun. Some mothers swear by frozen grapes, cut in half or small pieces of frozen banana or melon. But make sure the pieces are cut small enough so that there is no chance of choking and be extra vigilant when giving your baby food to teethe on.

The way to quiet teething pain quickly is with pressure or cold.

My child is asking about Father Christmas

TELL HIM THE TRUTH Children younger than about nine generally take Father Christmas, the Easter Bunny and the Tooth Fairy at face value. After that age, they start asking questions. Here is a good way to answer your child – and you must answer, because it's better to hear the truth from you than in the school playground. Tell your child that even if Santa is not exactly landing on roofs, the idea of Santa still exists and that everyone has a little Santa in them. Explain that in addition to receiving gifts, your child will now be part of the gift-giving process and will be able to help to pick out gifts for siblings and cousins. But make sure to tell your child not to tell other children about Santa. That job is up to their parents.

■ OUTSIDE CHILD CARE

I'm looking for a good nursery

OBSERVE, ASK QUESTIONS, DON'T SETTLE Try to find out as much as you can about local nurseries and give yourself plenty of time to assess each one that you consider. Here are some issues to keep in mind when evaluating nursery options:

- Make sure the nursery has an 'open door' policy (you are allowed to visit whenever you want). Visit as often as you feel is necessary to make an informed decision.
- Leave your child at home for the first visit, but take him or her on subsequent visits – even if your child is still a baby – to meet the nursery staff and the children.

- Find out what the ratio of staff to children is, what training and education are required of them and what type of educational programme is offered.
- Assess the physical setting. Is the place clean, well organised, safe and child-friendly? Is there enough play space and equipment? What kinds of meals are served?
- Spend time with the children at the centre. Are they clean, happy and active?
- Ask about the rules on punishments and make sure that you agree with them. Find out what happens when a child is ill.
- Interview the nursery director and the teacher whose class your son or daughter would be in.
- Trust your gut instinct. If you have a bad feeling about a place, don't choose it. It's not the place for your child.

I need to childproof my home for a family visit

TAKE A CHILD'S POINT OF VIEW If you don't have children, you don't have to worry about your windows being locked or electrical outlets being covered. But if you are suddenly playing host to young nieces or nephews for the weekend, you will have to childproof your home quickly. First, survey your home from a child's-eye perspective. Then try to eliminate all the hazards you can. Here's how:

- Put furniture in front of electrical outlets or fit accessible outlets with safety caps.
- Get a childproof lock for the bathroom. These inexpensive plastic locks are impossible for a tiny hand to unlock, but easy enough for adults.
- Put razors, creams and medicines out of reach of the children, preferably in a locked cabinet.
- Make sure all the windows are locked and that any window or door keys are not accessible to a child.
- If you are on an upper floor, move your furniture away from windows. Children love to climb up.
- Take any dangerous cleaning substances out from underneath the kitchen sink and store them up at a higher level.
- Finally, take care of your personal belongings. If you value your CDs, books, ornaments or antique furniture move them to a place where the little ones can't reach them.

I'm thinking of hiring a nanny

ASK QUESTIONS AND TRUST YOUR INSTINCTS A nanny or au pair will give your child individual attention in the secure setting of your home. But when hiring a nanny, keep these points in mind:

- Be sure to check a prospective nanny's references and work history carefully.
- At the interview, don't be shy about asking all the questions you want to. That's the only way to get to know her. Ask, for instance, why she went into this line of work and why she wants to care for your child in particular.
- Find out the candidate's approach to child rearing. Ask her what she would do in specific situations, such as an emergency or when your child won't eat or won't stop crying.
- Make sure you give your children time to interact with the prospective nanny or au pair.
- Always hire on a trial basis. Personalities often clash and a trial period makes it easier to fire the nanny should it come to that.
- As with a nursery, trust your instincts. Employ someone whom both you and your children like and are comfortable with.

■ PARTIES AND TRAVEL

I'm throwing a party for a horde of children

PLAN AHEAD AND KEEP IT SHORT Parties for children aren't just scaled-down versions of adult get-togethers. Keep these ideas in mind if you want all the guests at a birthday party to go home happy:

- Find out beforehand if any of your small guests are allergic to anything. Some children face life-threatening reactions when they eat certain common foods, such as peanuts. If a parent says a child is allergic, make sure you know exactly what you can and can't serve the child. Even better, get the parent to stay and chaperone the child.
- Make sure that the venue – either your home or another location – is safe for children and that they won't be able to venture away from the party on their own.
- Get plenty of adults to help to supervise the children. The younger the children, the more adults you will need to help to keep everything under control.

- Keep the party short. Young children need only about 45 minutes to play, eat cake and watch presents being opened.
- Plan the entertainment carefully. Some children are scared of clowns – or wizards – or magicians. Others are afraid to jump around on the inflatable bouncy castles that can be rented for parties. Make sure you have an attraction that most will like and plan to have alternative activities available.

I'm going to a theme park with children

SET GROUND RULES AND A MEETING SPOT If there's nothing quite like the thrill of a roller coaster, there's also nothing quite like the stress of taking a number of small children to a crowded, hot, expensive theme park with seemingly endless queues. Here's how to maintain your sanity and the children's, too.

- Before you go, make sure to call ahead and check the height restrictions for the rides. That way you'll avoid the unhappy spectacle of a child who can't go on any of the attractions.
- Also before you go, set the ground rules for crowded places. Tell the children that you will be watching out for them, but that they also have to watch out for you and for each other.
- Make the children easier to spot in a crowd by dressing them in the same brightly coloured shirts.
- If you're going with a big group do not put obvious name tags on the children. You don't want strangers calling out to them.
- Once you're there, designate a meeting spot in case anyone gets separated from the group. And point out the uniforms of the employees, so the children will know to whom they should go if they get lost.
- Take a pushchair. While pushing a tired child around is not exactly fun, it beats dragging a youngster by the arms.
- The three most important rules for theme parks are sunscreen, sunscreen and sunscreen. And make sure to apply it often.
- Bring along some frozen juice boxes, so they will be cold when the children get thirsty. And consider bringing a picnic. Food and drinks are very expensive once you get inside the park.
- Bring a change of clothes for the children even if it's not a water park.
- Bring a big towel or a blanket. It's handy for naps, drying off and relaxing in the shade.

TRICKS OF THE TRADE

Saving on tickets at theme parks
Prices for some theme parks are now running at more than £25 a person (slightly less for children). Clearly, a family outing can be very expensive. Save money by keeping an eye out for packages and special offers and buy your tickets in advance, either through the park or a travel agent or online. While one-day tickets will be the same price, multi-day tickets bought ahead of time are likely to be less expensive. Or if you go to the attraction frequently it could be worth investing in a season ticket.

On the road

■ CLOTHES AND PACKING

My clothes get jumbled up in my suitcase

PACK IN PLASTIC Self-sealing plastic bags are a veteran traveller's best friend. They're extremely lightweight, which is a plus when you have to haul your luggage through several miles of airport corridors. They're transparent, which makes baggage inspection go more easily and lets you find your possessions quickly in your hotel room. And they keep your clothes organised. Put underwear and socks in small bags and bulkier clothing into larger bags. Try www.transpack.co.uk or www.ziplock-bags.co.uk to buy the bags in large quantities.

My shirts come out of the suitcase crumpled

DRY-CLEANING BAGS ARE THE SOLUTION No one wants to look rumpled and dishevelled while travelling. But who has time for ironing, even if your hotel provides an iron? The key is to pack your shirts and blouses so that they emerge from your suitcase crease-free. First, be careful when folding your shirts or blouses. (If you pack them creased they will still be creased when you arrive at your destination.) Then lay a dry-cleaning bag out on a flat surface and slide one of the folded shirts inside the bag, all the way to the top. Stack a second shirt on top of the first one, but outside of the bag. Fold the bottom of the dry-cleaning bag over the second shirt. Then slide a third shirt inside the open end of the bag and put it on top of the second shirt. Pack this stack of shirts snugly in your suitcase, using the interior straps if possible, so they cannot slide around. With each shirt sandwiched between slippery plastic, the fabric will not bunch up and crease. This technique will work well with only one or two shirts as well. Just wrap the remaining plastic around them. If you need more than three shirts on your journey, lay out another plastic bag and start from the beginning.

To pack your clothes so that they emerge crease-free, try using dry-cleaning bags.

The clothes I'm travelling in are grimy

WASH THEM IN THE HOTEL SINK Even if you didn't schedule a stop at a self-service laundry into your tour of Paris, it's not a problem. Fill the sink in your hotel room with water that's an appropriate temperature for your fabric. Pour in a couple of tablespoons of shampoo. (Use ordinary shampoo that doesn't contain conditioner.) Drop your garment in and use your hand to agitate for 3 minutes. Let the water out of the sink, press the soapy water out of your garment and refill the sink with fresh water. Rinse the garment and press the water out again (don't wring). To accelerate drying, spread a bath towel across your bed or another clean surface, lay the garment on it flat and roll it up in the towel. After 15 minutes, either repeat with a fresh towel or hang the garment up to dry.

I'm travelling and my jewellery looks dirty

RESTORE THE GLEAM WITH TOOTHPASTE Smear a little toothpaste on a tissue and rub the jewellery gently with it. The toothpaste's mild abrasion will clean up jewellery in no time. Rinse under the tap.

■ COPING AWAY FROM HOME

There's no way I'll find the hotel exits in an emergency

LET YOUR SHOES POINT THE WAY When the alarms are blaring and smoke is filling the building, you don't want to hesitate in your hotel room doorway dithering over which way to turn to get to the emergency exit. So on arrival in your hotel room, take a few minutes to study the fire-exit diagrams. Then, when you're ready for bed, leave your handbag and shoes near your hotel room door. Point the shoes in the direction of the emergency exit in the corridor outside. If you ever have to evacuate in a hurry, you'll have a reminder of which direction to go to reach safety. And you can snatch up your shoes and bag on your way without wasting precious seconds.

I'm afraid of shaking hands and picking up something unpleasant

RUB ON AN ANTI-BACTERIAL GEL Whether you are at home or abroad, shaking hands is an efficient way to transmit germs. When you're

The successful suitcase
Photographer Karen Kasmauski knows all about packing a suitcase. Assignments for National Geographic have taken her to more than 32 countries on six continents. Here is her plan for successful packing:

• First, place heavy, flat objects, such as books and papers, in the bottom of the suitcase.
• Next, pack the clothes that need to lie flat – trousers, shirts and similar items. Secure them with the suitcase's interior straps.
• Pack the shoes on top of that, wrapped in plastic grocery bags.
• Add your cosmetics case or washbag.
• Pack underwear in one self-closing plastic bag and your socks in another. Use these to fill any holes in your suitcase's contents.
• Surround anything fragile with clothing for protection.

travelling, you may not always have access to a sink to wash your hands in. One solution would be to whip out an antibacterial hand wipe after a round of handshakes. But this approach would undoubtedly offend the people with whom you are trying to be friendly. A less conspicuous solution would be to carry a small bottle of antibacterial, 'waterless' hand gel and discreetly rub a bit into your hands after you've been shaking hands.

Antibacterial wipes do have a place in a traveller's germ-fighting kit. Use them to clean your hands before a meal or to wipe a toilet seat before you sit down.

I need to protect my camera from the rain

PUT IT IN A DISPOSABLE SHOWER CAP It would be a shame to let a good camera get ruined in the rain. On the other hand, it's a pity to miss photo opportunities because of a drizzle. Here is a quick – and free – solution. The next time you stay in a hotel, pick up one of the free, disposable shower caps that are provided in the bathroom. They often come in little boxes that fit easily in a camera bag. When it rains during an outdoor photo session, put the body of your camera in the shower cap, with the lens protruding through the circle of elastic. If the shower cap is clear, you'll be able to see through the camera's viewfinder. If not, make a small hole in the cap to give you access to the viewfinder. Pressing the shutter release should be no problem through the thin plastic. And manual winding can be done through the plastic, too, if your camera doesn't have an automatic film advance mechanism.

I can't keep my camera steady

MAKE A BEANBAG On the deck of a swaying, vibrating boat or aboard a fast-moving train, it's almost impossible to steady a camera, even on a tripod. Many photographers improvise a beanbag to stabilise their cameras. When travelling, they take along an empty cushion cover with a

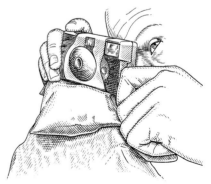

zip closing on one side. (A pillowcase would work, too.) When they reach their destination, they buy a temporary filling for the bag, such as corn kernels, popcorn, lentils or rice. The beanbag creates a platform for a camera on an uneven surface – a rock or a railing, for instance – and will cushion it on vibrating surfaces.

■ FLYING

I have missed my flight

BE EXTRA PLEASANT AT THE CHECK-IN DESK Whether you are flying for business or pleasure, nothing is quite as dismaying as missing your flight. But although you are going to be late getting to your destination, you may be able to soften the blow. It depends on what kind of flight you were booked onto. If you are on a package holiday and you miss your charter flight or you have bought a very cheap ticket, your options are likely to be limited. You may well have to buy another flight from a different airline to get you to your destination. Speak to the tour operator or airline first to see if anything can be done. No matter how stressed you feel, be polite and pleasant to the staff at the check-in desk.

If you were booked onto a scheduled flight you should be able to get onto the next *available* flight. It may not be the next flight but you shouldn't have to pay extra.

My flight has been cancelled

CALL THE AIRLINE'S HELPLINE When a flight is cancelled, save yourself the aggravation of waiting in the line at the reservation desk. Take out your mobile phone and dial the airline's helpline number to find out what your options are – either a seat on the next flight or assistance in securing a hotel room for the evening.

When you've missed your flight, it usually pays to be nice to the check-in staff.

If the problem is weather related, the helpline is likely to be tied up too, and you may be put on hold for a while. If that happens, try both tactics simultaneously: stay on hold while waiting in line with the rest of the crowd.

I have only minutes to change planes

BOOK A FRONT SEAT ON THE FIRST FLIGHT If you have to make a tight connection at an airport, make sure that your seat on your originating flight is as far forward in the plane as possible. Then you won't have to wait for as many passengers in front of you to get off the plane before you start your sprint across the airport.

I hate checking in my suitcase unlocked

SEAL THE LATCHES WITH GAFFER TAPE If you check your luggage onto a flight these days, you may be told to leave your bags unlocked for a security inspection. You may then imagine the baggage handlers tossing your suitcase around, the latches popping open and your underwear decorating the tarmac. Or, worse, someone groping through your baggage looking for valuables.

To cut your worries, try gaffer tape. Cover the unlocked latches of your suitcase with just enough tape to fit over the fastenings. This will prevent the latches from accidentally popping open but will

MAKING LAST-MINUTE TRAVEL ARRANGEMENTS

Back in the old days (pre-21st century), making last-minute travel arrangements was costly. Airlines and hotels charged more, because they had you over a barrel. Today, with Internet travel sites, last-minute booking is not only less expensive than it used to be, but in some cases it is also cheaper than booking ahead. Here's a look at some leading Internet travel sites and how they work:

- Expedia and Travelocity These two travel websites are easy to use. You type your travel dates and destination and the sites come back with your choices and prices. Prices are generally comparable with travel agent's prices, but they can vary wildly, from site to site and from moment to moment on one site. Always shop around before committing.

- Travelsupermarket.com This site allows you to find cheap flights, holidays and hotels from a range of UK airports and from all the different operators. You type in your preferred departure airport and destination, dates (giving three days flexibility) and how you want to travel. The site gives you details of a range of options from a number of other sites including Ebookers, Opodo, Expedia and Flightline.

- Lastminute.com This site allows you to be as flexible as you like. You can choose by date, destination and type of holiday – or all of these – and the site will come up with a wide range of destinations, holiday types and deals. Or you can select flight only or hotel only for your chosen destination. The site also highlights a range of 'last second' deals which are available within the next fortnight, some of which may be as little as two days away. Price is not the overriding factor on the site but there are a number of very good deals available especially if you are prepared to be flexible about where and when you travel.

- Priceline The ultimate in travel roulette. Say you want a hotel in New York. You go to Priceline, pick the area of New York you want to stay in, pick the star rating of the hotel and pick the price you are willing to pay. Within moments, you will find out if your bid has been successful. The same goes for flights: you pick from the dates and destination, enter a price you're willing to pay and roll the dice. Generally speaking, you can expect around 40 per cent off the prices you see on the the leading travel sites. You can do some advance research on Priceline by visiting biddingfortravel.com. This is a giant message board where people can post their Priceline adventures. If you see that someone was able to get a three-star hotel in New York for $44 (£26) on the same day that you are travelling, you will know that you won't have to bid much higher for your room..

allow a security officer to inspect the bag by peeling back the tape. If you use tape that matches the colour of your suitcase, the latches won't be as conspicuous to any criminal eyes who may be perusing a luggage-filled conveyor belt.

■ DRIVING PROBLEMS

I've hit a massive traffic jam

RELAX, DON'T FRET You're driving along and all of a sudden the traffic slows to a standstill. Accident, roadworks or simply a build-up of traffic, it doesn't matter; all you know is that you're stuck. Instead of getting cross, take it as an opportunity to relax. Try some deep-breathing exercises: inhale slowly and deeply through your nose, hold it for a moment and then slowly release the air through your mouth.

When you're feeling relaxed, here are some ways to pass the time:

Stuck in traffic? Make the most of it, to keep stress at bay.

- Sing along with the radio.
- As long as you are stationary, use your mobile phone to gossip with friends. Stop as soon as you start moving again.
- Put the car into neutral or park and read a book.
- Roll down your window and chat with the other people stuck in the same jam.
- Clean or tidy your car.

Above all, be thankful for this brief respite, during which no one can lean on you for anything.

I've lost control of my car

STEER WHERE YOU WANT TO GO To ensure that you are prepared if you ever lose control of your car, here are some pointers on what to do. First, stay calm. Next, determine whether it's the front or the back wheels that have lost traction. If your car refuses to turn, it's the front wheels that are not gripping. If your car seems to be going into a spin, it's the rear wheels.

For a front wheel problem, do the following: take your foot off both the accelerator and the brake and shift to neutral, but don't try

A deflating experience
The moment you get a flat tyre is no time to start pondering how you'll deal with the situation. Unless you're very handy, it's a good idea to join the AA or another road assistance company. You call when you're having trouble; they come out, usually within half an hour.

Another option is to keep in your boot a can of emergency tyre sealer/inflator, available at car parts suppliers for less than £10. These cans come with a short hose that fits onto your tyre valve, sending air and sealant into the tyre. The fix is only temporary. The air pressure in the tyre will be significantly less than normal and it won't last long. It is designed to give you enough time to get to a service station.

You must remember that you are still driving with a damaged tyre, so put your hazard lights on and keep your speed under 40mph (64kph).

to steer right away. As the wheels slide sideways, they will slow the vehicle and traction will return. As you gain traction, steer in the direction you want to go. Then put the transmission in drive or release the clutch and gradually accelerate.

The rear wheels are a little trickier: steer in the direction that the rear wheels are going. If your rear wheels are sliding left, steer left. If they're sliding right, steer right. Execute a little turn if it's a little spin, a bigger turn if you are in a bigger spin. You should also add some acceleration, not for speed but to transfer some weight to the back of the vehicle.

■ CAR CARE AND REPAIR

A pebble has made a chip in my windscreen

BUY A WINDSCREEN REPAIR KIT A pebble tumbles out of a dumper truck on the motorway, your windscreen smacks it at the maximum speed limit and your day is ruined. In fact, small chips and cracks are easy to repair. First, keep dust, mud, bird droppings and other dirt out of the crack, because they will interfere with the repair. Pull over and put some clear plastic tape over the windscreen crack until you can make a permanent repair. Then tend to the crack as soon as possible. Changes in temperature and everyday vibration caused by driving can worsen the crack. Go to a car parts supplier and buy a clear epoxy repair kit designed specifically for windscreens. They cost less than £10. Apply the adhesive according to the package directions.

Do-it-yourself fixes won't work well for cracks larger than around 30cm. For these big cracks, you will need to have the windscreen replaced by a professional.

My car has a scratch on the bodywork

COVER THE SCRATCH WITH NAIL VARNISH Rub your finger gently over the scratch. If you can't feel an indentation made by the scratch, you're in luck. Only the surface clear coat is damaged, not the paint layer. Go to a car parts supplier, pick up a polish (many have scratch-removing properties) and follow the package directions.

If you can feel the scratch on the surface of your car's finish, buffing and polishing will not help. The only solution is to paint over the scratch to make it less noticeable. Browse through the fingernail varnish you have at home, or visit a pharmacy or a department store. When you find a shade that matches the colour of your car, delicately paint over the scratch and let it dry. If you mess up the patch-up job, dab on a little nail varnish remover with a cotton bud to clean it up, let it dry and start again.

Auto parts suppliers also sell touch-up marking pens and coloured polishes that will disguise a scratch temporarily.

I have made a rip in the car seat

IT'S ANOTHER JOB FOR GAFFER TAPE If you have ripped your car's leather or vinyl upholstery, find some gaffer tape that matches the colour of the upholstery and cut a piece just large enough to cover the rip. Car parts suppliers sell tape in a wide range of colours. The tape will mask the wound until you can get it permanently repaired. Car parts suppliers also sell colour-matching adhesive repair kits for leather and vinyl upholstery.

Gaffer tape and do-it-yourself repair kits don't work quite as well on fabric. For large fabric tears, you will need the help of a specialist car upholstery repairer.

I'm worried that my child's car seat isn't secure

GET IT CHECKED OUT You never want to put your children at risk. But an badly installed car seat is doing just that. To find out if a car seat is set up properly, check out www.childcarseats.org.uk, a website sponsored by RoSPA, the Royal Society for the Prevention of Accidents (0121 248 2000). The site has detailed information on installation but also gives details of where you can go locally to check if you have put in your child's car seat correctly. Many local councils have safety officers who offer advice and checking as well.

My car has a dent

HAMMER OR SUCTION THE DENT OUT Here are two ways to fix a dent without taking your car to a repairer:

- If the dent is on or near the wheel arch, you will be able to tap it out with a hammer, but only after you unscrew the black plastic shields under the arch. To do this, make sure the emergency brake is in place. Next, using a small screwdriver, unscrew the four to six screws holding the shield in place.

PROBLEM STOPPER

Be ready for hazardous driving conditions
Most loss of driving control happens during winter, when snow and ice make driving dangerous. Here are some preventative measures you can take:
• Make sure your car is in good running order and the tyres have sufficient tread.
• Scrape all snow and ice off your car, including the roof, windows and windscreen wipers.
• Keep headlights free of snow, ice and mud.
• Brake carefully and gently on snow or ice.

Depending on the size of the dent, use either your fingers or a hammer to knock out the dent. If the dent is on the plastic shield itself, there is no need to take it off. Just get underneath it and push out the plastic with your fingers.

- If the dent is on the side of your car, you will need some suction to repair it. Find anything with a suction cup attached. Many automatic pencil sharpeners, for instance, have them on their bases. Most auto supply stores sell suction cups for pulling out dents. They cost about £7. Take the cup, place it directly over the dent and pull it off. The 'pop' sound indicates that you have pulled the body back into shape.

There's some car wax on my bumper

WIPE IT OFF WITH WD-40 Until they make car wax that comes off plastic car components easily, you will need the help of WD-40. Spray a little of it on to the wax and wipe it off with a rag or an old toothbrush. This also works for wax that gets into crevices.

I can't jump-start my dead car battery

POUR COLA ON THE TERMINALS If you've found a kind person to help you jump-start a reluctant car battery, but the engine still won't turn over, don't despair. The good news is that although a car battery might become extremely weak, it is never completely dead.

If the jump-start isn't working and there's a lot of corrosion around the battery terminals where you attach the cables, pour a can of cola on to the corroded area. The acid in the cola will dissolve the corrosion, improving your connection and increasing your odds of a successful jump-start. The cola also contains electrolytes, which will help to improve the electrical flow. Once you get home, wash the battery with a little water to get rid of the cola residue.

My car is speckled with tree sap

DAB THE SAP WITH SURGICAL SPIRIT Soap and water won't remove sap stuck to the finish of your car. But there is a simple solution. Pour a drop of surgical spirit directly on the sap spot, rub with your fingertips and watch the marks disappear. There is no need to rinse, either. The alcohol will just evaporate.

■ BICYCLES

My bicycle wheel is bent out of shape

BANG THE WHEEL AGAINST A TREE Remove the wheel from your bike and smack it against a tree or some other hard object like a bollard to bend it back into shape. Check your progress with each strike, so that you won't bend the wheel too far the other way. Replace the wheel on your bike and start pedalling. This is only a temporary fix; you will need to get a new wheel.

My bike tyre is flat and I don't have a repair kit

STUFF IT WITH LEAVES Pry one edge of the tyre (the 'bead') off the wheel rim of your bike. If you don't have a repair kit with you, you probably won't have bike tools to do this with, either, so try a pocket knife, some other piece of metal or your bare hands. Once one edge of the tyre is flopping outside the rim all the way around the wheel, gather a pile of leaves and moss and pack them tightly inside the deflated tyre. Squeeze the edge of the tyre back in place on the rim and start wheeling. The tyre may not be as firm as you're accustomed to, but it should get you back home.

Surprisingly, slamming your tyre against a tree is the quick way to straighten it enough to get back home.

My bike tyre has a split in it

LINE THE HOLE WITH A FIVER When a sharp rock or other item has left a gash in your bike tyre, you know that when you patch the inner tube (or use your back-up inner tube), it will pop through the hole in the tyre and burst again when you try to ride on it.

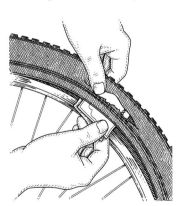

What you need is a strong but flexible material that you can place inside the tyre against the hole. And you'll find that paper money from your wallet will be just the ticket. Pry one edge of the damaged tyre off its rim. Pull out the inner tube and patch or replace it. Then place a note from your wallet against the gash inside the tyre. Press the tyre back onto the rim and reinflate the tyre.

PART EIGHT

Health and wellbeing

If you really have a serious medical problem, call the doctor. But everyone else can learn the best way to sneeze in public, how to cure a hangover, how to stop a nosebleed, how to avoid fainting, how to deal with a broken tooth, how to treat sunburn and much more.

- Common discomforts/328
- Minor health emergencies/341

Common discomforts

■ PERSONAL ANNOYANCES

I've got hiccups

CHANGE YOUR BREATHING PATTERN When you hiccup, your diaphragm tightens involuntarily. (The diaphragm is a dome-shaped wall of muscle and connective tissue between the chest and abdominal cavity that contracts when you breathe in and relaxes when you breathe out.) There are several ways to trick your lungs and diaphragm to get back to their regular cycle. Try any or all, until your hiccups stop:

Breathing into a paper bag is one quick way to end hiccups.

- Fill a glass with water, bend your head down and take a long, slow sip from the far side of the glass.
- Take a deep breath and hold it as long as you can. The build-up of carbon dioxide in your lungs relaxes the diaphragm.
- Hold a paper bag (never a plastic one) against your mouth and inhale and exhale into it. Again, this causes a build-up of carbon dioxide.
- Take nine or ten quick sips in a row from a glass of water.
- Eat something sharp-tasting, like a slice of lemon or a teaspoon of cider vinegar.
- Eat a big teaspoon of peanut butter.
- Or the classic remedy: put a teaspoon of sugar or honey stirred in warm water on the back of your tongue and then swallow.

I have bad breath

HAVE A DRINK AND SOME PARSLEY Bad breath is generally caused by bacteria growing in the mouth, not the remnants of your lunch. If you notice you have bad breath, swish water around your mouth and then drink lots more. A dry mouth is a haven for bacteria to thrive. A sugar-free mint or some gum will give your mouth a fresh flavour but will do little for the underlying cause. Try some sparkling mineral water or iced tea to freshen the somewhat unpleasant taste that sometimes develops. To discourage the build-up of bacteria in your mouth, brush your teeth at least twice a day and floss daily. Equally important, try cleaning your tongue. The tongue is like a bacteria magnet. Scraping it removes bacteria and makes your mouth feel more comfortable – you can buy a simple tongue scraper, or use the bowl of a teaspoon.

A wonderful natural deodorant for your mouth is parsley. Try putting parsley, basil or mint into salads, because many dressings use garlic and other smelly spices as main ingredients. Also good for bad breath are fennel, dill, cardamom and anise seeds.

If the problem is severe and won't go away, see your dentist in case of tooth or gum problems. If your mouth gets the all-clear, consult a doctor. Chronic bad breath is sometimes a sign of other health problems.

I sweat very heavily under my arms

BLOT UP THE MOISTURE AND APPLY AN ANTIPERSPIRANT There is a medical condition called hyperhidrosis – excessive perspiration – that affects 1 in 25 people. But for most of us, the sweat only pours out when we are tense, scared or really hot. If sweat is beginning to show through your shirt, excuse yourself, go to the cloakroom and towel down. Then apply an antiperspirant, rather than a deodorant. Many antiperspirants contain aluminium chloride, which causes the pores that release perspiration to close up. If you sweat heavily, look for one with 20 per cent aluminium chloride – ask your pharmacist to recommend a suitable brand. Next, if you have access to one, put on a T-shirt. Finally, drink some cold water to help to cool your body down and do what you can to calm yourself down.

My feet are very smelly

KEEP FEET CLEAN AND DRY Sweat itself doesn't smell – foot odour is caused by the bacteria that breed in sweat. Charcoal shoe inserts work (available at shoe shops and chemists), but they are only a temporary cure. If you are in a social situation in which foot odour is an issue, it's probably because you have taken your shoes off and the odour is probably coming from them, not your feet. Either put the shoes back on or move them far away. Dry the insides of the shoes with paper towels; if necessary, stuff them with paper towels and leave them there. Put on dry, fresh socks or take them off too.

If you have a problem with chronic foot odour, here are some effective remedies you can try:

PROBLEM STOPPER

Dealing with a sweaty problem
If sweating is a chronic problem for you, garment shields can offer a solution. These oblong, self-adhesive fabric guards are applied to the underarm area of your sleeve to create a barrier between your underarm and your dress or your blouse. You can usually buy garment shields from fabric shops or haberdashery departments.

- Wash your feet with water several times a day. A couple of times a week, soak your feet in warm, soapy water. When you do, brush between your toes with a soft brush. Pour in a cup or two of white vinegar to help disinfect your feet. Dry them well after washing.
- Avoid nylon socks, which do not let feet breathe. Also avoid cotton socks, which absorb and hold sweat. Instead, wear wool/synthetic combination socks, which wick away odour-causing sweat. To kill bacteria, it is a good idea to wash your socks in hot, not warm, water.
- Avoid shoes that don't breathe, such as those with plastic or synthetic linings.

My stomach is full of painful wind

CHEW HALF A TEASPOON OF FENNEL SEEDS Fennel seeds, which have a liquorice flavour, have been used for thousands of years to reduce wind and improve digestion. Caraway seeds have a similar effect. Here are a few other home remedies that may help to relieve wind:

- Make a cup of ginger tea by boiling slices of fresh ginger root or steeping ¼ teaspoon of powdered ginger in hot water for 5 minutes or so.
- Make peppermint tea, but only if you don't have gastric reflux or heartburn, since peppermint can affect the flap between the oesophagus and stomach. For most people with a healthy digestion, peppermint tea works like a charm and can be consumed three or four times a day as needed.
- Go for a good long walk. Walking is a particularly good way to encourage the dispersal of wind.

My ears are blocked with wax

CLEAN THEM WITH HYDROGEN PEROXIDE Earwax filters dust and other harmful particles out of the ear. Old wax is usually expelled by chewing motions, which push the wax, along with dead skin cells and bacteria, out of the ear. But as people age and there is less moisture in their wax, it can build up in the ear, hardening and causing blockage and pain. Don't use a cotton bud to clean it out; the swab can lodge the wax deeper in the ear canal and damage the eardrum. Instead, fill a dropper with hydrogen peroxide that is at body temperature or a little warmer. Lie down or tilt your head so the blocked ear is pointing up. Drip the peroxide into the ear until it feels full. Wait 3 minutes before tilting your head the other way over a washbasin or towel to let the peroxide drain out. Then tilt your head again and gently squirt warm water into your ear. Let it settle and then drain. Gently clean away the water and softened wax from your outer ear with a washcloth or cotton balls.

A few drops of olive oil can also do the trick. Let the oil work its way down into your ear. Leave it in for about an hour, or even overnight for really stubborn wax (protect your pillows with a towel), then gently squirt in some water to flush the oil out. In either case, finish up by using a hair drier to dry your ear.

Use the drier on the coolest setting and don't bring it any closer than 30cm from your ear.

■ SKIN PROBLEMS

My skin is dry and flaky

BATHE USING BATH OIL Normally, the body's natural oils, secreted from glands in the skin, help to keep it moist. But seasonal changes, such as drier air in winter, along with showering every day, can cause skin to dry out. The soaps we use wash away our natural oils, leaving the skin dry, flaky and irritated. The quick fix is to shower less often or at least cut back on the

WORLD-CLASS FIX

CUSHIONING A BAD SMELL

When Frank Lathrop of Houston, Texas, USA developed chronic flatulence as a side effect of a diabetes medicine, his employees became so tired of spraying air fresheners around to disguise the smell that they gave Lathrop an ultimatum – either he had to build himself a private office in the back of his manufacturing plant or they would resign. Lathrop's answer was to develop the Flatulence Filter. It looks like a normal seat cushion, but the grey tweed cushion contains a super-activated carbon filter. If the sitter passes some gas while sitting on the cushion, according to research published in July 1998 in the British Medical Association's *Gut,* a journal of gastroenterology and hepatology, the carbon filter will discreetly trap around 90 per cent of the odour-causing gas. The filter seat, Lathrop claims, is excellent for sufferers of gas-producing illnesses such as irritable bowel syndrome and colitis, as well as for generally flatulent people. His company also makes a filter pad, which fits inside underwear.

Acne control
Although it seems
counterintuitive, it is
best not to clean and
scrub your face too
much if you have acne.
Too much scrubbing
depletes the skin's
natural oils. This in
turn can cause the skin
to overproduce oil,
which can make the
acne worse.

amount of soap you use and the scrubbing you do. In addition, instead of showering, take a bath and use an emollient bath oil in the water for a while. The oil will help to replace the natural oils lost in the bath. This will be easier and more effective than trying to rub down your whole body with moisturising lotion.

I have a huge boil on my back

USE A WARM COMPRESS Boils are like massive pimples. Red, hot, painful and sometimes oozing pus, they can arise almost anywhere on the skin, usually with a hair follicle as its origin. As with pimples, never squeeze a boil. You risk spreading infection to other parts of the skin or even to the blood. Don't poke it or prick it with a pin. Instead, place a warm, wet compress on it for 10 minutes at a time, two to three times a day. These compresses will soothe the inflamed skin and possibly draw out the pus. You can use warm water or warm thyme or chamomile tea or a warm, moist tea bag by itself. If you can't reach the boil, soak as long as you can in a hot bath. Another approach is to dry it out by applying an acne medication containing benzoyl peroxide twice a day. Or apply tea tree oil, which is a natural antiseptic.

I have warts on my hands

USE GARLIC TO BATTLE THE WART Commercial wart removers work well and usually get rid of the wart in two weeks. But there are lots of effective home remedies that work too. For example, apply freshly crushed garlic directly to the wart and cover with a plaster. The caustic effect of the garlic will cause the wart to blister and fall off within a week. Apply new garlic every day, avoiding contact with healthy skin. (Smear the area around the wart with petroleum jelly to protect it.) Eating raw garlic or taking three garlic capsules a day may help the immune system to fight the virus.

Another remedy is to cover the wart with a small piece of gaffer tape and leave it there for six days. When you take the tape off, soak the wart in water for a few minutes and then use a disposable emery board or pumice stone to file down the dead, thick skin. Leave it uncovered overnight, then repeat the whole process. Other materials that people have used successfully to wither away a wart include vinegar, dandelion sap, ground vitamin C tablets, banana peel and lemon peel.

I have a deeply embedded splinter

USE A WART REMOVAL DISC Don't squeeze or gouge – you may cause infection. Buy a wart removal disc containing salicylic acid or other salicylic acid pads. (Some can be found designed for getting rid of corns on feet.) Buy a single pad if possible, because a pack will probably expire before you use it all up. The pad measures about 8 x 6cm. Use scissors to cut out a smaller pad, about 2.5mm square and place the sticky side over the hole where the splinter entered the skin. Cover this with a plastic sticking plaster and leave it for 6 hours. The salicylic acid in the pad will super-moisturise the skin. As the acid draws bodily fluid to the wound, the splinter will also be drawn to the surface. When the 6 hours are up, remove the plaster and pad. The head of the splinter should be exposed. Remove the splinter with a pair of clean tweezers, pulling in the opposite direction to the line along which the splinter entered.

If you can't get hold of a wart removal disc or similar treatment and the sliver is made from wood, soak the area of skin where the splinter is buried in a cup of warm water and 1 tablespoon of bicarbonate of soda. It should make the sliver swell up, making it much easier to remove. Repeat the soaking twice a day until the sliver emerges. Most splinters work themselves out in time, but seek medical advice if the surrounding area becomes infected.

I have a pimple on my face

USE EYEDROPS AND MAKE-UP Don't ever squeeze it. Squeezing pimples may cause an infection, create more inflammation and even lead to scarring. Instead dab an over-the-counter product containing salicylic acid or benzoyl peroxide such as Panoxyl on the spot.

If the pimple pops up just before a party or special event and you are desperate to disguise it, try this two-step approach for hiding it. First, apply some over-the-counter eyedrops (the kind meant to reduce redness in eyes) to the spot. The liquid will enter the skin, constrict the swollen blood vessels surrounding the pimple and reduce the redness. Then use make-up to cover the blemish. A green-tinted make-up will do the best job of hiding it, as green and red are on opposite sides of the spectrum.

Eyedrops are the quick way to take the redness out of an unsightly spot.

I have a cold sore

TREAT WITH ICE, ASPIRIN AND LYSINE Cold sores can be painful, annoying and, when they erupt, rather unattractive. They are caused

by a herpes simplex virus and are contagious when skin-to-skin contact occurs. Sometimes cold sores will go away only to return months later in the same place. That's because the virus hibernates in nerve cells within your body. Different things, such as emotional or physical stress, cold wind and sunshine, seem to trigger the re-emergence of cold sores.

Apply ice directly to the sore. It will bring down the swelling, ease the pain temporarily and, if done early enough, keep the sore from growing larger. Also consider taking half an aspirin tablet a day while you have a cold sore; studies show that that can cut the herpes infection's active time in half. Don't take aspirin if you have bleeding problems, indigestion or are taking blood thinners like warfarin. If you have it on hand, there is evidence that the amino acid lysine can help to heal cold sores. Take 3000mg daily until the sore goes away. You can also reduce the inflammation by dabbing the sore with the oil from a vitamin A or vitamin C capsule.

And if you want to go to a pharmacist, you can use an over-the-counter antiviral cold sore cream. Apply the cream with a sterile cotton bud instead of your finger to avoid infecting the sore. Don't use alcohol-based disinfectants. Finally, be careful not to touch your eyes after touching the cold sore (yet another reason to avoid touching it altogether). The virus can cause an eye infection.

I have a strange rash

TREAT AN ITCH Skin rashes crop up for many reasons and can be alarming. If it hurts, you should probably see a doctor about it. If it merely itches, you can probably treat it yourself. Two things can help to stop the itching: spreading hydrocortisone anti-itch cream on the rash and putting cool compresses on the rash. If the rash does not clear up in a few days, or spreads, see your GP.

By the time I got to see the doctor my rash had gone

TAKE A SNAPSHOT OF THE AFFECTED AREA You decide to see a doctor about a rash, but, like most rashes, blemishes and other skin conditions it is not a not life-threatening emergency, you have to wait a while before you get an appointment. By then, the condition has probably cleared up, making it harder for the doctor to suggest measures to stop it from coming back again. A solution is to take a photograph of the rash at its worst and show that to the doctor during your appointment.

■ NOT FEELING WELL

My back is killing me

ICE FIRST, HEAT LATER We're assuming that you don't have a chronic back condition, but rather muscle pain from overexertion, a sudden twist or a really bad night's sleep. As a pain reliever, ice works by blocking pain signals and reducing swelling. Several times a day, place an ice pack wrapped in a towel on the painful area for up to 20 minutes. Or use a bag of frozen peas. After 48 hours, switch to moist heat to stimulate blood flow and reduce spasms. Dip a towel in very warm water, wring it out and lay it over the painful area. Cover the towel with plastic wrap and put a heating pad on top of the plastic wrap. Leave it on for up to 20 minutes. You can repeat this three or four times a day for several days.

I feel like I'm going to be sick

SUCK A FRUIT LOLLY There are many reasons you might feel nauseated. You have to judge how serious this symptom is. Usually you can settle your stomach by sipping on something cool and carbonated, such as ginger ale. Fluids dilute the acidic secretions in the stomach and can reduce discomfort. Drink too much too fast and you might make things worse. A solution is to suck on a frozen fruit juice lolly, which is like taking little sips of juice.

I'm suffering from severe diarrhoea

DRINK WATER AND JUICES Depending on where you are and what you have recently eaten or drunk, you have probably ingested some sort of pathogen – a bacterium or virus, for instance. Most stomach bugs leave in two to three days. Assuming that your diarrhoea isn't bad enough to send you to the doctor, your main remedy is replacing lost fluids and electrolytes (body salts) by drinking lots of water and fruit juices. Also, black tea sweetened with sugar is effective; the tea contains astringent tannins that help reduce intestinal inflammation and the sugar improves sodium absorption. Tannin-rich blackberries have long been used for diarrhoea. Make blackberry tea from tea bags made with real blackberry leaves. Raspberry tea may be effective too. Or try capsules of the herb goldenseal, which appears to kill many of the bacteria that cause diarrhoea. Over-the-counter diarrhoea medicines can reduce the severity and dehydrating effects of

Here are three tips on how to avoid the dreaded hangover:

• **Avoid red wine** Red wine contains congeners, natural chemicals that play a role in the taste of a wine. They're also believed to cause the dreaded morning-after headache. White wine also contains congeners, but in much smaller amounts.

• **Alternate non-alcoholic beverages with your booze** This will not only cut your alcohol consumption in half but will also prevent dehydration, which contributes to your hangover. But avoid caffeine, a diuretic.

• **Eat foods cooked in grease before drinking** Fatty foods go a long way toward lining the inside of your intestines, which will slow down alcohol absorption.

diarrhoea. Another precaution is to make sure that you wash your hands frequently to prevent spreading the illness to others or reinfecting yourself.

I've woken up with a bad hangover

CONSUME MORE LIQUIDS AND EAT EGGS There is a bright side to hangovers. The dry-mouthed, head-throbbing, stomach-churning misery they induce is enough to keep most people from drinking too much for their own good. Here's what you can do to feel better:

- Drink lots of fluids. Alcohol is a diuretic, causing frequent urination and, ultimately, dehydration. As the body gets low on fluids, it draws water from all over the body, including the brain's outer membranes or dura, causing pain and discomfort. By drinking lots of fluids, you will both rid yourself of a cotton-wool mouth and rehydrate the rest of your body.
- Have a sports drink. One of the worst aspects of dehydration is the loss of important electrolytes, such as potassium and sodium, which causes pain and discomfort. Most sports drinks, such as Powerade and Lucozade Sport, contain potassium, sodium and other electrolytes that are lost in heavy physical activity – or heavy drinking.
- Eat eggs. Eggs contain an amino acid known as cysteine, which helps the body to get rid of toxins. This may be why you find eggs in many traditional hangover cures, including the legendary pick-me-up known as the Prairie Oyster (raw egg, brandy or vodka, olive oil and Worcestershire sauce). But make sure the eggs you consume are cooked. (See 'Avoiding Salmonella' on page 338.)
- Eat honey. Honey has lots of fructose, a sugar that helps to work the alcohol out of your system. It also contains vitamin B_6, which helps with hangover symptoms.
- Try ibuprofen. Ibuprofen, such as in branded products like Nurofen, is easier on the stomach than aspirin. But be careful: ibuprofen can upset the stomach, so use in moderation and avoid if you have bleeding problems or are taking blood-thinning drugs like warfarin. And there is evidence that ibuprofen and other over-the-counter pain relievers can cause serious side effects if a person consumes more than three drinks a day.

■ UNHYGIENIC CONDITIONS

I'm afraid I'll catch something in my GP's waiting room

KEEP YOUR HANDS CLEAN Doctors' waiting rooms can be dens of communicable diseases. You may have come in with a bad back, but you could very well leave with a cold. It isn't very likely that you will catch something that's floating in the air. Instead, it will come from a germ getting on to your hands and then entering your body when you touch your face. So:

You're less likely to catch a germ floating in the air than one you pick up on your hands.

- Be careful with your hands. While waiting, don't touch your mucous membranes – eyes, nose or mouth – after touching magazines, chair arms, doorknobs or anything else a sick person might have touched.
- Wash your hands. The minute you've left the room, wash your hands well. Ordinary soap is fine, as long as you're thorough, scrubbing for at least 15 seconds and rinsing well.
- Carry anti-bacterial wipes or gel. Alcohol-based wipes and gels are effective immediately against both bacteria and viruses (whereas other anti-bacterial agents often are not). Keep these handy in your purse or pocket. Use them to wipe off any surfaces you must touch, such as doorknobs if you're particularly worried, and use on your hands after you touch surfaces or shake hands. They also make a quick hand-cleaning alternative, in case you aren't near any soap and water.
- Avoid sneezes. Although even respiratory viruses are spread more often by transfer from hands to mucus membranes, sneeze droplets are airborne germ bombs. Be aware and do what you can to avoid them.
- Check your own germs. If you're sick, take precautions so that you won't spread your own germs in the waiting room. Wash your hands after blowing your nose or sneezing. Use alcohol wipes to clean anything after you have touched it. If everyone were more conscientious, the risk of catching something in a doctor's waiting room would be reduced.

I need to sneeze and I'm in a public place without a tissue

USE THE BEND IN YOUR ELBOW Sneeze or cough into the crook of your elbow, a part of the body that is unlikely to spread the germs to

others through contact. Contrary to your instincts, covering your mouth with your hands is not hygienic. If you are sick, you will end up with infectious microbes on your hands which can make others sick by touching doorknobs or shaking hands.

My 5 year old doesn't wash his hands for long enough

SING A SONG The simplest and most effective way to prevent the spread of infectious diseases, such as colds, flu and even hepatitis, is to wash your hands regularly before meals, after using the toilet, sneezing or blowing your nose. But you have to wash your hands properly, soaping them and scrubbing for at least 15 seconds, to wash away harmful microbes.

Get your children into the habit of singing a favourite song (ideally one with a few verses and choruses) while they wash their hands. The rule is that they're not finished scrubbing until the song is over. This makes washing more fun and more effective.

The changing-room floor at my local pool is always wet

WEAR FLIP FLOPS OR JELLY SHOES When you're in the gym changing room or in a public shower at the pool, wear something on your feet. Flip-flops work well because they are cheap, waterproof, lightweight and easy to slip on and off. This will help you avoid catching two common skin conditions, athlete's foot and verrucas.

Oh no! My child has head lice

WASH CLOTHES AND BEDDING, SHAMPOO HAIR Lice only happen to other people's children – until you find the little beasts on yours. A case of head lice does not necessarily mean you've been a neglectful parent or that you're lacking in the hygiene department. It simply means that your child – at school, football or a dance class – has come into contact with someone with lice.

Here's how to stop the problem. Wash all of the child's clothing, pjamas and bed linen in hot water (at least 60°C). If you have one, dry them on your tumble drier's hottest setting for at least 20 minutes. Vacuum carpets, upholstered furniture and the child's mattress to suck up any traces of lice, including their eggs.

Fortunately, lice – unlike much hardier fleas – can survive for only about a day without a human host, so anything you miss should soon die. Buy an over-the-counter pesticide-free lice removal kit at your local pharmacy. These kits usually include a removal shampoo and a fine-tooth comb for removing lice and their eggs or nits. Follow the directions carefully. For two weeks, inspect all family members daily for any traces of lice or nits. During these two weeks, have all family members avoid close head-to-head contact with the infested child.

■ MEDICATIONS

I'm going on holiday and want to keep my medication in order

PLAN AHEAD AND BRING YOUR BOTTLES Travelling takes us out of our routines, so taking regular medication requires planning. Here are some ideas for keeping it all under control while you are travelling:

- Keep a list of the prescription and non-prescription medicines and supplements you take. If you're flying, keep the list on you, not in your checked luggage.
- Never pack medicines in luggage that will be checked on a plane. Keep them in your hand luggage.
- Before departing, review dosage schedules and how travelling across time zones will affect when you take your pills.

- Take a copy of your prescription with you. Check local regulations at your destination – certain medications are illegal in some countries.
- Pack enough medicine to last the duration of the trip, plus at least an extra day's supply.
- If you use a pill dispenser, don't fill it until you arrive at your destination. Medicine containers have important information like medicine name, dosage, instructions and warnings. They also assure customs inspectors that you are not smuggling illegal drugs.
- Be careful where you keep your medicines as you travel. Heat and humidity can damage them, so never store medications in car glove compartments, car boots or beach bags.

My medicine cabinet is in a mess

GET RID OF OLD AND UNUSED PILLS AND MEDICINES A messy medicine cabinet is a potential health hazard, since old or unidentifiable medicines can be dangerous. Furthermore, if you don't stay on top of what's in your cabinet, you may be unaware of missing medicines – prescription and over-the-counter – that you may need one day. Here is a step-by-step strategy for keeping your medicine cabinet safe and up to date:

1 At least once a year, clean out your medicine cabinet, checking bottle labels for expiry dates.
2 Get rid of out-of-date medicines, those your doctor has told you not to take, medicines that have changed in smell or colour and those with missing or illegible labels.
3 Dispose of dangerous medicines safely. Don't throw them in the dustbin or flush them down the sink. Almost all pharmacies operate a service that allows you to drop off old and unused medicines that they will then get rid of safely.
4 Make sure medicine bottles have child-resistant caps and that the caps still work.

Minor health emergencies

■ URGENT SITUATIONS

I have scorched my finger on a hot pan

APPLY COLD, THEN ALOE VERA This advice assumes that you have a small first-degree burn, with damage only to the top layer of skin, leaving it red and painful. More serious burns need more specialist treatment. The most important action to take with any burn is to cool it as fast as possible by holding the area under cold running water for at least 10 minutes. If a tap is not available, any cold liquid is better than none. Cooling eases the pain and reduces the chance of scarring. After 10 minutes apply cool, moist cloths or a towel-wrapped ice pack. Over-the-counter pain relievers can help. Aloe-based moisturisers will soothe the skin. First-degree burns do not usually need medical attention and heal in about a week.

I've given myself a nasty paper cut

CLEAN AND COVER Small cuts are rarely a problem unless they get infected. Wash the area thoroughly, apply an antiseptic cream or spray and then cover with an adhesive plaster or liquid bandage. Cover it even if it isn't bleeding, because you still need to protect the exposed flesh from germs. An antiseptic should be reapplied four or five times during the first day for maximum protection.

I bit my tongue and it really hurts

RINSE WITH MOUTHWASH Gargling with a germ-killing mouthwash or a warm salt water solution will help to keep a tongue bite from getting infected and applying mouth ulcer or teething gel will reduce the pain. After that, you have to stop yourself from biting your tongue again. Because your tongue is swollen, be careful when chewing. Doctors recommend switching to soft foods until the swelling recedes. As with any cut, the swelling should go down within a few days and the tongue be completely healed within a few weeks.

A paper cut may hurt a lot, but all it needs is a little antibiotic cream and a plaster.

My child is crying because I have to remove a sticking plaster

SOAK IT FIRST WITH OLIVE OIL If the very thought of having a plaster ripped off sends shivers down your child's spine, there is a less painful way. Soak a cotton wool ball in olive oil and gently rub it over the plaster until it falls off. If you don't have olive oil handy, any cooking oil or bath oil will work just as well.

I've just ripped off the top of a fingernail

TRIM IT AND LEAVE IT If the rip is in the top half of the nail and the base of the nail remains securely in place, there is probably no damage to the skin underneath, so you can tend to it yourself. Otherwise, see a doctor. To fix a torn fingernail, take a nail trimmer and smooth out the edge to prevent it from catching on something and ripping further. Wash your hands and then leave the nail alone. Putting a plaster on it won't help; in fact, that will lock in moisture, which will soften the nail and make infection more likely. Rather, keep the nail dry and let it grow back at its own pace.

Someone on the train has a nosebleed

PINCH THE NOSE Nosebleeds happen for all sorts of benign reasons. If the person is elderly or has a serious health condition, such as heart disease, diabetes, high blood pressure or a blood clotting problem, seek medical help. If not, the nosebleed is probably not serious.

To stop the blood flow, get the person pinch the soft part of the nose firmly and breathe through the mouth. After 10 minutes release the pressure. If the bleeding has not stopped, reapply the pressure for up to two further periods of 10 minutes. If the bleeding continues, seek medical help.

■ EYE INJURIES

I've been hit in the eye

USE AN ICE PACK To reduce swelling and pain, put a cold cloth or an ice pack wrapped in a towel over the eye. Don't press on it. Keep it there for 15 minutes. If the eyeball itself is injured or if the eye continues to hurt or turns red or if you have blurred vision, double vision or a lot of new floaters (small specks floating across your field of vision), go to an accident and emergency department at once.

There's a speck of dirt in my eye

WASH IT OUT Don't rub your eye. You might scratch the cornea, the clear covering in front of the eye. Instead, gently lift the upper eyelid over the lower lid. Chances are the lower eyelashes will brush the speck off the inside of the upper eyelid. Blink several times to try to wash the speck out. If that doesn't work, flush it out with clean water using one of these methods: either hold your head under a tap and let the water irrigate your open eye or submerge your head in a basin full of water and blink rapidly. If these methods fail, keep the eye closed and go to accident and emergency or to the doctor. Left in place, a speck of dirt can scratch the cornea.

My husband has splashed chemicals into his eye

FLUSH THE EYES WITH CLEAN WATER Whatever the chemicals, acting fast is very important. You need to rinse the eyes with lots of clean water. If you are able to, hold his head under a tap and let the water flush the chemical from his eyes. Or bend his head and have someone pour clean water from a clean container into his eyes. Get him to use his fingers to hold the eyelids as far open as possible and roll his eyeballs during the rinsing. Rinse for at least 15 minutes. Once the chemical has been flushed away as much as possible, fill a clean sink, dip his whole face in the water and get him to blink

rapidly. If his eyes continue to hurt, go immediately to your nearest accident and emergency department. Do not bandage the eyes.

■ LIGHT-HEADEDNESS AND HEAD INJURIES

I feel as if I'm going to faint

LIE DOWN Fainting is a common occurrence. Many different stimuli trigger fainting in susceptible people. Some people faint when they stand for a long time in the heat. Others pass out when they see blood. Strong emotions, pain and stress can also cause fainting. Fainting results from a fall in blood pressure cutting down blood and oxygen flow to the brain. Before they actually faint, people often turn pale, begin sweating and generally feel terrible. An instant antidote is to lie down with your legs slightly raised. You need to get your heart above the level of your brain, so that oxygen-rich blood can get to the brain more easily. By lying down the minute you feel faint, you are more likely to remain conscious. If you don't lie down, you risk fainting and falling, and possibly injuring your head.

I feel dizzy

LIE DOWN If you have been exercising and you feel extremely dizzy, seek medical help right away. Dizziness during any kind of physical workout can be a sign of heart problems. Otherwise, feeling dizzy, like fainting, is fairly common. (If it happens more than once, however, see a doctor.) As with fainting, you should lie down, so that blood floods to your brain. If you're with someone, explain what you're doing, so that your companion can get help if the situation turns into an emergency. Take calming breaths and stay lying down until you feel completely normal.

My child has been hit on the head

STOP THE BLEEDING AND APPLY ICE Apply an ice pack directly to the wound to reduce swelling and alleviate the pain. If the wound is bleeding – and scalp wounds can bleed copiously – direct pressure with a clean cloth should stop the flow. Signs of a more serious head injury include seizures, loss of consciousness, nausea, strange behaviour and memory loss. If your child has any of these symptoms, go to an accident and emergency department at once.

My child is screaming on a plane

USE STEAM FROM HOT PAPER TOWELS IN A CUP If you've tried
everything – and your child still won't calm down, he or
she is probably suffering from ear pain, caused by
pressure changes in the ascending or descending plane. If
you've ever experienced ear canal pressure, you know how
much this can hurt. Don't bother trying to get your
youngster to yawn or swallow or do whatever it is you do to
equalise pressure in your own ears. Instead, try this: soak two
paper towels in hot (not boiling) water. Place each at the bottom
of a plastic cup and carefully cover the child's ears with the cups.
The hot air should help to even up the pressure and stop the pain.

*For instant relief
from an air-
pressure earache,
cover the ears
with plastic cups
containing hot,
wet paper towels.*

■ HOT WEATHER PROBLEMS

I'm overheated and I'm getting cramp

SIT STILL AND DRINK JUICE If it's hot outside and you're sweating a lot
from strenuous activity, your muscles, usually in the abdomen, arms
and legs, may begin to spasm, which can mean you are having heat
cramps. Heat cramps are caused by low salt and fluid levels in the
body. They can be a symptom of heatstroke (see page 230), which
can be serious. If you think you might have heatstroke or if you
have heart problems or are on a low-salt diet, seek medical attention
right away for heat cramps. Otherwise, here's what you can do to
make the cramps go away:

1 Stop what you're doing and sit quietly in a cool place.
2 Drink clear juice or a sports drink.
3 Don't go back to strenuous activity for a few hours.
4 If the cramps aren't gone in an hour, seek medical attention.

I've got badly sunburned

APPLY COLD COMPRESSES Despite applying SPF 45 and sitting under
umbrellas, we still get burned occasionally. Sometimes overexposure
to sun can even lead to second-degree burns.

If sunburn causes fever, fluid-filled blisters or severe pain or if the
burn affects an infant under the age of one, see a doctor. A doctor can
treat the burn and prescribe medicines to prevent infections or
scarring from the blisters. Otherwise, the pain should be over in a

How to beat the heat
Though we embrace hot weather in this country, you can have too much of a good thing – as in the deadly Paris heatwave of August 2003 which killed a large number of mainly elderly people. Follow this advice next time a heatwave hits to make sure it doesn't overwhelm you.

• **Find an air conditioner** If you don't have one in your home (most of us don't), during the hottest parts of the day, seek out cool public spaces, such as shopping centres and libraries.

• **Stay hydrated** Drink lots of water and other non-alcoholic drinks.

• **Dress sensibly** Wear lightweight, light-coloured, loose-fitting clothes.

• **Take it easy** Limit strenuous activity to the cooler parts of the day.

STAYING SAFE WHEN THERE'S LIGHTNING AROUND

A thunderstorm can be deadly. If you can hear thunder within 5 seconds of seeing lightning, you are in a lightning zone. Keep in mind that lightning is attracted to metal and water and will strikes tall things, such as trees and radio towers. Here's how to stay safe in a lightning storm.

If you are outside:

• Get away from water.

• Avoid fields, golf fairways and other wide open areas.

• If you can't get indoors, either wait in a car with the windows up or get to the lowest ground you can find and, instead of sitting, kneel or squat to minimise contact with the ground. If you feel your hair start to stand on end, drop to this position immediately.

• Stay off hilltops.

• Stand at least 2 metres from trees, gazebos, poles or other tall objects.

• Avoid metal objects such as golf clubs, fishing rods, garden furniture and gates.

• Remove golf shoes with spikes or steelcap boots.

• Wait at least 30 minutes after the last thunderclap or lightning strike before resuming your outdoor activity.

If you are inside:

• Stay away from windows and doors.

• Disconnect all non-essential electrical equipment, especially computers, stereos and televisions. Avoid using the telephone, except in emergencies. Your home's wiring attracts lightning.

• Avoid using sinks, baths or showers, since lightning can course through a home's plumbing.

few days and the skin should be fully healed in a week. To alleviate the pain of sunburn, apply cold compresses or have a tepid (not cold) shower or bath. Rub in moisturising lotion or aloe gel but not salve, butter or ointment. Do not pop blisters.

My child has a heat rash

FIND A SHADY SPOT Heat rash strikes on hot, humid days when a person, usually a young child, is sweating profusely. It appears as a red cluster of pimples, most likely on the neck and upper chest, in the groin, under the breasts and in elbow creases. The simple cure for heat rash is to cool off. Stay out of the sun and drink plenty of fluids. Place a wet flannel over the area, or soothe with calamine lotion. If the rash is very itchy, an antihistamine cream may help.

■ DENTAL EMERGENCIES

I have broken a tooth

PROTECT THE TOOTH IN YOUR MOUTH If a sizeable chip has come off, save it. Clean the injured area and apply an ice pack to it. Contact your dentist, who may be able to reattach the broken part. If you cannot get to the dentist right away, get rid of the chip. It will no longer be of use. But here is how to protect the broken tooth still attached to your jaw from infection or other problems: buy some dental (orthodontic) wax, the kind used by kids with braces and sold by pharmacies. Clean your mouth by brushing your teeth and swishing around some antiseptic mouthwash. Roll a small piece of the wax into a ball and stick it on the tooth. The wax will protect the exposed roots. If you can't find orthodontic wax, use a small piece of sugarless chewing gum until you can get to a dentist.

WORLD-CLASS FIX

DO-IT-YOURSELF DENTISTRY

During a photographic expedition in Antarctica, photographer Pat Keough bit down on a pebble in his porridge and split a molar in his lower jaw. He would not see civilisation for another month and a half, so he was forced to take matters into his own hands. Like many a handy person, his mind turned to gaffer tape.

To make a dental cap, Keough snipped a piece of gaffer tape 2.5cm long and 1.25cm wide. He used tissues to dry his mouth out, so the tape would bind with his teeth. Then he placed the tape over the top of the broken tooth and used his fingers to mould it into a snug fit. For stability and extra padding, he cut another piece of tape – 2.5cm square – and placed it over the broken tooth and the two neighbouring teeth as well. The result was not the most comfortable dental cap ever created, but it did prevent the broken tooth from cutting his tongue and it kept air away from the exposed nerve, reducing his pain. He spent the next few weeks chewing on the other side of his mouth and had to rebuild the gaffer tape dental cap about five more times.

Tips for whiter teeth

• **Chew sugarless gum after meals.** The gum and chewing action stimulate the flow of saliva, which helps to removes stains and stop bacteria growing.

• **Rinse with water after meals.** A quick rinse with clean water will flush stain-causing matter out of the mouth.

• **Use a straw.** The less contact that coloured liquids – tea, soft drinks and juices, for instance – have with your teeth, the better. The rule of thumb is that if it will stain your shirt, it will stain your teeth.

• **Drink clear fluids.** Try white grape juice instead of purple. Drink a lemon and lime soft drink instead of a cola. Even better, stick to water.

A filling has fallen out of my tooth

USE DENTAL WAX OR CHEWING GUM Old fillings sometimes fall out and when they do, they may expose a tooth's roots to food and to infection-causing bacteria. You may find it painful to eat or drink, especially cold drinks, and there may be sharp edges that catch on your mouth. Until you can get to a dentist, here's what to do: rinse your mouth, brush your teeth very gently, swish around a little antiseptic mouthwash and then plug the gap with a small ball of temporary filling material, available from chemists, dental wax (orthodontic wax) or sugarless chewing gum to protect the exposed roots. If you can't get a dentist's appointment straightaway, repeat this every time you eat or drink something, and last thing at night. A dab of clove oil on a cotton bud should help to ease any pain.

The crown has fallen off my tooth

ATTACH IT TEMPORARILY WITH DENTURE ADHESIVE First, find the crown. You will need to visit a dentist as soon as possible. But in the meantime, here is a quick solution: rinse the crown or cap in clean water and reattach it with denture adhesive, available at pharmacies and supermarkets. (An additional tip: to save money and avoid waste, look for a travel-size container of the denture adhesive.) This quick fix will re-establish your smile temporarily until the dentist can do it permanently.

My gums are extremely painful

RINSE WITH SALT WATER Gum pain is usually due to a build up of plaque on the teeth, harbouring bacteria and leading to gum soreness, swelling and bleeding. It's important to brush and floss regularly and to see a dentist fast to prevent further damage. In the meantime, try rinsing your mouth with a warm water solution of either salt or bicarbonate of soda. This will soothe the pain and help to prevent infection.

My teeth hurt when I bite into cold and sweet items

USE A TOOTHPASTE FOR SENSITIVE TEETH The cause is likely to be erosion of dental enamel or receding gums that expose tiny channels within the tooth called dental tubules. These lead to the tooth's nerve, which is exquisitely sensitive. When cold drinks, sweets and other substances – even cold air – come into contact with the nerve, you get a jolt of pain. Try using a toothpaste for sensitive teeth. These products contain ingredients that seal dental tubules, reducing the nerve's exposure. But toothpaste for sensitive teeth does not work overnight. Give it a couple of weeks.

If the pain continues, make an appointment with the dentist. At the same time, switch to a soft or extra-soft toothbrush and don't brush hard, because that can contribute to enamel erosion and gum loss. Your gums are important, not only in keeping out pain-causing substances, but in keeping out bacteria and preventing tooth decay.

Act fast. If you can get to a dentist as soon as you can, it may be possible to reimplant a dislodged tooth.

My child has knocked out a tooth playing sport

TAKE TOOTH AND CHILD TO THE DENTIST Young people are at especially great risk of losing teeth. (Each year millions of teeth are knocked out while youngsters play sports.) If your child – or anyone else – loses a tooth, act fast. If you get to a dentist soon enough (within 40 to 60 minutes), the tooth may be able to be re-implanted. (If it's a baby tooth, there is no need to replace it – just get your child's dentist to make sure that the permanent tooth underneath has not been damaged.) Locate the dislodged tooth. Hold it by the crown only. Do not touch the exposed roots. Rinse it with clean water, but do not rub it or touch the roots with anything. The best way to protect the tooth while travelling to the dentist is to put it back in its socket, cover it with gauze and have the owner bite down on it to hold it in place. Or you can store the tooth temporarily in cold milk, salt water or between your cheek and gum. The point is not to let it dry out. Immediately call your dentist, who may have an emergency number out of hours, or go to accident and emergency – if you act fast enough, it may be possible to reattach or repair the tooth

Index

**Extraordinary Fixes
for Everyday Things**

Editor
Lisa Thomas

Art Editor
Julie Bennett

Designer
Martin Bennett

Writer
Jeff Bredenberg

Consultants
Simon Gilham,
David Holloway,
Jonquil Lowe,
Sheena Meredith,
Mike Naylor

Proofreader
Barry Gage

Indexer
Marie Lorimer

Illustrators
Harry Bates (how-to),
Travis Foster (humour)

**Reader's Digest
General Books**

Editorial Director
Julian Browne

Art Director
Anne-Marie Bulat

Managing Editor
Nina Hathway

**Head of Book
Development**
Sarah Bloxham

**Picture Resource
Manager**
Christine Hinze

**Pre-press Account
Manager**
Dean Russell

**Product Production
Manager**
Claudette Bramble

**Production
Controller**
Katherine Tibbals

Colour origination
Colour Systems Limited

Printed and bound in China

To our readers

The information in this book has been carefully researched, and all efforts have been made to ensure accuracy and safety. Neither the author nor The Reader's Digest Association Limited assumes any responsibility for any injuries suffered or damages or losses incurred as a result of following the instructions in this book. Before taking any action based on information in this book, study the information carefully and make sure that you understand it fully. Test any new or unusual repair method before using it as a remedy or on a highly visible or valuable area or item. The mention of any product or website in this book does not imply an endorsement. All prices, sellers' names, product names and websites mentioned are subject to change and are meant to be considered as general examples rather than specific recommendations.

Extraordinary Fixes for Everyday Things
is published by
The Reader's Digest Association
Limited, 11 Westferry Circus,
Canary Wharf, London E14 4HE

Copyright © 2009 The Reader's Digest
  Association Limited
Copyright © 2009 Reader's Digest
  Association Far East Limited.
Philippines Copyright © 2009 Reader's
  Digest Association Far East Limited
Copyright © 2009 Reader's Digest
  (Australia) Pty Limited
Copyright © 2009 Reader's Digest
  India Pvt Limited
Copyright © 2009 Reader's Digest
  Asia Pvt Limited

The text is adapted from **Five Minute Fixes**
published by Reader's Digest
Association Inc. in 2005

Photographs All iStockphoto.com, except
the following: ShutterStock, Inc. (Andrew
Lewis) pp. 21, 41, 56, 61, 143, 144, 154, 163,
167, 170, 201, 210, 212, 214, 230, 235, 240,
256, 264, 290, 296, 299, 303, 314, 332,
336. ShutterStock, Inc. (Teamarbeit) pp.
105, 107, 110, 112, 114.

We are committed both to the quality
of our products and the service we
provide to our customers. We value your
comments, so please do contact us on
08705 113366 or via our website at
www.readersdigest.co.uk

If you have any comments or
suggestions about the content of
our books, email us at
gbeditorial@readersdigest.co.uk

ISBN: 978 0276 44570 5
Concept code: US4535/G
Book code: 400-462 UP0000-1
Oracle code: 250008289H.00.24